Mass Media
and
Society

Edited by
James Curran and Michael Gurevitch

Edward Arnold
A division of Hodder & Stoughton
LONDON NEW YORK MELBOURNE AUCKLAND

Introduction, Selections and Editorial Matter
© 1991 James Curran and Michael Gurevitch

Chapter 1 © Peter Golding and Graham Murdock
Chapter 2 © Liesbet van Zoonen
Chapter 3 © John Fiske
Chapter 4 © James Curran
Chapter 5 © Denis McQuail
Chapter 6 © Annabelle Sreberny-Mohammadi
Chapter 7 © Michael Schudson
Chapter 8 © Joseph Turow
Chapter 9 © Michael Gurevitch
Chapter 10 © Jay G Blumler
Chapter 11 © Judith Lichtenberg
Chapter 12 © Jack M McLeod, Gerald M Kosicki and Zhongdang Pan
Chapter 13 © John Corner
Chapter 14 © Sonia M Livingstone
Chapter 15 © Ien Ang and Joke Hermes
Chapter 16 © Todd Gitlin

First published in Great Britain 1991
Reprinted 1992

Distributed in the USA by Routledge, Chapman and Hall, Inc.
29 West 35th Street, New York, NY 10001

British Library Cataloguing in Publication Data

Mass media and society.
  I. Curran, James   II. Gurevitch, Michael
  302.23

  ISBN 0-340-55947-0
  ISBN 0-340-51759-X pbk

Library of Congress Cataloging-in-Publication Data

Mass media and society/edited by James Curran and Michael
Gurevitch.
    p.   cm.
  Includes bibliographical references and index.
  ISBN 0-340-55947-0 : $ 59.95.—ISBN 0-340-51759-X
(pbk.) : $19.95
    1. Mass media—Social aspects.   2. Mass-media—Political aspects.
I. Curran, James.   II. Gurevitch, Michael.
HM258.M26578   1992   91-23441
302.23—dc20   CIP

Typeset in 10/11pt Times by Rowland Photosetting Limited,
Bury St Edmunds, Suffolk
Printed and bound in Great Britain for Edward Arnold,
a division of Hodder and Stoughton Limited,
Mill Road, Dunton Green, Sevenoaks, Kent TN13 2YA
by Biddles Limited, Guildford and King's Lynn

Contents

List of contributors

Ien Ang, Senior Lecturer in Communication Studies (Murdoch University, Australia)

Jay G. Blumler, Emeritus Professor (University of Leeds), Professor of Journalism (University of Maryland)

John Corner, Senior Lecturer in Communication Studies (Centre for Communication Studies, University of Liverpool)

James Curran, Professor of Communications (Goldsmiths' College, University of London)

John Fiske, Professor of Communication (University of Wisconsin-Madison)

Todd Gitlin, Professor of Sociology (University of California, Berkeley)

Peter Golding, Professor of Sociology (University of Loughborough)

Michael Gurevitch, Professor, College of Journalism (University of Maryland)

Joke Hermes, Research Student (University of Amsterdam)

Gerald Kosicki, Assistant Professor of Journalism (Ohio State University)

Judith Lichtenberg, Associate Professor (University of Maryland)

Sonia M. Livingstone, Lecturer in Psychology (London School of Economics, University of London)

Jack McLeod, Maier-Bascom Professor of Journalism (University of Wisconsin-Madison)

Denis McQuail, Professor of Mass Communication (University of Amsterdam)

Graham Murdock, Reader in Sociology (University of Loughborough)

Zhongdang Pan, Assistant Professor of Communication (Cornell University)

Michael Schudson, Professor of Communication (University of California, San Diego)

Annabelle Sreberny-Mohammadi, Professor of Communication (University of Leicester)

Joseph Turow, Professor of Communication (University of Pennsylvania)

Liesbet van Zoonen, Lecturer in Communication (University of Amsterdam)

Acknowledgements

The publishers would like to thank the following for permission to include copyright material:

The Central Statistical Office for Table 1 from *Family Expenditure Survey*, 1989, reproduced with permission of the Controller of HMSO; the UNESCO Press for Tables 6.1 and 6.3 from *World Communication Report*, © UNESCO, 1989 and for Table 6.2 from *UNESCO Statistical Yearbook*, © UNESCO, 1989; Pergamon Press plc for permission to reproduce material from *Making Sense of Television: The Psychology of Audience Interpretation* by S M Livingstone, Copyright ©, 1990, Pergamon Press plc.

Every effort has been made to trace copyright holders of material reproduced in this book. Any rights not acknowledged here will be acknowledged in subsequent printings if notice is given to the publisher.

Introduction

Fourteen years have passed since the publication of *Mass Communication and Society* in 1977. That volume was produced and edited expressly for students of The Open University course of that same title. It was designed to offer the students a collection of essays aimed at supplementing other course materials, and the structure of the book therefore followed rather closely the structure of the course.

Like other Open University texts *Mass Communication and Society* was available also to students and academics outside the Open University. Shortly after the publication of the book we were gratified to discover that our collection of readings quickly reached an audience far wider than the one for which it was initially intended. We attributed this to the manner in which the book succeeded, more or less by accident, in identifying and defining the contours of the field at the time.

However, in spite of its longevity (over the years the book was reprinted nine times) we became increasingly aware of the 'creeping obsolescence' of the 1977 volume. We decided, therefore, to put together a revised edition. But as soon as we thought about it in detail, it became clear that a merely 'revised' edition would remain trapped in the models and paradigms of the 1970's and fail to come to terms with the extraordinary transformation of the field that has taken place since then.

This volume follows its predecessor in the sense that it has retained the same organising framework of three sections. It has also some of the same authors (in addition to younger ones who were still at school when its predecessor first appeared). And it is pitched at about the same level as before.

But it also differs from the 'first edition' in a number of ways. It has more overview articles in order to carry the expository load formerly taken by Open University course units. It relies less on reprints; all the essays for this book are written for it, though two appeared in different, earlier guises in journals. It is less parochial in feel (relatively speaking) in that it is not written, as before, almost entirely by British academics. But above all, it is different because it reflects and critically responds to the new revisionism that has developed in mass communications research during the last decade.

A critical review of revisionist scholarship is provided by James Curran (1990) in an essay whose origins go back to earlier discussions concerning the structure of the revised edition of *Mass Communication and Society*. The central theme of this essay is that the critical tradition in media research has imploded in response to an internal debate. This has led to an increasing repudiation of the totalising themes of marxism, a reassessment of the relationship of media organisations to the structure of social power, a stress on the audience as an active creator of meanings, and a shift from a political to a popular aesthetic. During the same period, some researchers in the liberal-pluralist tradition have reconsidered their position in response to attacks from radical critics; they have moved, in effect, against the flow of traffic coming the other way. The result is a redefinition of the field in which the traditional dichotomy between neo-marxist and liberal-pluralist perspectives have become less salient and also less sharply defined, while other perspectives – notably, feminism, theories of subjectivity and particularistic versions of pluralism – have gained increased prominence.

The other important shift of the field has been prompted by changes in the media industry, particularly television. The age of channel austerity has been replaced by an era of channel abundance, with the adoption of new TV technologies. The 1980's were also characterised by the dominance of conservative governments in many Western countries, and this led to sweeping changes in the regulatory structures governing television both in Europe and the United States. The upheavals of Eastern Europe and the Soviet Union in 1989–91 also engulfed its media, prompting a debate about how these should be reorganised and democratised. For all these reasons, a policy oriented discussion of the political and cultural role of the media and of so-called 'technologies of freedom' has assumed an importance that it lacked in the more static period of the mid 1970's.

This book reflects these different changes and trends in mass communication research. But it also comments upon and critically appraises them. This is done not by promoting one particular point of view but by staging a debate, both explicit and implicit, on the basis of which readers can form their own judgement. Thus, the first section provides general accounts of the role of the media in society, including normative liberal, postmodernist, feminist and neo-marxist perspectives by advocates of these different positions. The second section offers alternative views of the formative influences that shape the media, and analysis of recent changes in the media industries. The last section explores the role of the media in the social production of meaning, viewed from different perspectives and methodologies.

Within this formal organisation, there are a number of crisscrossing interconnections between different parts of the book. Some essays confront the viewpoint of other essays: others, still, complement and support one another. Identifying all these skirmishes and liaisons (some unplanned and unexpected) would be tedious. But it may be helpful nevertheless to point to certain running debates that recur in the book as a whole.

One area of engagement takes the form of a tacit debate about how to conceptualise the wider context in which the media are situated. The holistic framework of neo-marxism that characterised 1970's 'mainstream' critical research, and the totalising themes of radical feminism that characterised another branch of it, were rejected by many radical researchers in the 1980's and early 1990's in favour of a more complex and multi-faceted conspectus of society in which manifold relationships of power are said to be in play in different situations. This led to the adoption of a number of alternative models of society ranging from revised neo-marxist and socialist feminist perspectives of society through to postmodernism and a particularistic version of pluralism in which society is analytically disaggregated into a series of discrete instances.

The chapters in this book illustrate a variety of models in play. It may be helpful to pick out three chapters, however, since they exemplify strong revisionist currents in the field. The first is what might be described as a 'Foucauldian' analysis by Annabelle Sreberny-Mohammadi. She traces different stages in the debate about the media and third world: the initial, self confident conception of the media as an agency of modernisation in backward countries; the radical counterblast portraying western media domination of the third world as a form of cultural imperialism that was imposing western values; followed by the pluralist fightback pointing to two-way flows of communication between developed and developing countries, and emphasizing audience autonomy. Her conclusion at the end of this interesting resume is that the media in developing countries have an ambivalent role; they can be both instruments of social control and agencies of emancipation, an expression of global western power and a means by which local identities are revitalised. Underlying this conclusion is a reluctance to accept the nation state as an adequate conceptual category in the analysis of dependency and domination. But it also reflects a complex understanding of power relations in terms of gender, class, ethnicity and centre-periphery cleavages. In effect, indigenous audience responses to western media content are viewed by her as a response to and negotiation of manifold relations of power and multiple identities.

Streberny-Mohammadi is working out of a radical, class based paradigm. Similar arguments are also emerging out of radical feminist perspective. Liesbet Van Zoonen, for instance, attacks the view that the media project only sexist stereotypes that deny the true nature of women and suborn female audiences into passive acceptance of patriarchy. Instead, she argues, the essentialist conception of feminity underlying this approach should be replaced by a culturalist one; womens' pleasure in the media should be seen not as a process of passive victimisation and indoctrination but as a way in which women actively express something about themselves as women; and the media itself should be viewed as a site of negotiation between conflicting definitions of gender rather than as an unproblematic agency of patriarchy. This argument is carried further by Ien Ang and Joke Hermes who contest the validity of 'women' as a conceptual category for making sense of society, arguing that women have multiple identities with a variety of subjective responses to the media, which convey heterogeneous and contradictory meanings. Particularistic studies, properly contextualised, should replace 'generalised absolutes' and 'easy categorisation' in which feminists claim to know the interests of women and speak on their behalf.

Ang and Hermes's article exemplifies in the context of a feminist debate a wider set of arguments within the radical revisionist tradition. A view of the media as an agency of class domination (or, in its more qualified form, as an agency that tends to privilege representations of the world that sustain the interests of dominant power groups) was challenged partly on the grounds that audience produce their own meanings. The circuit of power is supposedly disconnected at the juncture between media and audience because people actively make sense of and interpret media content in terms of prior discourse positions. This stress on the 'resourcefulness' and 'productivity' of the audience was reinforced by the argument that meaning is not fixed but is produced through the interaction between text and the socially situated discourses of audiences; that most media texts can be interpreted differently; and that in general media content is more diverse and contradictory than was alleged during the heyday of critical analysis in the 1970's. In effect, an analysis emerging out of critical literary theory and ethnography came very close to a view of the 'obstinate' audience that was a key building block in American pluralist sociology and that served as the ground on which approaches such as 'uses and gratifications' flourished. Yet, ironically, it was precisely this pluralist tradition that the critical analysis of the 1970's was seeking to dethrone.

The extent to which audiences can be said to be active producers of meaning, and the implications this has for understanding the wider relationship of the media to society, are linked issues that form the second key area of engagement in the book. John Fiske provides an eloquent exposition of the view that 'bottom-up' meanings generated by audiences overpower 'top-down' meanings encoded in the media, although he dissociates himself from the extreme postmodernist view that people consume images without consuming their meaning. His position is not that dissimilar to the radical postmodern orientation of Ang and Hermes referred to earlier. Sonia Livingstone's essay also documents the active interpretive role of audiences, and in this sense can be read as supportive of Fiske's core argument.

Other essays attack, however, revisionist perspectives of the audience. The most directly confrontational is Todd Gitlin's essay which argues that celebration of audience automony is misconceived in two ways. It overstates the oppositional meaning of sub-cultural expression, and mistakenly equates cultural consumption with political activity. Style contests, in short, are mistakenly identified as the political expression of class war. John Corner attacks as oversimplified studies that emphasize the multiple meanings of media content. He argues that they often fail to distinguish between the relative openness and closure of meaning in specific texts, fail to differentiate between layers of meaning and different genres, and fail to analyse adequately the social context of meaning production. His reservations are echoed in Golding and Murdock's re-presentation of a political economy perspective. Jack McLeod, Gerald Kosicki and Zhongdang Pan's critical review of the empirical literature on media effects – though presented by them as a broadside in another battle – takes on an additional meaning in this context. Its implication is that the conception of the recalcitrant audience that dominated American social science in the 1950's – which recent revisionist thought is gravitating towards – needs to be heavily qualified in the light of evidence suggesting that the media have a selective, variable but important influence.

Another focal point of debate in contemporary media research revolves around the relationship of media organisations to the structure of power in society. Here a number of arguments are in play in what is becoming an increasingly complicated arabesque in which researchers in rival traditions inflect the same arguments and incorporate the same evidence in different ways. Simplifying greatly, neo-marxist researchers tend to stress capitalist state and economic determinations of the media, and the formative influence of the dominant class culture, while liberal-pluralist researchers tend to see media output as the product of relatively autonomous professionals responding to the social organisation of the media and the widely shared values and concerns of the public.

This battle ground is the third area of engagement in the book. What it indicates, however, is that the range of difference between rival perspectives is narrowing. Although this may partly reflect the personal views of the authors concerned, it is also a reflection of the general trend in this particular area of research. Thus, Peter Golding and Graham Murdock are at pains to distance themselves from simple instrumentalist and structuralist views of marxist political economy, and define 'economic determination' as an initial limitation and constraint on the general environment of communication activity. Schudson and Turow covering respectively news and entertainment organisations from a liberal-pluralist perspective nonetheless incorporate radical political economy arguments as a partially valid element in a broader picture.

There is another cluster of articles which, while relating to the debates above, can be viewed perhaps as a single group. They all discuss the public role of the media at a time of rapid transition and technical change. Denis McQuail maps alternative ways of conceptualising and judging the public performance of the media. James Curran argues that discussion of the democratic role of the media is dominated by old saws that need to be discarded, and suggests ways in which the media's democratic role can be reformulated and realised in practice. This discussion is continued in a sense by Judith Lichtenberg who defends the objective, professional model of journalism but in a form that differs from the way in which it is often interpreted in practice. Michael Gurevitch considers the wider implications of the creation of a 'global news room' and points to the way in which technological change impacts on, and potentially alters, 'older' patterns of power relationships both within the media industries and between the media and governments. And Jay Blumler critically assesses the functioning of the US broadcast system in the context of a large increase in the number of television channels. His analysis is of particular interest not least because American television is regularly held up either as a model of admiration or as a symbol of what to avoid.

In short, this book seeks to generate a debate between more traditional paradigms and new revisionist thinking, and to provide a commentary on some recent changes in the media. Our thanks go to contributors who have sought to define collectively but at some physical distance from one another the changing contours of mass communication research, and who have put up with requests for revisions and amendments. Our thanks go also to Lesley Riddle at Edward Arnold, whom it has been a great pleasure to work with.

Reference

CURRAN, JAMES, 1990: 'The New Revisionism in Mass Communication Research: A Reappraisal', *European Journal of Communication*, 5, pp. 135–164.

SECTION I

Mass Media and Society: General Perspectives

1

Culture, Communications, and Political Economy

Peter Golding and Graham Murdock

Everyone, from politicians to academics, now agrees that public communications systems are part of the 'cultural industries'. The popularity of this tag points to a growing awareness that these organizations are both similar to and different from other industries. On the one hand, they clearly have a range of features in common with other areas of production and are increasingly integrated into the general industrial structure. On the other hand, it is equally clear that the goods they manufacture – the newspapers, advertisements, television programmes, and feature films – play a pivotal role in organising the images and discourses through which people make sense of the world. A number of writers acknowledge this duality rhetorically, but go on to examine only one side, focusing either on the construction and consumption of media meanings (e.g. Fiske 1989) or on the economic organization of media industries (e.g. Collins, Garnham and Locksley 1988). What distinguishes the critical political economy perspective outlined here, is precisely its focus on the interplay between the symbolic and economic dimensions of public communications. It sets out to show how different ways of financing and organizing cultural production have traceable consequences for the range of discourses and representations in the public domain and for audiences' access to them.

Critical Political Economy of Communications – Straw Men and Stereotypes

Some terms become notoriously loose in practice, acquiring the status of cliché or slogan rather than analytical precision. One such term in our field is 'critical' analysis, often and wearily contrasted with 'administrative' research. The dichotomy between empirical (often implying simply quantitative) work and more theoretical concerns has become equated rather loosely with the distinction between administrative (meaning commissioned by the media companies by and large) and critical work (meaning broadly marxisant). The dichotomy has always been false and has been much lamented and regretted.

The approach we are outlining here is clearly critical, but in a sense which necessarily engages with empirical research, and which has no qualms about addressing issues of pragmatic and policy concern. It is critical in the crucial sense that it draws for its analysis on a critique, a theoretically informed

15

understanding, of the social order in which communications and cultural phenomena are being studied.

This is a characteristic which it shares with another major tradition of research – cultural studies. Both work within a broadly neo-Marxist view of society, both are centrally concerned with the constitution and exercise of power, and both take their distance from the liberal pluralist tradition of analysis with its broad acceptance of the central workings of advanced capitalist societies. (Curran 1990: 139). But this shared general stance conceals long-standing differences of approach, generated by the divergent intellectual histories of these traditions, and sustained by their very different locations on the contemporary academic map.

Whilst critical political economy has been institutionalized within faculties of social science, and draws its major practitioners from the ranks of people trained in economics, political science and sociology, departments and pro-grammes of cultural studies are still mostly situated in humanities faculties and pursued by scholars drawn from literary and historical studies. As a result, the two groups tend to approach communications with rather different interests and reference points, even when there is a strong desire to cut across disciplin-ary boundaries, as there often is.

Work on communications from within a cultural studies perspective 'is centrally concerned with the construction of meaning – how it is produced in and through particular expressive forms and how it is continually negotiated and deconstructed through the practices of everyday life' (Murdock 1989a: 436). This project has generated work in three distinct, but related areas. The first, and by far the largest, concentrates on the analysis of cultural texts, including those produced by the media industries. In contrast to transportation models, which see media forms such as thrillers, soap operas or documentary films as vehicles for transmitting 'messages' to consumers, cultural studies approach them as mechanisms for ordering meaning in particular ways. Where content analysis sees the meaning of say, a violent act in a television drama, as definable in advance and detachable from its position in the text or the programme's relation to other texts, cultural studies insists that its meaning is variable and depends crucially on the contexts supplied by the overall narra-tive, the programme's genre, and the previous publicity surrounding the show and its stars.

This emphasis on the relational dimensions of meaning and its consequent mutability is pursued in a second major strand in cultural studies research, which is concerned with the way that audience members interpret media artefacts and incorporate them into their world views and life styles. This ethnographic thrust celebrates the creativity of consumers, (see e.g. Willis 1990) and offers a powerful and necessary counter to simple 'effects' models. It views audience members as active subjects, continually struggling to make sense of their situation, rather than as passive objects of a dominant production system. This thrust is part of cultural studies' wider attempt to retrieve the complexity of popular practices and beliefs. As a powerful counter to the simpler notions of 'effects' and the dismissive critiques of popular culture as trivial and manipulative, it is clearly a very considerable gain. However, as we shall see, it can easily collude with conservative celebrations of untrammelled consumer choice.

In common with liberal defenders of the 'free market, the new populists of cultural studies focus on the moment of exchange when the meanings carried by texts meet the meanings that readers bring to them. In both styles of analysis, this encounter is removed from its wider contexts and presented as an instance of consumer sovereignty. For writers like John Fiske, it is also a signal of popular resistance of 'ideology countered or evaded; top-down power opposed by bottom-up power, social discipline faced with disorder' (Fiske 1989: 47). This romantic celebration of subversive consumption is clearly at odds with cultural studies' long-standing concern with the way the mass media operate ideologically, to sustain and support prevailing relations of domination. But even if this wider perspective is restored there is still the problem that cultural studies offers an analysis of the way the cultural industries work that has little or nothing to say about how they actually operate as industries, and how their economic organization impinges on the production and circulation of meaning. Nor does it examine the ways in which people's consumption choices are structured by their position in the wider economic formation. Exploring these dynamics is the primary task for a critical political economy of communications. In doing so we would be following Raymond Williams' injunction that 'we should look not for the components of a product but for the conditions of a practice' (Williams, 1980: 48).

Critical work, then, is not the opposite of administrative research, nor is it unambiguously opposed to the methods or concerns of cultural studies. Two central features of critical analysis take us a little nearer to a meaningful demarcation, firstly in terms of epistemology, secondly in terms of historicity.

The critical perspective assumes a realist conception of the phenomena it studies, in the simple sense that the theoretical constructs it works with exist in the real world, they are not merely phenomenal. For this reason critical analysis is centrally concerned with questions of action and structure, in an attempt to discern the real constraints which shape the lives and opportunities of real actors in the real world. In this sense critical theory is also materialist, in its focus on the interaction of people with their material environment and its further preoccupation with the unequal command over material resources and the consequences of such inequality for the nature of the symbolic environment.

Secondly, critical analysis is historically located. It is specifically interested in the investigation and description of late capitalism, which it defines as both dynamic and problematic, as undergoing change and as substantially imperfect. This historical anchoring of critical analysis is distinct from any approach which is essentialist, detached from the specifics of historical time and place.

In this chapter, however, we have a less ambitious objective, which is to describe the basic tenets of a critical political economy of the media. While this approach assumes a critical analysis of contemporary society, it is far from a full account.

What is Critical Political Economy?

Critical political economy differs from mainstream economics in four main respects. Firstly, it is holistic. Secondly, it is historical. Thirdly, it is centrally concerned with the balance between capitalist enterprise and public intervention. Finally, and perhaps most importantly of all, it goes beyond technical issues of efficiency to engage with basic moral questions of justice, equity and the public good.

Whereas mainstream economics sees the 'economy' as a separate and specialised domain, critical political economy is interested in the interplay between economic organization and political, social and cultural life. In the case of the cultural industries we are particularly concerned to trace the impact of economic dynamics on the range and diversity of public cultural expression, and its availability to different social groups. These concerns are not of course exclusive to critical commentators. They are equally central to political economists on the Right. The difference lies in the starting points of the analysis.

Liberal political economists focus on exchange in the market as consumers choose between competing commodities on the basis of the utility and satisfaction they offer. The greater the play of market forces, the greater the 'freedom' of consumer choice. Over the last decade, this vision had gained renewed credence with the governments of a variety of ideological hues. Born again in their faith in Adam Smith's hidden hand of 'free' competition, they have pushed through programmes of privatization designed to increase consumer choice by extending the scale and scope of market mechanisms. Against this, critical political economists follow Marx in shifting attention from the realm of exchange to the organization of property and production, both within the cultural industries and more generally. They do not deny that cultural producers and consumers are continually making choices, but they do so within wider structures.

Where mainstream economics focuses on the sovereign individuals of capitalism, critical political economy starts with sets of social relations and the play of power. It is interested in seeing how the making and taking of meaning is shaped at every level by the structured asymmetries in social relations. These range from the way news is structured by the prevailing relations between press proprietors and editors or journalists and their sources, to the way that television viewing is affected by the organization of domestic life and power relations within the family. These concerns are of course widely shared by researchers who are not political economists. What marks critical political economy is that it always goes beyond situated action to show how particular micro contexts are shaped by general economic dynamics and the wider structures they sustain. It is especially interested in the ways that communicative activity is structured by the unequal distribution of material and symbolic resources.

Developing an analysis along these lines means avoiding the twin temptations of instrumentalism and structuralism. Instrumentalists focus on the ways that capitalists use their economic power with a commercial market system to ensure that the flow of public information is consonant with their interests. They see the privately owned media as instruments of class domination. This case is vigorously argued in Edward S. Herman and Noam Chomsky's work, Manufacturing Consent: The Political Economy of the Mass Media (1988). They develop what they call a 'propaganda model' of the American news media, arguing that 'the powerful are able to fix the premises of discourse, to decide what the general populace is allowed to see, hear and think about, and to 'manage' public opinion by regular propaganda campaigns' (1988: xi). They are partly right. Government and business élites do have privileged access to the news; large advertisers do operate as a latter-day licensing authority, selectively supporting some newspapers and television programmes and not others; and media proprietors can determine the editorial line and cultural stance of the papers and broadcast stations they own. But by focusing on these kinds of strategic interventions they overlook the contradictions in the system. Owners, advertisers and key political personnel cannot always do so as they would wish. They operate within structures which constrain as well as facilitate, imposing limits as well as offering opportunities. Analyzing the nature and sources of these limits is a key task for a critical political economy of culture.

At the same time, it is essential to avoid the forms of structuralism which conceive of structures as building-like edifices, solid, permanent and immovable. Instead, we need to see them as dynamic formations which are constantly reproduced and altered through practical action. In his review of news studies, Michael Schudson argues that political economy relates the outcome of the news process directly to the economic structure of news organizations, and that 'everything in between is a black box that need not be examined' (Schudson 1989: 266). This is a misreading. Although some studies confine themselves to the structural level of analysis, it is only part of the story we need to tell. Analyzing the way that meaning is made and re-made through the concrete activities of producers and consumers is equally essential to the perspective we are proposing here. The aim is 'to explain how it comes about that structures are constituted through action, and reciprocally how action is constituted structurally' (Giddens 1976: 161).

This in turn, requires us to think of economic determination in a more flexible way. Instead of holding on to Marx's notion of determination in the *last* instance, with its implication that everything can eventually be related directly to economic forces, we can follow Stuart Hall in seeing determination as operating in the *first* instance (Hall 1983: 84). That is to say we can think of economic dynamics as defining the key features of the general environment within which communicative activity place, but not as a complete explanation of the nature of that activity.

Critical political economy is also necessarily historical, but historical in a particular sense. In the terms coined by the great French historian, Fernand Braudel, it is interested in how 'the fast-moving time of events, the subject of traditional narrative history' relates to the 'slow but perceptible rhythms' which characterize the gradually unfolding history of economic formations and systems of rule (Burke 1980: 94). Four historical processes are particularly central to a critical political economy of culture; the growth of the media; the extension of corporate reach; commodification; and the changing role of state and government intervention.

What Thompson describes as 'the general process by which the transmission of symbolic forms becomes increasingly mediated by the technical and institutional apparatuses of the media industries' (1990: 3–4) makes the media industries the logical place to begin an analysis of contemporary culture.

Media production in turn has been increasing, commandeered by large corporations and moulded to their interests and strategies. This has long been the case, but the reach of corporate rationales has been considerable, extended in recent years by a push towards 'privatization' and the declining vitality of publicly funded cultural institutions. Corporations dominate the cultural landscape in two ways. Firstly, an increasing proportion of cultural production is directly accounted for by major conglomerates with interests in a range of sectors, from newspapers and magazines, to television, film, music and theme parks. Secondly, corporations which are not directly involved in the cultural industries as producers, can exercise considerable control over the direction of cultural activity through their role as advertisers and sponsors. The financial viability of commercial broadcasting together with a large section of the press depends directly on advertising revenue, whilst more and more of the other 'sites where creative work is displayed' such as museums, galleries and theatres 'have been captured by corporate sponsors' and enlisted in their public relations campaigns (Schiller 1989: 4).

The extension of corporate reach reinforces a third major process – the commodification of cultural life. A commodity is a good which is produced in order to be exchanged at a price. Commercial communications corporations have always been in the business of commodity production. At first, their activities were confined to producing symbolic commodities that could be consumed directly, such as novels, newspapers, or theatrical performances. Later, with the rise of new domestic technologies such as the gramophone, telephone and radio set, cultural consumption required consumers to purchase the appropriate machine (or 'hardware') as a condition of access. This compounded the already considerable effect of inequalities in disposable income, and made communicative activity more dependent on ability to pay. Before they could make a telephone call or listen to the latest hit record at home, they needed to buy the appropriate hardware. As we shall see, the higher a household's income, the more likely it is to own key pieces of equipment – a telephone, a video recorder, a home computer – and hence the greater its communicative choices.

At first sight, advertising-supported broadcasting seems to be an exception to this trend, since anyone who has a receiving set has access to the full range of programming. Consumers do not have to pay again. However, this analysis ignores two important points. Firstly, audiences do contribute to the costs of programming in the form of additions to the retail price of heavily advertised goods. Secondly, within this system, audiences themselves are the primary commodity. The economics of commercial broadcasting revolves around the exchange of audiences for advertising revenue. The price that corporations pay for advertising spots on particular programmes is determined by the size and social composition of the audience it attracts. And in prime-time, the premium prices are commanded by shows that can attract and hold the greatest number of viewers and provide a symbolic environment in tune with consumption. These needs inevitably tilt programming towards familiar and well-tested formulae and formats and away from risk and innovation, and anchor it in common-sense rather than alternative viewpoints. Hence the audience's position as a commodity serves to reduce the overall diversity of programming and ensure that it confirms established mores and assumptions far more often than it challenges them.

The main institutional counter to the commodification of communicative activity has come from the development of institutions funded out of taxation and oriented towards providing cultural resources for the full exercise of citizenship. The most important and pervasive of these have been the public broadcasting organizations, typified by the British Broadcasting Corporation (the BBC) which has distanced itself from the dynamics of commodification by not taking spot advertising and by offering the full range of programming equally to everyone who had paid the basic annual licence fee. As the BBC's first Director General, John Reith, put it; public broadcasting 'may be shared by all alike, for the same outlay, and to the same extent . . . there need be no first and third class' (Reith 1924: 217–8). As we shall see however, this ideal has been substantially undermined in the last decade as the Corporation has responded to a fall in the real value of the licence fee by expanding its commercial activities in an effort to raise money. In a marked departure from the historic commitment to universal and equal provision, these include plans to launch subscription channels for special interest groups.

At the same time, the Corporation has also come under intensified political pressure, particularly in the areas of news and current affairs. Its always fragile independence from government has been challenged by a series of moves, ranging from well publicized attacks on the 'impartiality' of its news coverage to police seizures of film, and a government ban on live interviews with members of a range of named organizations in Northern Ireland, including the legal political party, Sinn Fein.

These attempts to narrow the field of public discourse and representation are part of a wider historical process whereby the state in capitalist societies has increasingly assumed a greater role in managing communicative activity. From its inception, political economy has been particularly interested in determining the appropriate scope of public intervention. It is therefore inevitably involved in evaluation competing policies. It is concerned with changing the world as well as with analyzing it. Classical political economists and their present-day supporters start from the assumption that public intervention ought to be minimized and market forces given the widest possible freedom of operation. Critical political economists on the other hand point to the distortions and inequalities of market systems and argue that these deficiencies can only be rectified by public intervention, though they disagree on the forms that this should take.

Arguments within political economy on the proper balance between public and private enterprise are never simply technical however. They are always underpinned by distinctive visions of what constitutes the 'public good'. Adam Smith ended his career as a professor of moral philosophy. He saw markets, not simply as more efficient, but as morally superior, because they gave consumers a free choice between competing commodities; only those goods that provided satisfaction would survive. At the same time, he saw very clearly that the public good was not simply the sum of individual choices, and that private enterprise would not provide everything that a good society required. He saw particular problems in the sphere of culture, and recommended various public interventions to increase the level of public knowledge and provide wholesome entertainment. Critical political economy takes this line of reasoning a good deal further, linking the constitution of the good society to the extension of citizenship rights.

The history of the modern communications media is not only an economic history of their growing incorporation into a capitalist economic system, but also a political history of their increasing centrality to the exercise of full citizenship. In its most general sense, citizenship is 'about the conditions that allow people to become full members of the society at every level' (Murdock and Golding 1989: 182). In an ideal situation, communications systems would contribute to these conditions in two important ways. Firstly, they would provide people with access to the information, advice and analysis that would enable them to know their rights and to pursue them effectively. Secondly, they would provide the broadcast possible range of information, interpretation and debate on areas that involve political choices, and enable them to register dissent and propose alternatives. This argument has been elaborated by the German theorist, Jurgen Habermas, in his highly influential notion of the 'public sphere'.

His historical narrative explains that in the early capitalist period a range of practices and institutions were evolved which facilitated rational and critical discussion of public affairs. This open arena of debate, in which the emerging newspaper press played a prominent role, especially in Britain, was, so Habermas argues, a feature found throughout industrializing western Europe. As critics have pointed out however, his view of the past is highly idealized. In the first place, like early enthusiasts of a 'free' commercial press, he is 'far too sanguine about the capacity of market competition to ensure the universal access of citizens to the media of communication' and fails to examine 'the inevitable tension between the free choices of investors and property owners and the freedom of choice of citizens receiving and sending information' (Keane 1989: 39). Secondly, this historic public sphere was an essentially bourgeois space, which largely excluded the working class, women and ethnic minorities.

Nevertheless, the idea of the public sphere is worth retaining, providing that we add that it needs to be open enough that all groups in the society can recognise themselves and their aspirations as being fairly represented. This general ideal of a communications system as a public cultural space that is open, diverse, and accessible, provides the basic yardstick against which critical political economy measures the performance of existing systems and formulates alternatives.

Political Economy in Practice: Three Core Tasks

In order to illustrate the concerns and distinctive priorities of a political economy of communications we briefly outline three areas of analysis. The first is concerned with the production of cultural goods, to which political economy attaches particular importance in its presumption of the limiting (but not completely determining) impact of cultural production on the range of cultural consumption. Secondly, we examine the political economy of texts to illustrate ways in which the representations present in media products are related to the material realities of their production and consumption. Finally, we assess the political economy of cultural consumption, to illustrate the relation between material and cultural inequality which political economy is distinctively concerned to address.

The Production of Meaning as the Exercise of Power

Philip Elliott, in a bleak reading of developments in Britain in the early 1980s, suggested that the public sphere has been seriously eroded by recent developments. Technological and economic developments were promoting 'a continuation of the shift away from involving people in societies as political citizens of nation states towards involving them as consumption units in a corporate world'. Intellectuals, in particular, were being robbed of those public forums in which they could engage in their culture of critical discourse' (Elliott, 1982: 243–244). A focal question for the political economy of communications is to investigate how changes in the array of forces which exercise control over cultural production and distribution limit or liberate the public sphere. In practice this directs attention to two key issues. The first is the pattern of ownership of such institutions and the consequences of this pattern for control over their activities. The second is the nature of the relationship between state regulation and communications institutions. We can briefly review each of these in turn.

The steadily increasing amount of cultural production accounted for by large corporations has long been a source of concern to theorists of democracy. They saw a fundamental contradiction between the ideal that public media should operate as a public sphere and the reality of concentrated private ownership. They feared that proprietors would use their property rights to restrict the flow of information and open debate on which the vitality of democracy depended. These concerns were fuelled by the rise of the great press barons at the turn of the century. Not only did proprietors like Pullitzer and Hearst in the United States and Northcliffe in the United Kingdom own chains or newspapers with large circulations, but they clearly had no qualms about using them to promote their pet political causes or to denigrate positions and people they disagreed with.

These long-standing worries have been reinforced in recent years by the emergence of multi media conglomerates with significant stakes across a range of central communications sectors. Rupert Murdoch's News International empire is a well known case in point. It includes major press and publishing interests in the USA, UK and Australia, as well as America's fourth largest television network, Fox, and a controlling stake in Britain's direct satellite broadcasting service, British Sky Broadcasting. Other important examples include Sony of Japan which owns CBS records and Columbia Pictures, and the Bertelsmann company of Germany, which controls RCA records and Doubleday books as well as a major domestic chain of newspapers and magazines.

The rise of communications conglomerates adds a new element to the old debate about potential abuses of owner power. It is no longer a simple case of proprietors intervening in editorial decisions or firing key personnel who fall foul of their political philosophies. Cultural production is also strongly influenced by commercial strategies built around 'synergies' which exploit the overlaps between the company's different media interests. The company's newspapers may give free publicity to their television stations or the record and book divisions may launch products related to a new movie released by the film division. The effect is to reduce the diversity of cultural goods in circulation. Although in simple quantitative terms there may be more commodities in circulation, they are more likely to be variants of the same basic themes and images.

In addition to the power they exercise directly over the companies they own, the major media moguls also have considerable indirect power over smaller concerns operating in their markets or seeking to break into them. They establish the rules by which the competitive game will be played. They can use their greater financial power to drive new entrants out of the marketplace by launching expensive promotional campaigns, offering discounts to advertisers, or buying up key creative personnel. Firms that do survive compete for market share by offering similar products to the leading concerns and employing tried and tested editorial formulae.

Historically, the main interruptions to this process have come from state intervention. These have taken two main forms. Firstly, commercial enterprises have been regulated in the public interest with the aim of ensuring diversity of cultural production, including forms that would be unlikely to survive in pure market conditions. British commercial television companies for example are required to make a range of minority interest programmes, even though they are not profitable. Secondly, cultural diversity has been further underwritten by various forms of public subsidy.

Over the last two decades however, this system has been substantially altered by privatization policies. Major public cultural enterprises, such as the French TF1 television network, have been sold to private investors. Liberalization policies have introduced private operators into markets which were previously closed to competition, such as the broadcasting systems of a number of European countries. And regulatory regimes have been altered in favour of freedom of operations for owners and advertisers. The net effect of these changes has been to increase greatly the potential reach and power of the major communications companies and to reinforce the danger that public culture will be commandeered by private interests. Charting these shifts in the balance between commercial and public enterprise and tracing their impact on cultural diversity is a key task for a critical political economy.

There are several dimensions to this process. Firstly, state agencies such as the army and police have become major users of communications technologies both for surveillance and for their own command and control systems. Secondly, governments and state departments have become increasingly important producers of public information in a variety of forms ranging from official statistics and daily press briefings to public advertising campaigns. Thirdly, governments have extended their regulatory functions in relation to, both the structure of the media industries (through restrictions on ownership and pricing for example), and the range of permissible public expression (through regulations relating to areas such as obscenity, incitement to racial hatred, and 'national security'). Finally, and most importantly, liberal democratic governments have widened the range of cultural activities that they subsidize out of the public purse, either indirectly, by not charging value added tax on newspapers for example, or directly, through various forms of grants. These range from the monies provided for museums, libraries and theatres to the compulsory annual licence fee for television set ownership which funds the BBC.

Broadcasting in Britain has evolved as a quasi-public institution, in which the ideals of public service have been translated into both law and custom and practice. The BBC, particularly under its first Director-General John Reith, construed itself as undertaking a mission to inform, educate, and entertain, in a potent if indistinct ideology which has been readily adopted by commercial broadcasting. Both see themselves as performing a role more akin to education or health than to conventional purveyors of commodities in the market place. The patrician overtones in such a self-assigned role, and the contradictions it generates for a medium dependent on advertising revenue, have undermined the credibility of this conception of broadcasting, and the enterprise culture of 1980s' Conservatism enthusiastically challenged the idea that broadcasting should be protected from the disciplines of the market, arguing that consumer choice and cultural independence were best guaranteed by liberating the broadcast media from state regulation.

Defenders of public service broadcasting have found themselves wrong-footed, appearing to support a bureaucratic and statist conception of communications which was far from the ideals of the 'public sphere'. In addition they seem to be ignoring the boundless potential of new technologies which might deliver the choice and communicative opportunities of an ideal 'public sphere' far more readily than the dead hand of state intervention.

The contribution of political economy to this debate is to analyze how and in what ways the relation between the media and the state has consequences for the range of expression and ideas in the public arena. For example what have been the consequences of the effective detachment of the BBC from market forces? Recent analysis would suggest that increasing pressure on the BBC to compete for income beyond the licence fee (now falling in real value and intended to form a decreasing proportion of the BBC's revenue up to the renewal of its Charter in 1996), has begun to restrict significantly the range of the Corporation's activities and output.

However, the state is not only a regulator of communications institutions. It is itself a communicator of enormous power. How this power is exercised is of major interest to a political economy of culture. Governments are inevitably anxious to promote their own views of the development of policy, and to ensure that legislative initiatives are properly understood and supported. In recent years this desire has fostered a rapid growth in communications activity, so that by 1990 the government was the second biggest advertiser in the country (see Golding, 1990: 95). Communications researchers have commonly analyzed this process as one of agenda-building, in which the state effectively gives subsidies to media organizations by reducing the effort required to discover and produce information for their audiences. As Gandy defines the term, an information subsidy 'is an attempt to produce influence over the actions of others by controlling their access to and use of information relevant to those actions' (Gandy, 1982: 61). In an increasingly public relations state the provisions of such subsidies can range from the entirely healthy distribution of essential information with which to explain and facilitate public policy to the nefarious management of news in which 'being economical with the truth' becomes an accessory of political life (see Golding, 1986).

The production of communications, however, is not merely a simple reflection of the controlling interests of those who own or even control the broad range of capital plant and equipment which make up the means by which cultural goods are made and distributed. Within the media are men and women working within a range of codes and professioanl ideologies, and with an array of aspirations, both personal and social. These ambitions can be idealized; much cultural production is routine, mundane, and highly predictable. But the autonomy of those who work within the media is a matter of substantial interest to political economists. Their aim is to discover how far this autonomy can be exercised given the consequences of broad economic structure we have described above, and to what extent the economic structure of the media prevents some forms of expession from finding a popular outlet and audience.

An example can illustrate the point. Successive Royal Commissions have remarked on the significant absence within the British media of a popular newspaper with political sympathies to the radical left. The last Royal Commission on the Press, for example, concluded that 'There is no doubt that over most of this century the labour movement has had less newspaper support than its right-wing opponents and that its beliefs and activities have been unfavourably reported by the majority of the press' (House of Commons, 1977: 98–9). 'There is no doubt', it went on, 'that there is a gap in political terms which could be filled with advantage' (ibid.: 110). Many journalists would sympathize with this view. As senior Fleet Street commentator Tom Baistow has lamented 'For millions of Left, Centre and agnostic Don't Know readers there is no longer any real choice of newspapers'. (Baistow, 1985: 57). To explain this, political economists will examine the impact of shifts in advertising support and ownership to discover why this gap exists and why, therefore, opportunities for the expression of radical views of the political left do not routinely find space in the organs of the British national press. To do so they will wish to go beyond these broad structural features, however, to assess the consequences for daily practice, routine news gathering and processing, journalistic recruitment and professional ideology, of these larger structures. This will require detailed study of the work of journalists, the way sources of varying power and authority engage in 'Agenda-building', and the link between what industrial sociologists have traditionally characterized as market situation and work situation.

The political economy of cultural production, then, is concerned with the concrete consequences for the work and nature of making media goods of the broad patterns of power and ownership which are their backdrop. To see where this takes us in the analysis of what gets produced we need to move on to the political economy of media output.

Political Economy and Textual Analysis

As we noted earlier, research in cultural studies has been particularly concerned with analyzing the structure of media texts and tracing their role in sustaining systems of domination. As it has developed, this work decisively rejected the notion that the mass media act as a transmission belt for a dominant ideology and developed a model of the communications system as a field or space, in which contending discourses, offering different ways of looking and speaking, struggle for visibility and legitimacy. But outside of televised political speeches, discourses are seldom available for public consumption in their 'raw' state. They are reorganized and recontextualized to fit the particular expressive form being used. Discourses about AIDS for example, might well feature in a variety of television programmes, ranging from public health advertisement, to news items, investigative reports, studio discussion programme, or episodes of soap operas or police series. Each of these forms has a major impact on what can be said and shown, by whom, and from what point of view. In short, cultural forms are mechanisms for regulating public discourse. We can distinguish two dimensions to this process. The first has to do with the range of discourses that particular forms allow into play, whether they are organized exclusively around official discourses, or whether they provide space for the articulation of counter-discourses. The second concerns the way that the available discourses are handled within the text, whether they are arranged in a clearly marked hierarchy of credibility which urges the audience to prefer one over the others, or whether they are treated in a more even-handed and indeterminate way which leaves the audience with a more open choice.

If cultural studies is primarily interested in the way these mechanisms work within a particular media text or across a range of texts, critical political economy is concerned to explain how the economic dynamics of production structure public discourse by promoting certain cultural forms over others. Take for example, the increasing reliance on international co-production agreements in television drama production – these arrangements impose a variety of constraints on form, as the partners search for subject matter and narrative styles that they can sell in their home markets. The resulting bargain may produce an americanized product which is fast moving, based on simple characterizations, works with a tried and tested action format, and offers an unambiguous ending. Or it may result in a variant of 'televisual tourism' which trades on the familiar forms and sights of the national cultural heritage (Murdock 1989b). Both strategies represent a narrowing of the field of discourse and inhibit a full engagement with the complexities and ambiguities of the national condition. The first affects a closure around dominant transatlantic forms of story-telling with their clearly marked boundaries and hierarchies of discourse. The second reproduces an ideology of 'Englishness' which excludes or marginalizes a whole range of subordinate discourses.

This general perspective, with its emphasis on the crucial mediating role of cultural forms, has two major advantages. Firstly, it allows us to trace detailed connections between the financing and organization of cultural production and changes in the field of public discourse and representation in a non reducible way, that respects the need for a full analysis of textual organization. Indeed, far from being secondary, such an analysis is central to the full development of the argument. Secondly, by stressing the fact that media texts vary considerably in their degree of discursive openness, it offers an approach to audience activity that focuses on structured variations in response. However, in contrast to recent work on audience activity produced within cultural studies, which concentrates on the negotiation of textual interpretations and media use in immediate social settings, critical political economy seeks to relate variations in people's responses to their overall location in the economic system (Murdock 1989c). Of course, this cannot explain everything we need to know about the dynamics of response, but it is a necessary starting point.

Consumption – Sovereignty or Struggle?

For political proponents of a free market philosophy communications goods are like any other. Since the best way of ensuring adequate distribution and production of the general commodities people want is through the market, so too, the argument follows, is this true for cultural goods. It is the truth or otherwise of this proposition that provides the analytical target for a political economy of cultural consumption.

Curiously, an influential version of this free market philosophy has had considerable currency in much work within recent cultural studies. In an attempt to contest the apparent simplistic determinism of a view which sees audiences as the passive dupes of all powerful media, some writers have asserted the sovereignty of viewers and readers, to impose their own meanings and interpretations on material which is 'polysemic' – that is capable of generating a variety of meanings. This analysis has tempted writers of very varying political or social presuppositions. For liberal pluralists it has refurbished the view that the checks and balances of cultural supply and demand, though admittedly uneven, are far from bankrupt. The customer, though perhaps a little bruised, is still ultimately sovereign. For writers with more critical or radical instincts, it is a view which has unleashed a populist romance in which the downtrodden victims caricatured by crude economic determinists are revealed as heroic resistance fighters in the war against cultural deception.

Consumer sovereignty is in any total sense clearly impossible – nobody has access to a complete range of cultural goods as and when they might wish, without restriction. The task of political economy, then, is to examine the barriers which limit such freedom. It construes such barriers being of two kinds, material and cultural. We can examine each of these in turn.

Where communications goods and facilities are available only at a price there will be a finite capacity to have access to them, limited by the disposable spending power of individuals and households. Spending on services generally has grown significantly in the last generation. In 1953/4 spending on services made up 9.5 per cent of household expenditure; by 1986 this proportion had risen to 12.7 percent (Central Statistical Office, 1990). All expenditure on personal and household services and on leisure goods and services amounted to over a third of household expenditure by 1988 (ibid.: 24). Within this global figure spending within the home has risen as a proportion, linked most significantly to the television set as an increasingly dominant hub of leisure time and expenditure. On average British adults in 1990 spent 24 hours a week watching television broadcasts, and an as yet uncertainly calibrated amount of time using television for related activities, such as viewing videos or playing computer games. As the range of hardware required for such activities grows, however, so too does the demand on private expenditure necessary to participate in them.

As Table 1 shows there is a marked difference in the ownership of home computers and videos between different income groups, a gap that is unlikely to diminish substantially due to two factors. First, income differentials themselves have sharply widened in the last decade. During the 1980s wage increases for the highest paid fifth of male workers were 42 per cent higher than for the lowest paid fifth (Low Pay Unit, 1988: 11). In addition the gap between

Table 1 Ownership of communications equipment among households
in different income groups (1989).

Household weekly	percentage owning		
income (£)	phone	video	home computer
46–60	64.3	13.9	0.8
81–100	73.9	25.9	6.2
126–150	83.9	42.6	6.9
151–175	83.9	55.4	11.2
176–200	87.2	65.5	14.1
226–250	96.2	75.4	25.8
276–325	96.2	80.5	29.4
376–450	98.6	85.2	33.1
over 550	99.7	77.7	34.3
All households	86.2	56.6	16.6

Source: Family Expenditure Survey 1989.

households dependent on social security benefits for their income and those in
the labour market has also increased. Together these changes meant that
between 1977 and 1987 the share of incomes (after allowing for all taxes paid
and benefits received) of the poorest fifth fell from 6.4% of the total to 5.1%,
while the share enjoyed by the richest fifth grew from 40% to 45% (Oppenheim, 1990: 127). The disposable spending power of different groups in the
population is thus significantly polarized. Secondly such goods require regular
updating and replacement, disadvantaging groups with limited spending power
and cumulatively advantaging the better off. Owning video or computer
hardware requires expenditure on software, owning a phone means spending
money on using it. Thus limited spending power is a deterrent not only to initial
purchase but to regular use.

However not all expenditure on communications goods involves expensive
acquisition of equipment. Television programmes can be viewed once you have
a set to watch them on, as most people do, while many cultural materials are
available as public goods; they are paid for from taxation as a common resource
– public library books, for example. This is not a static situation, however. For
political economists a shift in the provision and distribution of cultural goods
from being public services to private commodities signals a substantial change
in the opportunity for different groups in the population to have access to them.
If television channels, or individual programmes, are accessible by price, as is
envisaged for much of the new television structure heralded by the 1990
Broadcasting Act, then consumption of television programmes will be significantly governed by the distribution of household incomes. Similar considerations would come into play if, for example, public libraries were to make
greater use of powers to charge, as was proposed in a government green paper
in 1988, even though, at the time, such proposals were shelved (Office of Arts
and Libraries, 1988). By imposing the discipline of price on cultural goods they
acquire an artificial scarcity which makes them akin to other goods of consider-

ably greater scarcity. It is for this reason that the political economy of cultural consumption has to be especially concerned with material inequalities.

Critical political economy is not only concerned with material barriers to cultural consumption, however. It is also interested in the ways in which social location regulates access to the cultural competences required to interpret and use media materials in particular ways. One of the strongest empirical traditions within cultural studies – running from studies of youth subcultures to research on differential 'readings' of television texts – has concerned itelf with how social locations provide access to cultural repertoires and symbolic resources that sustain differences of interpretation and expression (Morley 1983). This emphasis on social experience as a cultural resource is important, but it can be oversold. Consumption practices are clearly not completely manipulated by the strategies of the cultural industries but they are equally clearly, not completely independent of them. Rather we need to see cultural commodities as the site of a continual struggle over uses and meanings between producers and audiences and between different consumer groups.

At the same time we need to go on to explore other links between people's loction in the productive system and their communicative activity. In pursuing this project, it is important to remember that 'production' is not the same thing as paid employment, it also includes domestic labour. Women's prime responsibility for the 'shadow Work' (Illich 1981) of shopping, cleaning, cooking and nurturing has fundamental consequences for their relation to the mass media. Not only are their choices often constrained by the prior demands of husbands and children, but the fact that no one else in the family is regenerating their affective resources, leads them to look for other ways of maintaining psychological support. For example, where men mostly use the telephone instrumentally, to 'get things done', women often use it expressively, to sustain social networks. What appears from the outside as trivial gossip, is experienced from the inside as an emotional life-saver.

Conclusion

People depend in large measure on the cultural industries for the images, symbols, and vocabulary with which they interpret and respond to their social environment. It is vital, therefore, that we understand these industries in a comprehensive and theoretically adequate way which enables the analysis of communications to take its place at the heart of socal and cultural research. We have argued that a critical political economy provides an approach which sustains such an analysis, and in so doing have illustrated in a preliminary way, the origins, character, and application of such an approach. Much remains to be done, both theoretically and empirically, however, before we can claim to have fully established a critical political economy of communications.

References

BAISTOW, T., 1985: *Fourth Rate Estate: An Anatomy of Fleet Street*. Comedia.
BURKE, PETER, 1980: *Sociology and History*. London: George Allen and Unwin.

CENTRAL STATISTICAL OFFICE, 1990: *Family Expenditure Survey 1988* HMSO.

COLLINS, RICHARD, GARNHAM, NICHOLAS and LOCKSLEY, GARETH, 1988: *The Economics of Television: The UK Case*. London: Sage Publications.

CURRAN, J., 1990: The new revisionism in mass communication research: a reappraisal *European Journal of Communication*. Vol. 5(2–3) pp. 135–164.

ELLIOTT, P., 1982: Intellectuals, the 'information society', and the disappearance of the public sphere. *Media, Culture and Society* Vol. 4. pp. 243–253.

FISKE, JOHN, 1987: *Television Culture*. London: Methuen.

FISKE, JOHN, 1989: *Understanding Popular Culture*. London: Unwin Hyman.

GANDY, O., 1982: *Beyond Agenda-Setting: Information Subsidies and public policy*. Ablex.

GIDDENS, ANTHONY, 1976: *New Rules of Sociological Method*. London: Hutchinson.

GOLDING, PETER, 1986: Power in the Information society. G. Muskens and C. Hamelink (eds.) *Dealing with Global Networks: Global Networks and European Communities* Tilburg, IVA.

GOLDING, PETER, 1990: Political communication and citizenship: the media and democracy in an inegalitarian social order in M. Ferguson (Ed.) *Public Communication: The New imperatives*. Sage.

HABERMAS, J., 1989: *The Structural transformation of the Public sphere*. Polity Press.

HALL, STUART, 1983: 'The problem of ideology – Marxism without guarantees'. In B. Matthews (Ed) *Marx: A Hundred Years On*. London: Lawrence and Wishart, pp. 57–85.

HALL, STUART, 1986: 'Media power and class power' in J. Curran et al (Eds) *Bending Reality: The State of the Media*. London: Pluto Press, pp. 5–14.

HERMAN, EDWARD, S. and CHOMSKY, NOAM, 1988: *Manufacturing Consent: The Political Economy of The Mass Media*. New York: Pantheon Books.

House of Commons, 1977: *Royal Commission on the Press: Final Report* Cmnd. 6810. HMSO.

ILLICH, IVAN, 1981: *Shadow Work*. London. Marion Boyars.

KEANE, JOHN, 1989: 'Liberty of the press' in the 1990s, *New Formations*, No. 8, Summer, pp. 35–53.

Low Pay Unit, 1988: *The Poor Decade: Wage Inequalities in the 1980s*. London: Low Pay Unit.

MORLEY, DAVID, 1983: 'Cultural transformations: the politics of resistance' in H. Davis and P. Walton (eds) *Language, Image, Media*. Oxford: Basil Blackwell. pp. 104–117.

MURDOCK, GRAHAM and GOLDING, PETER, 1978: Theories of Communication and Theories of Society *Communication Research* Vol. 5(3), pp. 390–456.

MURDOCK, GRAHAM, and GOLDING PETER, (1974): For a Political Economy of Mass Communications. R. Miliband and J. Saville (Eds) *The Socialist Register 1973* Merlin.

MURDOCK, GRAHAM, 1989a: 'Cultural Studies: Missing Links', *Critical Studies in Mass Communication*, Volume 6, No. 4, December, pp. 436–440.

MURDOCK, GRAHAM, 1989b: 'Televisual Tourism' in – Christian W. Thomsen (ed.) *Cultural Transfer or Electronic Colonialism?*, Heidelberg: Carl Winter-Universitatsverlag, pp. 171–183.

MURDOCK, GRAHAM, 1989c: 'Audience Activity and Critical Inquiry' in – Brenda Dervin et al (eds) *Rethinking Communication Volume 2: Paradigm Exemplars*. London: Sage Publications, pp. 226–249.

MURDOCK, GRAHAM and GOLDING, PETER, 1989: 'Information poverty and politcal inequality: citizenship in the age of privatized communications', *Journal of Communication*, Vol. 39, No. 3, Summer, pp. 180–195.

Office of Arts and Libraries, 1988: *Financing our Public Library service: Four subjects for debate* Cmnd. 324 HMSO.

OPPENHEIM, C, 1990: *Poverty: The Facts*. London: Child Poverty Action Group.
REITH, JOHN, 1924: *Broadcast Over Britain*. London: Hodder and Stoughton.
SCHILLER, HERBERT, I., 1989: *Culture Inc: The Corporate Takeover of Public Expression*. New York: Oxford University Press.
SCHUDSON, MICHAEL, 1989: 'The sociology of news production', *Media, Culture and Society*, Volume 11, Number 3, July, pp. 263–282.
THOMPSON, JOHN, B., 1990: *Ideology and Modern Culture: Critical Social Theory in the Era of Mass Communication*. Oxford: Polity Press.
WILLIAMS, R., 1980: *Problems in Materialism and Culture*. London: Verso.

2

Feminist Perspectives on the Media

Liesbet van Zoonen

With the current proliferation and fragmentation of feminist theory and politics, reviewing feminist perspectives on the media has become a hazardous task. A general overview of the field can hardly do justice to the variety of feminist discourse while advancing one's own particular approach inevitably excludes other, often equally valid feminist discourses. In this chapter I shall use both approaches. While I cannot deny my own political and academic preferences, I do hope to provide a framework general enough to understand historical developments and recent trends in feminist media studies.

How does feminist media theory distinguish itself from other perspectives such as postmodernism, pluralism, neo-marxism, etc.? Its unconditional focus on analyzing *gender* as a mechanism that structures material and symbolic worlds and our experiences of them, is hard to find in other theories of the media. Even by mid and late seventies mainstream communication scholars did not seem to be very interested in the subject 'woman'. 'And why should they? Before the advent of the women's movement these [sex-role] stereotypes seemed natural, "given". Few questioned how they developed, how they were reinforced, or how they were maintained. Certainly the media's role in this process was not questioned' (Tuchman, 1978: 5). Nor were critical communication scholars in the forefront of recognizing the importance of gender, as the account of the Women's Studies Group of the Centre for Contemporary Cultural Studies (CCCS) at Birmingham confirms: 'We found it extremely difficult to participate in the CCCS groups and felt, without being able to articulate it, that it was a case of the masculine domination of both intellectual work and the environment in which it was being carried out' (*Women Take Issue*, 1978: 11).

The situation has improved to a certain extent. There seems to be a hesitant acknowledgment of the necessity and viability of feminist approaches to the media. Academic journals of communications have published review articles of feminist media studies and sometimes devoted whole issues to it (*Communication*, 1986; Dervin, 1987; Foss and Foss, 1983; *Journal of Communication Inquiry*, 1987; McCormack, 1980; Rakow, 1986; Smith, 1983; Steeves, 1987; Van Zoonen, 1988). However, in 'general' reviews of main trends in communication theory and research one finds few traces of this growing body of feminist scholarship. To mention some arbitrary examples: in Denis McQuail's bestselling *Introduction to Mass Communication Theory* there is no reference to 'woman', 'gender', 'sexuality', or other feminist concerns. The revised second edition has one paragraph about feminist content analysis added. In special issues about communications research in western and eastern Europe published by the *European Journal of Communication* and *Media, Culture and Society* (1990) references to gender or feminism are all but absent.

In the field of cultural studies feminist concerns have gained more ground. Many innovating studies about 'women's genres' such as soap operas, romance novels and women's magazines and their audiences, have informed and have been informed by this approach (e.g. Hobson, 1982; Modleski, 1982; Radway, 1984; Winship, 1987). Moreover, authors such as Fiske (1987) and Morley (1986) addressing other issues in cultural studies, have incorporated gender in their research as one of the crucial mechanisms in structuring our cultural experiences and our outlook on daily life. Notwithstanding the succesful and inspiring conjunction of feminist and cultural studies, not all feminist studies are cultural studies, and not all cultural studies are feminist studies. I shall elaborate the former as I review different feminist perspectives later on. The latter brings me to a second distinctive feature of feminist media studies.

The feminist academic venture is intrinsically political. In the early years of the revived movement, a concurrence of research, writing and political activism was common practice. A typical example is Betty Friedan's research about the construction of the American cultural ideal of 'the happy housewife-heroine' in women's magazines and advertisements.[1] The book *The Feminine Mystique* (1963) was an immediate best seller and gave rise to a revival of the women's movement which had been dormant since the successful struggle for women's suffrage. One of the first 'second wave' feminist groups was the *National Organisation of Women*, headed by Betty Friedan. Not surprisingly, NOW declared the media to be one of the major sites of struggle for the movement: in the spring of 1970 approximately 100 women occupied the offices of *The Ladies Home Journal* demanding among other things a female editor in chief, a child care centre for employees and the publication of a 'liberated issue' to be compiled by the protestors. At least one feminist supplement to the *Journal* appeared. A nationwide research project monitoring television networks and local stations for sexist content was conducted with the intention to challenge the licence of any station with a sexist record when it came up for renewal before the Federal Communications Commissions (Hole & Levine, 1972: 264). Although by the beginning of the eighties much feminist research came from the academy, its political nature remained, therewith fundamentally undermining the dominant academic, paradigm, of objectivity, neutrality and detachment. For example, Tuchman (1978: 38) introducing one of the first volumes about women and the media, asks herself: 'How can the media be changed? . . . How can we free women from the tyranny of media messages limiting their lives to hearth and home?' The book concludes with a chapter discussing the policy implications of the research material presented. Numerous other academic publications conclude with recommendations for change (e.g. Creedon, 1989; Gallagher, 1980; Thoveron, 1986).

With its substantial project, it is the reciprocal relation between theory, politics and activism, the commitment of feminist academics to have their work contribute to a larger feminist goal – however defined, the blurred line between the feminist as academic and the feminist as activist, that distinguishes feminist perspectives on the media from other possible perspectives. Paradoxically, as I shall try to show in this review, the growing theoretical and empirical sophistication of feminist media studies has not only jeopardized its relevance for a critical feminist media politics but also diminished its potential as a comprehensive cultural critique. For example, as we acknowledge the pleasure women derive from watching soap operas, it becomes increasingly difficult to find moral justifications for criticizing their contribution to the hegemonic construction of gender identities. To disentangle this paradox I shall first discuss liberal, radical and socialist feminist discourses which share – in spite of their many differences – a social control model of communication, and a conceptualization of gender as a dichotomous category with a historically stable and universal meaning.

Liberal, Radical and Socialist Feminism

Classifying feminism in three neatly separated ideological currents, is certainly at odds with the present fragmentation of feminist thought. It seems hard to include, for example, postmodern and psychoanalytic trends satisfactorily in this tripartition. Also, feminist theory and practice is often rather eclectic, incorporating elements from different ideologies as circumstances and issues necessitate. As a result few feminist media studies can be unequivocally classified in one of the three categories. However, taken as ideal types – which I shall do here – they are indicative of the various ways in which feminists perceive the media. Although less dominant than in the seventies and early eighties, they still underlie many feminist selfperceptions and analysis.[2]

Liberal Feminism

In liberal feminist discourse irrational prejudice and stereotypes about the supposedly natural role of women as wives and mothers account for the unequal positon of women in society. General liberal principles of liberty and equality should apply to women as well. 'Equal Rights' or 'reformist' feminism are other labels for these principles which find their political translation in attempts to change legislation, in affirmative action programs, in stimulating women to take up non-traditional roles and occupations and to develop masculine qualities to acquire power. Such role reversal is much less strongly advocated for men.

Sex role stereotypes, prescriptions of sex-appropriate behaviour, appearance, interests, skills and selfperceptions are at the core of liberal feminist media analyses (Tuchman, 1978: 5). Numerous quantitative content analyses have shown that women hardly appear in the mass media, be it depicted as wife, mother, daughter, girlfriend; as working in traditionally female jobs (secretary, nurse, receptionist); or as sex-object. Moreover they are usually young and beautiful, but not very well educated. Experimental research done in the tradition of cognitive psychology tends to support the hypothesis that media act as socialization agents – along with the family – teaching children in particular their appropriate sex roles and symbolically rewarding them for appropriate behaviour (cf. Busby, 1975; Gallagher, 1980). It is thought that media perpetuate sex role stereotypes because they reflect dominant social values and also because male mediaproducers are influenced by these stereotypes.

The solutions liberal feminism offers are twofold: women should obtain more equal positions in society, enter male dominated fields and acquire power. With a time lag mass media will reflect this change. Meanwhile, media can contribute to change by portraying more women and men in non-traditional roles and by using non sexist language. The strategies liberal feminists have developed to reach these goals are many: teaching 'non-sexist professionalism' in Schools of Journalism (Van Zoonen, 1989); creating awareness among broadcasters and journalists about stereotypes and their effects; putting 'consumer pressure' on media institutions, especially on advertisers; demanding affirmative action policies of media institutions (cf. Thoveron, 1986). Liberal media strategies have had some unwarranted consequences. The emphasis on role reversal for women in particular has created a new stereotype of 'Superwoman', the response of commercial culture to the demands of liberal feminism. Women's magazines and advertisements portray her as an independent and assertive career woman, a successful wife and mother, who is still beautiful and has kept the body she had as a girl in perfect shape. Real women trying to live up to this image, end up suffering from serious burn out symptoms (Dowling, 1989).

Another unforeseen consequence of liberal strategies is showing painfully in developments in the media workforce. The numbers of female journalists have increased considerably in recent years with the United States in the forefront (MRTW, 1989). Sad enough however, as American researchers have observed 'a female majority in the field does not translate into superior power or influence for women: instead, it has been translated to mean a decline in salaries and status for the field' (Creedon, 1989: 3). In part these problems arise from liberal feminism's disregard for socio-economic structures, and power relations. Social conflict is presented as a difference of opinion which can be resolved through rational argumentation. This assumption is reflected in the emphasis on strategies which imply teaching and raising awareness of (male) mediaproducers, and in the rather optimistic belief that media-institutions can be changed from within by female mediaprofessionals. That men – as radical feminists would argue – or consumer capitalism – as socialist feminists would argue – have vested interests in maintaining their power over women, does not easily fit in the ideal of rational disinterested argumentation.

Radical Feminism

In radical feminist discourse 'patriarchy', a social system in which all men are assumed to dominate and oppress all women, accounts for women's position in society. Patriarchy is conceived to be the result of men's innately wicked inclination to dominate women, a genetically determined need which they can fulfil – in the last instance – by exercising their physical strength. Radical feminists have been in the forefront of exposing male abuse of women and politicizing issues formerly considered as private: sexual violence, wife battering, incest, pornography, and more recently, sex tourism and trafficking in women. It is obvious that men can have no place in radical feminist utopias. In order to free themselves completely women have to cut off all ties with men and male society, and form their own communities. Lesbianism therefore is necessarily following political choice – another example of the radical politicization of the personal.

Since mass media are in the hands of male owners and producers, they will operate to the benefit of a patriarchal society. Apparently this premise does not need further research, given the few media studies that have been conducted from a radical feminist perspective. The main focus is on pornography and rather polemical: 'Pornography exists because men despise women, and men despise women because pornography exists' (Dworkin, 1980: 289). In radical feminist media analyses the power of the media to affect men's behaviour towards women and women's perception of themselves is beyond discussion: 'Researchers may have been unable to prove a direct connection between any particular instance of media and any particular act, but *there can be no doubt* that media distortion contributes to a general climate of discrimination and abuse of women' (Davies et al., 1988: 6, author italics).

The media strategies of radical feminism are straightforward: women should create their own means of communication. Technological developments in print and audiovisual media made the proliferation of feminist writing, newsletters, magazines, radio and TV programmes, video and film groups possible. A host of feminist ideas would otherwise have not received a public forum (Kessler, 1984). Most media are produced by a collective of volunteers, who usually work without profits motives and share responsibilities. Radical feminist logic does not allow for hierarchies; they are thought to be a perversion of masculine society. Contributions are anonymous or signed with first names only since it is assumed that all women share the same kind of patriarchal oppression.

Radical media strategies have been more problematic than they seemed at first sight: the belief that women together – all innately good people – would be able to work without competition, hierarchy or specialization, and would write or film from the same source of essential femininity, proved an illusion. A constant feature of radical feminist media has been internal conflict about organization and editorial policy. Power differences, difference of opinion and interests appear to exist among women also, and are not a male preserve. Another dilemma has been posed by the inability of feminist media to attract readers and audiences beyond the feminist parish. While their self proclaimed aim often is to inform and mobilize larger audiences, movement media tend to fulfil more of a ritual function. With the waning enthusiasm for collective expressions of feminism, the circulation figures of feminist media declined rather dramatically resulting in the demise of many of them.[3]

In its pure form, radical feminist media analyses have not gained much ground. However, many elements of it are also found in other theories. Socialist feminism incorporates the concept of patriarchal ideology in its marxist analysis of women's position, without however adopting its essentialist stance. The conviction that differences between men and women are essentially biological has emerged in other feminist perspectives as well. French feminists drawing heavily from psychoanalytic theory have very sophisticatedly located the difference between men and women in the different structure of male and female genitals, considering, for example, classic linear narrative structure as an expression of masculine, goal oriented sexuality. French feminist theory has particularly influenced literary and film studies, but is rare in studies of mass media (e.g. Mattelart, 1986). The solution for women's position is not sought in withdrawing from patriarchal culture, but in creating new and legitimate spaces for the feminine voice, supposedly more process-oriented. This has been extremely successful in the area of women's writing, but the feminist avantgarde film of the seventies never acquired a large following (e.g. Pribram, 1988).

Socialist Feminism

Unlike radical and liberal feminism, socialist feminism does not focus exclusively on gender to account for women's position, but attempts to incorporate an analysis of class and economic conditions of women as well. Central concepts are 'the reproduction of labour' and 'the economic value of domestic labour'. Although not recognized as such, the nurturing, moral, educational and domestic work women do in the family is said to be indispensable for the maintenance of capitalism. Were all this labour to be paid, the profit margins of capitalism would be critically diminished (cf. Zaretsky, 1986). Socialist feminism shares with liberal feminism an emphasis on the need for women to take up paid labour. However, at the same time a fundamental restructuring of the labour market is called for, in which the average labour week is reduced to 25 hours so that women and men have time left to share nurturing and domestic responsibilities.

More recently, socialist feminism has tried to incorporate other social divisions along the lines of ethnicity, sexual preference, age, physical ability, since the experience of, for example, black, lesbian and single women did not fit nicely in the biased gender/class earlier model. This has resulted in an increasingly complicated and incoherent theoretical project, which until now has not produced a satisfactory account of the way material and cultural conditions interact. More and more, ideology in itself has become the main object of study. The work of Althusser, stating the relative autonomy of ideological *apparatuses* like the family, school, church and the media vis à vis the economic conditions, and the work of Gramsci analyzing how dominant ideology takes on the form of common sense (*hegemony*) have been particularly influential in socialist feminism. Cultural Studies approaches to gender and media that I shall discuss later, build on these concepts of ideology. Many authors (e.g. Steeves, 1987) place them in the same category. I suggest it is important to distinguish between socialist feminist discourse and cultural studies approaches due to their different conceptualizations of power. In socialist feminist discourse power remains located in socio-economic structures, be it mediated through the relatively autonomous level of ideology. Cultural studies approaches account for power as a discursive practice that can appear independent from material conditions. The distinction however is one of emphasis, both are reluctant to focus on gender exclusively and try to incorporate material and cultural conditons in accounting for women's position in society.

In its most crude form, the socialist feminist communication model of the seventies clings to radical models in which media are perceived to be ideological instruments presenting the capitalist and patriarchal society as the natural order. However, socialist feminism is distinguished by a much greater concern for the way in which ideologies of femininity are constructed in the media, and to whose avail. Much of its research consists of ideological analysis of mediatexts, using the analytic instrumentarium offered by structuralism and semiology (e.g. Coward, 1984). The solutions socialist feminism offers are not so much different from liberal or radical media strategies. Usually a double strategy is advocated: reforming the mainstream media as well as producing separate feminist media. What distinguishes the socialist call for female media producers, is an awareness of the middle class bias of that strategy, (e.g. Baehr, 1981) and the acknowledgement that at the same time structural changes in the organization of media labour are necessary. For example, a Dutch pressuregroup of feminist journalists campaigned rather successfully for affirmative action policies in journalism, increase of part time job possibilities, parental leave and childcare facilities at the newspapers office (Diekerhof et al., 1985).

Concepts of Gender and Communication

Strategies for change follow logically from liberal, radical and socialist feminist media analyses. They aim either at reforming existing media institutions and professions, or at creating new feminist 'institutions' and developing proper feminine and feminist interpretations of professionalism. However, with the privilege of hindsight, we are now in a position to observe how useful these strategies have been. It would appear that some of them have not been very successful. Some even seem to have been counterproductive, as in the case of American journalism becoming a female dominated field reduced in status and salaries. Such political disillusions are intricately linked to theoretical flaws which all three perspectives share. These flaws concern the conceptualization of gender as a dichotomous category with a homogeneous and universal meaning, and the premise of mass media being instrumental to the control needs of respectively, society, patriarchy, and capitalism.

Gender

Radical and liberal feminism share their appreciation of gender as an inevitable consequence of sex differences, consisting of two binary and universal canons of behaviour, characteristics and values found in either women – the feminine canon – or in men – the masculine canon. Femininity is supposed to be composed of emotionality, prudence, cooperation, communal sense, compliance, etc. Masculinity supposedly is its opposite: rationality, efficiency, competition, individualism, ruthlessness, etc. Liberal feminism has it that we learn to accept these canons as normal through women's mothering role in the family and through other socialization agents like the media, while radical feminism believes in the essential nature of these differences. Transgressions of this dichotomy, manifested for example in androgynous appearances like Grace Jones and Prince; in certain types of lesbian and homosexual culture; in the phenomenon of transsexuality; and more routinely in daily lives and experiences of women and men whose behaviour and characteristics do not fit easily in the feminine or masculine canon, are considered exceptions to the thus defined universal 'sex-gender system'.

Consider the 'sameness-difference' dilemma such a universal transcendent concept of gender runs into: for liberal feminism women are *essentially the same as men but not equal*, for radical feminism women are *essentially different from men and not equal*. (It is most easy to explain this dilemma by juxtaposing liberal and radical feminism. That is not to say, however that socialist feminism is less bothered by it). Liberal feminism urges women in particular to regain that sameness becoming equal in the process. Radical feminism tells women to celebrate their being different and to struggle for a social revaluation of femininity. Both solutions are intrinsically problematic. Liberal feminism implicitly accepts the values of the protestant work ethic basic to modern capitalism by telling women to leave their domestic world, enter the (male) workforce and develop the masculine features necessary to acquire power. Masculinity is advocated as an ideal to live up to, at the expense of human values traditionally associated with women. Role reversal might render equality to women, but in the process important 'feminine' values are dismissed and lost. This is an outcome no liberal feminist aspires to, it is thus argued that women should go public without forsaking their femininity. Moreover their supposedly moral superiority should feed and improve the degenerated public world (cf. Elshtain, 1981). In feminist media studies this liberal dogma is reflected in the call for more female journalists whose specific feminine input of concern for human relations and personal experiences would improve the current distanced and dehumanized news style (e.g. Neverla & Kanzleiter, 1984). There is a theoretical inconsistency here: whilst the essential sameness of women and men is used to legitimize demands for equality, difference enters again through the backdoor as women need their specific 'feminine' features to modify the egalizing consequences of the struggle for equality. The rather naive assumption that dominant masculine culture would easily make room for its necessary feminine complementation has more important practical consequences. As already mentioned, the recent increase of the number of female journalists in the US has not led to an increase in their influence, but instead to a devaluation of the status and the salaries of the field (Creedon, 1989: 3). The remaining option for liberal feminism then seems to be a mere adjustment strategy: equality as defined by dominant masculine culture; 'equal but the same'.

Radical feminist assumptions of essential differences between women and men, and their call for separate women's spaces and communities are equally problematic. They imply a return to an ontological explanation of human differences introducing a tyranny of biological destiny historically used to circumscribe women's place in society. As such radical feminism has the same totalitarian tendencies as its main antagonist patriarchal society. How, for instance, can radical feminism perceive women who do not conform to their supposedly innate femininity, other than as genetical deviations? (cf. Elshtain, 1981: 204–228). Radical feminist strategies inevitably condemn women to a marginal position: they will be either oppressed suffering from false consciousness within patriarchal society which is supposed to be beyond reform. Or they choose to step out of patriarchal society being free and true to their nature but remaining isolated and marginal, as for instance the lifecycle of radical feminist media illustrates. The problem is similar in psycho-analytic essentialist currents: 'For if, as some psychoanalytic theories appear to suggest, social subjects are determined, through family relations and language acquisition, *prior* to the introduction of other considerations, including race, class, personal background or historical moment, the social construct thus described is a closed system unamenable to other subject formations' (Pribram, 1987: 6). In radical feminist discourse the inevitable outcome of the sameness-difference dilemma is 'different but not equal'.

This paralyzing dilemma is a product of radical and liberal conceptualizations of gender as having universal and transcendent meaning. Feminist philosophers and historians have pointed to the historical specifity of the idea that men are political and rational, while women would be more personal, emotional and inclined to nurture. Landes (1988) locates the origins of these ideas in the work of Rousseau. Montesquieu and other philosophers of the French Revolution, who inspired republicans to banish women to the home and called men to their supposedly natural fulfilment in the world of politics. The resulting gendering of the public and the private sphere as we know it today, feeding many (feminist) discourses about the meaning of gender, can thus be considered to be a historically specific construction, by no means universal and transcendant. Thus not only has the French Revolution banished women to the family, it has also succeeded in imprisoning feminist theory and politics in its philosophical framework (cf. Van Zoonen, 1991, in press). An acknowledgement of the historical specifity of current dominant beliefs about women and men, opens up new ways of conceptualizing gender, not as universally given, but as socially constructed. The issue then, is no longer how to promote a certain type of femininity as in radical feminism, or how to dismiss femininity and masculinity altogether as in liberal feminism, but rather to analyze how and why particular constructions of masculinity and femininity arise in historical contexts, how and why certain constructions gain dominance over others and how dominant constructions relate to the lived realities of women and men.

Communication

Liberal, radical and socialist feminist discourse share an instrumental perspective on communication. Media are perceived as the main instruments in conveying respectively stereotypical, patriarchal and hegemonic values about women and femininity. They serve as mechanisms of social control: in liberal feminist discourse media pass on society's heritage – which is deeply sexist – in order to secure continuity, integration, order and the transmission of dominant values (Tuchman, 1978); radical feminism argues that patriarchal media serve the needs of patriarchal society by suppressing and distorting women's experiences which, if expressed in their true form, would seriously disturb the patriarchal set up (Mattelart, 1986); socialist feminism assumes that media present the capitalist, patriarchal scheme of things as the most attractive system available. Direct social control becomes unnecessary since dominant ideology has been translated into 'common sense' (*Women Take Issue*, 1978). Media fulfil the structural needs of respectively democratic, patriarchal and capitalist society by transmitting its distorted dominant values about women. What feminism of each kind advocates, is the transmission of the reality of women's lives instead: media should be instrumental to creating feminist utopias. Feminist value judgements are thus completely cast in future oriented political terms, with 'political' referring to the complete social set up. As a result 'good' media – contributing to feminist goals – and 'bad' media – maintaining the status quo, are easily distinguished. Supposedly, it is only a matter of time for women's collective awareness to surface resulting in a massive exchange of 'bad' women's magazines, romance novels, etc. for 'good' feminist media.

But anno 1990, having more than 20 years of organized feminism behind us, Utopia is still far from near. A variety of new women's magazines have entered the market successfully adapting to the fragmentation of a formerly unified female readership: girls, young women, older women, career women, rich housewives, the avid cook or gardener, ordinary working women, travelling women and the traditional housewife all happily subscribe to their own kind of women's magazine; romance novels have introduced new heroines profoundly touched by feminist calls for independence, but still longing for and always attaining heterosexual everlasting romance; soap operas like Dallas, Dynasty, Falcon Crest and its successors – a typical 1980s television genre – attract a predominantly female audience in spite of its 'overtly' sexist, patriarchal and capitalist content; and feminist media struggle with reaching a larger audience, attracting advertisers, maintaining their old audience, or suffer from internal conflict or simply boredom.[4] Obviously the feminist transmission model of communication cannot account for these developments, other than plaintively reproaching the avid consumers of the 'bad' media with 'false consciousness'. I suggest instead to ascribe this ineptitude to the realistic bend and the passive audience conception of the model.

Realism

It is obvious that many aspects of women's lives and experiences are not very well reflected by the media. Many more women work than media-output suggests, very few women are like the 'femme fatales' of soap operas and mini series, and women's desires consist of a lot more than the hearth and home of traditional women's magazines. A call for more realistic images of women might seem self-evident, but is quite problematic. Gender stereotypes for instance do not come out of the blue, but have social counterparts which many might perceive as 'real'. Thus a common negation of the accusation that media distort reality is: 'But many women are mothers and housewives?' Who can define the objective reality media should transmit? Feminists? They are divided among themselves as the previous paragraphs have only minimally illustrated. Women? They can even much less be considered a uniform category. As Brunsdon (1988: 149) duly argues: 'Thus for feminists to call for more realistic images of women is to engage in the struggle to define what is meant by "realistic", rather than to offer easily available "alternative" images. . . . Arguing for more realistic images is always an argument for the representation of "your" version of reality.'

A related problem of the 'reality reflection thesis' is the implication that media output has unequivocal meanings: they are either real or not real. This denies the complex and multiple meanings of media texts implied by the commercial logic of mass media needing to be popular among a variety of social groups and subcultures (cf. Fiske, 1987). In facing the dilemmas of the reflection thesis, feminist media studies have been profoundly influenced by cultural studies and by its own shift to a constructivist theory of gender. Although not a unified approach with a consistent program, cultural studies' central tenet of 'communication as a process through which a shared culture is created, modified and transformed' (Carey, 1989: 43), implies a conceptualization of media texts as sites of struggle over meaning (e.g. of gender), rather than as transparent cultural prescriptions. The reality media offer is a product of ongoing negotiation at the level of media-institutions, -texts and -audiences (Gledhill, 1988). As a result media texts are inherently 'polysemic' (Fiske, 1987) and construct diverging and sometimes conflicting articulations of femininity. Although it is often quite clear which articulations of femininity are to be preferred according to media producers (the dominant meaning of the text), the idea of a polysemic nature of media texts undermines the possibility of thinking of audiences as onesidedly and unambiguously affected by media. Which of the many meanings of the texts will they take up? This brings me to the second major problematic of the feminist transmission model of communication: its passive audience conception.

The Audience and 'US'

In feminist transmission models of communication audiences don't have much choice in interpreting media texts. Either they can accept them as true to reality, in which case they are successfully socialized (liberal feminism), brainwashed (by patriarchy) or lured to the idea that what they see and read is 'common sense' (socialist feminism). Or they see through the tricks mass media play on them and reject the sexist, patriarchal, capitalist representation of things. It seems clear that many feminists consider themselves among the latter 'enlightened' people raising themselves 'to the lofty pedestal of having seen the light' (Winship, 1987: 140). A deep gap is constructed between 'us' feminists, and 'them' the audience. Objectionable in particular are soap operas, romance novels, and women's magazines which create a 'cult of femininity and heterosexual romance' that – since these media are predominantly consumed by women – set the agenda for the female world. (cf. Ferguson, 1983). Such a strong conviction about the value (or rather lack of it) of these media for women's lives, is remarkably similar to the patriarchal attitudes of men knowing what is best for women. Dismissing women's genres for their supposedly questionable content, carries an implicit rejection of the women who enjoy them. That is obviously at odds with the feminist mission to acknowledge and gain respect for women's experiences and view-points. Moreover, it does not contribute to our understanding of how contending constructions of gender are articulated in such cultural phenomena. Why, then are these genres so popular among women? How do women use them to give meaning to their daily experiences? How do 'discourses of femininity' articulated in them interact with other non mediated discourses of femininity such as motherhood and sexuality (cf. Brunsdon, 1981).

The above questions have activated an unprecedented concern with the female audience, expressed in a boom of mainly ethnographic studies about female recipients of particular genres, soap operas and romance novels leading the field (see Ang and Hermes in this volume). However, the problem of 'us' feminists versus 'them' the audience is not solved by the ethnographic twist in feminist media studies and might in some cases even be intensified as the feminist researcher puts herself in the authoritative position of the all knowing expert of female media pleasures, while in the end still rejecting them as unproductive for 'the' feminist revolution. This is utterly problematic in Radway's by now almost classic study *Reading the Romance*. After respectfully analyzing the romance reading experiences of married working women, she claims that romance reading contains an act of protest against patriarchal culture. Briefly and bluntly summarized: by the social act of reading romance, women signal a time out for their domestic and caring labour; and by taking up romances in particular with their omnipresent androgynous hero capable of nurturing woman herself, they deny the legitimacy of patriarchal culture in which such men are quite hard to find. Radway now militantly concludes that '*we*, who are committed to social change' (my italics), should keep looking for and encouraging these traces of social protest: 'If we do not, we have already conceded the fight and, in the case of the romance at least, admitted the impossibility of creating a world where the vicarious pleasure supplied by its reading would be unnecessary.' (Radway, 1984: 222). In the end the only value of romance reading Radway acknowledges, is its potential – however far hidden – for the feminist revolution.

But what to make of those feminists who enjoy soap operas, who revel in harlequin novels and who are addicted to their weekly subscription of their favourite women's magazine, to mention just a few 'bad' genres. Winship (1987) addressing precisely this question in her analysis of women's magazines confesses that she has been a 'closet reader' of Cosmopolitan and Woman's Own for years, since a 'true' feminist is not supposed to derive pleasure from such ghastly products. Hers is one of the few examples of a study in which the personal experiences and pleasures of the researchers are an integrated element of the study, thus releasing the tension between 'us' and 'them'. As Skirrow (1986: 115) has argued: 'In investigating popular culture the only way not to feel like a snooping health investigator, sniffing out whether someone's environment is fit to live in, is to examine some aspect or form of it which evokes passionate feeling in oneself.'[5]

Feminism and Cultural Studies

From the points of criticism to feminist transmission models of communication that I laid out in the previous paragraphs, the contours of a 'cultural feminist media studies' project emerge. Though it would be hard to defend the existence of a well defined theoretical and empirical program, to which a majority of feminist communication scholars adhere, it does seem justified to say that cultural studies approaches are gaining momentum given the growing number of publications in this vein (e.g. Baehr & Dyer, 1987; Brown, 1990; Gamman & Marshment, 1988; Pribram, 1988; Shevelow, 1989).

My own formulation of its theoretical premises would start from Harding's (1986: 17) definition of gender 'as an analytic category within which humans think about and organize their social activity, rather than as a natural consequence of sex-difference, or even merely as a social variable assigned to individual people in different ways from culture to culture'. Such a conceptualization of gender implies that its meaning is never given but varies according to specific cultural and historical settings, and that its meaning is subject to ongoing discursive struggle and negotiation, the outcome having far reaching socio-cultural implications. This struggle over meaning is not a mere pluralistic 'debate' of equal but contending frames of reference. It is circumscribed by existing ethnic and economic power relations, and by the fact that 'in virtually all cultures, whatever is thought of as manly, is more highly valued than whatever is thought of as womanly' (Harding, 1986: 18).

What part do media play in the ongoing social construction of gender? Much depends on their location in economic structures (e.g. commercial vs. public media), on their specific characteristic (e.g. print vs. broadcast), on the particular genres (e.g. news vs. soap opera), on the audiences they appeal to and on the place they occupy in those audiences' daily lives. But obviously all media are among the central sites in which struggle over meaning takes place. Stuart Hall's (1980) encoding-decoding model is a good starting point in case. According to Hall the production structure yields an 'encoded' text which does not constitute a closed ideological system but in which contradictions of the production process are discounted. The thus encoded structure of meaning is brought back into the practices of audiences by their similar but reverse 'decoding' process. Encoding and decoding need not to be symmetrical, i.e. audiences don't need to understand media texts as producers have intended them. In fact, a certain 'misunderstanding' is likely, because of 'the a-symmetry between the codes of "source" and "receiver" at the moment of transformation in and out of the discursive form. What are called 'distortions' or 'misunderstandings' arise precisely from *the lack of equivalence* between the two sides of production' (Hall, 1980: 131, original italics). Gledhill's (1988) analysis of meaning production as cultural negotiation at the level of institutions, texts and audiences builds on the encoding/decoding model.

Institutional negotiation results from conflicting frames of reference within media organizations. 'Creative' personnel is guided mainly by professional and aesthetic logic, while managing directors predominantly have economic and ideological interests in mind. D'Acci's (1987) analysis of the American police series *Cagney and Lacey*, featuring two female detectives, illustrates the intricate interplay between institutional and textual negotiations indicative of the complexities and contradictions of the encoding process. Having a female buddy pair at the heart of the series satisfied two institutional needs at once: to revitalize the popular but somewhat stale genre of police series, and to respond to social changes caused by the women's movement. In practice these two claims were not easily realized. A continuous struggle between the writers and the network accompanied the production of the series, the conflicts all boiling down to the question how to reconcile the treatment of feminist issues with the commercial interest of the network to keep away from controversial topics.

The negotiations about an episode in which unmarried career cop Cagney thinks she is pregnant shows how diverging frames of reference enter at the level of script development. The writers did not even consider to let Cagney have an abortion, anticipating that the network would never allow that solution. So a miscarriage was proposed, but the network rejected the story anyway, not wanting 'to shine the spotlight on pregnancy and the problems of an unmarried pregnant woman' (D'Acci, 1987: 219). Obviously, negotiation at this point concerns the ideological implications of the script. The networks countered the writers with a proposal of a story in which Cagney (in her late thirties) has to decide whether she will ever have children. This was unacceptable to the writers for its lack of narrative resolution, the negotiation here being about professional standards of sound scripts. Finally, the contending claims were reconciled by letting Cagney *think* she is pregnant. As becomes clear by the end of the episode, she is not. How her pregnancy could happen and what she means to do about it, is hardly discussed in the rest of the episode, since that would involve such politically and socially explosive issues as birth control and abortion. A rather dim narrative remains to which each woman can bring her own experiences with (un)wanted pregnancies and 'career/children' dilemmas. D'Acci's analysis of Cagney and Lacey is a rare exception to the tendency within feminist media studies to focus on gender only as explaining particularities of media content.

Negotiations at the level of texts concern the availability of meanings in a text as expressions of the encoding process, and as a result of independent and unpredictable interactions between contending elements in the text. Next to that textual interactions allow audiences to take up different 'subject positions'. To take another analysis of Cagney and Lacey as an example: Clark (1989) argues that the series' narrative form, representational codes and structures of looking, empowers women and encourages women-identified constructions of meaning. The series combines the linear narrative of the police series – a crime usually related to such feminist issues like sexual harassment, rape, prostitution, etc. is committed and solved – with the more circular structure of the soap opera. Integrated in the linear narrative is the personal life of the heroines which follows a more open and fragmented course. In that narrative the emphasis is on process rather than action, on dialogue rather than solution: 'We don't know from any cause effect structure what Chris [Cagney] will decide about marriage or how MaryBeth (Lacey] will cope with having breast cancer' (Clark, 1990: 119). What we do see are their considerations, their ideas and feelings which are extensively played out, while the outcome of their deliberations (not to marry, what kind of treatment to take) does not get much emphasis. According to Clark representation of the decision making *process* 'invites the participation of the spectator to complete the process of meaning construction in ways that are meaningful to her'. (119)

Textual analysis such as described above, utilizing concepts from psychoanalysis, structuralism and semiotics, has been quite common in film studies (Pribram, 1988) but more and more television text are being analyzed in a similar vein. For example, Ang (1990) analyzes how the textual construction of Sue Ellen, one of the major female characters of *Dallas* provides several imaginary subject positions for women: Lewis (1989) and Kaplan (1988) discuss how music videos appeal to a gendered audience; Holland (1987) and

Van Zoonen (1991) examine the significance of women newsreaders for the ongoing construction of traditional femininity. Older research about romance novels and women's magazines can also be considered part of this body of work (Modleski, 1982; McRobbie, 1982, Winship, 1987).

The concept of polysemic media texts should be embraced with caution, however. In spite of its essential ambiguity, the range of meanings and subject positions a text offers is not infinite. 'Encoding will have the effect of constructing some of the limits and parameters within which decodings will operate' (Hall, 1980: 135). So most texts do have a 'preferred reading' which, given the economic and ideological location of most media, will tend to reconstruct dominant values of a society – unless we are dealing with alternative media which should also be thought of as polysemic and encoded, within a rather different set of constraints, however. Moreover, meanings in texts need to be activated by real audiences before they can take on any social significance. The negotiation over meaning at the level of audience 'reception' has the most radical potential. 'Reception' implies two related sets of audience practices: use and interpretation.

In Hall's encoding-decoding model three hypothetical positions from which audiences may interpret television texts are identified: the viewer who takes up a *dominant-hegemonic* position reads the texts in terms of its encoding which makes the model symmetrical; the *negotiated positions* entail many more contradictions since the negotiating viewer accepts the global sense of the dominant encoding, but lets her own logic prevail at a more situated level; the most radical reading comes from an *oppositional position* in which the reader/ viewer recognizes the text as inflected with dominant codes and recodes it within her own alternative frame of reference. Hall's hypothetical positions have been empirically validated by Morley's (1980) research on *Nationwide Audience*, a British current affairs program which indeed proved to be subject to a variety of interpretations of the audience. The situation in which audiences actually turn on the televsion set or pick up a magazine – their social use of media – circumscribe their interpretations. Some examples illustrate this: Bausinger (1984) describes a family in which the man returns home from work and immediately turns on the TV, seemingly to watch the news, but effectively expressing a desire to be left alone. Gray (1987) observes how watching rented videos and discussing soap operas form an important part of the friendship of a group of neighbours: 'These popular texts (. . .) give a focus to an almost separate female culture which they can share together within the constraints of their positions as wives and mothers' (Gray, 1987: 49). Ang and Hermes (in this volume) present a detailed analysis of studies about gender and reception.

The concept of negotiated meaning and the emphasis on reception practices implies acknowledgement of gender construction as a social process in which women and men actively engage. In transmission models of communication women are perceived as victims of dominant culture as expressed in media messages. Supposedly, they are bombarded by disempowering images all but alien to their true selves. The interaction between media and female audiences thus takes on the form of a one way street. However, people do not only take media as expressions of dominant culture, they also use media to express something about themselves, as women or as men. Being a woman (or a man) implies 'work' since modern society offers so many distinct and sometimes contradicting subject positions (cf. Rakow, 1986). In each social situation an appropriate feminine identity has to be established and expressed. Women can use media to pick up and try out different feminine subject positions at the level of fantasy. But the actual use of media can also be expressive as the glossy existence of expensive 'life style' magazines, read by many not so well off readers, proves. Another illustration comes from Turkle's analysis of the reticence of women to bother about the relatively new social domain of information technologies. She argues that 'women use their rejection of computers (. . .) to assert something about themselves as women . . . It is a way to say that it is not appropriate to have a close relationship with a machine' Turkle (1988: 50). Although many men reject information technologies for exactly the same reason, the attitude of women takes on extra meaning considering the continuous social construction of gender differences.

Feminist Media Politics Reconsidered

The concepts of gender as a social construction and culture as negotiated meaning, release feminist media studies from many of the tensions of transmission models of communication. Paralyzing debates about the autonomous gendered contribution of individual female media producers become redundant by giving precedence to the institutional context of media production. The multiple realities of media texts are acknowledged as is the relative autonomy of audiences to accommodate them to their own situation. Women are taken seriously as active creators of their own daily lives and experiences, instead of being 'medicalized' as helpless victims of dominant culture. By way of conclusion, in true feminist tradition of undermining certainties rather than advancing them, I would like to raise some new problems associated with current theoretical and empirical practices of feminist media studies. Since the field is fully in motion, I can only call attention to them and consider some possible angles from which to approach them. Offering definite and authoritative solutions is beyond my capacity and my conviction that feminism should develop in mutual deliberation, not by the prescriptions of academic 'elites'.

I'll begin with a relatively easy problem of empirical emphasis. In spite of the theoretical recognition that gender construction involves both women and men, we have focused on constructions of femininity in media and genres that are read and appreciated predominantly by women; soap operas, romance novels and women's magazines. Alongside this focus we have limited our attention to implied and actual female audiences of those genres, more often than not drawn from traditional family situations. The knowledge we have accumulated by now, concerns a very particular group of media consumed by a very particular group of women. This is a focus born out of necessity since these are precisely the genres and audiences that have been neglected by mainstream research. An academic community preoccupied with such prestigious issues as new communication technologies, the future of public broadcasting or the effects of political communication, does not come down very easily to the more profane level of media use in the daily lives of 'ordinary women'. But consider the implicit message of our research focus: do we really think *gender* is only constructed in 'women's media'? How about the constructions of masculinity found in sports programs, war movies, Playboy and Penthouse, to ventilate just a few stereotypes about men. How do men use those media to construct their gender identity, to express that they are not women? And to cut across the dichotomy of 'women's' and 'men's' media: how do men's 'feminine' activities such as reading a women's magazine or enjoying a soap opera relate to dominant constructions of masculinity?

With some exceptions men and masculinity have managed to remain invisible in media research: 'This has always been its ruse in order to hold on its power. Masculinity tries to stay invisible by passing itself off as normal and universal. (. . .) If masculinity can present itself as normal it automatically makes the feminine seem deviant and different' (Easthope, 1986: 1). Moreover, the focus on the reception of soaps, romances and women's magazines seriously narrows our potential for articulating a comprehensive cultural critique for we tend to ignore whole areas of social and cultural practice: at the level of institutional negotiation, of the production of actual texts there is little research that goes beyond the observation that women work in a male dominated field: at the level of textual negotiation there are many genres we do not know much about yet, e.g. news and current affairs, quality and popular press, sports, quizzes, etc. New media developments and 'the information society' do attract considerable funding for Research and Development, but have only recently gained feminist attention (e.g. Jensen, 1989, Van Zoonen, 1990). I have called the narrow focus of current feminist media studies a relatively easy problem, since its solution involves in theory a 'mere' incorporation of new fields of attention (transforming mainstream studies seems less likely). In practice however, given the minimally triple burden of feminist academics (with personal, feminist and academic responsibilities) this might not be an easy task at all.

There is a more fundamental problem to culturalist feminist media studies. As the importance of specific contextual and textual features for the construction of meaning suggest, it seems unlikely that from this field a general theory of gender and media that goes beyond abstract premises, will emerge. For our understanding of contemporary cultural processes, fragmented and unpredictable as they are, I suggest this a pro rather than a contra. But the particularist shift in theory and research does raise some disturbing questions about the political nature of feminist media studies, precisely the feature which I suggest determines the exceptional nature of the feminist academic project. If meaning is so dependent on context, can we still pass valid feminist judgements about the political tendencies and implications of texts? For we don't know how audiences will use and interpret texts A feminist judgement of obvious textual oppression does not need to be shared by other (female) audience groups. If one interpretation is not by definition better or more valid than another, what legitimation do we have to discuss the politics of representation, to try to intervene in dominant culture?

The above problem has been recognized and responded to in several ways: Ang (1985: 135) proposes to consider the fantasies and pleasures involved in watching *Dallas* as independent and relatively isolated dimensions of subjectivity, making daily life enjoyable in expectation of feminist utopias: 'Fiction and fantasy, then function by making life at present pleasurable, or at least liveable, but this does not by any means exclude a radical political activity or consciousness' (Ang. 1985: 136). A radical activity that applies to the politics of representation in a very limited sense. Ang's argument implies that as feminists we are allowed to produce new fantasies and fictions ourselves, but we should not interfere with the pleasures of the audience, since 'no fixed standards exist for gauging the "progressiveness" of a fantasy' (ibid). Brown (1990) does not follow this reticence to evaluate soap operas and the like. She appreciates 'soap operas, like women's talk or gossip and women's ballads as part of women's culture that exists alongside dominant culture and that insofar as the women who use these cultural forms are conscious of the form's otherness, they are practising feminine discourse'. According to Brown 'feminine discourse' implies acknowledgement of women's subordination often expressed in parodic form by making fun of dominant culture. Feminine discourse thus implies an act of resistance, albeit with cultural tools provided by the dominant order. Brown's appropriation of women's pleasure is useful for it implies a conception of politics that incorporates power relations in the private domestic sphere of media consumption. For example, women's televisual pleasures tend to be ridiculed by other (male) family members and often have to yield to sports and other male favourites. Brown's notion that research can contribute to the legitimation of women's fantasies can thus mean quite a relief in the here and now of daily life. However, Brown's appraisal of feminine discourse borders on simple populism, for how women's 'nomination, valuation and regulation' of their own pleasure relate to the dominant social order, remains undiscussed.

The problems of cultural relativism and populism are not privileges of feminist media studies, but haunt each contemporary attempt to formulate a progressive cultural critique. Schudson (1987: 66) discusses the new validation of popular culture in academic research and wonders how to respond to it: 'I end up caught between a belief that the university should be a moral educator, holding up for emulation some values and texts (and not others), and a reluctant admission that defining the basis of moral education is an unfinished often unrecognized task.' Schudson's doubts can be translated almost literally to the dilemmas of a contemporary feminist media critique: where can a feminist media critique derive legitimacy from and how do our academic efforts contribute to feminism's larger political project? If current research has taught us anything, it is that general judgements and strategies are not likely to gain much support or to be successful. The strategical implications of our research are much less self evident as they were in the case of liberal, radical and socialist feminism. However, I will attempt to conclude with some possibly relevant general considerations and questions.

I suggest a feminist media critique should start from the reception of specific genres in specific social context. To give an example: genre codes and conventions of news produce a relatively closed structure of meanings when compared to soap operas for instance. Considering that news claims an unambiguous relation with reality – a claim many people think justified – we need quite a different set of moral considerations from which to develop evaluations and strategies when analysing news, which may not be applicable in the case of soap operas. Acknowledging that news too is a social construction, would it still be very inappropriate to expect a decent and ethical representation, of, for example, feminist issues and the women's movement?

Another issue that might be explored is a consequence of the importance given to audience-text relations. Does it not seem logical, now that we are assuming and finding actively interpreting audiences, to develop strategies aimed at the 'semiotic empowerment' of female media recipients? Schudson (1987) makes a similar point when he argues that a task for the universities should be to educate readers in reading critically and playfully. I do not mean anything like making female audiences aware of the 'true' sexist, patriarchal of capitalist meanings of a text. But rather I refer to the pleasurers of discovering multiple and sometimes contending constructions in a text, a pleasure that I would gather is not so much different for academics and 'ordinary women'.[6] Finally, we should not define our sense of 'a larger feminist poltical project' too narrowly. Our own academic work is still inevitably political, for unfortunately the relation between gender and culture is, as yet, far from being a legitimate and integrated academic concern, with the exception of a few enlightened places.

Notes

1   'Construction' is not a label that Friedan would have used, but the word summarizes her project in the vocabulary of current feminist theory.
2   The reader with a more specific interest in connecting authors and studies to perspectives is referred to Steeves (1987).
3   My discussion of the policies and problems of feminist media is based on knowledge of the Dutch situation but I would be surprised if the gist of this analysis does not apply to other western countries as well.
4   See note 3.
5   I am indebted to Joke Hermes for this passage.
6   At least from my experience in teaching extramural courses about advertisements and soap operas.

References

ANG, I, 1985: *Watching Dallas: Soap Opera and the Melodramatic Imagination*, London: Methuen.
ANG, I, 1990: 'Melodramatic Identifications: Television Fiction and Women's Fantasy', pp. 75–88 in M. E. Brown (ed.) *Television and Women's Culture: The Politics of the Popular*, London: Sage.
BAEHR, H, 1981: 'Women's Employment in British Television', *Media, Culture and Scoiety*, 3(2), 125–34.
BAEHR, H. and DYER, G., 1987: *Boxed In: Women and Television*, London: Pandora.
BROWN, M. E., (ed.) 1990: *Television and Women's Culture: The Politics of the Popular*, London: Sage.
BRUNSDON, C., 1981: 'Cross roads: Notes on a Soap Opera', *Screen*, 22(4), 32–37.
BRUNSDON, C., 1988: 'Feminism and Soap Opera', pp. 147–50 in K. Davies, J. Dickey and T. Stratford (eds) *Out of Focus: Writing on Women and the Media*, London: The Women's Press.
BUSBY, L., 1975: 'Sex-role Research on the Mass Media', *Journal of Communication*, autumn, 107–131.
CAREY, J., 1989: *Communication As Culture: Essays on Media and Society*, Boston: Unwin Hyman.

CLARK, D., 1989: 'Cagney & Lacey: Feminist Strategies of Detection', pp. 117–133 in M. E. Brown (ed.) *Television and Women's Culture: The Politics of the Popular*, London: Sage.

Communication, 1986: 'Feminist Critiques of Popular Culture', 9(1).

COWARD, R., 1984: *Female Desire: Women's Sexuality Today*, London: Paladin Books.

CREEDON, P., (ed.) 1989: *Women in Mass Communication: Challenging Gender Values*, London: Sage.

D'ACCI, J., 1987: 'The Case of Cagney and Lacey', pp. 203–226 in H. Baehr and G. Dyer (eds) *Boxed In: Women and Television*, London: Pandora.

DAVIES, K., DICKEY, J., and STRATFORD, T., (eds) 1988: *Out of Focus: Writing in Women and the Media*, London: The Women's Press.

DERVIN, B., 1987: 'The Potential Contribution of Feminist Scholarship to the Field of Communication', *Journal of Communication*, autumn 1987, 107–120.

DIEKERHOF, E., ELIAS, M, and SAX, M., 1985: *Voor zover plaats aan de perstafel*, Groningen: Meulenhoff.

DOWLING, C., 1989: *Perfect Women*, New York: Summit Books.

DWORKIN, A., 1980: 'Pornography and Grief', pp. 286–291 in L. Lederer (ed.) *Take Back the Night*, New York: William Morrow.

EASTHOPE, A., 1986: *What a Man's Gotta Do: The Masculine Myth in Popular Culture*, London: Paladin Books.

ELSHTAIN, J., 1981: *Public Man, Private Woman*, Oxford: Martin Robinson.

European Journal of Communiction, 1990: 'Communications Research in Europe: The State of the Art', 5(2–3).

FERGUSON, M., 1983: *Forever Feminine: Women's Magazines and the Cult of Femininity*. London: Heinemann.

FISKE, J., 1987: *Television Culture*, London: Methuen.

FOSS, K., and FOSS, S., (1983): 'The Status of Research on Women and Communication', *Communication Quarterly*, 31, 195–204.

FRIEDAN, B., 1963: *The Feminine Mystique* London: Penguin Books.

GALLAGHER, M., 1980: *Unequal Opportunities: The Case of Women and the Media*, Paris: Unesco.

GAMMAN, L., and MARSHMENT, M., (eds) 1988: *The Female Gaze: Women as Viewers of Popular Culture*, London: The Women's Press.

GLEDHILL. C., 1988: 'Pleasurable Negotiations', pp. 64–79 in E. D. Pribram (ed.) *Female Spectators: Looking at Film and Television*, London: Verso.

GRAY, A., 1987: 'Behind Closed Doors: Video Recorders in the Home', pp. 38–54 in H. Baehr and G. Dyer (eds) *Boxed In: Women and Television*, London: Pandora.

HALL, S., 1980: 'Encoding/decoding', pp. 128–138 in S. Hall, D. Hobson, A. Lowe and P. Willis (eds) *Culture, Media, Language*, London: Hutchinson.

HARDING, S., 1986: *The Science Question in Feminism*, London: Cornell University Press.

HOBSON, D., 1982: *Crossroads: The Drama of Soap Opera*, London: Methuen.

HOLE, J. and E., LEVINE, 1972: *Rebirth of Feminism*. New York: Quadrangle.

HOLLAND, P., 1987: 'When a woman reads the news', pp. 133–150 in H. Baehr and G. Dyer (eds) *Boxed In: Women and Television*, London: Pandora.

JANSEN, S., 1989: 'Gender and the Information Society: A Socially Structured Silence', *Journal of Communication* summer, pp. 196–215.

Journal of Communication Inquiry, 1987: 'The Feminist Issue, 11(1).

KAPLAN, E., 1988: 'Whose Imaginary? The Television Apparatus, the Female Body and Textual Strategies in Select Rock Videos on MTV', pp. 132–156 in E. D. Pribram (ed.) *Female Spectators: Looking at Film and Television*, London: Verso.

KESSLER, L., 1984: *The Dissident Press: Alternative Journalism in American History*, London: Sage.

LANDES, J., 1988: *Women and the Public Sphere in the Age of the French Revolution*. London: Cornell University Press.

LEWIS, L., 1990: 'Consumer Girl Culture: How Music Video Appeals to Girls', pp. 89–101 in M. E. Brown (ed.) *Television and Women's Culture: The Politics of the Popular*, London: Sage.

MATTELART, M., 1986: *Women, Media, Crisis: Femininity and Disorder*, London: Comedia.

MCCORMACK, T., 1978: 'Machismo in Media Research: A Critical Review of Research on Violence and Pornography', *Social Problems*, 25 (5), pp. 544—555.

MCQUAIL, D., 1933, 1987: *Mass Communication Theory: an Introduction*, London: Sage.

MCROBBIE, A., 1982: 'Jackie: An Ideology of Adolescent Feminity', pp. 263–283 in B. Waites, T. Bennett and G., Martin (eds) *Popular Culture: Past and Present*, London: Croom Helm.

Media, Culture and Society (1990) 'The Other Europe?', 12(2).

MRTW (Media Report to Women) (1989) 'Women gained editorship in 1988, pp. 3–4, March/April.

MODLESKI, T., 1982: *Loving with a Vengeance: Mass Produced Fantasies for Women*, London: Methuen.

MORLEY, D., 1980: *The Nationwide Audience: Structure and Decoding*, London: British Film Institute.

MORLEY, D., 1985: *Family Television: Cultural Power and Domestic Leisure*, London: Comedia.

NEVERLA, I. and G. KANZLEITER, 1984: *Journalistinnen*. Frankfurt: Campus Verlag.

PRIBRAM, E D., (ed.) 1988: *Female Spectators: Looking at Film and Television*, London: Verso.

RADWAY, J., 1984: *Reading the Romance: Women, Patriarchy and Popular Literature*, Chapell Hill: University of North Carolina Press.

RAKOW, L., 1986: 'Rethinking Gender Research in Communication'. *Journal of Communication*, winter, pp. 11–26.

SCHUDSON, M., 1987: 'The New Validation of Popular Culture: Sense and Sentimentality in Academia', *Critical Studies in Mass Communication*, 4, pp. 51–68.

SHEVELOW, K., 1989: *Women and Print Culture: The Construction of Femininity in the Early Periodical* London: Routledge.

SKIRROW, G., 1986: 'Hellivision: an analysis of videograms', pp. 115–143 in C. MacCabe (ed.) *High Theory, Low Culture*, London: Methuen.

SMITH, M. Y, 1983: 'Research Retrospective: Feminism and the Media', pp. 213–227 in E. Wartella and D. C. Whitney (eds.) *Mass Communication Review Yearbook*. London: Sage.

STEEVES, H. L., 1987: 'Feminist Theories and Media Studies', *Critical Studies in Mass Communication*, 4, 95–135.

THOVERON, G., 1986: 'European Televised Women', *European Journal of Communication*, 1, pp. 289–300.

TUCHMAN, G., 1978: *Hearth and Home: Images of Women and the Media*, New York: Oxford University Press.

TURKLE, S., 1988: 'Computational Reticence: Why Women Fear the Intimate Machine', pp. 41–62 in C. Kramarae (ed.) *Technology and Women's Voices: Keeping in Touch*, London: Routledge.

VAN ZOONEN, L., 1988: 'Rethinking women and the news', *European Journal of Communication*, 1, pp. 35–52.

VAN ZOONEN, L., 1989: 'Professional Socialization of Feminist Journalists in the Netherlands', *Women's Studies in Communication*, in press.

VAN ZOONEN, L., 1990: 'Intimate Strangers?: Toward a Cultural Approach of Women and New Media', pp. 43–53 in GRANITE (eds) *For Business Only? Gender and New Information technologies*, Amsterdam: SISWO.

VAN ZOONEN, L., 1991: 'A Tyranny of Intimacy? Women, Femininity and Television News', in P. Dahlgren and C. Sparks (eds) *Communications and Citizenship*, London, Routledge.

WINSHIP, J., 1987: *Inside Women's Magazines*. London: Pandora Press.
    Women Take Issue, 1978: Women's Studies Group, Centre for Contemporary Cultural Studies, London: Hutchinson.

ZARETSKY, E., 1976: *Capitalism, the Family and Personal Life*, London.

3

Postmodernism and Television

John Fiske

Those who give us brief working definitions of postmodernism (e.g. Hebdige 1988, Gitlin 1989) agree on the fuzziness of the term and the difficulty of finding any consensus among its users. In this essay I make no attempt to emulate them, partly because they have done it better than I could, and partly because applying postmodernism to television requires me to be selective, not comprehensive, in my use of its constitutive elements. Television and popular culture have tended to be marginal in most postmodern theory, which has been more concerned to articulate its break with modernism in the 'highbrow' arts, particularly architecture, painting and literature. More recently Deleuze has written extensively on cinema, but of the primary postmodern theorists, only Baudrillard (1983a & b, 1987) has addressed the mass media and popular culture directly, so it is his brand of postmodernism that I shall discuss in this essay. Of course, there have been a number of more general applications of postmodern theory to television (e.g. Connor 1989, Grossberg 1987 and 1988, Kaplan 1987, Wollen 1986, Wyver 1986) but on the whole television as a cultural medium has not figured centrally in the debates around postmodernism. There are, I believe, good reasons for this. For while contemporary television exhibits many postmodern stylistic features, and postmodern theory can offer us many provocative insights into the textuality of television, there are important schools of television scholarship that provide strong counter-arguments. In this chapter, then, I wish to look at those features of postmodernism which offer most potential for the study of television and then to discuss their limitations.

One of the characteristics of 'modernism' (i.e. that which preceded the postmodern) was its belief that understanding social experience was both possible and the proper enterprise of art. Often the aim of this understanding was to produce a 'grand narrative', a coherent theory capable of explaining the multifarious and apparently unrelated facets of experience (e.g. marxism, structuralism or pychoanalysis). Other modernist movements, such as the avant-garde, tried to produce this understanding via the shock value of powerful and contradictory images. In the study of television as discourse, the modernist 'grand narratives' centred around the issues of mimesis, of representation, of ideology and of subjectivity. Let me summarize these briefly before moving on to postmodernism. The core argument in theories of representation is that, despite appearances, television does not represent (re-present) a piece of reality, but rather produces or constructs it. Reality does not exist in the objectivity of empiricism, but is a product of discourse. The television camera and microphone do not record reality, but encode it: the encoding produces a *sense* of reality that is ideological. What is re-presented, then, is not reality but ideology, and the effectivity of this ideology is enhanced by the iconicity of television by which the medium purports to situate its truth claim in the objectivity of the real, and thus to disguise the fact that any 'truth' that it produces is that of ideology, not reality. Television, therefore, works in the semiotic domain in the same way as the industrial system does in the economic. The industrial system does not merely produce and reproduce commodities: what it finally and inevitably reproduces is capitalism itself. So, television, in its production of televisual reality, reproduces not objective reality, but capitalism, even if ideologically rather than materially. The mimetic approach rests on the assumption that an image is, or at least ought to be, a reflection of its referent. It is based upon a transparency metaphor that constructs the camera lens as a window through which to view the world. However, because this magic window can record and circulate widely the image of what we see through it, it reverses the true, or logically correct, relationship between image and referent: it makes the image more important than the referent. The result of this is the development of a whole industry of 'image manipulation' that focuses on the reproduction and circulation of the image rather than any truth value it might have. Indeed, this notional truth value is often directly subverted by the practice of staging reality for its image-effect. Such 'untruthful' practices make it harder, the argument runs, for people in an image-culture to distinguish between image and referent.

These two theoretical approaches have little in common except a belief that there is a 'reality', however problematic, that differs essentially from its photographic image. In the theory of representation, however, this 'reality' is defined in terms of historical materialism, whereas the mimetic approach defines it in terms of positivism. Theories of representation offer an ideological critique of television's construction of reality: what it misrepresents or mystifies is its own ideological practice and therefore the relationship of the ideological to the real: its critical point of comparison, therefore, is with other, competing, more politically acceptable, senses of reality. For mimetic theories, however, the critique focuses on photography's deviation from or replacement of an absolute truth, and its critical comparisons are with truer, more accurate images of the real. Representational theories locate the epistemological problems of the television in its ideologically determined discursivity, mimetic theories locate them in its relationship to an empiricist reality.

However, in one way or another, both argue that the camera is an agent of misrepresentation. They both oppose the common sense apothegm that the camera cannot lie by arguing, on the contrary, that the camera does nothing *but* lie. Subjectivity theory extends theories of representation beyond the 'public' world of ideology and its sense of reality to the more private world of consciousness. Freud's and Lacan's theories of the subconsciousness intersect neatly with Marx's theory of ideology as false consciousness. Subjectivity theories argue that ideology works to produce what we may call a 'false subconsciousness'. Subjectivity is the inscription of the social-ideological upon the individual; it is where ideology becomes practised or lived. Subjectivity determines the position from which we make sense of ourselves, of our social relations and of our social experience. The dominant ideology works to reproduce itself in our subjectivities, so, regardless of our material social conditions, all of us who are subjects of capitalism, have to a greater or lesser degree, subjectivities inscribed with white, patriarchal bourgeois ideologies. More recent theories of subjectivity take better account of the contradictions both within the dominant ideologies, and between dominant ideologies and the material conditions of the people, by splintering the relatively coherent homogeneity of earlier accounts into theories of split and multiple subjectivity. But all of them focus on the way that dominant ideologies are reproduced in the subconsciousness of social subjects. All of them seek some form of 'grand narrative' to explain how ideology does not just re-present itself in its pictures of reality, but reproduces itself in the subjectivities upon and within which those representations work. Ideological reproduction and representation are part and parcel of the same process.

Baudrillard, however, side steps the misrepresentation/reproduction problem by defining it as a non-issue. In his postmodernist theory images and reality (whether a reality of social relations or of an empiricist universe) do not have different ontological statuses: there *is* no difference between image and reality. The consequence of this is that we now live in an age which Baudrillard (1983b) characterizes as one of the simulacrum. The simulacrum is for him an 'imploded' concept, by which he means one whose meaning derives, not from a sense of difference, but from the collapse or implosion into each other of the terms which, in the preceding age of representation, used to constitute the difference necessary for the production of meaning. The concept 'image' is not an implosive one, for its sense depends upon its difference from 'referent': similarly, the concept of 'reproduction' requires that of the 'original'. The simulacrum, however, is both the reproduction and the original, both the image and the referent imploded into a single concept.

In this account there can be no original reality whose image is reproduced on millions of screens. Margaret Thatcher smiling into the TV camera and making an off-the-cuff remark for the microphone as she walks between the helicopter and the waiting car is not a piece of reality whose image is transmitted to our television screen. She is her own image. Her hairstyle does not pre-exist its TV image and seeing it 'live' is no more authentic an experience than seeing it on the screen. The smile, the hairstyle and the comment would not be there if the TV cameras were not, if the viewers were not. The smile, the hairstyle and the comment exist simultaneously and similarly on the TV screen and on the helipad, there is no difference of ontological status between them, nor is there any way in which one could be said to precede or reproduce the other. Each is as real or as unreal as the other. So when the minority who keep electing Thatcher vote they are not voting for a real woman whose images had been reproduced around the nation *ad nauseam*, nor, on the other hand, are they voting for an image that can be tested for accuracy by its relation to a real person. Margaret Thatcher, whether experienced on the TV screen, the convention platform or the helipad, is a simulacrum, and she can be nothing else. This Thatcher simulacrum is not 'unreal' so she can and does perform real political acts. The simulacrum denies not reality, but the difference between the image and the real. Thatcher's political power is the *same* as her image power, her power to *do* is the same as her power to *seem*. What the simulacrum produces is the 'hyperreal', a concept into which are imploded the previously distinct concepts of image, reality, spectacle, sensation, meaning. The hyperreal has no origin in either reality or its images, but it constitutes the postmodern condition by describing both the real within which we live and our sense or experience of it as a single concept.

By using such elusive and deliberately ill-defined terms, Baudrillard is attempting to account for the key defining condition of our era: our society is image-saturated. The saturation is such as to produce a categorical difference, rather than one of degree, between our age and previous ones. In one hour's television viewing, one of us is likely to experience more images than a member of a non-industrial society would in a lifetime. The quantitative difference is so great as to become categorical: we do not just experience more images, but we live with a completely different relationship between the image and other orders of experience. In fact, we live in a postmodern period when there is no difference between the image and other orders of experience.

New York is not a real city, it is hyperreal. As we approach it for the first or the millionth time, there is no original authentic reality for us to experience, New York *is* its images on TV and cinema screens, on calendars and posters, on T-shirts and coffee mugs, through the windows of the bus about to descend into the Lincoln tunnel or from the deck of the Staten Island Ferry. Walking down Broadway is not a different order of experience from enjoying its cinematic representation. In postmodernism the image has broken free from the constraints of both mimesis and representation: it cannot be controlled by either reality or ideology. A simulation is the implosion into a single concept of image-reality-ideology that prevents the latter two terms of the triad from acting as final explanations or guarantors of the first. If a simulation is real in itself and not dependent upon its relationship to reality or ideology it becomes available for any use at any time in any context.

The loss of both 'reality' and 'ideology' as grounding bases for images is another facet of the loss of the 'grand narrative'. A key consequence of this loss is the fragmentation of experience and its images. Postmodern culture is a fragmented culture, the fragments come together for the occasion and are not organized into stable coherent groupings by an external principle. Television is particularly suited to the culture of the fragment, for its continuous 'flow' (Williams 1974, Altman 1986) consists of relatively discreet 'segments' (Ellis 1982, Fiske 1987) following one another in a sequence dictated by an unstable mix of narrative or textual requirements, economic requirements, and the requirements of varied popular tastes. Watching fifteen minutes of a soap opera, for example, will involve short scenes from up to five different narrative strands, commercials for half a dozen different products, promos for other TV shows and possibly current news headlines. Fragmentation overpowers any attempts to provide coherence within the sequence. Such fragmentation can be enhanced, of course, by using the remote control to 'graze' other channels during the ad breaks, or during the narrative lines in which the viewer is less interested.

Even television news, which attempts to tell the 'truth' (a grand narrative) about a reality that it still insists is different from and precedes its representation of it, shows postmodern characteristics. A story on a political kidnapping in the Middle East, for example, may well contain images that vary widely in their relationship to what 'really' happened: the studio anchor, the reporter on the spot after the event, pictures of the street after the event, file footage an editor has deemed appropriate, family snapshots or graduation photographs of the victims, commentary by an 'expert', artist's impressions of the event or of the kidnappers, computer graphics – all of these confuse the possible relationships between an event and its representation, and their conventionality suggests that they are not representing a unique event so much as reproducing familiar images. The images of Middle-East unrest are not separable from that unrest, not least because the kidnapping occurred only because of, and for, the media coverage. The kidnapping was a simulacrum in that it was at one with its representation, and thus there could be no contradictions between the different modes of its representation (file footage, live footage, artist's reconstruction etc.) for in the absence of any ontological difference between image and referent, there can be no 'true' mode of representation against which to measure others. Any image is as 'true' as any other, and thus there are no contradictory differences between them.

These postmodern images, which are not only escape referentiality and ideology, also escape the textual discipline exerted by organizing concepts such as genre, medium or period. They can be and are culled from any genre, any medium, any period. The postmodern sensibility does not experience this bricolage of apparently unrelated images as in any way cacophonous or contradictory, for unrelatedness is a function solely of the system of categories that we use: dispensing with organizing concepts such as genre, period or medium destroys the possibility of producing contradictions. In this, postmodernism differs significantly from avant-gardist modernism, despite the apparent similarity of their bricolage of images. For postmodernism the crucial part of the play of images is the sensuality of their surfaces. Postmodernism refuses a 'deep' meaning that underlines the surface; like poststructuralism it refuses the difference between the signifier and the signified and thus avoids the debate of which is the more significant. The object of 'depth analysis' (ideological, structuralist or psychoanalytic) is the determining structures that lie beneath our experience of both society and culture, and that organize our social consciousness: in refusing depth, postmodernism is denying the power or even the existence of these organizing structures.

One outcome of this denial is the stylistic device of pastiche. Pastiche is the re-imaging of the signifier: it may be thought of as parody without the parodic dimension. A scene from *Miami Vice* may be a pastiche of a music video: it may reproduce its style, not in order to comment on it or mock it (as a parody would), but simply to look like it. Parody depends on a difference between the original and its parodic reproduction: pastiche denies such difference. In pastiche images or styles from one period, genre or medium can be reproduced in another without that change of category having any significance (as it does in both parody and avant-garde modernism, for instance). Indeed, in postmodernism there can be no categorical transgression because there are no categorical boundaries to transgress. The shift is not one of significance but of spectacle. Equally, because simulacra do not have origins, there is no way in which a pastiche can change or differ from an original and cannot then be said to parody, subvert or criticize it. The signifying emptiness of pastiche is another sign of postmodernism's rejection of organizing structures. Quite consistent with this is its refusal of genre, for 'genre' is a way of organizing texts into a structure of similarity and difference. Because the textual is never totally autonomous from the social, the denial of generic structure is not just a textual refusal, it functions in the social as well. Genres are not only ways of organizing textual products, they are also ways of organizing their social circulation.

Via taste, whose function is to match the cultural product to the social position of its consumer, genres organize social identities in structures of similarity and difference. Soap opera, as a genre, not only organizes and controls the images that constitute it and differentiate it from other genres, but also organizes and controls the social meanings of femininity and domesticity that distinguish its fans. Extensions of the genre, such as the inclusion of popular singers and music performances extend and change the social allegiances of its viewers. The implosion of generic difference implies an implosion of social difference.

The complex societies of late capitalism require a wide social diversity but attempt to control and discipline this diversity in their own interests. The production and definition of social difference from above is a means of social discipline. This elaborated system of distinction and difference in the social domain is reproduced in and by an elaborated system of material goods in the economic domain and of cultural goods in the cultural domain. So the indiscipline of postmodernism's refusal to accept generic categories implies a refusal of discipline not only in images, but also in social and economic conditions. This refusal of the disciplinary order has, in theory at least, a liberatory potential. But the constraints imposed by the material conditions of social life are not always as easily evaded as those of the postmodern image. The more that a social group is materially and politically deprived in a society, the greater the constraint. The social and cultural fluidity proposed by postmodernism can most easily be achieved by those with relatively high economic and cultural capital. The refusal of generic categories may be, indeed is, a refusal of order and the resultant fragmentation of the image flow is a refusal of structure: order and structure are, we must remember, the basis not only of meaning systems, but also of social systems. In theory, those who have most to gain from such a refusal of order are those who are most oppressed by the existing one. But this emancipatory potential is much more easily achieved by those who are less economically and culturally disadvantaged.

Baudrillard (1983a) attempts to explain this problem by redefining the masses and their relationship to the social order. In earlier theories of mass culture, the masses were seen as alienated individuals whose historically 'real' social relations of class had been broken by contemporary capitalism. The masses thus had no stable place in the social order from which to base any resistance, and were thus vulnerable to ideological imposition. For Baudrillard, however, the alienation of the masses does not result in their vulnerability and passivity, instead it results in their freedom to refuse the social order. In particular they can consume images without consuming their meanings, whether referential or ideological. He argues that this refusal of meaning is the only resistance possible for the masses. It is an articulation of difference between the masses and the social order, but unlike the difference produced by alienation, this difference is resistant because it is a bottom-up product.

The problem with this account is that it admits of no differences within the masses, only of difference between them and the social order. This is symptomatic of the social origin of postmodernism as a style and a theory: its account of culture is most convincing for those in dominant social formations. It is not a critical theory, nor a materialist one. Postmodernism is both an aesthetic style and a theoretical account of its own aesthetic practices. Representational and mimetic theories provided modes of analysis of cultural practices that lay outside their epistemological framework. By bringing to bear upon cultural practices a level of analysis that those practices sought to repress they set up critical, political and contestatory relationships between the critique and its object of criticism. Postmodernism works within an epistemology whose modes of practice and modes of analysis and theorizing enter a mutually endorsing relationship with each other. Its implosive refusal of difference – whether between image and reality or between image and meaning – constructs its own imploded universe that denies the validity of any order of knowledge or being outside it from which a critique can be mounted. It is, ultimately, a self-protective *-ism*.

To critique anything we need to stand outside it, to bring to bear upon it an analytical lens from a different epistemology, and I wish to critique postmodernism from the perspective of social materialism. For, even in late market capitalism, which has brought the end of neither history nor socialism, there are still materialist ways of understanding both social experience and the role of meanings of that experience that have a validity and explanatory power that postmodernism denies them. From a materialist point of view, then, postmodernism, particularly in its Baudrillardian inflection, has suspiciously symptomatic similarities with old fashioned aestheticism. This aestheticism sought to *distance* art from life: it sought to establish an aesthetic distance between the art object and the mundanity of everyday life that worked to emphasize the transcendent qualities of art and to detach it from its immediate social and historical context. It also established a critical distance between the artwork and its reader/spectator that delegitimated socially and historically situated reading practices in favour of a transcendent appreciation or aesthetic sensibility. Bourdieu (1984) argues that this distance from everyday life in the domain of aesthetics is the equivalent of a freedom from immediate necessity in that of economics. Making art into a self-sufficient universe that is detached from the everyday is a practice of the elite who can afford to ignore the constraints of material necessity and who thus construct an aesthetic that not only refuses to assign any value to material conditions but actually validates only those art forms that deny, transcend and contradict them. Its anti-materialism is sustainable only from a position of privilege. So, too, Baudrillard's refusal to assign any significance to material conditions seems sustainable only from a position where those conditions are not ones of continuous constraint and oppression.

The various formations of the socially subordinate, which comprise the majority of our society, do construct and circulate their own popular cultures – they are far from being the cultureless, vulnerable mass that theoretical positions as diverse as those of élite humanism, political economy and postmodernism have constructed them; instead, there are active, productive, intensely experience cultures which are as crucial to the daily life of the people as are the material conditions which delimit that life. Popular culture is less a culture of art-objects and images, and more a set of cultural practices by which art is imbricated into the routines and conditions of everyday life. This intersection between the images produced and circulated by the media industries and everyday life is absent from representational, mimetic and postmodern theories of the image. All of these focus their theoretical lens upon macro-structural relationships whether between the image and ideology, the image and reality, or the image and other images. None of them look at the concrete, contextualized practices at the intersection between socially produced images and socially positioned people.

Leal (1990), for instance, studies an *entourage* of cultural objects around the TV set in the working class suburban home of newly urbanized peasants in Brazil. One set of objects is that of family photographs placed on the TV set: there are large portraits of absent family members – either dead or still living in the country: stuck into their frames are small ID photos of family members who have made the transition to urban life. The ID photo is an image not just of the family member but of his or her urban modernity; the composite image of the ID and the portrait photograph is an image of social mobility, of the transition between the rural past and the urban future. The images on the television screen in this context are always, whatever else they may be, images of the modern, the urban, the future. A soap opera in these conditions of reception and reproduction is, as Leal (1988) shows, a quite different cultural product from the same soap opera received and reproduced in middle class Brazilian homes.

Cho and Cho (1990), in their study of Korean women in the US watching Korean soaps on video tape, show how the social conditions of the women and the meanings and pleasures produced from the soap opera intertwine inextricably. One particularly controversial story line in the soap opera followed a wife's reaction to her husband's affair, and her decision to divorce him. Cho and Cho show both how subversive it is to represent this decision sympathetically and how many women watching used the narrative in their daily struggles to increase the space of their own control within the repressive patriarchy of a Korean marriage. They also show how the women's experience of US television with its more active and more empowered women was a factor in their production of meaning from the Korean soap and its transformation into their behaviour within the specific conditions of their own marriages. For many US viewers, the *Cosby Show*, for example, may be a reactionary representation of patriarchal bourgeois family ideology; but, when the show is received in the social condition of Korean women, its relatively greater gender equality and its humorous revelation of masculine fallibility and cunning offered progressive, if not actually radical, meanings. The Korean soap opera's story of the wife divorcing because of her husband's infidelity contained an image of the mistress driving off in the car given her by the errant husband. To an American women this might not seem a particularly intense or significant image. To many Korean women, however, the image of a woman driving a car is, according to Cho and Cho, a radical image of liberation: to Korean women in the US, the radical, liberatory dimension of the image remains, but is inflected with a sense of its achievability; this utopian fragment, for these women, has the status not of an impossible dream but an almost immediately achievable one, and in the US their husband's refusal or reluctance to let them drive lost whatever credibility it may have had in Korea.

Williams (1988), too, in her study of mainly black working class people in Washington found their culture exhibited a contradictory mix of creativity and constraint. Their poverty oppressed them materially – their apartments were small, their mobility limited so that they rarely went beyond their immediate neighbourhood. One strategy of coping with these material constraints was to pack into them a density of cultural experience, to produce a densely woven texture. So small apartments were filled with memorabilia and souvenirs that carried unique personal memories and meanings, a walk down the street to the shops was packed with meaningful encounters, gossip, and familiar places and their intense micro-histories of the events and people associated with them. Television, too, was part of this texture. It tended to be left on continuously, its sounds and images woven into the packed apartment and into the routines, experiences and conversations that filled the constraints of everyday life till they almost burst. Soap operas, such as *Dallas*, were particularly popular because their densely woven texture of emotions, experiences and familiar characters was easily assimilated into the texture of everyday life. The more affluent incomers into the neighbourhoods, however, consumed more space – their houses were larger, they moved freely through the city and beyond – and in their consumption of space were able to experience the cultural variety that the poor packed into the minimal spaces of their lives. The affluent may indeed, have had a more mobile, postmodern experience of Washington, the poor had a materially constrained and contextually experienced one. The constraints were real, and the images that entered into them were real ways of living within these constraints. Neither postmodernism's referent-free images, nor poststructuralism's infinite deferral of meaning can be found in the use of images in the lives of the subordinated. Indeed, the socially oppressed seek only those images which can be relevantly grounded into the material conditions of their social existence. It is in the conditions of reception that a materialist theory of images must be sought.

Homeless Native Americans in a shelter in Madison derive great pleasure from watching old Westerns on television; their pleasure peaks at the moment of the Indian's triumph, when they have taken the homestead or the wagon train; so at that moment they switch off the set, before the inevitable white restoration and retribution. Australian Aboriginals read Rambo as a member of the Third World in conflict with the white officer class (Fiske 1989a), and African Americans at the turn of the century read Buffalo Bill's touring Wild West Show not as a story of white progress and civilization, but one of Indian genocide that paralleled their own history (Lipsitz 1989).

Such freeing up of meanings from those preferred by their conditions of production, or from their work within and for the dominant ideology may, on the face of it, appear to be an example of postmodernism's refusal of ideology, its refusal of the historical. Such instances do provide evidence to support Baudrillard's claim that the resistance of the masses lies in their ability to consume images without their meanings, for the meaning-bearing function of images is their power-bearing function. But the rejection of the top-down meaning is not the whole story, for the gap created is then filled with a bottom-up meaning that is relevant to the material social conditions of those who produce it. Images are not meaningless surfaces, they are rather resource banks from which meanings can be made and remade. As an account of popular culture, Baudrillard's theory of the refusal of meaning simply stops too soon.

Similarly, postmodernism's emphasis on the sensual pleasure of the signifier explains much of the popular pleasure in spectacle, but, it too, stops too soon. A popular spectacle cannot be understood simply in terms of the sensations of the surface. A popular spectacle is incomplete unless and until people participate in it. The spectacle in the western of Native Americans destroying the white homestead or wagon train not only refuses the white meanings of the savage that has to be civilized, but can be and *is* enjoyed intensely by certain formations of the subordinate as a spectacle of their own vitality, opposition and empowerment. This spectacle works partly on the plane of the affective, it stimulates pleasurable feelings of empowerment and vitality whose significance lies in their intensity or texture, but it can also stimulate people to produce context-specific meanings that are transposable directly into their everyday lives. Many of the Korean women soap opera fans studied by Cho and Cho (1990) made meanings that transferred directly to their own marriages. These transformations were sometimes behavioural, such as in the case of the woman who came to realize that she had as much right to the family money as her husband, and so went out and spent as much on herself as he did on fishing gear. On other occasions they took verbal form, as in the case of the woman who tried to persuade her husband that in order to prevent their marriage suffering the same end as the one on the soap opera, he would have to allow her to develop a career of her own when they returned to Korea.

Such context specific meanings are the result of popular productivity: they are produced by the people from the images available to them, they are transformed into the people's words and behaviour, and in their new form are textured into the conditions of their everyday lives. We should not think of these meanings as *affecting* everyday life, as if they entered a causal relationship with it; rather they are *part* of everyday life. Their production and circulation is a necessary popular practice of the same order as the tactics of creating popular spaces within the place of the dominant order, whether these places be the crowded apartment block, the city street or even the most tightly regulated of all, the workplace. Postmodernism is a movement which, as Jameson (1984) has argued, is a product of late capitalism. But within late capitalism, it has been centred on the cultural elite – members of the 'creative' professions, including academics. There are few indications that people living under conditions of deprivation or subordination, who comprise the majority, live a postmodern life style with a postmodern consciousness.

We must remember, too, that as such movements are not universal in the society that has produced them, neither are they totally determined by their historical conditions. It is not an essential characteristic of signs and sign systems that they convey, defer or refuse meaning: Refusing to conform to generic or other forms of organization is not an action of late capitalist sign systems in themselves. The way sign systems are put to work in a particular socio-historical position is the result of how they are used by positioned social agents. The term 'social agents' grants to people in capitalist societies a degree of agency, by which I mean their ability to recognize their own social interests in however incomplete or unarticulated a form, and the power to act to promote those interests within social determinations which circumscribe their sphere of agency but which can also be affected and modified by that agency. Social agency is not a product of individualism, but a product and activity of social formations. The agency of the cultural elites may well promote its interests by celebrating the freedom of the sign from any constraint (of meaning, ideology, discipline) and in so doing celebrate their own individual creativity and freedom, whether in the production, use, re-use or interpretation of postmodern texts. Such a celebration of freedom expressed an individual creativity is a highly political depoliticization of culture, for it refuses to acknowledge the most fundamental of all constraints that have to be transcended for its freedoms to be achieved – the constraints of economic necessity and of socio-political subordination. It also disguises the social distinction between those who are able to evade these constraints and those who are not. For those whose material conditions of life remind them everyday of the omnipresence of these constraints, postmodernism is not an option.

Postmodern theory can, however, explain *some* elements in the culture of subordinated social formations. Its account of how signs are not tied to their conditions of production nor to their dominant conventions of use, its separation of the signifier from a systematically determined relationship with the signified and its consequent loosening of the links between ideology and representation are all helpful in explaining how it is that subordinated people can exercise their social agency in the cultural sphere by making their contextually relevant meanings out of the signs produced and distributed by the dominant Other.

There may also be an equivalent in the overtly political sphere. The belief of many activists that politics is best fought today on multiple, local, even fragmented sites and issues, rather than on a more singular national agenda can be seen as an example of a postmodern shift of emphasis from the grand narrative to the fragment. Postmodern radical politics may well be a fragmented politics, but provided that this fragmentation is not random but accommodates the specificities of the material social conditions that localize each case, it can be an effective politics. The failure of the concept of a final 'reality' or 'truth' to hold up in postmodern conditions does not require us to dispense with any notion of reality at all, but rather to reformulate the concept into one of multiple, differently experienced realities within which people live their everyday lives. These realities are ultimately structured by late capitalism, but emphasizing their fragmentation over their structuration leads us to seek the greatest significance in the differences between their specificities, in their discontinuities with the structure, and in their localization. Denying totally the existence of a ground narrative or overdetermining structure, as more extreme postmodernism does, can only entrench the status quo. But shifting one's theoretical and political focus away from the grand structure to the multiple fragmented experiences in which it is made material, offers a potentially more progressive inflection of postmodernism because it takes better account of the material conditions of the everyday lives of the subordinated.

Where Baudrillard's postmodernism fails, therefore, is in two key areas. It fails to recognize that the socially subordinate, at least, *do* make meanings, do put them into social circulation and do use them as resources in their daily lives.

It fails to recognize, too, that the dominant sign systems, which are used in the production of their bottom-up meanings, are not totally evacuated of their meanings of domination: far from it. Bottom-up meanings are produced in a structural relationship to top-down ones. The agency of the subordinate, social or cultural, is always exerted within a system that works to confine, contain or repress it. The evacuation of meaning, which characterizes much postmodern and poststructuralist theory, can be seen, then, as a strategy of the cultural élite to avoid recognizing its own implication in the structures of domination which are inherent in all capitalist societies, however late. Postmodernism must be judged by the uses to which it is put. I do not believe that we can, or should, reject it altogether, for it does offer unique and valuable insights into contemporary culture. I do believe, however, that we should reject any use made of it which divorces those insights from politicized accounts of the ways in which everyday life is lived in late, or developing, capitalist societies. The postmodern needs grounding in social materialism.

References

ALTMAN, R., 1986: 'Television/Sound', in T. Modleski (ed.) (1986) *Studies in Entertainment: Critical Approaches to Mass Culture*, Bloomington and Indianapolis: Indiana University Press.

BAUDRILLARD, J., 1983a: *In the Shadow of the Silent Majorities*, New York: Semiotext (e).

BAUDRILLARD, J., 1983b: *Simulations*, New York: Semiotext (e).

BAUDRILLARD, J., 1987: *The Evil Demon of Images*, Sydney: Power Institute.

BOURDIEU, P., 1984: *Distinction: A Social Critique of the Judgement of Taste*, Cambridge, MA: Harvard University Press.

CHO, M. and CHO, C., 1990: 'Women Watching Together: an ethnographic study of Korean soap opera fans in the US', *Cultural Studies* 4:1, 30–44.

CONNOR, S., 1989: *Postmodernist Culture: An Introduction to Theories of the Contemporary*, Oxford: Blackwell.

DELEUZE, G., 1986: *Cinema 1: The Movement-Image*, Minneapolis: University of Minnesota Press.

DELEUZE, G., 1989: *Cinema 2: The Time-Image*, Minneapolis: University of Minnesota Press.

ELLIS, J., 1982: *Visible Fictions*, London: Routledge.

GITLIN, T., 1989: 'Postmodernism: Roots and Politics' in Angus, I., and Jhally, S. (eds) (1989) *Cultural Politics in Contemporary America*, pp. 347–260, New York and London: Routledge.

GROSSBERG, L., 1987: 'The In-Difference of Television', *Screen* 28: 2, 28–66.

GROSSBERG, L., 1988: 'It's a Sin: Politics, Post-Modernity and the Popular' in L. Grossberg et al. (1988) *It's a Sin; Essays on Postmodernism, Politics and Culture*, Sydney: Power Publications, pp. 6–71.

HEBDIGE, D., 1988: *Hiding in the Light*, London and New York: Comedia/Routledge.

JAMESON, F., 1984: 'Postmodernism, or The Cultural Logic of Late Capitalism', *New Left Review*, 146, July/August, 53–92.

KAPLAN, E. A., 1987: *Rocking Around the Clock*, London and New York: Routledge.

LEAL, O., 1990: 'Popular Taste and Erudite Repertoire: The Place and Space of Television in Brazil', *Cultural Studies*, 4:1, 19–29.

LEAL, O. and OLIVER, R., 1988: 'Class Interpretation of a Soap Opera Narrative: The

Case of the Brazilian Novella "Summer Sun"', *Theory, Culture and Society*, 5, 81–89.

LIPSITZ, G., 1989: *Time Passages: Collective Memory and American Popular Culture*, Minneapolis: University of Minnesota Press.

WILLIAMS, B., 1988: *Upscaling Downtown: Stalled Gentrification in Washington, D.C.*, Ithaca and London: Cornell University Press.

WILLIAMS, R., 1974: *Television: Technology and Cultural Form*, London: Fontana.

WOLLEN, P., 1986: 'Ways of Thinking About Music Video (and Post Modernism), *Critical Quarterly* 28: 1 and 2, pp. 167–70.

WYNER, J., 1986: 'Television and Postmodernism' in Lisa Appignanesi (ed.) (1986) *Postmodernism: ICA Documents 5*, London: ICA.

4

Mass Media in the Public Interest:
Towards a Framework of Norms for Media Performance

Denis McQuail

Abandoning Theories of the Press

The purpose of this chapter is to move the discussion of media (or press) theory a stage or two beyond the stagnation which has set in since the mid-century, when the idea of a social theory of or for the press was given extensive attention, especially in the work of Sebert and colleagues (1956), in the wake of the American Commission on the Freedom of the Press (Hutchins, 1947). The work of Siebert was in part advocacy of a liberal model of a reformed free press operating 'responsibly' in a modern democracy, but it was also a codification of stages of history of the press (from the 'authoritation' to the 'libertarian') and also a marking of difference between western freedom models (responsible or not) and the soviet communist model, in which the media were assigned clear functions in society, as propagator, educator, mobilizer.

The 'Four Theories of the Press' have often been invoked as a framework. The present author added two more – 'development' theory and 'democratic-participant', to take account of other realities and other models (McQuail, 1983). Merrill (1971) argued that there were really only two fundamental kinds of theory of state-press relations, authoritarian or libertarian, a view which might have found some support both from conservative critics of intervention in the freedom of the media and from some critical theorists who would place all established media, state or commercial, in the 'authoritarian' category. Hachten (1981) added the concepts of 'revolutionary', 'developmental' and 'Western' to two of the original four (communist and authoritarian). Altschull (1984) said there were basically three models – 'market', 'marxist' and 'advancing', corresponding to the division into three 'worlds' – First, Second and Third'. In his view, each kind of system, in different ways, ensured that media were responsive to their paymasters and each had somewhat different versions of what might constitute freedom and responsibility.

More recently, Picard (1985) made a determined effort to distinguish, within the category of 'Western' models, a distinctive 'social democratic' version of press theory, which, in contrast to 'social responsibility' and 'libertarian' (free market) theory, provides legitimation for public intervention, or even for collective ownership to ensure true independence from vested interests, access and diversity of opinion. Whatever else, it is clear that there are always likely to be alternative, inconsistent and changing conceptions of the norms appropriate to the relations between media and their own society.

The attempt to formulate consistent 'theories' of the press is bound to break down, for reasons other than the underlying differences of interest and political ideology present in any society. The frameworks offered have generally derived from a simple and outdated notion of 'the press', which provides (mainly political) news and information and have failed to come to terms with the great internal diversity of mass media types and services and with changing technology and times. There is, for instance, little of relevance in any of the variants of theory which might realistically be applied to the cinema, or the music industry, or the video market, or even a good deal of sport, fiction and entertainment on television, thus to much of what the media are doing most of the time. It is hardly plausible that these phenomena should lie entirely outside the scope of social-normative thinking. In fact, these are often the aspects of media performance that have been especially the subject of normative discourse, without much benefit of theory of the kind described.

The confusion over the status and possible application of normative theory has been made worse by their: high level generality; their lack of direct connection with actual media systems and often the lack of correspondence between normative pretensions and reality of performance; their mixing of ideas about structure with notions of good, or bad, performance. In many, if not most, countries, the media do not constitute any single 'system', but are composed of many separate, overlapping, often theoretically inconsistent elements. For instance, values of independence and impartiality can be pursued with equal chance of success (or lack of it) by systems based either on principles of the free market or under strict public control. The practical utility of the four (or more, or less) theories has always been extremely doubtful and is even more so at a time when media technologies and distribution systems are multiplying and when there is less consensus about basic values than in the past.

Towards Principles of Media Performance

Of course, the verbal constructions which the theories comprised were largely confined to the pages of academic theory and had no status in law, regulation, self-regulation or policy. For decades, specific normative issues concerning the media have been fought out in the political and judicial arenas of most nationally societies. A wide-ranging body of principle concerning what media ought, or ought not, to do in their public capacity, however much contested, has slowly been developed. This is to be found in laws, regulations, court decisions, reports of commissions in sofar as it concerns what society expects of the media. The extensive regulation of broadcasting (and even its deregulation) have produced a very large body of proscription and prescription which has largely been ignored in the earlier tradition of theorising referred to above. The media themselves have produced yet more numerous codes of journalistic practice (Nordenstreng and Topuz, 1989) and there has also been a gradual extension of regulation and of the normative discourse to the international level (globally and regionally).

Some things have not changed fundamentally. There is still potential conflict between the media and those who exercise political or economic power and the mass media still tend to occupy a contested terrain of 'public space', such that their conditions of operation and actual performance remain of no less concern than in the past. There are still winners and losers as a result of what the media do. There are still first and second class citizens in the media audience, nationally and globally. There are still enormous variations in the informational, cultural and professional quality of what the media do. The implication of these remarks is that there is still a wide-ranging and actively disputed set of 'public interest' claims, based on relevant values relating to public communication, to be laid against the media structures and what they do. It follows that there is more scope for communication research and a need for theory to go with it.

The aim here is to suggest a different point of departure, an alternative to the 'plus or minus four theory' approach. The starting point and the empirical source for the rather loose framework of norms and principles of media performance proposed is to be found in the proliferating 'media politics' of recent decades. As far as the question of norms for media is concerned, a signal difference between now and the immediate post-war decade is the enormous expansion of mass media, a corresponding rise in public debate and, as noted already, the wider range of criteria against which their performance is likely to be judged.

The Concept of a 'Public Interest' Endures

Underlying the proposal for a normative framework is a fundamental presumption, that the media do serve the 'public interest' or 'general welfare', whether by design or chance. This means, in practice, that mass media are not the same as any other business or service industry, but carry out some essential tasks for the wider benefit of society, especially in cultural and political life. For this reason, the media can legitimately be held accountable for what they do or do not do and be liable to some claims that they do things which they might not choose to do. This presumption is, to some extent, invited by the media themselves which often, albeit selectively, claim to exercise a significant public role. Although the view has its opponents, it also has good credentials and in modern times, the presumption has often been acted on by way of commissions of enquiry, public intervention of various kinds (legal or economic).

To make such assumptions about media accountability is not to claim that there is a single known form which the media should take if they are to fulfil the public interest, or that some particular goals or effects are more 'in the public interest' than others. It does not imply, either, that the media are obliged to conform to popular will or carry out some particular mission. It is simply to say that in democratic societies there are likely to be grounds on which an argued claim can be made, by reference to some of the values indicated below, according to specific circumstances, that media should do or should not do some particular thing, for reasons of wider or longer term benefit to the society.

While the concept of the public interest has been slippery and controversial (see Held, 1970), a simple definition, drawn from the field of public planning says that something 'is in the public interest if it serves the ends of the whole society rather than those of some sectors of the society' (Banfield, 1955). Without some guiding assumption of this kind about the public task of the media, it is quite pointless for those outside the media to bother with normative principles, or for those inside to claim to be putting them into practice. Once it is made, however, it becomes quite useful, even necessary, to have some ordered version of the range of relevant performance criteria on matters which might affect the public life of society. The criteria for assessing the media presented below are limited by their origin. The countries from which they derive are politically pluralistic, predominantly capitalist, the media arrangements in force often divergent. Even so, the structure and operation of the media have often been hotly debated and public control of media has often been advocated on grounds of the 'public interest', as have deregulation and the further extension of the free market. This led to quite wide-ranging enquiry and debate. In general, the limits of action, if not of debate and advocacy, have been set by the status quo of property ownership and the guidelines of electoral democracy. Within these limits, a quite diverse set of expectations from, or on behalf of, 'society' has been articulated in different fora, in most countries. It is the expressions of these expectations which provided the materials from which to construct the framework offered below, even if the wealth of source material cannot possibly be acknowledged.

Locating the Foundations of Principle

The normative framework suggested is based on first principles – in the sense that it derives from basic social and political values which are relevant to communication but which obviously have a much wider range of reference to issues of public concern. The more specific norms for media performance which represent the application of these principles are not always consistent and the preference for one norm over another will vary from place to place and case to case. For this reason, there can be no single coherent body of normative theory, nor do we need one, especially if we work 'up' from media performance to media system rather than from 'society' 'down' to its media system.

Insofar as societies do have coherent ideologies, we are likely to discover a parallel ideology for the media as well. The option of following a consistent line of theory remains open, but the alternative, ad hoc and fragmentary, approach has some advantages, especially if it is true that ideologies are temporarily in retreat and certainly if media are tending towards the adoption of more universal, transnational, forms and practices. The strategy adopted here is to draw (without specific acknowledgement) on the large universe of public policy debate about media of the last fifty years, in order to find the terms which widely expressed public expectation from (and sometimes public purpose for, or criticism of), the media. It is quite explicitly *not* the intention here to advocate the special claim of any particular value or set of values, but to try to represent fairly the evaluative ideas and terms which are actually encountered in public debate and in regulations concerning media performance. These comprise, in effect, the terms of a particular policy *discourse*, whose meanings are rooted in typical and recurring circumstances of the working of mass media. As with any discourse (here meaning an identifiable and dedicated form of language usage), the terms are interrelated and overlapping and their specific meanings are dependent on their place in a larger frame of reference. The framework sketched is, first of all, an attempt to say what are its component elements. It is also a map of *space* occupied by public expectations and evaluative orientations towards the media, showing key distinctions and interrelations.

Although the source material has an empirical basis, there is no purely 'empirical' way of drawing such a 'map', nor is there likely to be any uniquely correct solution to the task. What is offered is no more than one proposal, accompanied by argument and explanation, for arranging the most frequently occurring normative terms and ideas in a single, logically interrelated, structure. The most difficult task is to find an entry point – to identify the irreducible core, the most economical statement of key principles, from which other sub-principles can be derived or to which they can be related. This is also the point where there is most chance of a subjective input, the personal views and 'bias' of the author of any such proposal. Some such bias is bound to have crept in.

Identifying Basic Values for Communication in Society

Fortunately, the discussion of media performance is not universal and freely floating, but rooted in time and place and it is reasonable to suppose that the core principles at stake largely coincide with the core values of modern western society. While there are many variants and alternative interpretations, it is proposed to name these as: *freedom*; *justice/equality*; *order/solidarity*.

Freedom as a value in civil society has often been defined in terms of communication rights: of belief, speech, movement, assembly, association, access to information. The most hated denials of freedom have been those which impinge on the identity and integrity of individuals and their rights to self-expression. The most practical instruments for protecting freedom and combating tyranny have involved using the means of communication to claim rights, criticize power-holders, advance alternatives. Legal guarantees of fundamental Human Rights always name freedom of expressions and the right to receive information as an essential principle (for instance Article 10 of the European Convention on Human Rights).

The value of equality, which corresponds in part with the idea of justice (equality of rights and before the law, fairness of social arrangements), is connected with public communication in less direct, but no less crucial ways. In brief: the expression of grievances and processes of justice require adequate channels of communication and the means of publicity; the potential to communicate and to receive communication is a social good which should be fairly and universally if not strictly equally, available; democratic political process designed to increase public welfare and equity also require the services of public channels of communication; the full concept of citizenship pre-supposes an informed and participant body of citizen (Golding, 1990). Most generally, if we suppose there to be a 'right to communicate', then it implies an equal individual claim to hear and to be heard. The fact that modern mass media have, in practice, appropriated and almost monopolized a good many of the real opportunities for public communication does not diminish the claim.

The third basic value, that of order, although equally fundamental, is open to more divergent definitions and evaluations than either freedom or equality. It was, nevertheless, coupled with both, under one of its several names, in the slogan of the French Revolution: liberté; egalité; fraternité. It was also a key term, in the sense of the solidarity of workers, in the socialist and social reform meanings of the nineteenth and twentieth centuries. It is usually regarded as a precondition for a just and civilized society. It is a central communication value: the interdependence and collective life of a society or community derive from, and depend on, communication processes and calls for communicative expressions of identity and belonging. Any social order, whether or not based on freedom and equality, can only be maintained over time through processes of public communication. The notion of order is, nevertheless, ambiguous because of its association with control, with hierarchy and subordination.

It is clear that the three basic values do often come into conflict with each other and an appeal to one may be used to counter an appeal to another. Freedom is not easy to reconcile with order and equality may call either for limits on freedom or may be inconsistent with hierarchical forms of order. Such tensions are often reflected in public debates about the structure, regulation and performance of mass media, reminding us of the lack of any consensus either over the way in which the values should be applied or over their relative order of precedence. The space occupied by the discourse of public communication is continually contested by opposing claims and interests.

The elements of a normative framework offered here do not provide a completely coherent or closed system of communication values. The aim is only to offer a pragmatic *description* of the field of values, choices and alternatives which have commonly been invoked and argued for in public debate about public communication. In the following paragraphs, the various elements which have been identified by this three-fold division of basic values are discussed in terms of their implications for media performance. The terms set out are intended to help generate more specific and testable criteria of performance.

Freedom as a Public Communication Value

Freedom is a condition, rather than a criterion, of performance and does not readily lend itself to either prescriptive or proscriptive statements. It refers primarily to rights to free expression and the free formation of opinion. However, for these rights to be realized there must also be access to channels and opportunities to receive diverse kinds of information. Media freedom also leads to positive benefits for the everyday needs of social organization. For instance, the *credibility* of any news and information supplied is largely dependent on confidence that it is not unduly or secretly influenced by partisan or vested interests (of government, advertiser, proprietor, source, etc.). Freedom is also thought to require and promote a diveristy of channels and thus more choice for the 'consumer' of information and other media services. Press independence is also a precondition of the exercise of the 'watchdog' role

– exercising public vigilance in relation to those with most power, especially government and big business. Other practical benefits include: openness to new ideas; a readiness to make access available to different voices in the society. Free media will be prepared, when necessary, to offend the powerful, express controversial views, deviate from convention and from the commonplace. Freedom of communication has a dual aspect: offering a wide range of voices and responding to a wide-ranging demand. Similar remarks apply to the cultural provision of media, where independence will be associated, other things being equal, with creativity, originality and diversity. These ideas bring us to an interface and overlap with benefits offered under the heading of 'Equality'.

This brief discussion has sought to make a connection between the following: structural conditions (legal freedom to publish); operating conditions (real independence from economic and political pressures and relative autonomy for journalists and other 'communicators' within media organizations); opportunities for 'voices' in society to gain access to channels; benefits of quality of provision for 'receivers' – according to criteria of relevance, diversity, reliability, interest, originality and personal satisfaction. The main elements discussed can now be expressed as the first set of components in a larger normative framework, as follows. It has to be emphasized that these are only *theoretical* benefits from freedom, logically linked. They may not be realized in practice because of inconsistencies of claims and limited opportunities (see Lichtenberg, 1990).

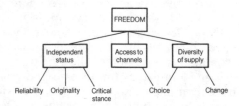

Fig. 4.1   Freedom as a media performance principle

Equality as a Public Communication Value

The basic value of equality has to be translated into more specific meanings when it is applied to the mass media. As a principle, it underlies several of the normative expectations which have already been referred to. In relation to communication and political power, it is equality which requires that no special favour be given to power holders and that access to media should be given on a fair, if not always an equal, basis to contenders for office and, in general, to oppositional or deviant opinions, perspectives or claims. In relation to business clients of the media, equality requires that all legitimate advertisers be treated on the same basis (the same rates and conditions). Equality implies, in such matters, that the normal principles of the market should operate freely.

It is equality which supports policies of universal provision in broadcasting and telecommunications and of sharing out the costs of basic services. Equality will support the expectation of fair access, on equivalent terms, for all alternative voices (the diversity principle again) that meet relevant crteria. In short, equality calls for an absence of discrimination or bias in the amount and kind of access available to senders or receivers, as far as is practicable. The real chances of equality are likely to depend on the level of social and economic development of a society and the extent of its media system. There will have to be *enough* space on different and mutually independent channels, for any degree of equality to be realized in practice.

The principle of diversity (also identified as a major benefit of freedom), which can be derived from these meanings of communication equality, is especially important because it underpins the normal processes of progressive change in society (the periodic replacement of ruling elites, the circulation of power and office, the countervailing power of different interests), which pluralistic forms of democracy are supposed to deliver. In accounting for diversity of *provision*, the extent to which real alternatives are on offer can be measured according to several alternative yardsticks: type of media (e.g. press, radio, TV, etc.); function or type (e.g. entertainment, information); the level of operation (national, regional, local, etc.); the audience aimed at and reached (differentiated by income, age, etc.); language, ethnic or cultural identity; politics or ideology. In general, a media system is more equal in character, the more diverse the provision according to the criteria mentioned.

Two basic variants of the 'diversity-as-equal-treatment' principle have been identified. According to one version, a literal equality should be on offers – everyone receives the same provision or chances for access as sender. This applies, for instance, where contending parties receive equal time in an election, or in those countries (such as Canada or Belgium) where separate language groups receive an equivalent media service. An alternative, more usual, version means only a 'fair', or appropriate, allocation of access and treatment. Usually, fairness is assessed according to the principle of proportional representation. Media provision should proportionately *reflect* the actual distribution of whatever is relevant (topics, social groups, political beliefs etc.) in the society, or reflect the varying distribution of audience demand or interest. The differentiation of media provision (content) should approximately correspond to the differences at source or to those at the receiving end.

A consideration of equality as an evaluative principle also takes us into the territory of objectivity, although this has other meanings and potential sources of support, especially those provided by the value of *independence* and by trends to professionalism and autonomy. Most centrally, objectivity is a particular form of media *practice* and also a particular attitude to the task of information collection, processing and dissemination. The main features are: adopting a position of detachment and neutrality from the object of reporting (thus an absence of subjectivity or personal involvement); lack of partisanship (not taking sides in matters of dispute); attachment to accuracy and other truth criteria (e.g. relevance, completeness); lack of ulterior motives or service to a third party. The process of observing and reporting should, thus, not be contaminated by subjectivity, nor should it interfere with the reality being reported on. In some respects, it has an affinity, in theory at least, with the ideal of rational, 'undistorted' communication advocated by Habermas (1979).

This version of an ideal standard of reporting practice has many advocates and has become the dominant model for the role of professional journalists (Wilhoit & Weaver, 1985). It has links with the principle of *freedom*, since independence is a necessary condition of detachment and truthfulness. Under some conditions (e.g. political oppression, crisis, war, police action), the freedom to report can only be obtained in return for a guarantee of objectivity. The link with *equality* is just as strong: objectivity requires a fair and non-discriminatory attitude to sources and to objects of news reporting – all should be treated on equal terms. Additionally, different points of view on matters where the facts are in dispute should be treated as of equal standing and relevance, other things being equal. Objective treatment or presentation may in practice be achieved by allowing equal space or time for alternative perspectives on, or versions of, facts.

In the set of normative interactions which develop between media and their operating environments, objectivity may be crucial. Agencies of state and advocates of various interests are able to speak directly to their chosen audiences by way of the media, without undue distortion or intervention by the mediators themselves and without compromising the independence of chan-nels. Because of the established conventions of objectivity, media channels can distance their editorial content from the advertising matter which they carry and advertisers can do likewise in respect of editorial content. In general, media audiences appear to understand the principle of objective performance well enough and its practice helps to increase their credence and trust in information and opinions which the media offer. The media themselves find that objectivity gives their own news product a higher and wider market value. Finally, because the objectivity standard has such a wide currency, it is often invoked in claims and settlements concerning bias or unequal treatment.

The main sub-principles related to the value of equality can now be entered, as follows in Fig. 4.2.

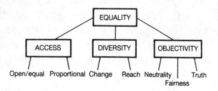

Fig. 4.2 Equality as a media performance principle

Order as a Public Communication Value

The ambiguous standing of the order concept in dicussions of media and society has alredy been noted. From the standpoint of established authority, the media are often viewed as potentially disruptive of the normal 'order' of the society, although they are also indispensable to the maintenance of order, in the wider sense of social 'harmony' and the normal running of things. From the point of view of individuals and the component sub-groups of society, mass communi-cation can also have both positive and negative tendencies. It helps in forming and maintaining personal identity and group cohesion, but it can be a source of disturbance or threat when it intrudes with alien values or as an instrument of constraint. Theory of mass communication draws attention to the dual effect of media in society – both centrifugal and centripetal, differentiating and uniting (Carey, 1969; McQuail, 1987).

In many public policy debates, there are several matters which regularly recur under the heading of 'order' in its widest sense, especially: the wish to retrain any impulse to individual or collective disorder; the protection of children and other vulnerable groups from moral or cultural harm; the positive motive of promoting education and traditionally valued culture; the question of cultural autonomy for language groups, regions and national cultures.

The concept of order is used here in a rather elastic way, to apply to symbolic (cultural) orders such as religion, art, customs, etc. as well as to forms of social order (community, society, established structures of relations). This broad distinction is also cut across by a distinction of perspective – from 'above' and 'below', as it were. This distinction is essentially that between established authority of society on the one hand and individuals and minority groups on the other. It also corresponds approximately to the distinction between order, in the sense of control, and order in the sense of solidarity and cohesion – the one 'imposed', the other voluntary and self-chosen. These ideas about order can be arranged as follows.

Any complex and viable social system will exhibit all the sub-aspects of order which are shown here. There will be mechanisms of social control as well as voluntary attachments, often by way of membership of component groups in society. There will be a sharing of common meanings and definitions of experience as well as much divergence of identity and actual experience. Shared culture and solidaristic experience tend to be mutually reinforcing. The relationship between mass communication and these different concepts has been handled in theories of media and society in divergent, though not logically inconsistent, ways (McQuail, 1987). Functionalist theory attributes to mass media a latent purpose of securing the continuity and integration of a social order (Wright, 1964) by promoting cooperation and a consensus of social and cultural values. Critical theory has usually interpreted mass media as agents of a dominant, controlling, class of power-holders who seek to impose their own definitions of situations and their values and to marginalize or delegitimize opposition. The media are often seen as serving conflicting goals and interests and as offering conflicting versions of an actual or desirable social order. The assessment of media in terms of order is, consequently, more dependent on the choice of perspective than is the case in respect of concepts of freedom and equality. The question '*Whose* order?' has first to be settled. In practice, most media assessment has tended to adopt a conventional standard, shaped by the dominant perspective (of established authority). As a result, more attention has usually been paid to *disruption* of order (conflict, crime, deviance, etc.) than to the failings of the established order as perceived by more marginal, or minority, social and cultural groups in society.

The complexity of concepts, points of view and evaluative principles which can be deployed in this territory is also an obstacle to research and some simplification is needed, at the risk of drawing somewhat arbitrary lines of demarcation. The solution adopted here is, first, to acknowledge a distinction between the *social* and the *cultural* domains (as in Fig. 4.3). The social order can, in turn, be treated under two alternative headings – one relating to social control, generally the view 'from above', another to the more solidaristic aspects of order – mutuality, cooperation, voluntarism, balance, etc. The social control aspect of media performance can usually be recognized either by way of very 'negative' portrayals of conflict, disorder and deviance or in the differential access and positive support given, symbolically, to established 'order' institutions and authorities – the law, church, school, police, military, etc.

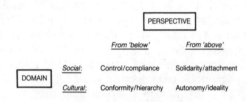

Fig. 4.3   Ideas concerning order

The second sub-principle (that of solidarity) involves a recognition that society is composed of many sub-groups, different bases of identity and of different interests. Standing against a unitary perspective of consensual good order in a nation state are a number of alternative perspectives on what is a desirable social order. Some groups may have no attachment in the social order beyond their own immediate social context and experience. A viable normative expectation from mass media is that they will sympathetically recognize such a perspective, providing some access and symbolic support for the relevant groups. In general, this (normative) theoretical position will encompass a generally outward-looking and empathetic orientation to social groups and situations which are marginal, distant or deviant, from the point of view of a dominant national society. This implies several possible expectations from the media. Firstly, it refers to media provision which supports the aspirations of sub-groups in society, either by giving access or positive forms of representation. The principle of *empathy* refers to the extension of sympathy to individuals or groups, the public recognition of shared risks, sorrows and hardships, the linking of private and local experience to wider experience. There is also a reflection here of aspects of media work which have been referred to as 'pro-social' in their tendency – generally content which is held to reinforce 'positive' social values, including those of caring for others and extending understanding to the marginal and even deviant in society, as well as to outsiders.

The domain of the 'cultural' is clearly not easy to keep separate from some of the matters just mentioned. As used here, the term refers to any set of symbols organized by way of language or in some other meaningful patterning. We can locate cultures in any of three main ways: as characteristic of a set of people, identifiable by language, gender, class, ethnicity, etc; or as a set of activities (work, home-related; politics; sport, etc.); or as represented in and by forms and artefacts (books, films, types of performance, genres, etc.). The first of these three is already largely covered under the 'social' designation referred to above, although 'people' are identifiable, not only as groups, but by their symbolic cultural characteristics – usages, customs, language artefacts, etc. Media assessment has typically been directed either at matters of cultural 'quality' or of 'authenticity' in relation to the group.

The subdivision of the sphere of the cultural, for present purposes of constructing a clear framework, is not easy to accomplish in a neat way, although line of division might be as follows: between a 'dominant', official or established culture and a set of possible alternative or sub-cultures. In practice, the former implies a hierarchical view of culture, according to which cultural values and artefacts which have been 'certified' by established cultural instit-utions will be relatively privileged, compared to 'alternative' cultural values and forms. Typically, such an established culture will imply a set of absolute cultural values and certifiable quality standards. The cultural virtues of the 'alternative' perspective will, in contrast, be relative, based only on personal perceptions of attractiveness, relevance and familiarity.

The component normative principles relating to 'order' can now be summarized, as in Fig. 4.4.

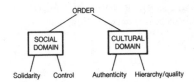

Fig. 4.4   Order and its main component principles

Interrelations of Principle in an Overall Framework

These three basic principles of freedom, equality and order have been worked out separately in terms of their implications for media performance. Neverthe-less, they are intimately connected and inevitably overlapping. Thus, the main concepts of Access and Diversity appear both under the heading of 'freedom' and under that of 'equality'. While the order principle stands somewhat apart, the connection between the 'solidaristic' component of order and equality is very strong and, in practice, solidaristic communication values can only be realized by 'access' to channels and by some degree of diversity in the media system.

The logic of the composition of the framework involves a progression of increasing specificity from the most abstract and general level (the three basic values), to the implications of these for media system and performance (independence, diversity, etc.), to yet more specific sub-principles or concepts which provide a link to the application of assessment procedures and research. In conclusion, the three main component elements can be brought together to offer a view of the upper levels (really the foundations) of the unified framework of principle.

From these key terms, quite a large number of more specific terms can be derived for application in the empirical assessment of media performance (as in Stone, 1987; Lemert, 1989; McQuail, 1991). The main conclusion of this chapter is that the practice of media criticism and of media research, as well as of regulating and deregulating media have between them, almost fortuitously,

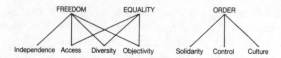

Fig. 4.5   Summary framework of principles of media performance

provided the essential building blocks for a quite comprehensive, flexible and changing 'social theory of the media', relevant to our times and of practical value in the ever widening circle of public discussion of the role of the mass media in society. Of course, the apparent coherence and symmetry of the framework of media norms is illusory. The key principles embody potentially deep fissures and inconsistencies, depending on how they are interpreted. They can be mutually contradictory and the sub-principles of media performance can always be defined according to self-interest. This means that there can be no straightforward 'reading-off' of 'the public interest' from this framework. All claims about what is in the public interest have to be specific, based on evidence and argued out in some relevant political forum.

References

ALTSCHULL, J. H., 1984: *Agents of Power: the role of news media in human affairs*, New York: Longman.

BURNS, T., 1977: *The BBC: public institution and private world*, London: Macmillan.

CAREY, J., 'The communication revolution and the professional communicator', in P. Halmos, ed., *The Sociology of Mass Media Communicators*, pp. 23–38. Keele: University of Keele. *Communcators*, pp. 23–38. Keele: University of Keele.

GOLDING, P., 1990: 'Political communication and citizenship', in M. Ferguson, ed., *Public Communication.*, pp. 84–100. London: Sage Publications.

HABERMAS, J., 1979: *Communication and the Evolution of Society*, Boston: Beacon Press.

HACHTEN, W., 1981: *The World News prism: changing media, clashing ideologies*. Ames, Iowa: Iowa State University Press.

HUTCHINS, R., 1947 *A Free and Responsible Press*. Chicago: University of Chicago Press.

LEMERT, J., 1989: *Criticizing the media*. Newbury Park, Calfornia: Sage Publications.

LICHTENBERG, J., (ed.), 1990: *Democracy and the Mass Media*, Cambridge: Cambridge University Press.

MCQUAIL, D., 1983 and 1987: *Mass Communiction Theory: and introduction*. London: Sage Publications.

MCQUAIL, D., 'Media Performance assessment in The Public Interest', pp. 111–147 in J. A. Anderson, ed., *Communication Yearbook 14* Newbury Park: Sage Publications.

MERRILL, J. C., 1974: *The Imperatives of Freedom*. New York: Hastings House.

NORDENSTRENG, K. and H. TOPUZ, (eds), 1989: *Journalist: status, rights and responsibilities*. Prague: IOJ.

PICARD, R. G., 1985: *The Press and the Decline of Democracy*. Westport, Conn.: Greenwood Press.

SIEBERT, F. T. PETERSON and W. SCHRAMM, 1956: *Four Theories of the Press*. Urbana: University of Illinois Press.

STONE, P., 1987: *Examining Newspapers*. Newbury Park, California.
WEAVER, D. and WILHOIT, G. C., 1986: *The American Journalist*. Bloomington: University of Indiana Press.
WRIGHT, C. R. 'Functional analysis and mass communication', *Public Opinion Quarterly*, 24, 1960, pp. 606–620.

5

Mass Media and Democracy: A Reappraisal

James Curran

Introduction

New times call for new thinking. Countries in eastern Europe are redesigning their media systems, with one eye cocked to the west in search of new ideas and models (as well as investment). The domination of public service broadcasting in western Europe is weakening in response to a combined commercial and political onslaught. And the rapid expansion of TV channels is transforming the media landscape in a way that calls for an intellectual adjustment.[1]

This chapter attempts therefore to do more than merely provide a textbook-style summary of traditional liberal arguments about the democratic role of the media.[2] It also assesses their relevance for today. Much liberal commentary derives from a period when the 'media' consisted principally of small circulation, political publications and the state was still dominated by a small, landed elite. The result is a legacy of old saws which bear little relationship to contemporary reality but which continue to be repeated uncritically as if nothing has changed. It is time that they were given a decent funeral.

Discussion of the democratic role of the media is bound up with a debate about how the media shoud be organized. Traditionalist conceptions were framed partly in order to legitimate the 'deregulation' of the press, and its full establishment on free market lines (Curran 1978). Calling into question traditionalist thought thus casts doubt on the free market programme that it was intended to legitimate. But the process of going back to first principles and reappraising the democratic role of the media also raises questions about the adequacy of conventional public service alternatives to the market.

This reappraisal concludes with a revised conception of the democratic role of the media, and a proposal for a new way of organizing the media. This may well be rejected in favour of better considered alternatives. But whatever view is taken, the general subject of the media and democracy clearly requires a removal van to carry away lumber accumulated through the centuries. What should be removed, what should take its place, and how the intellectual furniture should be rearranged is something that needs to be critically assessed.

Habermas and the Public Sphere

A good starting point for rethinking the democratic role of the media is provided by a recently translated study by Jürgen Habermas (1989), which has acquired almost a cult following in the United States and northern Europe.[3] In brief, Habermas argues that the development of early modern capitalism brought into being an autonomous arena of public debate. The economic independence provided by private property, the critical reflection fostered by letters and novels, the flowering of discussion in coffee houses and salons and, above all, the emergence of an independent, market-based press, created a new public engaged in critical political discussion. From this was forged a reason-based consensus which shaped the direction of the state.

Habermas traces the evolution of the 'bourgeois public sphere' – a public space between the economy and the state in which public opinion was formed and 'popular' supervision of government was established – from the seventeenth century to the first half of the nineteenth century. Thereafter, he argues, the public sphere came to be dominated by an expanded state and organized economic interests. A new corporatist pattern of power relations was established in which organized interests bargained with each other and with the state, while increasingly excluding the public. The media ceased to be an agency of empowerment and rationality, and became a further means by which the public was sidelined. Instead of providing a conduit for rational-critical debate, the media manipulated mass opinion. It defined politics as a spectacle, offered pre-digested, convenience thinking and conditioned the public into the role of passive consumers.

Although Habermas was careful to argue that participation in the public sphere, in its classical phase, was restricted to the propertied class, he has come under attack for idealizing this period of history (Mortensen 1977; Hohendahl 1979; Curran 1991). He has also been criticized for his characterization of the media and the public sphere in the subsequent period (Fraser 1987; Dahlgren 1991).[4] There are, perhaps, good grounds for questioning the value of Habermas's study as historical scholarship. But it offers nevertheless a powerful and arresting vision of the role of the media in a democratic society, and in this sense its historical status is irrelevant. From his work can be extrapolated a model of a public sphere as a neutral zone where access to relevant information affecting the public good is widely available, where discussion is free of domination by the state and where all those participating in public debate do so on an equal basis. Within this public sphere, people collectively determine through the processes of rational argument the way in which they want to see society develop, and this shapes in turn the conduct of government policy. The media facilitates this process by providing an arena of public debate, and by reconstituting private citizens as a public body in the form of public opinion.

The lingering question left by Habermas is how can this model – supposedly realized by a restricted class in the early nineteenth century – be universalized during the era of mass politics in a highly differentiated, organized capitalist society? The answer, we suggest, is that the public sphere cannot be re-established through a simple process of enlargement – by enabling those who were formerly excluded to participate in it. Rather, the public sphere and the role of the media in relation to it has to be reconceptualized and re-incarnated in a new form. But, first, we will consider more conventional accounts of the democratic role of the media.

Public Watchdog

Traditionalist liberal thought argues that the primary democratic role of the media is to act as a public watchdog overseeing the state. This is usually defined as revealing abuses in the exercise of state authority, although it is sometimes extended to include facilitating a general debate about the functioning of government. This watchdog role is said to override in importance all other functions of the media, and to dictate the form in which the media should be organized. Only by anchoring the media to the free market is it possible to ensure the media's complete independence from government. Once the media becomes subject to public regulation, it will lose its bite as a watchdog and may even be transformed into a snarling rotweiller in the service of the state.

This particular view seems to have become the cornerstone of a new consensus in the United States. For instance Kelley and Donway, two American political scientists of conservative sympathies, have recently argued that any reform of the media, however desirable, is unacceptable if it is 'at the cost of the watchdog function. And this is the inevitable cost. A press that is licensed, franchized or regulated is subject to political pressures when it deals with issues affecting the interests of those in power' (Kelley and Donway 1990: 97). This argument is restated in a different form by a political scientist of centrist views, Stephen Holmes: 'Doesn't every regulation converting the media into a "neutral forum" lessen its capacity to act as a partisan gadfly, investigating and criticizing government in an aggressive way?' (Holmes 1990: 51). Even commentators with strongly reformist views appear to entertain the same fears. 'I cannot envision any kind of content regulation, however indirect', writes Carl Stepp, an astringent critic of the American media, 'that wouldn't project government into the position of favouring or disfavouring some views and information over others. Even so-called structural steps aimed at opening channels for freer expression would post government in the intolerable role of super-gatekeeper' (Stepp 1990: 194).

These arguments have paved the way for the increasing deregulation of American broadcasting. During the last decade, American TV channels have been 'freed' from the obligation to provide a mixed schedule of programmes and from the fairness doctrine requiring public affairs to be reported from contrasting viewpoints. Rules restricting chain ownership of TV stations have been relaxed, and the requirement on cable TV companies to carry over-the-air channels has been dropped. Even the principle of license renewal of broadcasting stations, the coping stone of what residual regulation remains, is now being questioned.

What happened in the United States has begun to happen in Britain, though in the latter case in the teeth of considerable opposition. As in the United States, it was argued with great force that public regulation of broadcasting inhibited critical surveillance of government (Adam Smith Institute 1984; Veljanovski 1989). As Rupert Murdoch (1989: 9) succinctly put it, 'public service broadcasters in this country [Britain] have paid a price for their state-sponsored privileges. That price has been their freedom'. This rhetoric paved the way for a move towards deregulation. The 1990 Broadcasting Act authorized the auctioning of TV and radio franchises (with some quality safeguards), the expansion of the private broadcasting sector and the relaxation of content controls on commercial TV and radio. However, the basic infrastructure of public service broadcasting – the BBC and regulatory agencies enforcing public duties on private broadcasters – survived intact (Curran and Seaton 1991).

Part of the reason why the free market-public watchdog argument has had such resonance in both Britain and the United States is that it is based on premises that are widely accepted in relation to the press. In the United States, the Supreme Court, citing the First Amendment, even struck down in 1974 a press right of reply law in Florida partly on the grounds that its effect was to inhibit criticism of public officials and chill robust political debate (Barran 1975). A similar line of reasoning has been regularly invoked in Britain to keep the press free of public intervention. For instance, the last Royal Commission on the Press opposed any form of selective newspaper subsidy because 'It would involve in an obvious way the dangers of government interference in the press'. 'No public body', it added, 'should ever be put in a position of discriminating like a censor between one applicant and another' (Royal Commission on the Press 1977: 126).

These arguments highlight a fundamental inconsistency at the heart of the media system of both countries: the primacy of the watchdog role has been upheld in the press but not in broadcasting. Thus, the right of reply to partisan attack has been authorized in American broadcasting, ironically with the support of the Supreme Court, even though this was outlawed in the American press (Lichtenburg 1991). Similarly, British commercial broadcasting is still run on the basis of regulatory agencies 'discriminating like a censor between one applicant and another' in awarding franchises, even though this is judged to be unacceptable in print journalism.

For a long time, this inconsistency was tolerated by free market advocates on the grounds that broadcasting was a technically disabled medium (Royal Commission on the Press 1977: 9; cf Horwitz 1991). It was limited by the scarcity of frequencies on the electromagnetic spectrum, and had to be run consequently in the public interest or, as it was argued in the United States, managed in a way that accommodated the interests of those not awarded a franchise. In contrast, there are no physical constraints on the number of press titles that can be published. But this pragmatic justification for public service broadcasting crumbled in the 1980s with the widespread adoption of new TV technology (Pool 1983). The diffusion of fibre-optic cable TV in the United States meant that most areas had many more TV channels than newspapers to choose from. Although Britain was not cabled so extensively, the introduction of high-powered satellite TV resulted in British viewers having access to approximately the same number of TV channels as national newspapers. The door thus swung open to the deregulation of public service broadcasting in both countries. A similar pattern occurred elsewhere with cable and satellite TV generating an unprecedented choice of TV channels.

Private Media as Public Watchdog: A Reassessment

The traditional public watchdog definition of the media, in the context of an expanding broadcasting system, thus has a seemingly compelling logic. It legitimates the case for free market reform of broadcasting, while justifying the continued, unfettered capitalist organization of the press. There seems to be, at first glance, much to commend this approach. Critical surveillance of government is clearly an important aspect of the democratic functioning of the media. Exposure of the Watergate burglary cover-up during the Nixon presidency or lesser known exploits (outside their country) such as disclosure of state involvement in the illegal sale of Bofors guns in Sweden or Nikiforov's exposure of local state corruption in the USSR, leading to his murder in 1989, are all heroic examples of the way in which the media performed a public service by investigating and stopping malpractice by public officials.[5]

However while the watchdog role of the media is important, it is perhaps quixotic to argue that it should be paramount. This conventional view derives from a period when the 'media' were highly politicized and adversarial. Most modern media are now given over mainly to entertainment. Coverage of public affairs accounts for only a small part of even news media content, and only a proportion of this takes the form of critical scrutiny of government.[6] In effect, the received wisdom means defining the role of the media in terms of what it (save for a few exceptions) does *not* do most of the time.

The traditional approach appears time-worn in another way. It defines the watchdog role of the media as applying only to the state. This antiquated formulation derives from a period when the state was unrepresentative, corrupt and potentially despotic, and free speech and a free press were viewed as a defence against absolutism (e.g. 'Cato' 1720). This analysis came to be framed by a simplistic conception of society in which conflict was thought to exist primarily between the individual and the state, and between ignorance and enlightenment (Curran 1978). This ignored the exercise of power through structures other than the state, and so paid no attention to the role of the press as a defence against exploitation in the private sphere – most notably in the home and the economy. Clearly, a broader definition of the watchdog role of the media is needed. The media should be seen as a source of redress against the abuse of power over others. But as soon as this broader definition is adopted, it weakens the case for the free market.

As a consequence of the take-over boom of the last three decades, a large number of media enterprises are now tied to core sectors of finance and industrial capital. For example, during the period 1969–1986, nine multi-national conglomerates bought over 200 newspapers and magazines in Britain with a total circulation of 46 million at the time of purchase (excluding publications resold to each other) (Curran and Seaton 1988). Similarly, much of the press in the United States, Australia, New Zealand, Germany, France and Sweden – to mention only those countries for which evidence is readily to hand – have been bought by or have major shareholdings in non-publishing corporations (Bagdikian 1990; Chadwick 1989; Farnsworth 1989; Tunstall and Palmer 1991; Hadenius and Weibull 1986). The trend towards privatization has also resulted in television becoming increasingly embedded in the corporate structure of big business. Diversified conglomerates increasingly dominate the new TV industries based in Europe, and control commercial television in Australia (Tunstall and Palmer 1991; Chadwick 1989). A similar trend is developing in the US (Kellner 1990). For example, Japan's Matsushita Electric Industrial Company acquired in 1990 MCA, a major Hollywood producer of TV programmes, following the pattern set by General Electric's acquisition of the US network, NBC, in 1986.

One of the consequences of this changing pattern of ownership is that media enterprises have sometimes refrained from criticizing or investigating the activities of the giant conglomerates to which they belong (Hollingsworth 1986; Curran and Seaton 1991; Bagdikian 1990). In exceptional cases, parent companies have even stepped in to suppress indirect criticism of their interests. Thus Toshiba, one of Japan's leading nuclear contractors, withdrew in 1988 a record attacking Japan's nuclear programme which had been commissioned by its Toshiba-EMI music subsidary (Murdock 1990). The free market thus compromises rather than guarantees the editorial integrity of commercial media, and impairs in particular its oversight of private corporate power.

More importantly, changes in the ownership of the media have affected its relationship to government. One 'school' of researchers argues that media conglomerates are, in effect, independent power centres which use their political leverage to pursue corporate gain. Thus Chadwick (1989) argues in an important study that a number of entrepreneurs formed a tactical alliance with the Labour government in Australia in the late 1980s as a way of securing official permission to consolidate their control over Australia's commercial TV and press. This resulted in an unprecedented number of editorial endorsements for the Labour party in the 1987 election, as well as opportunistic fence-sitting by some traditionally anti-Labour papers. Similarly, Bagdikian also claims that media conglomerates turned a blind eye to official corruption and failed programmes during the Reagan era in order 'to protect a political ally' (Bagdikian 1990: X). In a more detailed analysis, Tunstall and Palmer (1991) argue that the policy of major media combines in Europe can be explained partly in terms of their pursuit of 'regulatory favours' (by which they mean principally the abolition or waiving of official media regulation). By implication, media conglomerates are not independent watchdogs serving the public interest but self-seeking, corporate mercenaries using their muscle to promote private interests.

Another political economy tradition argues that the transformation of media ownership is part of the emergence of an information-cultural complex with close ties to government (Schiller 1989; Herman and Chomsky 1988). The stress here is less on the individual interactions between media corporations and government, and more on the way in which the integration of the media into capitalism has encouraged it to endorse, sometimes critically, discourses supportive of capital. As one recent study puts it, 'it is because of the control of media institutions by multinational capital (big business) that the media have been biased towards conservatism, thus furthering what they perceive as their own economic interests' (Kellner 1990: 172). This approach contains a number of internal variations – some more persuasive than others[7] – and rarely confronts directly the liberal conception of the media as a public watchdog. But the thrust of this research, whether explicit or implicit, is that conglomerate media are not a source of *popular* control over government but merely one means by which dominant economic forces exercise informal influence over the state.

Critical scrutiny of government can also be blunted by political partisanship. In free market theory, partisanship on the right is balanced by partisanship on the left so that there is always a substantial press ready to expose government failure, whichever party is in office. But this theory begins to break down when parties of the right are in government and the press, as in most of Europe, is overwhelmingly right-wing. Although conflicts can occur between right-wing papers and right-wing governments, the tendency is for criticism to be reined in out of partisan and patriotic loyalty. In extreme cases, this can result almost in the suspension of critical judgement. The intrepid watchdog tradition did not find in Lord Matthews, for instance, a notable exponent. 'I would find myself in a dilemma', he declared, 'about whether to report a British Watergate affair because of the national harm. I believe in batting for Britain' (cit. Hollingsworth 1986: 31). At that time, Lord Matthews controlled the third largest press group in Britain.

The assumption at the heart of traditional theory that the free market nurtures fearless newshounds is thus open to question. This said, radical accounts that stress the 'incorporation' of commercial media by big business also need to be viewed critically. Their emphasis on the material transformation of the media is not always balanced by an analysis of countervailing influences within media organizations that make for *relative* journalistic independence. In reality, the need for audience credibility and political legitimacy, the self-image and professional commitment of journalists, and normative public support for journalistic independence are all important influences militating against the subordination of commercial media to the business and political interests of parent companies. This is well illustrated by the extraordinary battle that took place in the *Observer*, a British Sunday newspaper, owned by the multinational conglomerate, Lonrho.

In April 1984 Lonrho's chief executive, Tiny Rowland, told the *Observer* editor, Donald Trelford, not to run a story about atrocities committed by the Zimbabwe army in the dissident Matabele province. Rowland was already worried about his deteriorating relationship with the government in Zimbabwe where Lonrho's investments contributed some £15 million to group profits. The radicalism of the post-colonial government headed by Robert Mugabe represented an obvious threat to Lonrho interests, and Lonrho had also made the strategic mistake of bankrolling Mugabe's unsuccessful rival, Joshua Nkomo, in a recent election. Although Rowland denies accusing his editor of 'trying to destroy my business in Zimbabwe', there seems little doubt that he was seeking to safeguard his company's corporate interests when pressing for the Zimbabwe report to be withdrawn.

Donald Trelford defied his proprietor and published the story on 15 April, 1984. He was backed unanimously by his staff, and by the paper's independent directors appointed at the time of Lonrho's take-over of the *Observer*. In the protracted row that followed (in which Lonrho allegedly cancelled advertising in its own paper), Trelford offered to stand down. This put the proprietor in a difficult position. To have accepted would have undermined the credibility of the paper, added to its unprofitability, and generated appalling publicity for Lonrho. To refuse meant entrenching the editor's position and losing proprietorial authority. For a time, Rowland toyed with the idea of selling the paper. But in the end, he settled for a face-saving exchange of letters and confirmed Trelford's appointment. The sanction of publicity in effect prevented a powerful conglomerate from manipulating a subsidiary company. But it did not prevent Lonrho from exerting pressure on the *Observer* on subsequent occasions, when senior editorial resistance was not always so determined (Curran and Seaton 1991).

Public Media as Watchdogs: A Reassessment

Public service broadcasting organizations have also resisted editorial interference for much the same reasons. Their audience credibility and strategic long-term interests, the self-conception and self-respect of their journalists, have all encouraged a defence of their autonomy from government. There is also in many liberal democracies general support within the political elite for the principle of broadcasting independence, partly for reasons of self-interest. Ministers know that one day they will need access to broadcasting when they are voted out of office. Some broadcasting organizations are also difficult to capture because power within them is decentralized and dispersed or protected by an internal system of checks and balances. But the ultimate defence of public service broadcasting autonomy is public support. On a number of occasions, in countries ranging from Germany and Britain to Israel and Australia, public disapproval has stopped politicians from asserting increased political control over broadcasting in a way that directly parallels the saga at the *Observer*.[8]

Indeed, recent British experience points to a perplexing conclusion that, both partly supports and challenges the arguments advanced by free market traditionalists. On the one hand, British broadcasting lost some degree of autonomy during the 1980s in response to a sustained onslaught from a radical right-wing government (Cockerell 1989; Leapman 1987; Schlesinger et al., 1983). Yet, despite this, it continued to expose government to more sustained, critical scrutiny than the predominantly right-wing national press. This produced escalating conflict between government ministers and broadcasters, in contrast to their generally harmonious relationship with the press.

The contrast between press and broadcasting is illustrated by the furore over an ITV documentary, *Death on the Rock*, which suggested that a British army SAS unit had unlawfully killed members of the IRA in Gibraltar, and that this was being concealed in the official version of events. The Foreign Secretary, Sir Geoffrey Howe, asked the ITV regulatory authority, the IBA, to prevent transmission of the programmes on the grounds that it would prejudice the official inquest that was due to take place. The IBA refused, and the programme was transmitted on 28 April 1988. The then prime minister, Mrs Thatcher, described her feelings about the programme 'as much deeper than being furious', and her displeasure was echoed in much of the press. 'TV Slur on the SAS' was the *Daily Star*'s headline (29 April 1988) 'Fury Over SAS "Trial by TV"', reported the *Daily Mail* (29 April) which also published a TV review calling the programme 'a woefully one-sided look at the killings'. The *Sunday Times* ran several articles seeking to rebut the accusations levelled in the programme, in which it questioned the veracity of the programme's main witness and the professionalism of the programme makers.

This public flak failed to intimidate. Thames Television, the makers of the programme, convened an enquiry headed by Lord Windlesham (a former Conservative Northern Ireland Minister) which concluded that, 'taken as a whole "Death on the Rock" did not offend against the due impartiality requirement of the IBA and the Broadcasting Act 1981'. Although making some criticisms, this internal report hailed the programme as 'trenchant' and its makers as 'painstaking and persistent'. (Windlesham and Ramptom 1989: 143). The programme duly won several prizes including the BAFTA award, the TV industry's top prize symbolizing the broadcasting community's rejection of government and Conservative newspaper criticisms. As a final snub, the programme was screened again in 1991 as a part of a celebratory season to mark the 35th anniversary of the investigative TV programme series, This Week, in which 'Death On the Rock' had first appeared.

This illustrates the way in which a complex reality can deviate from the script written by traditionalist ideologues. State-linked watchdogs can bark, while private watchdogs sleep. Yet, often, both can remain somnolent.

This points to a dual problem. Public service broadcasting offers a number of levers that can be manipulated by politicians, although the position varies slightly in different countries (Browne 1989; Etzioni-Halevy 1987; Kuhn 1985 (a); Golding and Elliott 1979). Broadcasting authorities can be 'packed' with government supporters; financial pressure can be exerted by a government refusing to increase public funding; public flak can be generated by government in an attempt to drive a wedge between broadcasters and the public; informal and formal representations can be made to promote self-censorship; broadcasting organizations can also be threatened with being legislated out of existence or being reformed root and branch. Both financial and legislative sanctions have become more pressing at a time of rising broadcasting costs, increased TV competition and the legitimation of political opposition to public service broadcasting.

But private media organizations owned by conglomerates are also vulnerable. Indeed it is sometimes easier for the public watchdog role of the media to be subverted in the deregulated than in the regulated sector of the media. Owners of private media have greater legitimacy within their organizations than do government ministers seeking to influence public sector broadcasting organizations. Although this legitimacy does not extend to the promotion of narrowly defined corporate interests, it certainly underwrites influence on broader editorial concerns that affect critical surveillance of government. The owners of private media also have more direct control over the hiring and firing of senior personnel. They are not obstructed in the same way as government ministers by mediating agencies designed to prevent their interference: independent directors – the equivalent of public trustee members of broadcasting authorities – are the exception in private media. Public concern about manipulation of private media is also less well developed than it is in relation to public media, and so provides a less adequate form of protection.

In short, the complex issues raised by the public watchdog functioning of the media cannot be resolved by a simple, unthinking, catechistic subscription to the free market. What is needed are practical measures which will strengthen the role of the media as a watchdog rather than a complacent endorsement of one system.

Consumer Representation

However, the public watchdog perspective is essentially negative and defensive. It usually defines the role of the media in terms of monitoring government, protecting the public, preventing those with power from overstepping the mark. It thus stops short of the more positive, Habermasian conception of the media as an instrument of the popular will. But there is one strand within traditional liberal thought with affinities to Habermas's approach. This defines the role of the media as that of the 'fourth estate'. Some Victorian commentators argued that newspapers were subject to the equivalent of an election every time they went on sale, in contrast to politicians who were elected only infrequently (Boyce 1978). Consequently, they claimed, the press was a fully representative institution, and should be accepted as a partner in the process of government. As Thomas Carlyle argued, the press should be deemed 'a power, a branch of government, with inalienable weight in law-making' derived from the will of the people (Carlyle 1907: 164).

This argument was reformulated in the twentieth century in less assertive terms around the concept of the sovereign consumer. The core premise is that 'the broad shape and nature of the press is ultimately determined by no one but its readers' due to the hidden hand of the free market (Whale 1977: 85). Media owners in a market-based system must give people what they want if they are to stay in business, and this ensures that the media as a whole reflect the views and values of the buying public and act as a public mouthpiece. This particular argument has been given mythological force in traditional histories of the press (e.g. Siebert, Peterson and Schramm 1956). In the case of Britain, the received account is that the press progressed through three main stages (e.g. Aspinall 1973; Koss 1981 and 1984). In the first phase, it was subject to state censorship and functioned almost as an extension of the state. In the second stage, it was dominated by the political parties and served as an extension of the party system. In the third and final stage (dating from the 1940s), the press came to be managed by market-led pragmatists who sought to maximize sales rather than further a political viewpoint. This established allegedly the consumer as the ultimate controller of the press, and transformed newspapers into representatives of the public rather than of organized political interests.

A sophisticated variation of the consumer representation thesis is to be found also in critical, revisionist American sociology. As exemplified by Alvin Gouldner (1976), it acknowledges weaknesses in the traditional free market argument but nonetheless endorses its central conclusion. Gouldner draws attention to the existence of 'huge, immensely capitalized and increasingly centralized media' and argues that, in general, 'ownership generates a set of limits patterning the media in directions supportive of the property system'. Yet, he goes on to make a stark distinction between the market-based media system which he views as ultimately liberating, and public ownership of the media which he equates with the Soviet model and 'a catastrophic regression of rationality'. The grounds for making this manichean distinction is two-fold:

public ownership leads, in his view, to the fusion of official and media definitions of reality, whereas the market liberates the media even from those who run it. The mainspring of this liberation is supposedly the drive to make a profit. It propels 'leading publishers to tolerate (and promote) a counter-culture hostile to their own *long*-term property interests . . . They will and have sold an adversary culture that openly alienates masses of youth from their parents and government because, and so long as, it is profitable'. There is thus, according to Gouldner, 'the essential bourgeois contradiction between producing anything that sells, on the one side, and allowing only what is supportive of existing institutions, on the other'. This is resolved in favour of short-term gain so that 'in the end, the system subverts itself because there exists no protection of its own *future* that might rule out quick turnover profits at the cost of the system as a whole' (Gouldner 1976: 157).

There is thus a solid corpus of literature, written by people from different disciplines and from different theoretical perspectives, which all advance essentially the same argument: the free market produces a media system which responds to and expresses the views of the people. Like all persuasive mythologies, it contains an element of truth. But its overall conclusion is nonetheless profoundly misleading – for at least six different reasons.

First, market dominance by oligopolies has reduced media diversity, audience choice and public control. In most western countries, there has been a long term reduction in the number of competing newspapers, and an increase in local monopoly and chain ownership (Hoyer, Hadenius and Weibull 1975; Rosse 1980; Curran and Seaton 1981). This has been paralleled by a long term consolidation of centralized control of magazine, record, book, and film production (Locksley and Garnham 1988; Garnham 1990; Murdock 1990; Bagdikian 1990). The picture in the case of TV is more mixed because oligopolistic control of commercial TV has been prevented or mitigated in some countries by regulatory controls.

The scale of this oligopolistic domination of the media can be illustrated by the experience of Australia, Britain and the United States. In Australia, two men (Packer and Murdoch) controlled in 1989 84 per cent of the sales of the thirty best selling magazines; Murdoch controlled in 1988 a remarkable 63 per cent of metropolitan daily circulation, 59 per cent of Sunday circulation and 55 per cent of surburban local circulation; and three men (Lowy, Bond and Skase) almost totally dominated in 1989 the commercial TV market (Chadwick 1989). In Britain, the top five companies in each media sector controlled in the mid-1980s 93 per cent of national newspaper sales, 66 per cent of video rentals, 59 per cent of record, cassette and CD sales, 53 per cent of local evening sales, 45 per cent of ITV transmissions, and 40 per cent of book sales (Curran and Seaton 1988). In the USA, three companies control about two-thirds of the TV market; three publishers dominate the national news magazine market; and most of the local press is controlled by chains (Blumler 1989; Bagdikian 1990).

Free market apologists emphasize two things in relation to these trends. They point out correctly that the movement towards market domination by a few corporations in certain markets has not been continuous and uninterrupted (Royal Commission on the Press 1977; Burnett and Weber 1988). Some also point to the expansion of part of the media system and argue that this is reviving competition. The growth of specialized magazines, computerized newsletters, desk-top publishing, local radio stations and, above all, TV channels are all cited as evidence of endogenous market regeneration (Pool 1983; Compaine 1985; Dahlgren 1991). These are important qualifications. But what they overlook are three powerful countervailing and interrelated trends that are resulting in increasing domination of the media as a whole in a national context, and increasing market power in an international context. Since 1960, there has been a rapid acceleration of mergers and acquisitions of corporations in different media sectors, producing major multi-media combines. The general trend towards privatization of broadcasting, and the growth of the new TV industries, has also enabled media conglomerates to expand into a sector where their growth had been curtailed previously. And there has been a further shift towards the integration of the global market in TV programmes, books and business information (following trends already well established in the film and record sectors), which has enabled some companies to extend their market reach.

These trends have coalesced to produce private concentrations of media power that are unprecedented. The most far-flung is Murdoch's News Corporation which controls a newspaper empire stretching east-west from Boston to Budapest and north-south from London to Queensland, an extended magazine and book empire incorporating Triangle and Harper Collins, and a TV and film empire including Fox TV and Twentieth Century Fox in the US and five satellite TV channels transmitted by British Sky Broadcasting in Europe. Major European-based conglomerates include the Bertelsmann group which has a massive book-TV-film-radio-magazine empire in Germany, including both the RTL Plus television channel and Germany's largest cable TV company, in addition to the American book and record majors, Bantam and RCA, amongst other foreign media interests; Berlusconi's Fininvest group which controls 27 Italian TV stations, extensive press and film interests in Italy in addition to television holdings in France (Channel 5), Germany (Telefunf), Spain (Telecinco) and Canada; and the British-based Maxwell Communications Corporation which controls a major group of newspapers extending from the United States to eastern Europe, book companies including the New York publisher, Macmillan, as well as TV interests in Britain, France and Spain. These are matched by major conglomerates like Time-Warner, International Thompson and Sony based respectively in the US, Canada and Japan. The enormous resources commanded by these conglomerates, their large economies of scale, and extensive domination of linked markets, has undermined the functioning of the market as a free and open contest, a level playing field in which all participants have an equal chance of success.

The second, related flaw in the consumer representation thesis is that the rising capitalization of the media industries has restricted entry into the market.[9] In Britain, for example, it currently requires in start-up and run-in costs over £20 million to establish a new national daily newspaper, over £30 million to establish a new cable TV station, up to £50 million to acquire a major ITV franchise and over £500 to establish a new satellite TV business. It is still possible to enter more cheaply the marginal media sectors – such as local free sheets, local radio stations and specialist magazines – but these have much less influence by comparison with the commanding heights of the communications industry. It is also possible to attempt to launch into the main deregulated media sectors with a relatively small capital outlay, and even to maintain a nominal presence by operating on a very small budget with manageable losses. But low investment often leads to low quality and high price, a combination that usually marginalizes these ventures from the outset.

The heavy capitalization of the media industry has created, in effect, a zone of influence in which dominant economic forces have a privileged position, and to which other significant social forces are denied direct, unmediated access. As Nicholas Garnham comments: 'we would find it strange now if we made voting rights dependent upon purchasing power or property rights and yet access to the mass media, as both channels of information and fora of debate, is largely controlled by just such power and property rights' (Garnham 1986: 47).

It is in this context that free market celebration of the recent expansion of some media sectors needs to be assessed critically. The belief is that more media outlets have produced more diversity and choice. But what this increasingly fashionable argument ignores is that prevailing market structures determine and impose limits on the 'diversity' generated by expansion. More need not necessarily mean more of the same, as some left-wing critics maintain. But what it does mean is that choice is always *pre-structured* by the conditions of competition. In a contemporary context, this means a class filter imposed through the high costs of market entry; an unequal relationship between large and small competitors; often oligopolistic market domination; and the constraints imposed by catering for the mass market. The consequences of this pre-structuring can be briefly illustrated by recent changes in American television and the British press.

In the United States, a large increase in the number of TV channels has expanded cultural and genre diversity. The basic diet of the networks has been expanded by counter-programming independent stations and, above all, by cable TV stations making available a choice between cops and robber series, sit coms, chat shows, game shows, soaps, classic comedy TV shows, stand-up comics, Hollywood film classics, art house movies from Europe, newish American films, childrens' cartoons, foreign language programmes for ethnic minorities, and much more besides. But what it has failed to achieve is a corresponding increase in the ideological diversity of public affairs programming. The burgeoning number of local independent stations provides, according to Entman's pioneering research, 'little political information, let alone accountability news' (Entman 1989: 110). CNN has introduced two new news channels, which provide instantaneous coverage within much the same ideological framework as the three news networks (CBS, NBC and ABC). What none of the new commercial enterprises has done is to offer a leftish 'take' on the news. Indeed, the greatest political diversity is to be found significantly in the current affairs output of PBS and a relative newcomer, C-Span, both non-profit organizations outside the economic market, which are undercapitalized and marginalized.

Similarly, the recent expansion of the British national press has led to more consumer choice without substantially expanding its ideological range. The introduction of cost-cutting new technology led to the launch of seven new national papers between 1986 and 1990. But market leaders forced up costs by increasing paging and promotion in a deliberate attempt to squeeze out competition. In the event, only four new nationals survived: a pornographic, depoliticized Sunday paper (*Sunday Sport*), a Conservative tabloid bought by Rupert Murdoch (*Today*) and two centrist papers catering for an advertising-rich, elite audience (*Independent* and *Independent on Sunday*). As a consequence, the chasm between editorial and public opinion[10] in Britain persisted.

In short, distortions in the market require the media representation thesis to be heavily qualified. When this thesis was first advanced, it had considerably more validity than it has now. It really was the case in the pre-industrial phase of the press that almost anyone could set up, so to speak, their trestle table in the free market place of ideas. This produced a choice between ideologically diverse papers – conditions in which the 'public' could exercise significant influence over the press and be represented by it (Curran 1977). This has long ceased to be the case even if traditional free market arguments continue to be advanced as if nothing has changed.

The third flaw in the consumer representation thesis is that it ignores the way in which the relationship between media and audiences has been transformed since the nineteenth century. The audiences for 'popular' media have become much larger and also more heterogeneous in terms of their political and social composition: they no longer necessarily have a shared set of beliefs or common interest that can be 'represented'. The rise of entertainment content in news media has also reduced the desire for political reinforcement as a motivation for media consumption. A view of the media, fashioned during a period when politicized newspapers served highly differentiated audiences, no longer corresponds to the reality of the contemporary media. The *Sun*, the biggest selling daily in Britain, illustrates the change that has taken place. It devotes less than 15 per cent of its *editorial* content to public affairs news and comment, and sells to a politically divided audience of over 10 million readers. While it can be argued plausibly that the *Sun* connects to structures of feeling among its readers (Holland 1983), it certainly does not represent them in a political sense. Thus only 41 per cent of its readers voted Conservative in the 1987 general election – the choice insistently recommended by the paper. (Harrop 1988)

Fourth, the revisionist claim that media controllers subordinate their ideological commitments to the imperatives of the market is only partly true. It is based on selective arguments that simplify and misrepresent a complex situation. Thus, it is claimed that the dispersal of share ownership is producing a divorce between ownership and control of the media; that the new breed of media controllers are market-led pragmatists; and that the media, in a competitive environment, must submit to the rule of the consumer. In fact, a large number of communications conglomerates – including very large and extended ones – are still controlled by a single shareholder or family (Herman and Chomsky 1988; Murdock 1982). A significant number of media controllers – such as Springer, Hersant, Maxwell and Black – are ideologically committed rather than politically neutral businessmen. Above all, the rise of entertainment and the growth of oligopoly has increased the relative political autonomy of media owners in relation to the market.

All three points are illustrated by Rupert Murdoch's career. (Munster 1985; Leapman 1983). He has generally controlled the media enterprises he has invested in; his views have become increasingly right-wing, particularly since the early 1970s; and, in advancing his beliefs, he has skilfully negotiated the currents of the market rather than being swept passively along by them. Thus, on occasion, he has bowed to strong market signals: he refrained, for example, from changing the character of the radical New York magazine, *Village Voice*. At other times, he has trimmed when it has seemed advantageous to do so: the Victoria *Sun* and the New South Wales *Herald* both backed the right-wing Labour leader, Bob Hawke, in the 1987 election when it was in Murdoch's corporate interest to allow editorial flexibility. He also bent prudently to the wind when new technology facilitated the emergence of a new competitor, the London *Independent*: his appointment of an independently minded Conservative journalist, Simon Jankins, as editor of the *Times* in 1990 was a belated recognition that the *Times*'s Thatcherite politics was causing it to lose readers to the new paper. Yet, whenever possible, he has pushed his papers to the right by hand-picking editors with right-wing views and by bombarding inherited, politically centrist editors with aggressively worded right-wing advice (Evans 1983: Giles 1986). Indeed what has been most striking about these displays of ideological commitment has been his willingness to move some of his papers – such as the London *Sun*, *Sunday Times* and *Times* – to the radical right in opposition to the views of the majority of its readers (Curran and Seaton 1991). To see Murdoch as a passive absorbent of market dictates is to adopt too mechanistic and simplistic a view of the market: it also underestimates Murdoch's innovative ability and the strength of his convictions.

Fifth, the concept of sovereign consumer control ignores the variety of influences which shape media content. The familiar image of the trader in the marketplace of ideas, which regularly recurs in free market rhetoric, ignores the reality of highly bureaucratized media organizations, with fixed routines and structures, whose journalists rely heavily on a restricted range of sources. It simply overlooks, in other words, the voluminous sociological literature which shows the varied ways in which audience pressures are selectively interpreted, 'refracted' and even resisted within media organizations.[11]

Sixth, the idealized notion of market democracy ignores the central financial role of advertising in commercial broadcasting and the press. Critics of advertising tend to focus on the direct editorial influence exerted by advertisers through the witholding of advertising support for ideological reasons, and the pressure that this generates on media clients to accommodate to or anticipate advertisers' ideological concerns (Hoch 1974; Barnouw 1978; Bagdikian 1990). The extent of this influence is relatively small and tends to be exaggerated, certainly in Britain (Blumler 1986; Curran 1980). The more important way in which advertisers shape the media is by weighting the economic value of audiences. The structure of the press is oriented more towards upscale than downscale audiences because the former generates a larger advertising subsidy per reader (Curran 1986). This is true to a lesser extent of commercial television because programmes select and deliver audiences with less precision than press publications. However, advertisers still distort television because they tend to reward high ratings rather than intensity of audience demand. This generates strong pressure on general interest channels to aim for the middle market and to conform to middle market values and perspectives (Gitlin 1983; Brittan 1989).

There is also a more general sense in which the traditional conception of the media as a public representative does not seem to fit the contemporary media. A view formed when most media were partisan and 'spoke for' clearly defined constituencies seems less appropriate to market-based news systems, as in the US, which are predominantly bi-partisan and define themselves in terms of disseminating 'information'.

The view of the media as a public tribune thus seems almost obsolete. Yet, it is still worth clinging on to the notion of the media as a representative agency. The market also has a role to play in making media organizations responsive to the public. What is needed is a new formulation that fits changed circumstances and a revised conception of the media's democratic role.

Information Role

In addition to the concept of the media as a watchdog and representative, commentators have also stressed its 'informational' role. This is usually portrayed in terms of facilitating self-expression, promoting public rationality and enabling collective self-determination. These different functions of the media can only be fulfilled adequately, it is argued, through the processes of a free market.

Thus, the free market is supposed to promote a culture of free thinking democracy. No one should be subjugated, the argument goes, to another's will but should be able to express freely what they think to whomever they want. This freedom, essential to self-realization, is safeguarded allegedly by the right to publish in a free market.

The free market is also equated with efficiency in the pursuit of the public interest. The freedom to publish ensures that all significant points of view are in play in the public domain, and that a wide range of information is made available from diverse and antagonistic sources. This makes for good judgement and wise government. Originally, this claim was advanced in an assertive form based on the assumption that truth would confound error in an unrestricted debate. But in response to the decline of naive empiricism, this argument came to be reformulated in a more circumspect way. Typical of this more cautious approach is the American jurist, Oliver Holmes's much quoted contention 'that the ultimate good desired is better reached by free trade in ideas – that the best test of truth is the power of the thought to get itself accepted in the competition of the market . . .' (cit. Barran 1975: 320). This argument has been presented in a variety of guises. The free market mobilizes the collective intellectual resources of the nation. It fosters public rationality by enabling collective judgements to be made in the knowledge of alternative courses of action. Or, more simply, 'a free marketplace of ideas has a self righting tendency to correct errors and biases' (Kelley and Donway 1990: 90).

The market system is also celebrated as the best possible way of facilitating self-government. Free market media inform citizens from a variety of viewpoints; they keep open the channels of communication between government and governed, and between different groups in society; they provide a neutral zone for the formation of public opinion. In short, the processes of the market are central to the exercise of popular sovereignty.

These hosannas have come increasingly under attack even within the camp committed to the market system. One line of criticism has been that *market failure* has limited individual freedom of expression, and consequently prevented public debate from being adequately informed by diverse sources. As the influential Hutchins Commission argued as long ago as 1947, after surveying the development of the American media: 'the right of free public discussion has therefore lost its earlier reality' (Commission Report reprinted 1974). This then prompted the argument that public rationality has been impaired, and collective direction has been weakened, because people with something useful to say have not always been given a chance to say it. As the American political theorist, Alexander Meiklejohn, put it: 'self-government is nonsense unless the 'self' which governs is able and determined to make its will effective' (Meiklejohn 1983: 276).

Critics also opened up another line of attack, arguing that the *inherent* characteristics of the market deplete the informational role of the media. The British equivalent of the Hutchins Commission – the 1947–9 Royal Commission on the Press – claimed that the press was failing to inform adequately the people because it was a product of the market. 'The failure of the Press to keep pace with the requirements of society', it concluded, 'is attributable largely to the plain fact that an industry that lives by the sale of its products must give the public what the public will buy' (RCP 1949: 177). By implication, the inadequacy of the press was merely a reflection of the inadequacy of the public, printed large. This paternalistic judgement was subsequently reworked in a form that alleged that the presssure to maximize sales and ratings led to common denominator provision that underestimated the abilities of the public (Hoggart 1957; Thompson 1974). This very British debate was superseded by a less overtly moralistic analysis, on both sides of the Atlantic, which highlighted some of the characteristics of news produced within a market oriented system: information that is simplified, condensed, personalized, decontextualized, with a stress on action rather than process, visualization rather than abstraction, stereotype rather than human complexity, (Gitlin 1983; Newcomb 1987; Inglis 1990).[12] Since many of these criticisms were predicated on the assumption that these deficiencies were a by-product of processing news as a commodity for the mass market, they were an attack, by implication, on the notion that market processes safeguard the informationl role of the media.

Professional Responsibility Model

At this point, it is worth following a short detour. Across the horizon loomed at a convenient moment the figure of the media professional, with the perfect timing of the American cavalry riding to the rescue. It is no coincidence that both the Hutchins Commission and the Royal Commission of the Press concluded at about the same time that media professionalism was the solution to the shortcomings that they diagnosed. Journalists were urged to adopt the mantle of the professions. In this way, the media would be able to fulfill its informational role and serve the public interest (Commission 1974; RCP 1949).

Their reports were followed by a series of ringing public endorsements of professional responsibility. The cult of professionalism became a way of reconciling market flaws with the traditional conception of the democractic role of the media. It asserted journalists' commitment to higher goals – neutrality, detachment, a commitment to truth. It involved the adoption of certain procedures for verifying facts, drawing on different sources, presenting rival interpretations. In this way, the pluralism of opinion and information, once secured through the clash of adversaries in the free market, could be recreated through the 'internal pluralism' of monopolistic media. Market pressures to sensationalize and trivialize the presentation of news could be offset by a commitment to inform. The democratic role of the media could thus be rehabilitated without structural reform.

The ideology of professional responsibility has found numerous celebrants for a variety of reasons, not all noble.[13] But at its core is a seductive idea: professionalism means that the journalist's first duty is to serve the public. It proposes – certainly, as presented by its more radical advocates – that journalists should act as a counterweight to forces, both internal and external, that threaten the integrity of the media, including media controllers, advertisers, publicists and government.[14] By emphasizing accuracy and facticity, media professionalism seems to be defining the role of the media in a way that will assist people to make up their own minds for themselves. Professionalism is thus seemingly a philosophy of empowerment rather than of control; professional self-interest appears, in this case, to coincide with the public interest.

But professional commitments cannot exist in a vacuum. Journalists operate within certain structures which influence – and can distort – their definition of professionalism, (Tuchman 1978; Schlesinger 1987; Bevins 1990). The exercise of professional judgement also presupposes a high degree of autonomy. Although most American journalists stress their operational freedom, the evidence suggests that journalistic autonomy has declined in the US since the early 1970s, particularly in large news organizations (Weaver and Wilhoit 1986). Journalistic autonomy has also been revoked or curbed by interventionist media managements elsewhere. (Ericson, Baranec and Chan 1987; Curran and Seaton 1991). Put simply, professionalism is not assured within media organizations which do not have as their central goal the realization of professional norms. This is, indeed, one of the arguments for public service broadcasting.

Professionalism is also vulnerable because it is not clear on what basis it is justified. Journalism does not have the entry requirements, credentials and self-regulatory controls normally associated with a profession. Journalists have consequently an ambiguous status, and this can be a vocational weakness. A repeated criticism levelled against journalists is that their lack of critical engagement leads to tacit acceptance of the social order, and to over-ready adoption of the definitions provided by the powerful (Hall et al. 1978: Entman 1989; Abramson 1990). But this is inscribed within a particular set of professional beliefs which defines implicitly the role of a journalist as a subaltern one of mediating authoritatively-sourced information. Another version of professionalism stresses truth-seeking but this too is often interpreted in a restricted and defensive way. One truth-seeking strategy is the attempted 'scientization' of news reporting: the focusing on technical, strategic and insider perspectives of politics in a way that enables journalists to avoid being exposed as necessarily subjective participants in the political process (Hallin 1985). Reporting elections, for example, in terms of campaign strategies and game plans, as a glorified horse race rather than as democratic inquest, enables the journalist to take refuge in a 'neutral' form of interpretation. Another defensive strategy involves an almost mechanistic reliance on market-defined news values. This can lead to the manipulation of the media by publicists skilled at generating news bites and photo-opportunities, and exploiting the news codes operated by journalists (Gitlin 1991).

A further problem is that professionalism is itself ambiguous. It means different things to different people, and indeed different cultures. In the United States, TV news items on the major networks tend to take the form of structured, visually integrated, narrative texts whose meaning is relatively 'closed'. In Italy by contrast – and, indeed, in much of Europe – TV news tends to be more 'open', with more 'talking heads', in which greater prominence is given to contrasting interpretations of events (Hallin and Mancini 1984).[15] This divergence reflects the more dominant political and interpretive role of political parties in many European countries compared with the United States, and the more ratings-conscious commercialism of American TV. But it also reflects a different definition of professionalism, predicated on a different understanding of the place of broadcasters in society. In the US, the accent is on entertainment and disclosure – reporting news as a structured 'story' whose meaning is clearly signified by the reporter. In many European countries, greater emphasis is given to the role of broadcaster as a factual witness and passive mediator, who enables the viewer to have access to competing interpretations of the world.[16]

In sum, the ideology of professionalism does not provide an adequate way of realizing the democratic role of the media, although it is sometimes presented in these terms by critical writers in the free market tradition. This approach is misconceived partly because professional commitments need structures to support them, and partly because the code of professionalism is itself ambiguous. This ambiguity masks an unresolved debate about the democratic role of the media.

Defects of Traditional Perspective

This debate is unresolved partly because the traditional conception of the media's informational role fails to command allegiance even in purely theoretical terms. One shortcoming is that it ignores modern political structures, and focuses on the individual as the basic unit of analysis. The media protect the individual from the state; inform the individual as an elector; express public opinion, which is tacitly conceptualized as aggregated private opinion.

This perspective harks back to an almost pre-industrial conception of polity, in which the positive role of modern political parties, pressure groups and associations is overlooked. These provide a means of advancing individual interests within collectively organized society, afford a source of protection against the exercise of private economic power, organize political choice in a way that enables people to choose (in theory) between programmes as well as individuals, and provide a variety of means of influencing public opinion and exerting democratic pressure on the state. Traditional thought ignores the building blocks of modern liberal democracy and so has nothing constructive to say about how the media should relate to them and enhance their performance.

The second defect of the traditional approach is that it maintains an artificial and untenable distinction between information and representation. It does this by detaching information from its social context. Thus, the criterion for judging the successful functioning of the informational role of the media is normally held to be one of two things: the richness of media discourse defined in subjective terms of 'quality' or the number of media outlets which, as Horwitz (1991) shows in an admirable essay, is increasingly the yardstick being adopted in American jurisprudence.

Missing from this analysis is a recognition that ideas and systems of representation are part of the ideological arsenal which competing groups use to advance their interests. This point can be understood in a very simple and rudimentary way in terms of political agendas. Political parties on the right tend, in general, to emphasize law and order, defence and international relations because they are often seen by voters as being particularly strong on these issues. Parties on the left tend to emphasize welfare and employment because these are areas where they are often rated more highly. Rival political parties consequently vie with each other at election time to get broadcasters to make their 'issues' the dominant themes of election coverage. How broadcasters respond to – and, in effect, arbitrate between – these rival agendas can have a significant influence on the outcome of tight elections.[17]

A comparable but more complex process of contestation takes place between social groups. Different ways of signifying and making sense of society, different linguistic codes and conceptual categories, different chains of association and versions of 'common sense' privilege the interests of some social groups while disadvantaging others. Put another way, the media's informational role is never purely informational; it is also a way of arbitrating between the rhetorical claims of rival interests – in a form that has an indirect outcome in terms of the allocation of resources and life opportunities between different social groups.

The case for media diversity is thus not simply that it promotes a rational debate based on awareness of alternatives. It is also a way of promoting social equity in which divergent social groups have the opportunity to define their interests in their own terms and promote them in the public domain. It is in this context that the role of the media in forming a consensus should be understood. Traditionalists argue that the media should facilitate social agreement through the dissemination of accurate information and contrary opinion. This is an entirely reasonable proposition on the face of things. But it can mask, in reality, a process of manipulation in which one class or social coalition is able to naturalize and universalize its interests because it dominates the channels of cultural production. The media may give the appearance of distributing accurate information and facilitating a debate based on conflicting argument. Indeed, it may actually be doing both these things. But by confining this debate to 'legitimate' areas of controversy, and by grounding it on assumptions that do not challenge the structure of social power, it may also be engineering a contrived form of social consent.

The third limitation of the classical liberal model – and, one that is often alluded to – is that it overstates the rationality of public discourse. As Chafee (1983: 294) puts it, 'I can no longer think of open discussion as operating like an electric mixer . . . Run it a little while and truth will rise to the top with the dregs of error going down to the bottom'. His reservations were based on distortions in the distribution of information, the outpouring of information on a scale that is impossible for any one individual to assimilate and, above all, the subjective element in making judgements (cf. Peterson 1956). This last point has been highlighted by research emphasizing non-rational elements in opinion formation, and by studies emphasizing the highly selective way in which people assimilate communications (Tan 1985; Graber 1988). In reality, public discourse does not follow the rational pathways of the classic liberal model.

This has wider implications that tend to be ignored. Entertainment is usually omitted from conventional analysis of the media's democratic functioning because it does not conform to a classic liberal conception of the rational exchange between the rulers and ruled. But in fact media entertainment is one means by which people engage at an intuitive and expressive level in a public dialogue about the direction of society (Curran 1991). Media entertainment is in this sense an integral part of the media's 'informational' role.

There is another reason why entertainment is wrongly excluded from traditional accounts. This stems from the conventional assumption that the sole purpose of the public debate staged by the media is to effect changes of government policy and exercise democratic control over the state. But this implies too narrow a definition of public dialogue, and too restricted a definition of its purpose, rooted in a conventional distinction between private and public spheres which the slogan 'politics is personal' rightly challenges. Public dialogue should encompass the common processes of social life: its outcome should be to revalidate or revise social attitudes patterning social relationships. Media fiction is one important dimension in which this dialogue takes place.

The fourth weakness of the traditional model is, of course, that it fails to distinguish between the legal right to publish, and the economic reality limiting that right in real terms. For reasons that have already been given, limitations on market entry restrict individual freedom of expression. But it also restricts – and this is a category that does not feature in traditional analysis – freedom of group expression. Whole groups in society, not merely individuals, have restricted access to the public sphere through the media. This has undermined, in turn, self-government in the interests of all. It has limited the ability of sections of the community to voice effectively their interests, their opinions, their view of relative priorities. And this has prevented other groups from responding to, indeed even sometimes being aware of, these different definitions.[18] The democatic process for making collective judgements about the development of society has thus been weakened because it has not been, in an adequate and attainable sense, collective.

Media and the Public Sphere

Implicit or explicit in these criticisms are suggestions for rethinking the informational role of the media. At the cost of some repetition, it may be helpful to draw together briefly the main arguments into an ordered whole.

The public dialogue staged by the media system should be informed by a diversity of values and perspectives in entertainment as well as public affairs coverage. By generating a plurality of understandings, the media should enable individuals to reinterpret their social experience, and question the assumptions and ideas of the dominant culture. It should also enable everyone, on the basis of diverse perspectives and sources, to decide for themselves how best to safeguard and advance their welfare in collective as well as individual terms, and to set in the balance rival definitions of the public interest and claims based on equity.

This will be emancipatory in a number of ways. It will give subordinate classes increased access to ideas and arguments opposing ideological re-presentations that legitimate their subordination, and enable them to explore more fully ways of changing the structure of society to their advantage. Media fiction that enables people to explore imaginatively what it is like to be other people, in different circumstances and with different formative experiences, is also likely to promote empathy and understanding rather than the opposite. However, the key rationale for pluralism is not progressive social engineering: it is empowerment, giving people the right to define their normative vision of the world and their place in it through access to alternative perspectives of society.

Another (and complementary) democratic function of the media system is to act as an agency of representation. It should be organized in a way that enables diverse social groups and organizations to express alternative viewpoints. This goes beyond, however, simply disseminating diverse opinion in the public domain. Part of the media system should function in a way that invigorates civil society. It should assist collective organizations to mobilize support; help them to operate as representative vehicles for the views of their supporters; and aid them to register effective protests and develop and promulgate alternatives. In other words, the representational role of the media includes helping to create the conditions in which alternative viewpoints and perspectives are brought fully into play.

This implies a break from a 'postmodernist' approach in which the act of media consumption is equated with political activity; the private holding of a political opinion is equated with political activism; and the guiding democratic force in society is deemed to be enlightened public opinion in 'the public sphere' shaped by the interplay of argument and evidence in the mass media. This is a recipe for control from above, given the extent to which mass media are currently influenced by dominant elites, even if media audiences display a healthy degree of independence.

One way to step out of this seductive framework is to visualize the public sphere as a core surrounded by satellite networks and organized groupings. The core public sphere is the public space where all interests interact with one another in seeking to establish agreement or compromise about the direction of society. Feeding this core are a number of umbilical cords that connect it to the life force of civil society – different interpretive communities with a shared normative conception of society (such as greens, feminists and marxists), different organized groupings (such as political parties and pressure groups), different sub-cultures (such as those of ethnic minorities), and different social strata with distinctive interests and social experiences (which are only partly organized and articulated). The representative role of the media can be conceptualized in relation to this. One part of the media system should provide a public arena of debate roughly coterminous with society in which different interests are represented; another should provide channels of communication linking organized groups and social networks to this public arena; another part should facilitate the functioning of these groups within their respective constituencies; and a further part should be composed of unaligned channels of communication between the common public sphere and different social strata and congeries of individuals.

The third democratic function of the media is to assist the realization of the common objectives of society through agreement or compromise between conflicting interests. The media should contribute to this process by facilitating democratic procedures for resolving conflict and defining collectively agreed aims. For example, the media should brief the electorate about the political choices involved in elections, and so help to constitute elections as defining moments for collective decision about the public direction of society. The media system should also facilitate organized representation by giving due publicity to the activities, programmes and thinking of organized groups in addition to the formal processes of government and party opposition. But the media system is itself also an important mechanism for collective self-reflection. By staging a public dialogue in which diverse interests participate, the media should also play a direct role in assisting the search for areas of common agreement or compromise. It should also provide an adequate way in which people can engage in a wider public discourse that can result in the modification of social attitudes affecting social relationships between individuals and groups.

One problem arising from this conception of a democratic media system is that it will probably make the attainment of national agreement more difficult. Indeed, it will almost certainly reinforce existing centrifugal and fissiparous tendencies within society. A genuinely pluralistic media system implies enabling dissident groups within the working class to command effective communications resources, fostering sectional loyalties (whether in the form of class, ethnic, gender or other group solidarities), and staging an open public debate that weakens adherence to dominant political and social norms. This is in marked contrast to the experience of most countries where the media are usually integrated into the hierarchy of power and where the media function as agencies of social integration and control.

However, there are various ways in which the centrifugal impact of a pluralistic media system can be mitigated without subtracting from the pluralist commitment that underpins it. One conventional and legitimate way is, of course, to establish a legal framework that lays down acceptable (but minimal) limits to freedom of expression, such as restrictions on incitements to racial hatred. Another is to impose fairness rules on some media so that the range of representations it mediates reflects the broad balance of contending forces in society. This is a way of anchoring part of the media system to the central social forces in society. And by arguing that the media system should have a core component – a common space that links together divergent groups – this approach also builds in a stabilizing element. Underlying this is a desire to replace societal agreement based on domination with a more equitable system of public dialogue in which conflicts of interest are brought into the open and resolved in a democratic, non-violent way.

What might this media system look like in terms of structure and organization? What kinds of journalism would it foster? These questions beg further questions in the sense that the design of any media system needs to take into account the generation of pleasure and cultural provision, which are issues that lie outside the terms of reference of this essay. Any prescription based only on what serves the democratic needs of society can only be a partial input to a larger debate. But with this qualification in mind, what does a re-evaluation of the democratic functioning of the media imply in terms of concrete practice?

Towards a Working Model

The outline set out below may seem to American eyes detached from political reality. But although it does not exist in any country as a functioning model, it draws upon and composites features derived from the practice of different European countries. Indeed, it is proposed in this form precisely because it works with the grain of what is attainable.

The model can be viewed at a glance in Figure 5.1. It has a core sector, surrounded by media organizations which are organized on different principles. The core sector of general interest TV channels reaches a mass audience and provides a common forum of societal debate. It offers an opportunity for different classes and groups to take part in the *same* public dialogue about the direction of society. It provides scope, therefore, for them to interact with one another and engage in a reciprocal discussion. It also provides a single emporium in which individuals can explore where their self interest lies, and relate this to rival definitions of the common interest. Lastly, it offsets the particularistic features of the rest of the media system by providing a common symbolic environment which reinforces ties of mutuality.

Fig. 5.1 Model of a democratic media system

The peripheral sectors are composed of media reaching more differentiated audiences, and are organized in a way that is designed to produce a vigorous plurality of competing voices. One sector consists of private enterprise organizations; another sector promotes the maximimum journalistic and creative freedom; a third sector is dominated by media linked to organized interests; and the fourth fosters innovation within a modified market system. The diversity of these media is designed to feed into and invigorate the core system; it entrenches a system of balance and checks that promotes pluralism; and it strengthens the democratic institutions of civil society.

Core Media

In principle, the best way to organize the core sector is to set up competing public service organizations (whether in the form of publicly owned or publicly regulated commercial organizations). Potentially, this offers the best prospect of opening up broad social access to the airwaves, and enabling viewers to plug into different views and perspectives. It also creates the framework in which general interest channels maintain a high priority to news and current affairs programmes, and fulfil wider social objectives in its cultural provision. The system of payment for public service organizations also ensures that there are no second class citizens excluded by price from the general forum of public debate. A deregulated commercial system will, by contrast, tend to restrict the range of views and social interests represented on general interest channels, give lower priority to public affairs coverage and subordinate social objectives to maximizing audiences.

But the theory of public service broadcasting does not necessarily correspond to reality. One problem is that government can undermine the independence of public broadcasting institutions, and restrict the public debate conducted through their channels. The travails of the French broadcasting system provide a particularly stark cautionary tale in this respect, although government control has diminished during the last decade (Thomas 1976; Kuhn 1985). Two models (with various national differences) have been developed to tackle this problem. One is a corporatist model in which diverse representative groups are incorporated into the command structure of broadcasting. The other is a neutral civil service model in which broadcasting is established as a depoliticized system staffed by impartial 'public servants'. Both approaches are viable.

A successful corporatist strategy for preventing official control is exemplified by the German broadcasting system. Its core public service institutions are decentralized confederations in which opposed political tendencies are locked into a system of mutual checks and balances. This has produced organizations which it is impossible for government to capture without the equivalent of a prolonged, house-to-house battle against broadcasters with powerful political allies. Right-wing politicians in Germany have sought to get round this problem by seeking to establish a private enterprise sector, modelled on the American system, on the grounds, partly at least, that this would be inherently sympathetic to their political outlook. But this has been blocked by Germany's Constitutional Court which has insisted on commercial TV organizations being run on pluralistic public service lines. A highly complex system deliberately fashioned to prevent a repetition of Germany's past history, which has been protected by constitutional guarantees and public support, has frustrated every serious attempt to impose government control, (Williams 1976 and 1985; Browne 1989; Porter and Hasselbach 1991 (a) and (b)).

The alternative civil service model, typified by the British system, has also succeeded in sustaining, as we have seen, a critical relationship to government. But the limited official inroads made during the 1980s suggest that further insulation between government and broadcasters is needed. One insulating device is to limit government financial control by linking rises in the license fee to the national earnings index: another is to limit government powers of appointment to broadcasting authorities by 'franchising' representative national organizations and broadcasting staffs to elect some members.

A second, more intractable problem is that public service broadcasting organizations tend to be dominated by elites (even if they offer more ideologically 'open' and diverse systems of representation than commercial TV in the United States). The German and British broadcasting systems both exemplify this weakness. Thus, the output of British broadcasting has tended to be structured in terms of the assumptions of dominant power groups (Glasgow University Media Group 1976, 1980 and 1985), although its minority and fictional output has been more heterodox (Schlesinger et al. 1983; McNair 1988). The ideological range of its programmes has also expanded during periods of heightened political conflict (Curran 1990) and widening social debate (Tracey 1983). But the concept of the impartial public servant seems to lead to the mediation of a narrow range of discourses, particularly during periods of relative consensus. The German broadcasting system, by contrast, is more overtly pluralistic. German broadcasters have a public duty, in the words of the 1987 German inter-state broadcasting agreement, to grant 'means of expression to the significant political, ideological and social forces and groups' in society, and this is reinforced by pluralistic representation on broadcasting authorities. But in practice, its definition of pluralism is overdetermined by the major political parties.

Both systems can be improved. Broadcast representation in Germany should include more nominees from the new social movements, while ideological and cultural diversity should be adopted in Britain as an explicit public service goal. But the fine tuning of broadcast rules and structures can achieve only limited improvements. This is because the nature of the public dialogue conducted through public service TV relates to the wider public debate taking place in society. The basic strategy that has been adopted, as we shall see, is to improve core public service broadcasting by reinvigorating the debate on which it draws.

This entails regenerating sectionalist media. To offset their particularistic effect, it may be desirable to impose a public duty on public service core organizations to promote empathy and understanding between groups through the expression of diverse values and perspectives in its fictional output. It has an integrative impact, moreover, almost by virtue of its functioning as a mass audience medium. By mediating public events to a large undifferentiated audience, by providing a common stock of shared experience and by offering up common symbols of identification to be shared and also exchanged, core public service institutions serve as a focal point of collective unity and reinforce ties of social association in society (Peters 1989; Scannell and Cardiff 1991).

Brief reference should also be made to the potential impact of the new TV industries on public service broadcasting. Satellite and cable television threaten to disperse the TV audience and, consequently, to fragment the forum of societal debate established through public service television. Secondly, it also threatens to destabilize the economy of national public broadcasting systems by establishing a new distribution system for globally syndicated programmes. This undercuts the cost of making programmes for national audiences and bypasses existing protectionist arrangements. Its longterm effect could be to encourage some public service broadcasting systems, with falling audiences and revenues, to rely increasingly on cheap imported programmes. Beyond a certain point, this would reduce their capacity to facilitate collective self-reflection in a national context.

But public service organizations remain both dominant and resilient in most countries (Collins 1989). At the end of the day, a mechanism is available for the protection of national public service broadcasting, should this seem advisable. Cross-frontier, satellite broadcasting is subject to internationally agreed controls – in the context of Europe through the EEC and the Council of Europe – and these can be revised. But a satisfactory case for strengthening these controls has yet to be made.

Civic Media Sector

Diversity of representation – in its dual sense of representing the world and representing interests – is best secured by having well articulated viewpoints in play in the public domain that journalists, subject to the constant pressure of reaching tight deadlines, can readily draw upon. It is also facilitated by the efficient organization of competing interests so that journalists know whom to contact and where to go in order to provide a fully balanced account. Strengthening the civic media sector will help in both respects.

The civic media sector can be seen in summary form as being composed of three tiers. The top tier consists of media (such as party controlled general interest newspapers) which are linked to collective organizations but are aimed, in principle at least, at a general audience with the intention of winning wider support. They are usually adversarial in approach, and provide a way of sustaining and renewing a particular perspective of society that reflects the commitments and priorities of an organized group. The second tier consists of sub-cultural media (such as magazines for gays and lesbians) which relate to a constituency rather than an organized group. But they can have nonetheless an important organizational role. They can foster a positive collective identity, promote a sense of group unity and project goals that can only be realized through collective action.[19] The third tier consists of organizational media (for example, a national trade union journal or a newsletter of a local parents association) which serve as channels of communication between members of a group. These can provide a link between leaders, activists and supporters, reinforce commitment to the organization, relay information relevant to its functioning, and provide an internal forum for developing new ideas and strategies.

The civic media sector is in trouble. The party political press has wilted in many countries in the face of competition from entertainment oriented tabloids (Hoyer, Hadenius and Weibull 1975). Advertising has contributed to a lopsided development of the specialist press by heavily subsidizing the growth of publications that deliver a desired target market (such as doctors or those interested in home improvements), while providing much less support for subcultural media with a less defined or useful readership in marketing terms (Curran 1986). The large increase in private spending on corporate business media has also contributed to a lop-sided development of organizational media.

The civic media sector can be reinvigorated in two ways. One strategy is to give large social and political groups control over part of the minority broadcasting system. This could include: direct control over radio stations, time share and part use of technical facilities of a minority TV channel, must carry rules for cable TV operators. There are precedents, however, for a more assertive version of this approach in polarized or 'pillarized' societies. Italy has given, in effect, two TV channels to rival political parties (Sassoon 1985); the Netherlands has allocated control of two TV channels to rival programme-making organizations, each representing distinctive cultural, political and religious traditions, on the basis of the size of their membership. (McQuail and Siune 1986; Browne 1989).

The other (though not mutually exclusive) approach is to establish a public agency, funded by an advertising tax, to assist the launch or development of civic media. The agency could have all-party representation, and assist those projects which most contribute to the vigour of the civic media. It could function as a modified version of the Swedish Press Subsidies Board (Hulten 1984).

Professional Media Sector

Journalists working for adversarial media linked to organized interests function partly as propagandists. Those working for traditional public service organizations operate within certain constraints; they tend to adopt a detached rather than committed stance, with a stress on mediating competing truths rather than revealing the truth. Those working for profit-driven organizations often define professionalism in terms of market values. All these different approaches contribute to the plurality of perspectives that a healthy media system should promote. But there is also a need for an additional voice – that of the independent, truth-seeking journalist – operating within an environment that encourages journalistic autonomy.

Establishing a professional sector also represents a way of establishing a section of the media that speaks to the public in a different way. It can relate to society not in terms of organized groupings – as public service broadcasting and the civic media do in different ways, nor in terms of audience ratings and sales as in the case of commercial media – but as an aggregation of individuals in a voice and idiom that it can define.

What voices emerge will depend on how journalists and programme makers respond to the opportunities given to them. But there is a vacuum that needs to be filled: the revival of a radical, unaligned, populist style of truth seeking in fiction and its equivalent in journalism. During its heyday in late nineteenth century Europe and America, its effect was to expand the boundaries of social conscience by highlighting the plight of the vulnerable, and of those who, due to their lack of organization, were not in a strong position to assert a claim on the rest of society.

The professional sector will not simply add to the diversity of the media system. It also builds into it an important watchdog element. Public service broadcasting is linked to the state; the market sector is dominated by big business; the civic sector – or, at least, the most influential part of it – is controlled by collectively organized interests. There is a need for a professional sector which is a bedrock of independence and which can be relied upon to maintain a critical surveillance of all power centres in society, and expose them to the play of public opinion.

An institutional setting needs to be established that will enable programme makers to work in conditions of maximum freedom. This could take the form of two skeletal organizations – one controlling a minority TV channel, and the other a minority radio channel – which would commission rather than make programmes. This would ensure that programmes were made mostly in small, informal production companies. Members of boards running the two channels could be elected by people working in the radio and TV industries in order to assert their independence from government. Funding for the two channels could be supplemented by spectrum fees charged annually on commercial TV and radio franchise holders as a way of relieving market pressure. The aim, in short, is to create the ideal conditions for two showcase channels run by the broadcasting industry.

Private Enterprise Sector

Competition between commercial media encourages responsiveness to aggregate audience demand. Its presence within the system thus provides a countervailing and corrective influence to that of other forces – ranging from the journalism profession to organized interests – that will shape the rest of the media system. The tendency of private enterprise media to privilege right-wing perspectives will also contribute to the diversity of the media as a whole.

A private enterprise sector also strengthens, to some extent, the watchdog role of the media. The conventional assumption that it is a wholly independent check on the government is, as we have seen, mistaken. But a private enterprise sector is vulnerable to government influence in a different way from organizations formally linked to the state. And in this difference, there is a modest measure of security.

A substantial private enterprise sector should have a major presence in the press and perhaps the new TV industries. A *deregulated* commercial, over-the air TV sector should not be established, however, because it would undermine the pluralism of the rest of the broadcasting system. It would scoop advertising revenue needed to sustain alternatives. It would also generate pressure on its rivals to converge towards the middle market at the expense of minority provision and minority perspectives.

Social Market Sector

A major deficiency of the market sector is that it no longer functions in the way that it is supposed to in theory. Market domination and economies of scale limit competition; high entry costs exert a form of ideological control; restrictions on market choice reduce audience influence.

One response to this problem, exemplified by the Swedish press subsidies system, is to modify the ground rules of competition so that the free market is re-established as a level playing field. Its centrepiece is a complicated re-distributive system, finetuned over the years, which supports low circulation papers with a graduated subsidy. It has succeeded in helping to maintain press diversity without leading to government control (Hulten 1984; Picard 1988; Strid and Weibull 1988).

An alternative approach – and one that is more easily realizable in societies that lack Sweden's tenacious social democratic culture – is to establish a social market sector as a way of regenerating the market system. Its central role is to incubate new forms of competition, rooted in social forces underrepresented in the market, as a way of extending real media choice.

This objective can be furthered in three ways. Innovatory forms of media organization can be established in a way that extends diversity of output. A successful example of this is the establishment in Britain of Channel 4 with a remit to innovate and serve minorities, funded through advertising and a guaranteed safety net income from the main commercial TV network. The Channel 4 model – a cross-subsidized centre of innovation operating in a competitive context – can be extended to other media.

Second, a public funding agency can be established to fund challenges to the media conglomerates from groups with limited resources and a reasonable prospect of success. One sector where such an agency can have a considerable impact is local radio, where entry costs are still relatively low.

Third, tough anti-monopoly measures can be introduced to limit market domination by the major conglomerates. This can take the form, not merely of setting ceilings for expansion, but of curbing excessive cross-media concentration through enforced divestment. But if this is to result in a broadening of the social base of media ownership, a public agency has to be in place to assist underfinanced groups to acquire divested media. Otherwise, anti-monopoly controls could merely lead to one media conglomerate selling to another which is eligible as a purchaser under the new monopoly rules.

Retrospective

Implicit in this prescription is a complex set of requirements for a democratic media system. It should empower people by enabling them to explore where their interest lies; it should foster sectional solidarities and assist the functioning of organizations necessary for the effective representation of collective interests; it should sustain vigilant scrutiny of government and centres of power; it should provide a source of protection and redress for weak and unorganized interests; and it should create the conditions for real societal agreement or compromise, based on an open working through of differences rather than a contrived consensus based on domination. This can be best realized through the establishment of a core public service broadcasting system, encircled by a private enterprise, social market, professional and civic media sectors. These latter will strengthen the functioning of public service broadcasting as an open system of dialogue, and give added impetus to the collective, Do-It-Yourself tradition of civil society. In short this represents a reworking, in a contemporary context, of Habermas's historical idyll with which we started this chapter.

112   *James Curran*

Notes

1   My thanks to the staff and students at the Department of Communications, University of California, San Diego for helpful suggestions incorporated into this chapter.

2   'Liberal' is a confusing word, meaning different things in Britain and the United States. It is used here in its British historical sense, and refers to the body of thought developed by liberals in the eighteenth and nineteenth centuries. For an account of their thinking in nineteenth century Britain, see Boyce (1978) and Curran (1978); and for the eighteenth century, in both Britain and America, see Holmes (1991).

3   Recent studies of the media which have drawn heavily upon Habermas include, among others, Dahlgren (1987); Elliott (1986); Garnham (1986); Hallin and Mancini (1991); Keane (1989); Scannell (1989); and Skogerbo (1990).

4   Indeed, Habermas himself revised implicitly his earlier, pessimistic assessment by emphasizing subsequently audience adaptation and resistance to mediated meanings. See Habermas (1984: 391ff.) which confusingly was translated and published in English before his first book (1989).

5   It should be noted, however, that exposés of state illegality occurred in state-linked media in Sweden and the USSR, while broadcasting in the US (then subject to more regulation than now) also played a role in the Watergate saga. In reality, investigative journalism is not confined to free market media.

6   Estimates for the proportion of public affairs content in contemporary media are provided by Curran and Seaton (1991); Strid and Weibull (1988); and Neumann (1986) cit. Abramson (1990).

7   A useful, evaluative survey of different approaches in the political economy tradition is provided by Murdock (1982). A persuasively circumspect presentation of the radical political economy approach is provided in the essay by Golding and Murdock in this volume.

8   This is particularly well documented in Etzioni-Halevy's (1987) comparative study. For additional information about the British government's failed attempt to suppress a 'Real Lives' documentary about sectarianism in northern Ireland – with striking parallels to the *Observer* saga – see also Leapman (1987).

9   The two arguments are linked in that market dominance has forced up market entry costs.

10   This is illustrated by the difference between editorial and electoral opinion. Thus, in the 1987 general election, the Conservative press accounted for 72 per cent of national daily circulation, although the Conservative Party gained only 43 per cent of the vote.

11   Michael Schudson's chapter in this volume provides a useful summary of this literature. For a striking account of the way in which journalists can both resent and resist audience pressure, see Gans (1979).

12   A good example of this approach is provided by Hallin (1991) who shows that the average 'sound bite' on American network TV news declined from over forty seconds in 1968 to under 10 seconds in the 1980s.

13   For iconoclastic accounts of media professionalism, see in particular Schudson (1978), Schiller (1981), Tuchman (1978) and Elliott (1978).

14   This leads logically to a demand either for industrial democracy (see Ascherson (1978)) or for legal protection of journalistic autonomy (see Baistow (1985)). Though these arguments are seductive, they also raise a problem. Journalists tend to share the same news values, and to hunt in packs and develop group judgements. The greater empowerment of journalists across all media could lead potentially, therefore, to greater editorial uniformity. Partly for this reason, the proposal at the end of this chapter adopts a deliberately selective approach to underwriting journalistic control.

15   Hallin and Mancini's penetrating essay relates to only one European country, Italy, which has a distinctive TV system and political culture. But there are affinities, nevertheless, between TV news in Italy and other European countries.

16   This definition was made particularly explicit in Germany, following a wide public debate about the role of the broadcaster. See Williams (1976).

17   For an example of the way in which media agenda setting and 'priming' can affect election results, see Iyengar and Kinder (1987).

18   A minor but telling illustration of the way in which different groups can be ignorant of what the other thinks, even though they live cheek by jowl in ostensibly integrated communities, occurred when I conducted jointly two group discussions in an East Anglian village for the Eastern Counties Newspapers Group. When asked about what most concerned them, the first group of working class couples said that they were worried about the lack of good job prospects for their children, the lack of leisure facilities for the young, and the problem of social discipline among teenagers. The second group of middle class couples were mainly concerned about the environment and the threat of increased urbanization in the area (which would generate a wider range of jobs and more 'leisure facilities') and were convinced that the first group fully shared their concerns. When informed that this was not the case, they were visibly taken aback, with some arguing rightly that the local paper should have alerted them to what other people in the community were feeling. This may seem to illustrate an aspect of rural, socially stratified England. But other monopoly papers also fail to provide an adequate channel of communication between social classes in their local community. For example the *Los Angeles Times*, arguably one of the best daily papers in the United States, with enormous resources at its disposal, is nevertheless quite extraordinarily uninformative about what members of Los Angeles's large underclass are thinking and feeling.

19   For the way in which media for sexual minorities can have an indirect but important organisational role, see Gross (1989).

References

ASPINALL, ARTHUR, 1973: *Politics and the Press, c. 1780–1850*. Brighton: Harvester.

ABRAMSON, JEFFREY, 1990: 'Four Criticisms of Press Ethics' in Judith Lichtenberg ed. *Mass Media and Democracy*. New York: Cambridge University Press.

ADAM SMITH INSTITUTE, 1984: *Omega Report: Communications Policy*. London: ASU.

ASCHERSON, NEAL, 1978: 'Newspapers and Internal Democracy' in James Curran ed. *The British Press*. London: Macmillan.

BAISTOW, TOM, 1985: *Fourth-Rate Estate*. London: Commedia.

BARRON, JEROME, 1975: *Freedom of the Press for Whom?*. Ontario: Midland Book.

BAGDIKIAN, BEN, 1990: *The Media Monopoly*. 3rd edition, Boston: Beacon Press.

BEVINS, ANTHONY, 1990: 'The Crippling of the Scribes', *British Journalism Review*, 1, 2.

BLUMLER, JAY, 1986: 'Television in the United States: Funding Sources and Programme Consequences' in West Yorkshire Media in Politics Group, *Research on the Range and Quality of Broadcast Services*. London: HMSO.

BLUMLER, JAY, 1989: 'Multi-Channel Television in the United States: Policy Lessons for Britain', Markle Foundation Report (mimeo).

BOYCE, GEORGE, 1978: 'The Fourth Estate: The Reappraisal of A Concept' in George Boyce, James Curran and Pauline Wingate eds. *Newspaper History*. London: Constable.

BROWNE, DONALD, 1989: *Comparing Broadcast Systems*. Ames, Iowa State University.

BRITTAN, SAMUEL, 1989: 'The Case for the Consumer Market' in Cento Veljanovski ed. *Freedom in Broadcasting*. London, Institute of Economic Affairs.

BURNETT, ROBERT and WEBER, ROBERT, 1988: 'Concentration and Diversity in the Popular Music Industry, 1948–86'. Gothenburg: University of Gothenburg (mimeo).

CARLYLE, THOMAS, 1907: *On Heroes, Hero-Worship and the Heroic in History*. London, Chapman and Hall.

CATO, 1983: 'Of Freedom of Speech: That the Same is Inseparable from Public Liberty', *Cato's Letters*, No. 15, 4 February, 1720. Reprinted in Haig Bosmajian ed. *The Principles and Practice of Freedom of Speech*. 2nd edition, Lanham: University Press of America.

CHADWICK, PAUL, 1989: *Media Mates*. Melbourne: Macmillan.

CHAFEE, ZECHARIAH JNR, 1983: 'Does Freedom of Speech Really Tend to Produce Truth?' in Haigh Bosmajian ed. *The Principles and Practice of Freedom of Speech*. 2nd edition, Lanham, University Press of America.

COCKERELL, MICHAEL, 1989: *Live From No. 10*. 2nd edition, London: Faber and Faber.

COLLINS, RICHARD, 1989: 'Language of Advantage', *Media, Culture and Society*, 11, 3. *Commission on Freedom of the Press*, (Hutchins Report) Chicago, University of Chicago Press, 1947. Reprinted (ed. Robert Leigh) Midway Reprint, 1974.

COMPAINE, BENJAMIN, 1985: 'The Expanding Base of Media Competition', *Journal of Communication*, 35.

CURRAN, JAMES, 1978: 'The Press as an Agency of Social Control: An Historical Perspective' in G. Boyce, J. Curran and P. Wingate eds. *Newspaper History*. London: Constable.

CURRAN, JAMES, 1980: 'Advertising as a Patronage System' in Harry Christian ed. *The Sociology of Journalism and the Press*, Sociological Review Monograph 29. Keele: University of Keele Press.

CURRAN, JAMES, 1986: 'The Impact of Advertising on the British Mass Media' in R. Collins et al. eds. *Media, Culture and Society: A Critical Reader*. London, Sage.

CURRAN, JAMES, 1990: 'Culturalist Perspectives of News Organizations: A Reappraisal and Case Study' in Marjorie Ferguson ed. *Public Communication*. London: Sage.

CURRAN, JAMES, 1991: 'Rethinking the Media as a Public Sphere' in Peter Dahlgren and Colin Sparks eds. *Communication and Citizenship*. London: Routledge.

CURRAN, JAMES and JEAN SEATON, 1991: *Power Without Responsibility: The Press and Broadcasting in Britain*. 3rd edition, London: Routledge, 1988 and 4th edition, London, Routledge.

DAHLGREN, PETER, 1987: 'Ideology and the Public Sphere' in J. D. Slack and F. Fejes eds. *The Ideology of the Information Age*, Norwood, N.J.: Ablex.

DAHLGREN, PETER, 1991: 'Introduction' in Peter Dahlgren and Colin Sparks eds. *Communication and Citizenship*. London: Routledge.

ELLIOTT, PHILIP, 1978: 'Professional Ideology and Organisational Change: The Journalist Since 1800' in George Boyce, James Curran and Pauline Wingate eds. *Newspaper History*. London: Constable.

ELLIOTT, PHILIP, 1986: 'Intellectuals, the "Information Society" and the Disappearance of the Public Sphere' in Richard Collins et al. eds. *Media, Culture and Society: A Critical Reader*. London: Sage.

ENTMAN, ROBERT, 1989: *Democracy Without Citizens*. New York, Oxford University Press.

ERICSON, RICHARD, PATRICIA BARANEK and JANET CHAN, 1987: *Visualizing Deviance*. Milton Keynes: Open University.

ETZIONI-HALEVY, EVA, 1987: *National Broadcasting Under Siege*. London: Macmillan.

EVANS, HAROLD, 1983: *Good Times, Bad Times*. London: Weidenfeld and Nicholson.

FARNSWORTH, JOHN, 1989: 'Social Policy and the Media in New Zealand' in *Report of the Royal Commission on Social Policy*. Vol. 4, Wellington, NZ: Government Printer.

FRASER, NANCY, 1987: 'What's Critical about Critical Theory? The Case of Habermas and Gender' in Seyla Benhabib and Drucilla Cornell eds. *Feminism as Critique: On the Politics of Gender*. Minneapolis: University of Minnesota Press.

GANS, HERBERT, 1979: *Deciding What's News*. London: Constable.

GARNHAM, NICHOLAS, 1986: 'The Media and the Public Sphere' in Peter Golding, Graham Murdock. and Philip Schlesinger eds. *Communicating Politics*. Leicester: Leicester University Press.

GILES, FRANK, 1986: *Sunday Times*. London: John Murray.

GITLIN, TODD, 1983: *Inside Prime Time*. New York: Pantheon.

GITLIN, TODD, (ed.) 1986: *Watching Television*. New York: Pantheon.

GITLIN, TODD, 1991: 'Blips, Bites and Savvy Talk: Television and the Bifurcation of American Politics' in Peter Dahlgren and Colin Sparks eds. *Communication and Citizenship*. London: Routledge.

GLASGOW UNIVERSITY MEDIA GROUP, 1976: *Bad News*. London: Routledge and Kegan Paul.

GLASGOW UNIVERSITY MEDIA GROUP, 1980: *More Bad News*. London: Routledge and Kegan Paul.

GLASGOW UNIVERSITY PRESS, 1985: *War and Peace News*. Milton Keynes, Open University Press.

GOLDING, PETER and PHILIP ELLIOTT, 1979: *Making the News*. New York, Longman.

GOULDNER, ALVIN, 1976: *The Dialectic of Ideology and Technology*. London, Macmillan.

GRABER, DORIS, 1988: *Processing the News*. 2nd edition, White Plains, NY: Longman.

GROSS, LARRY, 1989: 'Out of the Mainstream: Sexual Minorities and the Mass Media' in Ellen Seiter et al. eds. *Remote Control*. London: Routledge.

HABERMAS, JÜRGEN, 1989: *The Structural Transformation of the Public Sphere*. Cambridge: Polity.

HABERMAS, JÜRGEN, 1984: *The Theory of Communicative Action*. Vol. 1, Boston: Beacon Press.

HADENIUS, STIG and LENNART WEIBULL, 1986: *Massmedier*. Stockholm: Bonnier.

HALL, STUART, CHAS CRITCHER, TONY JEFFERSON and BRIAN ROBERTS, 1978: *Policing the Crisis*. London: Macmillan.

HALLIN, DANIEL, 1985: 'The American News Media: A Critical Theory Perspective' in John Forester ed. *Critical Theory and Public Life*. Cambridge, Massachusetts: MIT Press.

HALLIN, DANIEL, 'Sound Bite News' in Gary Orren (ed.) 1991 (forthcoming). *Blurring the Lines: Elections and the Media in America*. Glencoe: Free Press.

HALLIN, DANIEL and MANCINI, PAOLO, 1984: 'Speaking of the President: Political Structure and Representational Form in U.S. and Italian News', *Theory and Society*, 13.

HALLIN, DANIEL and MANCINI, PAOLO, 1991 (forthcoming): 'Summits and the Constitution of an International Public Sphere: The Reagan-Gorbachev Meetings as Televised Media Events', *Communication*.

HARROP, MARTIN, 1988: 'Press' in David Butler and Dennis Kavanagh, *The British General Election of 1987*. London: Macmillan.

HERMAN, EDWARD and CHOMSKY, NOAM, 1988: *Manufacturing Consent*. New York: Pantheon.

HOCH, P., 1974: *Newspaper Game*. London: Calder and Boyars.

HOHENDAHL, PETER, 1979: 'Critical Theory, Public Sphere and Culture. Jürgen Habermas and His Critics', *New German Critique*, 16.

HOGGART, RICHARD, 1957: *The Uses of Literacy*. London: Chatto and Windus.

HOLMES, STEPHEN, 1990: 'Liberal Constraints on Private Power?: Reflections on the Origins and Rationale of Access Regulation' in Judith Lichtenberg ed. *Mass Media and Democracy*. New York: Cambridge University Press.

HOLLAND, PATRICIA, 1983: 'The Page Three Girl Speaks to Women, Too', *Screen*, 3, 24.

HOLLINGSWORTH, MARK, 1986: *The Press and Political Dissent*. London: Pluto Press.

HORWITZ, ROBERT, 1991 (forthcoming): 'The First Amendment Meets Some New Technologies: Broacasting, Common Carriers, and Free Speech in the 1990's', *Theory and Society*.

HOYER, SVENNIK, STIG HADENIUS and LENNART WEIBULL, 1975: *The Politics and Economics of the Press: A Developmental Perspective*. London: Sage.

HULTEN, OLOF, 1984: *Mass Media and State Support in Sweden*. Stockholm: Swedish Press Institute.

IYENGAR, SHANTO and DONALD KINDER, 1987: *News That Matters*. Chicago: University of Chicago Press.

INGLIS, FRED, 1990: *Media Theory*. Oxford: Blackwell.

KEANE, JOHN, 1989: '"Liberty of the Press" in the 1990's', *New Formations*, 8.

KELLEY, DAVID and ROGER DONWAY, 1990: 'Liberalism and Free Speech' in Judith Lichtenberg, (ed.): *Mass Media and Democracy*. New York: Cambridge University Press.

KELLNER, DOUGLAS, 1990: *Television and the Crisis of Democracy*. Boulder: Westview Press.

KOSS, S., 1981 and 1984: *The Rise and Fall of the Political Press in Britain*. Vols. 1 and 2, London: Hamish Hamilton.

KUHN, RAYMOND, (ed.) 1985 (a): *The Politics of Broadcasting*. Beckenham: Croom Helm.

KUHN, RAYMOND, 1985 (b): 'France: The End of the Government Monopoly' in R. Kuhn ed., *The Politics of Broadcasting*. Beckenham: Croom Helm.

LEAPMAN, MICHAEL, 1983: *Barefaced Cheek*. London: Hodder and Stoughton.

LEAPMAN, MICHAEL, 1987: *The Last Days of the Beeb*. 2nd edition, London: Coronet.

LICHTENBERG, JUDITH 'Introduction' in J. Lichtenberg, (ed.) 1990: *Mass Media and Democracy*. New York: Cambridge University Press.

LOCKSLEY, GARETH and NICHOLAS, GARNHAM, 1988: 'Trends in Communication in Europe', *CCIS Working Paper No. 3*. London: Polytechnic of Central London.

MCNAIR, BRIAN, 1988: *Images of the Enemy*. London: Routledge.

MCQUAIL, DENIS and KAREN SIUNE (ed.), 1986: *New Media Politics*. London: Sage.

MEIKELJOHN, ALEXANDER, 1983: 'The Rulers and the Ruled' in Haigh Bosmajian ed. *The Principles and Practice of Freedom of Speech*. Lanham: University Press of America.

MORTENSEN, FRANDS, 1977: 'The Bourgeois Public Sphere – A Danish Mass Communications Research Project' in M. Berg et al. eds. *Current Theories in Scandinavian Mass Communication Research*. Greaa, Denmark: GMT.

MUNSTER, GEORGE, 1985: *Rupert Murdoch*. Ringwood, Australia: Viking.

MURDOCH, RUPERT, 1989: *Freedom in Broadcasting* (MacTaggart Lecture). London: News International.

MURDOCK, GRAHAM, 1982: 'Large Corporations and the Control of the Communication Industry' in M. Gurevitch, T. Bennett, J. Curran and J. Woollacott eds. *Culture, Society and the Media*. London: Methuen.

MURDOCK, GRAHAM, 1990: 'Redrawing the Map of the Communications Industries: Concentration and Ownership in the Era of Privatization' in Marjorie Ferguson ed. *Public Communication*. London: Sage.

NEUMANN, W., 1986: *The Paradox of Mass Politics*. Cambridge: Harvard University Press.

NEWCOMB, HORACE, (ed.) 1987: *Television: The Critical View*. New York: Oxford University Press.

PETERS, JOHN, 1989: 'Democracy and American Mass Communication Theory: Dewey, Lippmann, Lazardsfeld', *Communication*, 11.

PETERSON, THEODORE, 1956: 'Social Responsibility Theory of the Press' in F. Siebert et al., *Four Theories of the Press*. Urbana: University of Illinois Press.

PICARD, ROBERT, 1988: *The Ravens of Odin*. Ames: Iowa State University.

POOL, ITHIEL DE SOLA, 1983: *Technologies of Freedom*. Cambridge: Harvard University Press.

PORTER, VINCENT and SUZANNE HASSELBACH, 1991 (a): 'Beyond Balanced Pluralism: The Regulation of Broadcasting in the Federal Republic of Germany' in Peter Dahlgren and Colin Sparks eds. *Communication and Citizenship*. London: Routledge.

PORTER, VINCENT and SUZANNE HASSELBACH, 1991 (b): *Pluralism, Politics and the Market Place*. London: Routledge.

PETERSON, THEODORE, 1956: 'Social Responsibility Theory of the Press' in Fred Siebert et al. *Four Theories of the Press*. Urbana: University of Illinois Press.

ROSSE, J. N., 1980: 'The Decline of Direct Newspaper Competition', *Journal of Communication*, 30.

Royal Commission on the Press 1947–9 Report, 1949: London: HMSO.

Royal Commission on the Press 1974–7 Final Report, 1977: London: HMSO.

SASSOON, DON, 1985: 'Italy: The Advent of Private Broadcasting' in R. Kuhn ed. *The Politics of Broadcasting*. Beckenham: Croom Helm.

SCANNELL, PADDY, 1989: 'Public Service Broadcasting and Modern Public Life', *Media, Culture and Society*, 11, 2.

SCANNELL, PADDY and DAVID CARDIFF, 1991: *Social History of Broadcasting*. Vol. 1, Oxford: Blackwell.

SCHILLER, DAN, 1981: *Objectivity and the News*. Pennsylvania: University of Pennsylvania.

SCHILLER, HERBERT, 1989: *Culture Inc*. New York: Oxford University Press.

SCHLESINGER, PHILIP, MURDOCH, GRAHAM and ELLIOTT, PHILIP, 1983: *Televising 'Terrorism'*. London: Pluto.

SCHLESINGER, PHILIP, 1987: *Putting 'Reality' Together*. London: Routledge.

SCHUDSON, MICHAEL, 1987: *Discovering the News*. New York: Basic Books.

SKOGERBO, ELI, 1990: 'The Concept of the Public Sphere in a Historical Perspective: An Anachronism or a Relevant Political Concept?', *Nordicom Review*, 2.

STEPP, CARL, 'Access in a Post-Responsibility Age' in Judith Lichtenberg ed. *Mass Media and Democracy*. New York: Cambridge University Press.

STRID, INGELA and LENNART WEIBULL, *Mediesveridge 1988*. Goteborgs: Goteborgs University Press.

TAN, ALEXIS, 1985: *Mass Communication Theories and Society*. 2nd edition, New York: Wiley.

THOMAS, RUTH, 1976: *Broadcasting and Democracy in France*. London: Crosby Lockwood Staples.

THOMPSON, D., (ed.) 1974: *Discrimination and Popular Culture*. London: Heinemann.

TRACEY, MICHAEL, 1983: *A Variety of Lives*. London: Bodley Head.

TUCHMAN, GAYE, 1978: *Making News*. New York: Free Press.

TUNSTALL, JEREMY and PALMER, MICHAEL, 1981: *Media Moguls*. London, Routledge.

VELJANOVSKI, CENTO, 1989: 'Competition in Broadcasting' in C. Veljanovski ed. *Freedom in Broadcasting*. London, Institute of Economic Affairs.

WEAVER, DAVID and WILHOIT, G. CLEVELAND, 1986: *The American Journalist*. Bloomington: University of Indiana Press.

WHALE, JOHN, 1977: *The Politics of the Media*. London: Fontana.

WILLIAMS, ARTHUR 1976: *Broadcasting and Democracy in West Germany*. Bradford: University of Bradford Press.

WILLIAMS, ARTHUR, 1985: 'West Germany: The Search for the Way Forward' in R. Kuhn ed. *The Politics of Broadcasting*. Beckenham: Croom Helm.

WINDLESHAM, LORD and RAMPTON, RICHARD, 1989: *The Widlesham/Rampton Report on Death on the Rock*. London: Faber and Faber.

6

The Global and the Local in International Communications

Annabelle Sreberny-Mohammadi

Introduction

> After three thousand years of explosion, by means of fragmentary and mechanical technologies, the Western world is imploding. During the mechanical ages we had extended our bodies in space. Today, after more than a century of electric technology, we have extended our central nervous system itself in a global embrace, abolishing both space and time as far as our planet is concerned . . . As electrically contracted, the globe is no more than a village.
>
> McLuhan, *Understanding Media*, 1964, 11–12

> A Third World in every First World
> A Third World in every Third World
> And vice-versa
>
> Trinh Minh-ha, 1987

Contemporary rhetoric suggests that we live in a unitary world in which space and time have collapsed and the experience of distance imploded for ever. The antagonistic blocs of East and West are giving way to international markets, moneys and media. Germany is unified. A new and expanding 'Europe' looms. The centrifugal force of 'globalization' is the catchphrase of the 1990s. Yet at the very same time, in the same but different world, the centripetal forces of old and new tribalisms and nationalisms are at work and ethnic struggles are breaking out all over. Armenians confront Azarbaijanis, Serbs fight Croats, Mowhawk Indians confront Quebecois, there is violence between Umkatha and the ANC. Race-related violence increases in New York City, with a new Black-Asian dimension. The Soviet Union acts violently against Lithuania, putting perestroika in peril. Iraq invades and annexes Kuwait, and Arab-Americans fear discrimination, as do Muslims in Europe, and the world waits for 'high noon' on January 15, 1991. Far from the 'loss of the subject', identity seems to lie at the heart of politics in the late twentieth century.

Giddens, (1990, p. 64) defines globalization as 'the intensification of world-wide social relations which link distant localities in such a way that local happenings are shaped by events occurring many miles away and vice versa'. For Giddens, what he calls 'time-space distanciation' (p. 64), a theme developed at length in Harvey (1989), helps to create 'complex relations between *local involvements* (circumstances of co-presence) and *interaction across distance* (connections of presence and absence). In this stretching process of

118

relations, there are numerous modes of connection between different regions and contexts. Appadurai (1990) has described five such 'scapes' of interaction as the ethnoscape, the technoscape, the infoscape, the financescape and the mediascape – which are interconnected, even overlapping.

Much theoretical debate centres on how the current situation should be conceived and labelled. Some argue that there is a discernibly 'new' kind of economic-cultural structure to be called 'post-modernity' (Harvey 1989) while others argue that the evident changes of the last fifteen years simply reflect the supreme developpement and natural extension of global capitalism and prefer to call this structure 'late capitalism' (Mandel, Jameson 1990) or 'high modernity' (Giddens 1990). What is significant throughout these debates is that the role of communication and information have been finally and generally recognized as crucial elements in the new world order. Yet the role and shape of communications at the beginning of the 1990s is by no means very fixed or very clear, and neither are our theoretical models for explaining/exploring communications on an international scale. The rapidity and complexity of change in the media environment as we enter the 1990s seems to require a newer set of terms and vantage points than are offered by older perspectives, which often seem frozen in a bygone era. This chapter explores the dynamic tension between the global and local levels of analysis, as suggested by Giddens, as a provocative and useful construct which can help us uncover the deeply contradictory dynamics of the current moment. In the twin yet opposing processes of globalization versus localization, media play a central role and reveal the tensions between the macro and micro levels of socio-economic structures, cultures, and development dynamics.

A Brief Reprise of Older Models in International Communication:

Since the 1960s, the field of International Communication has been dominated by three successive intellectual paradigms: that of 'communications and development', that of 'cultural imperialism' and currently by a revisionist 'cultural pluralism' which is still searching for a coherent theoretical shape. It will be argued here that this third construct is itself full of contradictions, and that the 'global/local' model at least has the merits of putting 'contradiction' at the core of its construct. A brief reprise of these models is useful, both as intellectual history and to understand the different theoretical bases and implications of the models for current understanding.

'Communications and Development' emerged out of developmentalist thinking in the early 1960s. After the Second World War, the emergence of independent national political systems such as India, Algeria, Ghana, out of the grip of varied European colonialisms, spawned debates among Western academics about the nature of 'development' and the obstacles within such newly-independent nations to development. Some arguments focused on the lack of capital for investment, prompting such practical solutions as the World Bank and interest-bearing loans, under which results many developing nations are still groaning. Other arguments examined the lack of entrepreneurial vision and trained manpower, spawning education exchanges and training programs. The arguments developed by Daniel Lerner (1958) and Wilbur Schramm

(1964) focused instead on the Weberian/Parsonian 'mentalities' or conjeries of attitudes that were supportive or obstructive to change. They suggested that the traditional values of the developing world were the central obstacles to political participation and economic activity, the two key elements of the development process. The 'solution' for their analysis was the promotion of the use of communciations media to alter attitudes and values, embodied in 'media indicators' (minimum numbers of cinema seats, radio and television receivers, and copies of daily newspapers as a ratio of population necessary for development), which were adopted by UNESCO and widely touted in the developing world. This perspective has been roundly criticized for its ethnocentrism, its ahistoricity, its linearity, for conceiving of development in an evolutionary, endogenist fashion and for solutions which actually reinforced dependency rather than helping to overcome it.

The 'dependency' paradigm, developing initially in Latin America and building on older critiques of imperialism (Gunder-Frank 1964) instead recognized the global structures and interrelationships conditioning the 'development' of the Third World, particularly the multiple and diverse legacies of colonialism. It was particularly critical of the post-independence economic dynamics which kept Third World states in economic hock to the ex-imperial powers, and argued that 'development' could not be mere mimicry of Western structures but had to be conceived as an autonomous, self-chosen path that built on the rich/ancient cultures of the Third World. From within this broad, critical framework, the specific model of 'cultural imperialism' argued that, far from aiding Third World nations to develop, the international flows of technology transfer and media hardware coupled with the 'software' flows of cultural products actually strengthened dependency and prevented true development. The great merit of the models of 'cultural imperialism' (Schiller 1976; Matterlart, 1979) and 'media imperialism' (Boyd-Barrett 1977) was their recognition of *global* dynamics and relationships, taking their cue from much older models of imperialism, and the suggested linkages between foreign policy interests, capitalist expansion and media infrastructures and contents. This theoretical model spawned a wide variety of empirical studies which documented the imbalanced flow of media products – from news (Galtung and Ruge 1965) to films (Guback and Varis 1982) to television programming (Varis 1974/1984) – as well as the export of organizational structures (Katz and Wedell 1977) and professional values (Golding 1977) from the developed to the Third World. Behind its structuralist analysis and the descriptive mapping of international communications dynamics, a central assumption was that Western cultural values (often conflated to 'American' values) such as consumerism and individualism, expressed implicitly in a variety of media genre as well as directly through advertising, were being exported to and decisively altering Third World cultural milieux. Fears of 'cultural homogenization' and 'cultural synchronization' (Hamelink 1983) were voiced, and arguments made for Third World 'cultural disassociation' along the lines of Samir Amin's 'delinkng' from the global capitalist system as the only way toward autonomous development and protection of indigenous cultures. Criticism of this position have been made from quite divergent historical perspectives. One argument, looking back in time, suggests that the very term 'cultural imperialism' tends to obscure the many deep and diverse *cultural* effects of imperialism itself, including the export of religion, educational systems and values, European languages, and administrative practices, all of which have long ago and perhaps irretrievably altered the cultural milieux of the colonized (Sreberny-Mohammadi in Golding, forthcoming). Such an argument questions the utility of terms such as 'authenticity' and 'indigeneity' within a lengthy history of cultural contact, absorption and recreation, and suggests that a cultural debate which focuses mainly on modern media neglects other much older and deeper structures which may embody 'foreign' values but may also be the pillars of modernization.

Another strand of critique, looking forward to the new realities of the 1990s, suggests that, like the earlier arguments for 'communications and development', the 'cultural imperialism' model was based on a situation of comparative global media scarcity, limited global media players and embryonic media systems in much of the Third World. The speed-up of history, evidenced in the rapidity of changes in many areas of social life, is especially evident in the global spread of communication and information technologies and the advent of many new and diverse media actors over the past decade or so. In 1990, it is clear that the international media environment is far more complex than that suggested by the 'cultural imperialism' model whose depiction of a hegemonic media pied piper leading the global media mice appears frozen in the realities of the 1970s, now a bygone era.

Empirically there is a more complex syncopation of voices and a more complicated media environment in which Western media domination has given way to multiple actors and flows of media products. More nations of the South are producing and exporting media materials, including film from India and Egypt, television programming from Mexico and Brazil. For example, *TV Globo*, the major Brazilian network, exports telenovelas to 128 countries, including Cuba, China, The Soviet Union, East Germany, earning export dollars for Brazil, and its productions outnumber those of any other station in the world (Tracy 1988). Indeed the flow of televisual materials from Brazil to Portugal is one example of how contemporary cultural flows reverse the historic roles of imperialism, while Latin American telenovelas on Spanish television channels in the United States has been called 'reverse cultural imperialism' (Rogers and Antola). In another region and medium, the Indian film industry has an international reputation as the most productive – more than nine hundred films in 1985 – with an extensive export market (Dissanayeke 1988). India has also managed to keep a somewhat dualistic yet productive tension between high art film and a popular cinema, creating movies that reflect and reinforce different elements of India's rich cultural past as well as indigenizing invasive foreign elements into a distinctive Indian style (Binford, 1988). Television, too, has been successful at translating ancient Indian culture into popular contemporary televisual fare, the Hindu epic, the Ramayana, clearing urban streets and creating a huge demand for additional episodes over the 50 originally planned (Chatterji 1989). These Third World producers have become not only national producers but international exporters of cultural products, a process which revisionists claim has altered any one-way flow of Western material and the 'hegemonic' model of cultural imperialism (McNeely and Soysal 1989). These 'global pluralists' adopt an optimistic voice regarding the diversity of media producers and locales and the many loops of cultural flows that have merged (Tracey 1988; Boyd 1984). But the very rapidity of change on the international media scene makes it hard to discern long-term trends. The 'global pluralists' are correct to note the coming of age of many Thrid World media producers and the localization of some media production. Yet at the same time even stronger tendencies toward greater globalization and conglomeratization can be discerned, which I will document shortly.

There is also a conceptual challenge to the 'cultural imperialism' model, stemming from new modes of analyzing media effects which question the 'international hypodermic needle' assumption proferred by the 'hegemonic' model. Arguments about 'the active audience' and 'polysemy' (e.g. Fiske 1987) inserted into international communications debate suggest that diverse audiences bring their own interpretive frameworks and sets of meaning to media texts, thus resisting, reinterpreting and reinventing any foreign 'hegemonic' cultural products, the details of which we will again explore later. The 'global pluralism' model seems to suggest many independent and happy producers, somewhat evacuating issues of dominance, cultural appropriation and media effects. I think we need a fourth perspective, one that essentially recognizes and does justice to the dynamic tension between the global and the local, as suggested by Giddens, and the shifting terrains that they encompass. After Trinh Minh Ha (1987), I'll call this outlook 'the global in the local, the local in the global' and use the rest of the chapter to explore some of the evident contradictions and tensions between these two poles in different contexts. We could divide globalization in the media sphere into four separable elements: the globalization of media forms, of media structures, of media flows and of media effects. I'll examine them in turn.

1   Globalization of Media Forms

It is claimed that more and more of the world is wired as a global audience with access to electronic media. The 'success' of the spread of media distribution and reception systems is in evidence – by the end of the 1980s radio signals were globally available and transistors have overcome lack of infrastructure, while nationally-based television services have been established in all but the smallest and poorest of African and Asian countries.[1] Globally, the number of television receivers rose from 192 million in 1965 to 710 million in 1986. There are antennae in the Amazon jungle. China is the third largest producer of television receivers. Beyond RTV reception, video players/recorders (vcrs) have *potential* global reach, although a volume entitled *Video World-Wide* actually examines only 22 countries as well as 'the Gulf States', 'West Africa' and 'Southern and East Africa' and argues that there are only four truly 'video rich' areas in the world, Japan and South-East Asia; the 'Arab countries'; Western Europe, and North America (Alvarado 1988; see also Boyd et al. 1989). Thus, at least in terms of national involvement in electronic media production and distribution of public access to communications infrastructure, there has been significant development over the past two decades.

However, distribution is still extremely unequal. The global 'average' of 145 receivers per 1000 population actually ranges from a high of 783 per thousand in North America to a low of 13 per thousand in the non-Arab states of Africa. The global trend is in place, yet by no means 'achieved'. Global still does not mean universal.

Table 6.1 Television receivers, 1965–86

Continents, major areas and groups of countries	Total television receivers (in millions)			Television receivers per thousand inhabitants		
	1965	1975	1986	1965	1975	1986
World total	192.0	414.0	710.0	57.0	102.0	145.0
Africa	0.6	2.5	15.0	1.9	6.2	25.0
Americas	84.0	160.0	268.0	182.0	286.0	397.0
Asia	24.0	57.0	138.0	13.0	25.0	48.0
Europe (incl. USSR)	81.0	189.0	280.0	120.0	260.0	362.0
Oceania	2.4	5.5	9.0	137.0	262.0	360.0
Developed countries	181.0	373.0	564.0	177.0	325.0	472.0
Developing countries	11.0	41.0	146.0	4.7	14.0	39.0
Africa (excl. Arab States)	0.1	0.6	5.7	0.4	2.0	13.0
Asia (excl. Arab States)	24.0	56.0	130.0	13.0	25.0	45.0
Arab States	0.9	3.4	17.0	8.4	24.0	85.0
North America	76.0	133.0	209.0	355.0	564.0	783.0
Latin America and the Caribbean	8.0	27.0	59.0	32.0	84.0	145.0

Source: *Unesco Statistical Yearbook*, 1988.

2 Globalization of Media Firms

Central to any discussion of globalization has been the rise of a global market and the role of transnational corporations (TNCS) in adapting to, producing for and profiting from that. The media sphere has long had its global firms, which tend to become bigger and more powerful as the century winds to an end (Bagdikian 1990). Media moguls such as Rupert Murdoch, Sylvio Berlusconi and Henry Luce with the Warner Brothers have created corporate structures that span continents, combine holdings in broadcast, print and film production and also control distribution facilities such as satellites and cable networks. As an example, the merger in March, 1989, between Henry Luce and Harry and Jack Warner made *Times-Warner* the largest media corporation in the world. It has an assessed value of $18 billion, a workforce approaching 340,000, a corporate base in the United States, with subsidiaries in Australia, Asia, Europe and Latin America (Time Warner Inc., 1990) 1989 revenues were over $10 billion during 1989 from activities in magazine and book publishing, music recording and publishing, film and video and cable television. Time Warner is thus a prime example of a growing global corporate structure which is highly vertically integrated – controlling the production process from the conception of a film idea to the building in which it will be shown, for example – and diversifying horizontally to have stakes in other related leisure and information holdings. By Time Warner's own analysis, vertical integration has numerous benefits, including 'creative synergies' and economies of scope and scale; 'optimal levels of promotion' which prevents separate companies having a 'free ride" on the promotional activities of others'; enables companies to 'be responsive to the desires of consumers'; and allows companies to accept greater financial risk than firms which operate in individual industry segments, thus being able to support projects of questionable commercial value. Access to global markets essentially reinforce and multiply the economies of scale.

Time Warner's own materials readily describes the company as 'a vertically integrated global entity' (Time Warner 1990, p. 47). Indeed, large corporations have not been slow to recognize the positive public value attached to the notion of 'globalization' as a unifying process of recognition of a common humanity, and coolly to adopt it for their own purposes. Thus, as part of its own self-marketing, on Earth Day – April 22, 1990 – a day devoted to global awareness and ecological concern, Time Warner launched a new logo and a new motto: 'The World is Our Audience'. In similar fashion, Sony justifies its development of American-based holdings by appropriating a famous radical grassroots slogan 'Think Globally, Act Locally' for its own purposes. Thus Sony USA writes 'It is Sony's philosophy that global corporations have a responsibility to participate actively in the countries in which they operate, a philosophy of "global localization". This means thinking globally while acting locally – being sensitive to local requirements, cultures, traditions and attitudes'. (Sony USA, p. 1) (Note that Sony employs 100,000 worldwide, enjoys an annual consoli-

Table 6.2   Selected major information and communication groupings.
Total Media turnover – Top 15 Corporations out of 78 listed by UNESCO.

Group	County	Ranking-media	Media sales	Press, publishing, recording (%)	Radio-TV, motion pictures (%)	Period
Capital Cities/ABC	USA	1	4 440	23	77	
Time	USA	2	4 193	61	39	
Bertelsmann	Germany, Fed. Rep. of	3	3 689	54	18	June-87
News Corp	Australia	4	3 453	58	32	June-88
Warmer Communica-tions	USA	5	3 404	49	51	
General Electric	USA	6	3 165		25	
Gannett	USA	7	3 079	88	12	
Times Mirror	USA	8	2 994	85	11	
Gulf + Western	USA	9	2 904	37	63	
Yomiuri Group	Japan	10	2 848	63	23	86
CBS	USA	11	2 762		100	
ARD	Germany, Fed. Rep. of	12	2 614		100	
NHK	Japan	13	2 541		100	March-88
Advance Publications	USA	14	2 397	92	8	
MCA	USA	15	2 052	8	92	

NB Of the 78 firms listed by UNESCO *in the complete table* not one was based in the Third World.

dated sales of about \$16.3 billion, and has its stock sold in exchanges in ten countries). These global giants clearly see themselves as part of a current phenomenon and are quick to point out the increasingly international activities of competitors.

Some try to debate the extent of this process of consolidating a few vertically-integrated global media giants and their power to control the creation, production and distribution of worldwide information and communication. Thus, Murdoch's News Corporation argues against the notion that the emergent pattern is of 'international media holdings by relatively few media forms', by arguing that 'multinational media companies have emerged but they are too numerous to be characterized as "few"' (NTIA, 1990, p. 5). But this appears nothing more than a quibble; of the thousands of corporations active in the media business worldwide, this group of global media moguls is clearly no more than a handful. While accurate and extensive comparative data is still hard to find, a UNESCO-compiled table for seventy-eight firms listed for their total 1987 media turnover (including press and publishing, television, radio and cinema) shows that only seven had turnover of more than three billion dollars, with 15 having turnover of more than 2 billion dollars (UNESCO 1989, p. 104).

Of the seventy-eight firms listed in the complete table, not one was based in the Third World. Forty-eight were US or Japanese, while the rest were Western European, Canadian or Australian. Already in 1988, the combined revenue of five such giants (Bertelsmann AG; News Corp; Hachette; and pre-merger Time inc. and Warner) was estimated at \$45 billion, or 18 per cent of the \$250 billion worldwide information industry. (See Table 6.2.)

Many of these corporations are American, and for many sectors of the American culture industries, international sales are now a crucial source of income. In 1989 foreign revenues accounted for 38% of total revenues for the American motion picture industry and helped to keep the value gap between imported film and film exports at \$3 billion dollars. Ted Turner's Cable News Network is received by the Kremlin and the Islamic Republic, and *Dallas* enjoys an international audience in over 90 countries, and US corporations have shown interest in cultural products being included in GATT talks and terms of trade (Time Warner 1990, p. 62).

Yet clearly by 1990 not all this global expansion is conducted by American or European-based firms, the usual assumption of the 'cultural imperial' thesis. There is considerable inter-capitalist rivalry, and foreign interests have discovered both the lucrative domestic US market, still the single largest in the world, and the global resonance of American popular culture. A few recent examples would be the globalization of Hollywood, involving the purchase of Columbia Pictures and Tri-Star Pictures by Sony, the Japanese giant which had already bought Columbia Records in 1988 (the context for the Sony America slogan discussed above); the purchase of MGM/United Artists by Pathe SA, an Italian company; the purchase of 20th Century Fox by Rupert Murdoch's Australian-based News Corporation, and in November 1990, the purchase of MCA Inc, which includes Universal Studios, Universal Pictures and MCA Records by the Japanese firm Matsushita.

The dynamic of foreign firms buying US media outlets extends well beyond film-making into many other media: Murdoch's News Corporation owns newspapers in Boston and San Antonio, Harper Row books, and Triangle

Publications which publishes *TV Guide*, the largest circulation magazine in the United States; International Thomson Group, based in Canada, owns 116 daily newspapers in the United States; the British-based Maxwell Communications owns Macmillan Books; Bertelsmann AG, the West German giant, owns RCA and Arista Records, while the Dutch firm N.V. Philips owns Polygram, Island and A&M Records.

The increasing complexity and transnationalization of global media markets has, somewhat tardily, become the focus of a recently launched study by the National Telecommunications and Information Administration (NTIA), a section of the US Department of Commerce in Washington, DC. Entitled *Comprehensive Study on the Globalization of Mass Media Firms*, in February 1990 it invited input in order to 'better formulate US communications policy in a rapidly changing information environment' (NTIA 1990). Culling through the responses which NTIA has provided, and from which much of the above factual evidence is drawn, it rapidly becomes clear that the US-based media/culture coporations are concerned essentially with two phenomena that affect their access to international media markets. The first is the newly defined and instituted European cultural policy which they interpret as a set of trade barriers to the free flow of American cultural products. The second is the problem of media piracy, significantly but not solely in the Third World. Yet it is abundantly clear that Europe is viewed as the most promising media market, with very little interest paid to or in media development in the Third World, other than chagrin at the media free ride that many Third World societies have enjoyed. Thus these frequently cited examples of media 'globalization' actually reveal its very limited coverage. These processes involve corporate actors of the North, interested in Northern media products and audiences, with marginal amounts of the production or circulation occurring among the peoples of the South. It seems quite evident that the production and promotion strategies of these global media firms would do little to alleviate the global imbalance in media availability, and rather exacerbate the global imbalances between the media rich and the media poor.

3   Global Media Flows

Globalization has often been applied to the spread of Western mediated products across the globe, from which few places seem immune. There is much anecdotal evidence of the use of Western cultural products, sometimes in somewhat improbable and erstwhile 'remote' places. Ouderkirk (1989) describes trekking up the highest Guatamalan mountains in search of some remote and authentic Qeche Indians and hearing some stirring music which as she approached turned out to be old Beatles tapes! Pico Iyer's (1989) travelogue talks about 'video nights in Kathmandu' and elsewhere in Asia, encountering 'Ike and Tuna Turner' sandwiches in the heart of the people's Republic of China, Burmese musicians playing songs by the Doors, as well as countless Asian remakes of Rambo movies. The film *Bye Bye Brasil* amusingly reflects on the public abandonment of traditional performing arts for television as it spread into the hinterland of Brazil. Recent visits to the Islamic Republic of Iran revealed considerable use of American videos such as *Robocop* and

Maximum Overdrive and audiotapes of Madonna and Michael Jackson, all brought in via the black market from Dubai (Sreberny-Mohammadi and Mohammadi 1991).

As already mentioned, much early work supportive of the 'cultural imperialism' hypothesis provided descriptive mappings of unequal global flows, and much international debate in the 1970s–80s focused on this notion, as an indicator of global domination and threat to indigenous cultural survival. This culminated in the UNESCO mass media declaration, the report of the Macbride Commission and the formulation of a tenet of the New International Information Order as moving from a merely 'free' flow to a 'free and balanced' flow of communication (although no adequate empirical measures of such balance have ever been devised).

Trade Barriers and Piracy: Local Strategies vis-a-vis the Global

Two different strategies have been devised to deal with the imbalanced flow, one of which involves limitations and trade barriers to cultural imports. Limits on the amount of imported programming and vetting of imported materials exist in Brazil, India, Iran and elsewhere in the Third World. But now that Europe appears to be moving toward an albeit voluntary continental policy for 1992, transnational corporations are extremely worried. Time Warner argues that it faces formidable trade barriers, 'some of which are clothed in the garb of "cultural" measures ostensibly designed to protect the cultural sovereignty and artistic heritage of the country in question'. (Time Warner 1990, p. 48). The corporation proclaims a certain sensitivity: 'Although we must be sensitive to the cultural environment and needs of every locale in which we operate, trade barriers can only be justified to the limited extent that they are truly necessary to protect indigenous cultures that would otherwise be overwhelmed by the cultural products of other countries' but in the very next paragraph the tone changes: 'The cultural issue is appearing with alarming frequency in the international marketplace, and must be roundly rejected' (Time Warner 1990, p. 48). Its main concern, shared by other media multinationals, is the new European initiative in the *Television without Frontiers* directive which suggests a 50 per cent quota on imported programming by October 1992 where possible (although this is non-binding) and defines a 'European' television company, one where the production and control of production is in an EC state or as a majority of the total cost of production is borne by a producer or co-producer from the EC states or those states privy to the Council of Europe convention. Thus even the possibility of transnationals developing co-productions with Europeans is limited to a minority financial and creative capacity, a trade limitation in Time Warner's eyes. There are also European Community initiatives to promote the EC audiovisual industry and cultural uniqueness of member states as well as the development and standardization of hardware such as HDTV. While Koreans are chastized for putting live snakes in cinemas showing US-made films, and Brazil and Egypt are noted for developing policies promoting homemade cultural production, from the statements of Time Warner and other corporations it is evident that essentially they see Europe as the problem, not the Third World. The former presents an already well-developed media market with a substantial population possessing considerable disposable income, a market to which US-based firms want ready access. Thus a closer examination of corporate 'globalization' strategies reveals highly preferred locales and areas of acute disinterest, depending on the already existing level of insertion of the populations within global capitalism.

The Third World is problematic to transnationals mainly because of its video piracy, an ingeniously literal understanding of the 'free' flow concept. Yet while this means lost revenues to multinationals, such piracy often affects embryonic industries at home, and thus undermine alternative national cultural production. It is apparent that the still limited and unregulated media markets of the Third World are not especially attractive to transnational culture brokers, which perhaps ironically gives Third World media systems a chance to produce for themselves and escape the Western cultural net, a *force majeure* for delinking.

Media localization: The Newest Argument

At the same time as these dynamics of globalization have been established, an opposing tendency is concurrently at work, as a consequence of, and often in reaction to, the former; that is the dynamic of localized production and the indigenization of cultural products already referred to above. The evidence about such trends is patchy and somewhat contradictory. Varis in his two studies of television flows in 1973 and 1984 concluded that few national systems had made major transitions to self-reliance in television programming. Increasing counter-evidence and counter-argument to the few 'positive' cases is being advanced. At a Summer 1990 meeting of communication researchers in Brazil, Latin American researchers argued that despite the proliferation of media, television programming has become more North American; that 99 per cent of the films shown on Brazilian television are American, and that cheap packages of old movies and TV shows are 'dumped' and thus flood the Latin American media scene (Osava 1990). Oliveira argues that Brazilian homemade television is even more commercial than American programming with 'merchandising' of products a central part of telenovela content, encouraging a consumerist way of life of which the United States is the most advanced example (Oliveira 1990). The same can be said of Peruvian media. India's film industry is being severely challenged by the spread of vcrs and video piracy, the importation of Western movies and the closure of cinemas as running costs rise and audiences dwindle (Mohan 1990). Cross-fertilization between Western cinema and television – predominantly American and British – with the popular Indian cinema is creating more 'hybrid' cultural forms, like a new film genre wryly described as the 'curry eastern' (Jain, 1990).

Evidence suggests that when a choice is available, domestic production is preferred over imported, as telenovelas garner larger audiences than imported American soaps not only in Brazil but elsewhere in Latin America (Rogers and Antola). But in such a process, fears of hybridization and creolization exist, that the 'authenticity' of a culture is damaged and undermined in its contact with Western culture industries and its adoption of genres foreign to domestic cultural tradition. Some counter that the Latin telenovela is a truly indigenous and independent genre (Straubhaar 1981), building on internal cultural forms and breaking with the mimicry of Western genre that Tunstall forewarned. But

Oliveira argues that this 'indigenization' of media often seems to enhance not diversity but domination by corporate concerns. Tunstall in *The Media are American* (1978) pointed out that the importation of media systems to the Third World included not only media hardware but also Western forms and genres, which he suggested would lead to precisely such 'hybrid' concoctions. But we must ask what is this pristine image of culture that lurks behind this argument? Human history is a history of cultural contact, influence and recombination, as is in evidence in language, music, visual arts, philosophical systems; perhaps media flows merely reinforce our mongrel statuses.

More to the point, evidence suggests that this 'newer' model of cultural indigenization may have been severely overstated and certainly presented in a far too naive manner. Much of this so-called indigenous production is created by large corporations, and deeply infused with consumption values, one of the basic critiques of the 'cultural imperialism' perspective. Another point of direct relevance to the 'localism' claim, is that the level of this media production is at the level of the nation, either through state-supported or national corporate networks. Thus in such arguments the 'local' is really the 'national', while the truly local (sub-cultural, grassroots, etc) is ignored. This 'national' culture may privilege urban life-styles over rural, may barely represent minority languages and tastes, even disallowing such diversity in the name of 'national unity'; it may produce mediated culture within a narrowly-defined ideological framework that fits the politics of the regime of the day. The case of Iran suggests that tradition required defending at the moment that it was already challenged, so Islam as 'cultural identity' was constructed to oppose the Shah and the influx of foreign cultural values and products, only to be used after the revolution as an ideological weapon against all political opponents (Sreberny-Mohammadi 1990). National agendas are not coincidental with truly 'local' agendas, and real concerns arise as to whether 'national' media cultures adequately represent ethnic, religious, political and other kinds of diversity. In international relations, the 'national' level may be local vis-a-vis the global level, but in domestic relations, the 'national' is itself a site of struggle, with a variety of 'local' identities and voices in contention.

Cultural Products in the Global Economy

The *new revisionism* also seems to have exaggerated the size/amount of this 'localized' production, which is perhaps of financial significance for national economies in the Third World, but is barely yet reflected in international statistics. There are immense difficulties involved in cross-national calculations and comparisons of media, information and cultural production and flow statistics (Braman 1990). UNESCO has made a major effort to compile international data in *World Communication Report* published in 1989. Taking this information for the moment at face value, it provides important indicators of the extent of the changes the 'global pluralists' suggest. For example, information on 'total turnover for information and communication' for selected major information and communications groupings which includes equipment, services, and cultural products, clearly shows the continuing dominance of US and Japanese firms. (See Table 6.3).

These comprise 67 per cent of the top 25 companies, 66 per cent of top 50 companies and 67 per cent of the top 100 companies; European firms, by contrast, comprise 28 per cent of top 25, and 26 per cent of the top 50 (with Canada the only other nation included), and 26 per cent of the top 100 companies. Other commonwealth countries begin to appear in the second fifty, while Korean and Brazilian companies appear at positions 83, 91 and 94. Of 304 organizations listed by UNESCO in a ranked table of major information and communication groupings, Globo placed 301. Thus the exemplar of *Rede Globo* and Brazilian cultural production as a counter to 'cultural imperialism' as a net exporter of cultural products is cut to size. Simply summarized, the US, Japan and Western Europe dominate in this agglomerate category.

If hardware and software areas are parcelled out, does the picture look any different? Not significantly. The table for 'total media turnover' for major information and communication groupings provides a remarkably similar picture to the above.

Half of the first 25 companies, of the first 50, and of the total of 78 companies for which statistics are presented, are US companies. (See Table 6.2). No Third World media corporation penetrates this 'top 78'. Now, of course, such figures represent the total dollar value of communications output, and say nothing specific about *export* dollar values, but they do dampen the optimistic hailing of major Third World cultural producers. While the map of global cultural flows is more complex in 1990, it is not as yet fundamentally realigned. But what about the question of 'effects'?

4   Global Media Effects?

Media effects is one of the most disputed areas of domestic media research so there is no reason to expect any greater unanimity about effects at the international level. The 'cultural imperialism' thesis did tend to suggest a 'hypodermic needle' model of international effects, 'American' values being injected into Third World hearts and minds. Recent work, building on reception theory and models of the active audience, is giving a more nuanced view of international effects as mediated by pre-existing cultural frameworks and interpretative schema. Thus, despite their book's title, (*The Export of Meaning*) Leibes and Katz (1990) argue that meaning is not exported *in* Western television programming but created *by* different cultural sectors of the audience in relation to their already-formed cultural attitudes and political perceptions. Others (Beltran, Oliveira) argue that it is not so much national American values that are exported but rather more generalized capitalist consumption values (which, of course, America best epitomizes) reinforced by advertising and prevailing development orientations. For them, globalization portends homogenization which, while useful for milk, produces a culture that tastes bland and is not even good for you!

What is often omitted from discussions on effects, are the deeper shifts in cultural orientations and patterns of sociability, in modes of perception and information-processing, that the advent of media create everywhere, albeit in different forms relative to the pre-existing local culture; that is to say it is the very 'fact of television', as Cavell (1982) calls it, in our social lives, not so much its content, that is most often overlooked.

Table 6.3 Selected major information and communication groupings. Total turnover for information and communication.

Group	Country	Ranking-information and communication	Information and communication sales	Total sales	Information and communications (%)	Period
IBM	USA	1	54 217	54 217	100	March-88
NTT	Japan	2	40 926	40 926	100	March-88
ATT	USA	3	37 458	33 598	111	
Matsushita	Japan	4	24 683	34 832	71	March-88
Deutsche Bundespost	Germany, Fed. Rep. of	5	20 185	28 960	70	
NEC	Japan	6	19 622	19 622	100	March-88
Philips	Netherlands	7	19 253	26 023	74	
British Telecom	UK	8	17 344	17 344	100	March-88
France Telecom	France	9	16 650	16 650	100	
Toshiba	Japan	10	16 106	17 824	90	March-88
Lucky Gold Star	Korea, Rep. of	83	2 791	11 474	24	86
CBS	USA	84	2 762	2 762	100	
TRW	USA	85	2 721	6 821	40	
Apple	USA	86	2 661	2 661	100	September-87
ARD	Germany, Fed. Rep. of	87	2 614	2 614	100	
US Sprint	USA	88	2 592	2 592	100	November-87
TDK	Japan	89	2 586	2 586	100	May-87
Toppan Printing	Japan	90	2 584	3 800	68	
Samsung	Korea, Rep. of	91	2 581	14 193	18	85
NHK	Japan	92	2 541	2 541	100	March-88
Ford Motor	USA	93	2 500	71 643	3	
IBL	UK	300	501	501	100	86
Globo	Brazil	301	500	500	100	86
Nippon Telecommunication Corstruction	Japan	302	500	500	100	March-87
Talt	USA	303	500	500	100	
JTAS (Jydske Telefon)	Denmark	304	500	500	100	

Groups 11–82 and 94–299 have not been included in this table.

The arrival of media in Third World settings is finally being examined by anthropologists (although there is never an index listing for 'media' or 'television' in a cultural anthropology textbook, despite the fact that most Third World societies are now mediated in some way) and communications researchers. Ethnographic studies are beginning to show the rich play between the pre-existing culture and the new quasi-international culture and the shifts in social relations that the latter may foster. In an ethnographic study conducted in various sites across Brazil, Kottak (1990) explored how television alters patterns of sociability, usage of time, creates conflicts within the family and alters the gender balance, themes also explored in the comparative work on family use of television compiled by Lull (1988). Kottak suggests the need to investigate media impact over time, finding in Brazil an early mesmerization with the television set with a later development of selectivity and critical distance, negative attitudes toward television increasing with higher income and years of exposure.

Other ethnographic work suggests the slippery boundaries of the 'global' and 'local'. Abu-Lughod (1990) has studied the impact of what she calls 'technologies of public culture' on the Awlad 'Ali, the Western Desert Bedouin in Egypt. Although these bedouin have been quite marginal to mainstream Egyptian culture, they were by no means culturally or politically untouched before these technologies arrived; indeed, they often made their money from selling post-war scrap metal and from smuggling goods between pre-Qaddafi Libya and Egypt. Abu-Lughod examines the impact of tape-players, radios and television on Awlad 'Ali life, saying that their use does not eliminate sociability but in fact brings people together for long periods of time. Such use does realign social relationships, mixing the sexes and tempering age differences at home, while video shows in local cafes kept young men away from the home and gave them greater exposure to media. In line with reception theory, she argues too that these technologies do not destroy distinctive cultures because 'it is not just that people themselves seem to embrace the technologies and actively use them for their own purposes, but that they select, incorporate and redeploy what comes their way' (p. 8) although she notes that so far at least the amount of truly *foreign* programming available is extremely limited. If anything, new technologies such as cassettes have helped to revitalize Bedouin identity as distinct from Egyptian culture through recordings of poetry and song. The urban middle-class Egyptian lifestyles revealed on soap operas present a different set of options to Bedouin women, specially the possibility of marrying for love and living independent of the extended family, so that the dominant Egyptian mediated culture is used as a language of resistance against the authority of tribal elders. Also embedded in such programming are consumer values, for electronic durables as well as products for a newly sexualized femininity, drawing the bedouin further into the Egyptian political economy. Yet at the same time, in a contradictory manner, Egyptian radio and television carries more transnational messages about Islam, which is gaining in popularity, and which provides an antidote both to capitalist urban Egyptian values as well as the local bedouin identity. (Abu-Lughod, p. 11)

Hannah Davis (1990) describes life in a small Moroccan agricultural town of 50,000 people and notes how 'symbols from different worlds overlap: a picture of the king of Morocco hangs next to a poster of the Beatles. The sounds of a religious festival outside . . . mingle with the televised cheering of soccer fans . . . in the morning we watch a holy man curing a boy, then stop off at the fair where we see a woman doing motorcycle stunts; in the evening we watch an Indian fairy tale or a Brazilian soap opera or an Egyptian romance' (p. 13). She remarks 'it is not the contrast between the elements that is striking; it is the lack of contrast, the clever and taken-for-granted integration' (p. 12). As in much of the Middle East (the world?!) public space is male space, and thus it is the women who gather round the television and VCR at night, watching Egyptian, Indian and 'French' – here the generic term used for Western – films. Egyptian films were romances that reduced the women to tears, while the Western films elicited 'gasps of suprise, horrified hiding of the eyes, fascination or prurience', with American sexual shamelessness being both admired and feared, imitated and denigrated. The transcultural mix of symbols is apparent when one young girl organizes a traditional religious feast yet defiantly appears wearing a denim skirt and earrings; thus, such symbols may be used in personal struggles to 'define, test or transform the boundaries' of local lives (p. 17).

Such examples reveal the complex (re)negotiation of identity(ies) vis-a-vis the 'dominant' and the 'foreign' cultures, both of which shift in focus depending on the specific locale of the actor. The above examples pose a number of different pairs of relations in which the site of the 'local' and the image of the 'global' are differently defined: rural/urban; Bedouin/Egyptian; Moroccan/ Egyptian; bedouin/French; Moroccan/American and so forth. This work reveals again the post-modern 'bricolage' of assorted cultural icons from different locations and time periods which circulate inside the non-industrialized world, yet invites no simple reading of the effects of these encounters. Iran is again a useful example of the way in which cultural icons can become deeply invested with one set of ideological connotations in one moment of political struggle, and invested with completely the opposite connotations at a subsequent but differently defined political moment. Thus religious language, traditional symbolism and mythology were popularly (re-)adopted as part of the revolutionary struggle against the Shah, but with the new repression of the Islamic Republic a popular cultural underground began to produce hard liquor and circulate Western videos as part of a new resistance (Sreberny-Mohammadi and Mohammadi, forthcoming). Thus a 'sign' of resistance – the veil, for example – at one point in time can become a 'sign' of oppression at another. The detail of such anthropological/ethnographic work extends the 'localist' focus, and show the complexity and range of reactions to and uses of contemporary global cultural encounters. They warn us against generalized assumptions about media/cultural effects, that the 'foreign' may emanate from the urban capital, a Western country other than the US and perhaps even from a Third World media producer of very different cultural background but whose depictions of social life in the process of development can reverberate across the South.

One other basic shift that the global flow of mediated products and the establishment of culture industries in the Third World creates, is that documented by Horkheimer and Adorno toward consumption of mass-produced culture. That is culture, from being local lived experience becomes media product, with the implicit danger that what is not reflected on television no longer has cultural worth. One last neglected 'effect' is important to consider. It has been argued that media development in the West has moved through a set of 'stages' during which one form of communication and its preferred modality of discourse has been dominant. These have been described by Ong as orality, chirography/typography and the period of the dominance of electronic media which he labels 'secondary orality'. Yet in the Third World there is evidence that the middle stage, at least as measured by mass literacy and circulation of printed materials, may be 'jumped', with societies moving directly from a predominantly oral culture directly into the 'secondary orality' of electronic media. We have paid little attention to this new and different kind of cultural formation. The 'communications and development' model tended to collapse history, suggesting the development of newspapers, cinemas, radio and television all at once, while the 'cultural imperialism' model has given most attention to electronic media. Yet if print is connected to the development of rational logical thinking (Ong), to the development of modern ideologies not linked to church or aristocracy (Gouldner), and the growth of a public sphere, open debate and active citizenry (Habermas), then the limited if non-existent development of this mode of communication in developing countries has profound political and social consequences which have barely been acknowledged. Analysis of the uses of different media by class and gender in Third World societies, and the power relations which develop is another rather ignored area of research (Sreberny-Mohammadi 1991).

Conclusion

If nothing else, the chapter has shown the complexity of the global contemporary media/culture spectrum at the start of the twenty-first century, and the range of theoretical constructs that have been used to explain, and base policy on the international role of media, particularly in the 'Third World'. The 'mood' of contemporary analysis can be quite varied. One position is that of the happy post-modernist who sees that many kinds of cultural texts circulate internationally and that people adopt them playfully and readily integrate them in creative ways into their own lives, and that cultural bricolage is the prevailing experience as we enter the twenty-first century. Another is the melancholy political economist who sees the all-pervasive reach of the multinationals and wonders how long distinctive cultures can outlast the onslaught of the western culture industries. Somewhere in between lies the cautiously optimistic fourth-Worlder who sees in the spread of media the possibilities for revitalization of local identities (ethnic, religious, class, etc) and their use as tools of political mobilization vis-à-vis both national and global forces. But we have also seen the slippery nature of the linguistic terms used in international communications analysis: that 'global' rarely means 'universal' and often implies only the actors of the North; that 'local' is often really 'national' which can be oppressive of the 'local'; that 'indigenous' culture is often already 'contaminated' through older cultural contacts and exists as a political claim rather than a clean analytic construct. The bi-polar model suggests either imbalance/domination, the political-economy perspective, or balance, the 'global pluralist' perspective, whereas the real world reveals far greater complexity.

Cultural boundaries are not etched in stone but have slippery divisions dependent on the self-adopted labels of groups. What seems clear is that, far from an end to history, or the loss of the subject, identity politics and cultural preservation are going to be amongst the hottest issues of the next century that will be fought out internationally and intra-nationally, with profound political and economic consequences. The apparent triumph of late capitalism in 1989–90 and the demise of the so-called second world of state socialism, suggest that ideological politics in the classic sense is going to be less important than the revival of identity politics in the future. Yet at the same time as the demise of a single master narrative of global progress is trumpeted in some quarters, in others the old indicators of a single path to 'development' are still utilized, and even adopted with greater eagerness by Third World societies yearning for 'progress'. It is likely that in the next decade we shall see a revival of intense debate about development, and the unresolved role of culture within that process, neo-Lernerian arguments for the positive role of media systems as part of national development encountering arguments for more thorough-going Third World economic disassociation and delinking from the global capitalist economy (Amin 1990), as well as fourth world/indigenist culture arguments for the maintenance of local identities (Verhelst 1990). These levels may themselves be in conflict, for a strong 'national' position taken in relation to international economic and cultural forces may lead to repression of 'local' forces and voices in relation to that 'national' level. Inter-state relations are not coterminous with inter-cultural relations, and the political and conceptual agenda of the twenty-first century is going to be how to cope with these various levels of actors and processes. It is here that conceptual leakage in the global/local framework of analysis is most evident, highlighted by the particularly complex set of issues raised by mediated cultural flows which poignantly reveal in their electronic presence the absence or porousness of boundaries. In the bipolar model it is the 'national' level of analysis that becomes invisible. Yet it is national policy-making that helps define a cultural identity, provides the regulatory framework for media organizations – the state providing direct funding and control in many Third World nations – and cultural trade policy, as well as defining the domestic public sphere and the extent to which diverse voices will or will not be heard. As Giddens himself underscores in much of his work, nation-states are the key political systems of the modern world, controlling the structures – legal, administrative, financial, military, surveillance, and informational – in which we all live and which are now involved in transnational dynamics – a capitalist world economy, the world military order, systems of inter-governmental organizations, transnational political movements, etc – which both press in on and explode the meaning of national boundaries (Giddens 1985). Indeed, as Giddens argues, the world-wide system of nations states exists in constant tension with the global capitalist economy.

It seems that we require a third-term, between the two terms of 'global', and 'local', that recognizes the separate level of 'state' structures and national policy-making' which is still the crucial level of political, economic and cultural decision-making. So much of current political cultural struggle centres precisely on (the memories of) the 'imagined communities' of nations and their claims to be 'states' (Anderson 1983). At issue in current political struggles – in the Soviet Union, Eastern Europe, the Middle East, Africa – is whether 'nations' do/should constitute homogenous cultural/ethnic bases or be political structures which allow heterogeneity and civic rights to flourish. While the latter was the basis for modern nation-states (Hobsbaum 1990) we increasingly hear demands for the former, raising questions about the appropriate relation between cultural rights and national boundaries, and whether narrowly-conceived ethnic states are really progressive. A bi-polar model such as globalization and localization too readily implies either dominance or balance. A triangular model, with the 'national' re-inserted, reflects the multiple and deeper tensions and contradictions that constitute the present world order.

Notes

1 UNESCO suggests that 39 countries and territories had not yet introduced a television service by 1988:
Africa: Botswana, Cameroon, Cape Verde, Central African Republic, Chad, Comoros, Gambia, Guinea-Bissau, Malawi, Rwanda, St Helena, Sao Tome and Principe, Western Sahara; North America: Anguila, Belize, Caymen Islands, Dominica, Saint Vincent and the Grenadines, Turks and Calcos Islands; South America: Malvinas, Guyana; Asia: Bhutan, East Timor; Europe: Holy See, Liechtenstein, San Marino; Oceania: Cook Islands; Fiji, Kiribati, Nauru, Niue, Norfolk Islands, Papua New Guinea, Samoa, Solomon Islands; Tonga, Tuvalu, Vanuatu.

References

ABU-LUGHOD, LILA, 'Bedouins, Cassettes and Technologies of Public Culture', *Middle East Report*, 159, 4, 7–12.
ALVARADO, MANUEL, (ed.), 1988: *Video World-Wide: An International Study, London/Paris*: Unesco/John Libbey.
AMIN, SAMIR, 1990: *Delinking*, Monthly Review Press.
ANDERSON, BENEDICT, 1983: *Imagined Communities*. London: Verso.
ANTOLA, L. and E. M. ROGERS, 1984: 'Television Flows in Latin America', *Communication Research*, 11, 2, pp. 183–202.
APPADURAI, ARJUN, Spring 1990: 'Disjuncture and Difference in the Global Cultural Economy', *Public Culture*. 2, 2, pp. 1–24.
BAGDIKIAN, BEN, Lords of the Global Village', *The Nation*, 248, 23, pp. 805–820.
BOYD, DOUGLAS, 1984: 'The Janus Effect? Imported Television Entertainment Programming in Developing Countries', *Critical Studies in Mass Communication*, 1, pp. 379–391.
BOYD, D., J. D. STRAUBHAAR and J. A. LENT, (eds), 1989: *Videocassette Recorders in The Third World*. Longman.
BINFORD, MIRA REYM, 1988: 'Innovation and Imitation in the Indian Cinema' in W. Dissanayeke (ed.) *Cinema and Cultural Identity*. Maryland, University Press of America.
BOYD-BARRETT, OLIVER, 1977: 'Media Imperialism: toward an international framework for the analysis of media systems', in J. Curran, M. Gurevitch and J. Woollacott, eds., *Mass Communication and Society*. London: Edward Arnold.
CAVELL, STANLEY, Fall 1982: 'The Fact of Television', *Daedalus*, III, 4, pp. 75–96.
CHATTERJI, P. C., 1989: 'The Ramayana TV serial and Indian secularism', *InterMedia*, 17, 5, pp. 32–34.
DAVIS, HANNAH, 'American Magic in a Moroccan Town', *Middle East Report*, 159: 19, 4, pp. 12–18.

DISSANAYEKE, WIMAL, 1988: 'Cultural Identity and Asian Cinema', in W. Dissanayake, ed., *Cinema and Cultural Identity*. Maryland: University Press of America.

FABRIKANT, GERALDINE, 'Studios look to Foreign Markets', *New York Times, March 7, 1990, Section D1*.

FISKE, JOHN, 1987: *Television Culture*. New York: Methuen.

GALTUNG, J. and RUGE, M., 1965: 'The Structure of Foreign News', *Journal of Peace Research*, 1, 64–90.

GIDDENS, ANTHONY, 1990: *The Consequences of Modernity*. Stanford University Press.

——, 1985: *The Nation-State and Violence*. Cambridge: Polity Press.

GOLDING, PETER, 1977: 'Media Professionalism in the Third World: the transfer of an ideology' in J. Curran, M. Gurevitch and J. Woollacott, eds, *Mass Communication and Society*. London: Edward Arnold/Open University.

GUBACK, THOMAS and TAPIO VARIS, 1982: *Transnational Communication and Cultural Industries*. (Reports and Papers on Mass Communication No. 92) Paris: UNESCO.

GUNDER-FRANK, ANDRÉ, 1964: 'The Development of Underdevelopment' in *Capitalism and Underdevelopment in Latin America*, New York: Monthly Review Press.

HAMELINK, CEES, 1983: *Finance and Information*, New Jersey: Ablex.

——, 1983: *Cultural Autonomy in Global Communications*, New York: Longman.

HARVEY, DAVID, 1989: *The Condition of Postmodernity*, Oxford: Basil Blackwell.

HOBSBAUM, ERIC, 1990: *Nations and Nationalism since 1780*, Cambridge: Cambridge University Press.

IYER, PICO, 1989: *Video Nights in Kathmandu*, New York: Vintage Press.

JAIN, MADHU, Spring 1990: 'The Curry Eastern Takeaway', *Public Culture* 2, 2.

JAMESON, FREDERIC, 1984: 'Postmodernism, or the cultural logic of late capitalism', *New Left Review*, 146, 53–92.

KATZ, E. and WEDELL, G., 1977: *Broadcasting in the Third World*, Massachusetts: Harvard University Press.

KOTTAK, CONRAD PHILLIP, 1990: *Prime-Time Society: An Anthropological Analysis of Television and Culture*, California: Wadsworth.

LERNER, DANIEL, 1958: *The Passing of Traditional Society*, New York: Free Press.

LIEBES, T. and E. KATZ, 1990: *The Export of Meaning*, Oxford University Press.

LULL, JAMES, ed. 1988: *World Families Watch Television*, California: Sage Publications.

*MANDEL, ERNEST, *Late Capitalism*.

MATTELART, ARMAND, 1979: *Multinational Corporations and the Control of Culture*, England: Harvester Press and New Jersey: Humanities Press.

MCLUHAN, MARSHALL, 1964: *Understanding Media*, London: Routledge Kegan Paul.

MCNEELY, CONNIE and YASEMIN MUHOGLU SOYSAL, Fall 1989: 'International Flows of Television Programming: A Revisionist Research Orientation', *Public Culture*, 2, 1: 136–145.

MOHAN, ANJOO, Sept–Oct 1990: 'Cinema fall prey to video pirates', *Development Forum*.

MINH HA, TRINH, 1987: 'Of Other Peoples: Beyond the "Salvage" Paradigm', in Hal Foster, ed., *Discussions in Contemporary Culture Number One*, Seattle: Bay Press.

NTIA (National Telecommunications and Information Administration), US Department of Commerce, 1990: *Comprehensive Study of the Globalization of Mass Media Firms*, February.

OLIVEIRA, OMAR SOUKI, June 1990: 'The Three-Step Flow of Cultural Imperialism: A Study of Brazilian Elites', paper presented at ICA Conference, Dublin, Ireland.

——, June 1990: 'Brazilian Soaps Outshine Hollywood: Is Cultural Imperialism Fading Away?'. Paper presented at ICA Conference, Dublin, Ireland.

OSAVA MARIO, May–June 1990: 'Foreign domination of TV perplexes Latin Americans', *Development Forum*.

OUDERKIRK, CATHLEEN, July 1989: 'Modern-day Mayans', *World Monitor*, 2, 7.

SCHILLER, HERBERT, 1976: *Communication and Cultural Domination*, White Plains: International Arts and Sciences Press.

SCHRAMM, WILBUR, 1964: *Mass Media and National Development*, California: Stanford University Press.

SONY, USA, May 30, 1990: *Comments in Response to Notice of Inquiry on Globalization of Mass Media Firms*, NTIA/OPAD.

SREBERNY-MOHAMMADI, ANNABELLE, 1991: 'Media Integration in the Third World: An Ongian Look at Iran', in B. Gronbeck, T. Farell and P. Soukup, eds, *Media, Consciousness and Culture*, California: Sage Publications, in press.

——, 'The Many Faces of Cultural Imperialism', in P. Golding, P. Lewis, and N. Jayaweera, eds., *Beyond Cultural Imperialism: The New World Information Order Debate in Context*, London: Sage Publications, forthcoming.

SREBERNY-MOHAMMADI, A. and A. MOHAMMADI, 1991: 'Hegemony and Resistance: Cultural Politics in the Islamic Republic of Iran', *Quarterly Review of Film and Video* (special issue on World Television), forthcoming.

STRAUBHAAR, JOSEPH D., 1981: 'Estimating the Impact of Imported versus National Television Programming in Brazil', in S. Thomas, ed., *Studies in Communication and Technology*, vol. 1, New Jersey: Ablex.

Time Warner Inc., May 30, 1990: *Comprehensive Study of the Globalization of Mass Media Firms*, Response to National Telecommunications and Information Administration Request for Comments, NTIA/OPAD.

TRACEY, MICHAEL, March 1988: 'Popular Culture and the Economics of Global Television', *Intermedia*, 16, 2.

TUNSTALL, JEREMY, 1977: *The Media are American*, London: Constable.

UNESCO, 1989: *World Communication Report*, Paris: UNESCO.

VARIS, TAPIO, 'The International Flow of Television Programs' *Journal of Communication*, Winter 1984: 143–152.

VERHELST, THIERRY, *No Life Without Roots: Culture and Development*, London: Zed Press, 1990.

SECTION II

Media Production

7

The Sociology of News Production Revisited

Michael Schudson

Social scientists who study the news speak a language that journalists mistrust and misunderstand.[1] They speak of 'constructing the news', of 'making news', of the 'social construction of reality'. 'News is what newspapermen make it', according to one study (Gieber 1964: 173). 'News is the result of the methods newsworkers employ', according to another (Fishman 1980: 14). News is 'manufactured by journalists' (Cohen and Young 1973: 97) in the words of a third. Even journalists who are critical of the daily practices of their colleagues and their own organizations, find this talk offensive. I have been at several conferences of journalists and social scientists where such language promptly pushed the journalists into a fierce defence of their work, on the familiar ground that they just report the world as they see it, the facts, facts, and nothing but the facts, and yes, there's occasional bias, sensationalism, or inaccuracy, but a responsible journalist never, never, never fakes the news.

That's not what we said, the hurt scholars respond. We didn't say journalists fake the news, we said journalists make the news:

> To say that a news report is a story, no more, but no less, is not to demean news, nor to accuse it of being fictitious. Rather, it alerts us that news, like all public documents, is a constructed reality possessing its own internal validity.
>
> Tuchman, 1976: 97

In the most elementary way, this is obvious. Journalists write the words that turn up in the papers or on the screen as stories. Not government officials, not cultural forces, not 'reality' magically transforming itself into alphabetic signs, but flesh-and-blood journalists literally compose the stories we call news. Once this is granted, social scientists say, all the rest follows. (Would you say that of science? the journalist might respond. Would you say that scientists 'make' science rather than 'discover' it or report it? Yes, the conscientious scholar must answer, we would say precisely that, and sociologists of science do say precisely that.)

This is not a point of view likely to make much headway with professional journalists. 'News and news programmes could almost be called random reactions to random events', a reporter told British sociologist Graham Murdock. 'Again and again, the main reason why they turn out as they do is accident – accident of a kind which recurs so haphazardly as to defeat statistical examination. (1973: 163). The study of the generation of news aims to find an order behind this sense of accident (and to understand as ideology, journalists' failure to believe in such an order).

The sociology of the production of news goes back some years. Max Weber (1921, 1946) wrote of the social standing of the journalist as a political person; Robert Park (1923), an ex-journalist himself, wrote about the generation of news and news itself as a form of knowledge, and Helen MacGill Hughes (1940) wrote an early study of human interest stories. But the formal study of how news organizations produce news products dates to the studies in the early 1950s of 'gatekeepers'.

Social psychologist Kurt Lewin coined the term 'gatekeeper' and several social scientists (White 1950; Gieber 1964) applied it to journalism. David Manning White studied a middle-aged wire editor at a small mid-western newspaper. He decided which wire service stories would run in the paper and which would not. For one week, 'Mr Gates' (as White called him) made available to the researcher every piece of wire copy, both those he rejected and those he selected to print in the paper. He then wrote down a reason for rejection on every story he turned down. Some of these reasons were not very illuminating – 'not enough space'. Others were technical or professional – 'dull writing' or 'drags too much'. Still others were explicitly political – 'propaganda' or 'He's too Red'. These last greatly influenced White's interpretation of gatekeeping although explicitly political, opinionated reasons for rejection amounted to just 18 out of 423 cases. Mr Gates admitted that he did not like President Truman's economic policies, that he was anti-Catholic, and that his views on these subjects affected his news judgement. So there is reason for White to conclude that 'we see how highly subjective, how based on the "gatekeeper's" own set of experiences, attitudes and expectations the communication of "news" really is'.

Can Mr Gates' judgement be attributed to personal subjectivity? If so, we would expect some variation among wire editors if a larger sample were studied. Walter Gieber found otherwise in a 1956 study of 16 wire editors in Wisconsin. All the editors selected news items in essentially the same way. Gieber found the telegraph editor to be

preoccupied with the mechanical pressures of his work rather than the social meanings and impact of the news. His personal evaluations rarely entered into his selection process; the values of his employer were an accepted part of the newsroom environment.

The telegraph editor, then, was not doing politics in selecting the news. He was doing a rote task. He was 'concerned with goals of production, bureaucratic routine and interpersonal relations within the newsroom' (1964: 175). Gieber's analysis is a refutation, not an extension, of White's.

The term 'gatekeeper' is still in use. It provides a handy metaphor for the relation of news organizations to news products. The problem with the metaphor is that it leaves 'information' sociologically untouched. It minimizes the complexity of newsmaking. News items are not simply selected but constructed. The gatekeeper metaphor describes neither this nor the feedback loops in which the agencies that generate information for the press anticipate the criteria of the gatekeepers in their efforts to get through the gate, like teenagers trying to figure out how best to talk and look in order to get admitted to X-rated movies or establishments that serve liquor. How do you 'pass' as an adult? How do you get a piece of information to 'pass' as news? The whole industry of public relations, which after the First World War emerged as a major intermediary between government and business on the one hand, and journalism on the other (Schudson 1978), trades on its expertise in knowing how to construct items that 'pass'.

If the gatekeeper model is ultimately as confused as it is suggestive, what approaches might work better? Three perspectives on newsmaking are commonly employed. The first is the view of political economy that relates the outcome of the news process to the economic structure of the news organization. Everything in between is a black box that need not be examined to understand the fundamental consonance between profit-seeking private industry, on the one hand, or state control, on the other, and conservative, system-maintaining news. This view appears in its most theoretically sophisticated and self-critical form in British media studies (Murdock 1982).

The second approach is that of mainstream sociology, the study of social organization and the sociology of occupations and occupational ideology that, unlike the standard political economy perspective, takes as the central problem for understanding journalism in liberal societies to be the journalists' professed autonomy and decision-making power. This perspective tries to understand how journalists' efforts on the job are constrained by organizational and occupational routines.

Third, but rarely explicitly developed, there is a 'culturological' or anthropological approach, if you will, one that emphasizes the constraining force of broad cultural symbol systems regardless of the details of organizational and occupational routines.

All three of these approaches have strengths and weaknesses I want to discuss here. All of them, even taken together, have so far fallen short of providing an adequate comparative and historical social science of news production.

The Political Economy of News

The political economy perspective is often characterized and caricatured as 'conspiracy theory' or as a rather simple-minded notion that there is a ruling directorate of the capitalist class that dictates to editors and reporters what to run in their newspapers. (Note that sociologists of news have overwhelmingly emphasized news in capitalist societies. This is obviously a limitation to any comprehensive understanding of news.) Since this ignores the observable fact that reporters often initiate stories of their own, that editors rarely meet with publishers, and that most working journalists have no idea who sits on the board of directors of the institutions they work for, in this form the political economy perspective is easily dismissed. However, its more sophisticated versions are essential to a general understanding of the production of news.

Here, as elsewhere, a key issue is what aspect of 'news' it is that one wants to explain or understand. Is it the conservative, system-maintaining character of news? This is more often than not the feature of news political economy scholars focus on – but there are many other possibilities. One of them, of course, appears to be the exact opposite – the press has sometimes been characterized as adversarial or even nihilistic, system attacking or system denigrating, government toppling or crime promoting. In other cases, there are finer features of news that analysts want to understand. Why does news seem to focus on individuals rather than systems and structures? Why does news appear to be so heavily dependent on official sources? Or analysts may focus on features of the literary character of news – why is there a 'summary lead' rather than a chronological opening to a news story? Why is a television sound bite in American network news usually no more than 10 or 15 seconds long? Why do city hall reporters summarize the highlights of official meetings rather than report the whole, often disorganized and desultory proceeding – and what consequences are there to thereby 'rationalizing' the portrait of the political process? (Paletz et al., 1971). Perhaps the most complex question of 'what to explain' concerns whether one should find distressing, and try to explain, the deviation of the media from 'fair' and 'objective' reporting or, instead, should find disturbing and try to understand how it is that 'fair', 'objective' reporting presents a portrait of the world in tune with the view of dominant groups in society. Thus critics have objected to the Glasgow Media Group's studies for castigating television news bias when the more important point may be that broadcast news programs 'achieve their ideological effectivity *precisely through* their observation of the *statutory* requirements of balance and impartiality' (Bennett 1982: 306).

The 'political economy' approach generally does not attend to these fine-grained questions but looks at the big picture. This is both its strength and its weakness. The link between the larger political economy of society and day-to-day practices in journalism is, as Graham Murdock has observed, 'oblique'. Still, he concludes, despite journalistic autonomy, 'the basic definition of the situation which underpins the news reporting of political events, very largely coincides with the definition provided by the legitimated power holders' (1973: 158).

For an American, that kind of conclusion was easier to come to before Watergate than after. As Peter Dreier (1982) observes, much of the interest in institutional or organizational-level analysis of the news emerged in the late sixties because 'instrumental' perspectives from political economy did not seem to describe the then current media activism. While one can argue that the outcome of Watergate was just what legitimated power holders in some circles wanted, it stretches the concept of 'legitimated power holders' to the breaking point if a two-term President at the centre of political life in Washington for two decades, is not among them. It is also a problem, as Dreier (1982) observes, to understand why, if the large corporations and the media work hand-in-glove, the corporations in the early 1970s should have been so vehemently and sincerely aghast at media coverage of politics, the environment, and business.

At the same time, there is normally little problem in demonstrating that, at least in broad terms, news 'coincides with' and 'reinforces' the 'definition of the political situation evolved by the political elite' (Murdock 1973: 172). The behaviour of the American press in questioning the Vietnam war and in bringing down President Nixon can be understood as happening only because the poltical elite was divided much more profoundly than it ordinarily is. Even then, the press seems largely to have gone about its normal business of citing official leaders – it just so happened that the officials were at odds with one another (Hallin 1986).

For understanding broad features of the news product, economic or political economic explanations are often well suited. Curran et al. (1980) ask why elite and mass-oriented newspapers provide such different fare when reader surveys find that different classes prefer to read similar materials. Their explanation centres on the value to advertisers of advertising in papers that attract a small, concentrated elite audience. The expense of having an ad reach what American advertisers now call an 'upscale' audience is lower if a large share of this audience can be reached through one publication – without having to pay the cost of reaching thousands of extraneous readers.

Explanations from political economy may be especially apt for understanding the broadly different stances different news organizations or types of organizations take toward audiences in the marketplace. While many discussions of the news media take up 'the media' as a relatively undifferentiated entity, they generally do so only by limiting attention to 'elite' or 'prestige' or 'national' news outlets. The production of news in alternative media are rarely examined (but see John Downing (1984) for a useful account of alternative media in the United States, Portugal, and Italy) and the popular press is more often dismissed out of hand than studied (this has been the fate even of an innovative paper like *USA Today*). It should be apparent, however, that private ownership, even coupled with a dominant profit orientation, is not a structural factor sufficient in itself to explain news production; the elite press and the popular press (or in the terms of Svendson and Mortenson (1980) studying Denmark, the omnibus press and the yellow press) differ too dramatically in what news they cover and how they cover it.

It is true that American media corporations are interlocked with other major corporations (Dreier and Weinberg 1979). It is equally true that fewer and fewer corporations control more and more of the American news media (Bagdikian 1989). Under these circumstances, it would be a shock to find the press a hotbed of radical thought. But, then, critical or radical thought in any society at any time is exceptional. That there could be a moment of critical upheaval in American society and in the American media in the late 1960s raises doubts about any political economic perspective that attributes power of Orwellian proportion to the capitalist class. That there has been a moment of astonishing reversal in Eastern Europe in 1989 raises related doubts about attributions of unlimited power to the socialist state. The ability of a capitalist class to manipulate opinion and create a close system of discourse is limited; ideology in contemporary capitalism is 'contested territory' as many analysts have observed. The ability of a socialist bureaucracy to create a closed system has limits, too, although its direct efforts to create one have often been stronger and have certainly been more explicitly advanced and have faced fewer legal or political impediments.

The most recent and comprehensive statement of a political economic perspective in the United States is Edward S. Herman and Noam Chomsky's *Manufacturing Consent* (1988). They offer what they call a 'propaganda model' of the mass media, the view that the media 'serve to mobilize support for the special interest that dominate the state and private activity' (1988: xi). For them, news serves established power and, although they recognize some variability in the American press, they do not locate any essential difference between the role of leading news institutions in the United States and *Pravda* in the Soviet Union (judging from half a dozen instances where they directly liken the American press to *Pravda*). For them this follows necessarily from the fact that the news is produced by a concentrated industry of several dozen profit-making corporations, an industry dependent on advertising for its profits, dependent on government officials for its sources, intimidated by right-wing pressure groups, and imbued with anti-communist ideology. Their 'propaganda model' is a blunt instrument for examining a subtle system, a system with more heterogeneity and more capacity for change than they allow. Still, their documented examples of American foreign affairs reporting distorted by an anti-communist consensus remain powerful, although not so persuasive as Daniel Hallin's evidence that news coverage of Central America (one of the key cases Herman and Chomsky take up) has been less dominated by an anti-communist frame of reference than foreign affairs reporting a generation earlier (Hallin 1983).

Because the political economic perspective is primarily the perspective of left-wing critics and analysts of the news media, it is perhaps not surprising that it tends often to paint the news media in liberal societies in the tones of news media in authoritarian regimes. Herman and Chomsky do so explicitly. This is rhetorically possible only in the absence of serious attention to the news media in authoritarian societies. Comparative study would force greater attention to the distinctive features in liberal capitalism that shape journalism – not only the obvious legal protections for an independent press but also the legal barriers. Soviet journalists, for instance, have easier access to industry and to conducting interviews on a factory shop floor than do their Western counterparts who are constrained by the legal standing of private property (Mills 1981: 178).

The political economy perspective in the Anglo-American literature has been oddly insensitive to political and legal determinants of news production; it has been more 'economic' than 'political'. British and American studies of Britain and the United States have taken a liberal democratic political framework for granted. In contrast, Rosario de Mateo's (1989) sketch of the newspaper industry in Spain during the Franco regime, the transition to democracy, and the full restoration of democracy makes it clear that private, profit-making newspapers under Franco put ideological purity as their first priority while private, profit-making newspapers in Spain today emphasize a profit orientation first and provide more opportunity for freedom of expression than the press under Franco. DeMateo's essay suggests, as does the book by William Hachten and C. Anthony Giffard on the press in South Africa (1984), that the legal framework for newswork requires greater attention in any systematic analysis of the political economy of news. The impact of the state upon journalism, both through legal regulation of the media and informal pressure and threats, varies greatly from one nation to another and can vary enormously from one period to another within the same nation.

In the case of South Africa, formal legal restraints on the press have been explicit. In the United States, the First Amendment provides unusually broad grounding for independent journalism, although other legal considerations, including the 'chilling effect' produced by the threat of libel litigation, influence journalistic conduct. While legal aspects of journalism have received serious study, especially in the United States with its First Amendment tradition, little of this work has been recognized, let alone actively integrated, into the British or American sociology of news. Sociologists, myself among them, have too casually taken for granted a liberal constitutionalism protective of journalistic prerogatives and encouraging of an active, even adversary, role for the press. The Eastern European transformations of 1989–90 should encourage new comparative work and may establish just what similarities and differences exist between state-operated media serving directly as agents of state social control and privately owned media operating more subtly in various roles in liberal societies, cheerleading the established order, alarming the citizenry about flaws in that order, providing a civic forum for political debate, acting as a battleground among contesting elites. Pnina Lahav and her colleagues have usefully surveyed press law in seven democratic societies. Lahav concludes that in countries like Sweden and the United States free expression is better protected than in countries like the United Kingdom, France, and the federal Republic of Germany with 'a more elitist attitude toward the press' (Lahav, p. 4).

If there is serious ideological contestation in liberal democracies (as Herman and Chomsky would deny), how does it take place? What institutional mechanisms or cultural traditions or contradictions of power provide room for debate and revision? The political economy perspective typically does not say. Intent on establishing connections among different key social institutions, political economy generally fails to describe formally what the disconnections are. In contrast, Daniel Hallin, borrowing from the work of Jurgen Habermans, has argued that the possibility for the media to offer dissenting views and to publicize scandalous news arises in part because they must attend as much to their own legitimation as to furthering the legitimation of the capitalist system as a whole (Hallin 1985). If they fail to attend to their own integrity and their own credibility with audiences, they may in fact 'simply become ineffective ideological institutions'. This, it appears, is exactly what has happened to official media in Eastern Europe; readers there are famous for recognizing that the only reading worth doing is reading 'between the lines'. In any event, the weaknesses in the political economy perspective lead necessarily to greater scholarly attention to the social organization of the news work and the actual practices of creating the news product.

The Social Organization of Newswork

In an influential essay (1974), Harvey Molotch and Marilyn Lester created a typology of news stories according to whether the news 'occurrence' is planned or unplanned and whether the planners of the occurrence are or are not also the promoters of it as news. If an event is planned and then promoted as news by its planners, this is a 'routine' news item. If the event is planned but promoted by someone different from the agent of the occurrence, it is a 'scandal'. If the event is unplanned and then promoted as news by someone other than its hapless instigator, it is an 'accident'.

This typology defines news by the way it comes to the awareness of a news organization. In none of the three news types is the occurrence a spontaneous event in the world that the news media discover on their own by surveying the world scene. For Molotch and Lester, it is a mistake to try to compare news accounts to 'reality' in the way journalism critics ordinarily do, labelling the discrepancy 'bias'. Instead, they seek out the purposes that create one reality instead of another. The news provides a 'reality' that is 'the political work by which events are constituted by those who happen to currently hold power' (1974: 111). Molotch and Lester reject what they call the 'objectivity assumption' in journalism – not that the media are objective but that there is a real world to be objective about. For Molotch and Lester, newspapers reflect not a world 'out there' but 'the practices of those who have the power to determine the experience of others' (1974: 54).

In what might these practices consist? Mark Fishman conducted a participant-observation study of newspaper work in a California newspaper with a daily circulation of 45,000 and a full-time editorial staff of thirty-seven (Fishman 1980). He finds that journalists are highly attuned to bureaucratic organizations of government and that *the world is bureaucratically organized for journalists* (1980: 51). That is, the organization of 'beats' is such that reports get the largest share of their news from official government agencies. 'The journalist's view of the society as bureaucratically structured is the very basis upon which the journalist is able to detect events' (1980: 51). One of the great advantages of dealing with bureaucracies for the journalist is that the bureaucracies 'provide for the continuous detection of events' (1980: 52). The bureaucrat provides a reliable and steady source of news.

One study after another comes up with essentially the same observation, and it matters not whether the study is at the national or local level – the story of journalism, on a day to day basis, is the story of the interaction of reporters and officials. Some claim officials have the upper hand (Gans 1979: 116; Cohen 1963: 267). Some media critics, including many government officials, say reporters do (Hess 1984: 109). But there is little doubt that the centre of news generation is the link between reporter and official, the interaction of the representatives of the news bureaucracies and the government bureaucracies. This is clear especially when one examines the actual daily practices of journalists. 'The only important tool of the reporter is his news sources and how he uses them', a reporter covering state government in the United States told Delmer Dunne (1969: 41). Stephen Hess confirms this in his study of Washington correspondents. He found reporters had conducted 3,967 interviews for 865 stories sampled and that Washington reporters 'use no documents in the preparation of nearly three-quarters of their stories' (Hess 1981: 17–18). Hess does not count press releases as documents – these are, of course, another means of communication directly from official to reporter. Knowing sources, Gaye Tuchman observed, is a mark of professional status for reporters. She cites one reporter saying of another, 'He's the best political reporter in the city. He has more sources than anyone else' (1978: 68). It is clear that the reporter-official connection makes news an important tool of government and other established authorities. Some recent work, accordingly, examines news production from the viewpoint of the news source rather than the news organization (Cook 1989). The corollary to the power of the government source or other well legitimated sources is that 'resource-poor organizations' have great difficulty in getting news coverage (Goldenberg 1975). If they are to be covered, as Todd Gitlin's study of SDS indicated, they must adjust to modes of organizational interaction more like those of established organizations (Gitlin 1980).

There has been much more attention to reporter-official relations than to reporter-editor relations, a second critical aspect of the social organization of newswork. Despite some suggestive early work on the ways in which reporters engage in self-censorship when they have an eye fixed on pleasing an editor (Breed 1955: 80), systematic sociological research has not been especially successful in this domain. Certainly case studies of newswork regularly note the effects – usually baleful – of editorial intervention (Crouse 1973: 186; Gitlin 1980: 64–5; Hallin 1986: 2). Frands Mortensen and Erik Svendsen (1980) pay explicit attention to various forms of self censorship in Danish newspapers. Generally, however, studies do not look at the social relations of newswork from an editor's view. This may have something to do with rhetorical forms of understanding the news process that social scientists have unconsciously borrowed from film and fiction portrayals of journalism or it may have to do with the greater glamour of and greater access of reporters compared to editors. In any event, most research has focused on the gathering of news rather than on its writing, rewriting, and 'play' in the press. There has been little work, for instance, on the production of headlines, although informal observation suggests that headlines often misrepresent stories in the direction of conventional thinking or toward the editorial preferences of the newspaper.

This is particularly unfortunate when research suggests that it is in the *play* of a story that real influence comes. Hallin (1986), Herman and Chomsky (1988) and Lipstadt (1986) all argue that in the press of a liberal society like the United States lots of news, including dissenting or adversarial information and opinion, gets into the newspaper. The question is *where* that information appears and how it is inflected. Hallin interestingly suggests there was a 'reverse inverted pyramid' of news in much reporting of the Vietnam war. The nearer the information was to the truth, the farther down in the story it appeared (1986: 78).

If one theoretical source for the sociology of news has been symbolic interactionism or social constructionist views of society (as in the work of Molotch and Lester, Tuchman and others), a complementary source has been organizational or bureaucratic theory. If, on the one hand, the creation of news is seen as the social production of 'reality', on the other hand it is taken to be the social manufacture of an organizational product, one that can be studied like other manufactured goods. This latter point of view is evident, for instance, in Edward Jay Epstein's early study (1973) that grew out of a political science seminar at Harvard on organizational theory. That seminar took its working assumption to be that members of organization 'modified their own personal values in accordance with the requisites of the organization' (1973: xiv). One should therefore study organizations, not individuals, to analyze the 'output' they product – in this case, news. Epstein's study, based on field work at national network news programmes in 1968 and 1969, emphasized organizational, economic, and technical requirements of television news production in explaining the news product. Epstein's study, like many others, finds the technical constraints of television news particularly notable. These, of course, have changed radically and rapidly in the past two decades – a serious historical account of this technological revolution remains to be written. A broadly comparative sociology of news would observe how the absence of some technical and logistical features of news production taken for granted in advanced economies limits news coverage in developing nations. In Ghana, for instance, poor communication between cities and rural areas, including the frequent breakdown of lorries carrying newspapers to the countryside, helps confine reporting to urban areas and issues (Twumasi 1985).

Who are the journalists in news organizations who cover beats, interview sources, rewrite press releases from government bureaus, and rarely (but occasionally) take the initiative in ferreting out hidden or complex stories? If the organizational theorists are generally correct, it does not matter who they are or where they come from; they will be socialized quickly into the values and routines in the daily rituals of journalism. Initial evidence from a cross-national survey by Colin Sparks and Slavko Splichal (1989) apparently supports this view: despite different national cultures, despite different patterns of professional education, and despite different labour patterns of journalists (some in strong professional associations or unions, some not), the stated professional values of the journalists surveyed do not differ greatly from nation to nation. The structural sources of these professional values, however, may differ significantly. Jane Leftwich Curry suggests in her study of pre-1989 Poland that Polish journalists' strong attachment to professionalism 'defies traditional Western theories' of socialist media (1990: 1). At the same time, she suggests that Polish professionalism is a product not of the autonomy of journalists but of 'the unpleasant push and pull of political forces' journalists are subjected to (1990: 207). Professionalism is a set of values and practices that protect the Polish journalist from manipulation by the Communist Party, government bureaucrats, and the sponsoring organization of each newspaper or journal.

Professional values notwithstanding, there is great interest among at least some American scholars in ascertaining the social backgrounds of media personnel as clues to the kind of bias they will bring to their work. Studies by S. Robert Lichter, Stanley Rothman, and Linda S. Lichter, culminating in *The Media Elite: America's New Powerbrokers* (1986) made the case that news in the United States is 'biased' in a liberal direction because journalists at the elite news organizations are themselves liberal. Their survey of 240 elite journalists finds a pattern familiar from earlier work – that many of these journalists describe themselves as liberals and tend to vote Democratic. They argue that these national journalists are a 'homogeneous' liberal, cosmopolitan band with growing wealth and power. Yet 'homogeneous' scarcely describes a group in which 54 per cent call themselves liberal, 46 per cent moderate or conservative (Lichter et al. 1986: 28). The group is more socially liberal (53 per cent say adultery is not wrong) than economically liberal (only 13 per cent think government should own big corporations). American elite journalists fully accept the framework of capitalism although they wish for it to have a human face.

The real problem in Rothman and Lichters' approach is that it offers no convincing evidence that the news product reflects the personal views of journalists rather than the views of the officials whose positions they are reporting (Gans 1985). American journalists in leading news institutions are generally very committed to their ideology of dispassion, their sense of professionalism, their allegiance to fairness or objectivity as it has been professionally defined. They have a professional commitment to shielding their work from their personal political leanings. Moreover, their political leanings may be weak. Several observers find leading American journalists not so much liberal or conservative as apolitical. Michael Robinson and Margaret Sheehan (1983) interviewed CBS and UPI reporters and found that most seemed to be moderates or just not very political. Stephen Hess came to a similar conclusion in studying Washington reporters: '. . . Washington reporters are more apolitical than press critics contend. The slant of Washington news is more a product of the angle from which it is observed than from ideology' (1981: 115).

What is fundamental in organizational approaches, as opposed to the social-compositional approach of Rothman and the Lichters, is the emphasis on (a) constraints imposed by organizations despite the private intentions of the individual actors and (b) the inevitability of 'social construction' of reality in any social system. The latter point is crucial. Many (though not all) analysts from a social organizational perspective abandon any strong claim that there is a 'reality' out there that journalists or journalistic organizations distort. News is not a report on a factual world; news is 'a depletable consumer product that must be made fresh daily' (Tuchman 1978: 179). It is not a gathering of facts that already exists; indeed, as Tuchman has argued, facts are defined organizationally – facts are 'pertinent information gathered by professionally validated methods specifying the relationship between what is known and how it is known . . . In news, verification of facts is both a political and a professional accomplishment (1978: 82–83).

Culturological Approaches

For Molotch and Lester and Tuchman, the fact that news is 'constructed' suggests that it is *socially* constructed, elaborated in the interaction of the news-making players with one another. But the emphasis on the human construction of news can be taken in another direction. Anthropologist Marshall Sahlins has written in a different context that 'an event is not just a happening in the world; it is a *relation* between a certain happening and a given symbolic system' (1985: 153). Molotch and Lester, Tuchman, and others who emphasize the 'production of culture' do not focus on the cultural givens within which everyday interaction happens in the first place. These cultural givens, while they may be uncovered by detailed historical analysis, cannot be extrapolated from features of social organization at the moment of study. They are a part of culture – a given symbolic system, within which and in relation to which reporters and officials go about their duties.

This 'cultural' perspective on the news has not been codified nor established as any sort of 'school'. Indeed, I think that most understandings of the generation of news merge a 'cultural' view with the social organizational view. It is, however, analytically distinct. Where the organizational view finds interactional determinants of news in the relations between people, the cultural view finds symbolic determinants of news in the relations between 'facts' and symbols. This does not mean that the culturologist must repair to universal categories – although this is one possibility. Frank Pearce, for instance, in examining media coverage of homosexuals in Britain (1973), takes as a theoretical starting point anthropologist Mary Douglas's view that societies like to keep their cultural concepts clean and neat and are troubled by 'anomalies' that do not fit the pre-conceived categories of the culture. Homosexuality is an anomaly in societies that take as fundamental the opposition and relationship of male and female; thus homosexuals provide a culturally charged topic for story-telling that seeks to preserve or reinforce the conventional moral order of society – and its conceptual or symbolic foundation. News stories about homosexuals, Pearce says, may be moral tales, 'a negative reference point . . . an occasion to reinforce conventional moral values by telling a moral tale. Through these means tensions in the social system can be dealt with and "conventionalized"' (1973: 293).

If Mary Douglas is one theoretical reference point for Pearce, Sigmund Freud is another (though unstated). Pearce cites R. D. Laing's observation that people enjoy reading the kind of material to be found in the sensational press because it enables them to experience vicariously pleasurable feelings they are otherwise forbidden to discuss or imagine. 'These pleasurable sensations that we have denied but not annihilated', Pearce writes, 'may be lived through again by means of the sensational newspaper' (1973: 291).

Incidentally, this sort of observation brings into the analysis the news institutions' sense of their audience, something relatively rare in the sociology of news. Of course, there is a large literature in communication studies on the 'uses and gratifications' audiences get from the mass media. But these studies are rarely invoked by analysts to explain why we get the sort of news we do. Is this an important omission? Perhaps not. Journalists typically know very little about their audience. American journalists underestimate the size of their working class audience (Gans 1979: 238–9). Soviet journalists overestimate the education level of their readers and underestimate the proportion of women in their audience (Remington 1988: 167). Herbert Gans found that the reporters and editors he studied at news weeklies and network television programmes 'had little knowledge about the actual audience and rejected feedback from it. Although they had a vague image of the audience, they paid little attention to it; instead, they filmed and wrote for their superiors and for themselves, assuming . . . that what interested them would interest the audience' (1979: 230). Neither American nor Soviet journalists show much interest in learning more about their audiences. But journalists, like other writers, address an 'implied audience' and it would be instructive to know more about how this image of the reader is constructed in the journalists' minds.

A culturalist account of news helps account for generalized images and stereotypes in the news media – of predatory stockbrokers just as much as hard-drinking factory workers – that transcend structures of ownership or patterns of work relations. In Paul Hartmann's and Charles Husband's analysis of British mass media coverage of racial conflict, for instance, they note that 'The British cultural tradition contains elements derogatory to foreigners, particularly blacks. The media operate within the culture and are obliged to use cultural symbols' (1973: 274). This is just the sort of observation I would call 'culturalist' or 'culturological', and here it seems a necessary element in explanation.

A culturalist account of news would also seem relevant in understanding journalists' vague renderings of how they know 'news' when they see it. The

central categories of newsworkers themselves are 'cultural' more than structural. Stuart Hall, in his essay on news photographs, tried to define the
indefinable 'news values' or 'news sense' that journalists regularly talk about.
He writes:

> News values' are one of the most opaque structures of meaning in modern society.
> All 'true journalists' are supposed to possess it: few can or are willing to identify
> and define it. Journalists speak of 'the news' as if events select themselves. Further,
> they speak as if which is the 'most significant' news story, and which 'news angles'
> are most salient are divinely inspired. Yet of the millions of events which occur
> every day in the world, only a tiny proportion ever become visible as 'potential
> news stories': and of this proportion, only a small fraction are actually produced as
> the day's news in the news media. We appear to be dealing, then, with a 'deep
> structure' whose function as a selective device is un-transparent even to those who
> professionally most know how to operate it
>
> (1973: 181)

This seems to me exactly right, at least for Western journalism. In the Soviet
Union, at least in the first instance, the matter is much simpler – 'the party's
conception of newsworthiness becomes the journalists' (Remington
1988: 169), although there is evidence even in pre-Gorbachev days that Soviet
journalists held professional values distinct from party directives (Mills, 1981).
Gaye Tuchman's observation on American journalists parallels Hall's on the
British when she writes that 'news judgement is the sacred knowledge, the
secret ability of the newsman which differentiates him from other people'
(1972: 672). The question is what to make of it. It seems to me too simple,
though common now, to label this as 'ideology' or the 'common sense' of a
hegemonic system. It makes of human beliefs and attitudes a more unified,
intentional and functional system than they are. Many beliefs that ruling
groups may use for their own ends are rooted much more deeply in human
consciousness and are to be found much more widely in human societies than
capitalism or socialism or industrialism or any other modern system of social
organization and domination. Patriarchal and sexist outlooks, for instance,
may well be turned to the service of capitalism, but this does not make them
capitalist in origin nor does it mean that they are perfectly or inherently
homologous to capitalist structures or requirements for their preservation.

A specific example may illustrate the many dimensions of this problem.
Why, Johan Galtung and Mari Ruge (1970) ask, are news stories so often
'personified'? Why do reporters write of persons and not structures, of
individuals and not social forces? They cite a number of possible explanations,
some of which are 'cultural'. There is cultural idealism – the Western view that
individuals are masters of their own destiny responsible for their acts through
the free will they exercise. There is the nature of story-telling itself, with the
need in narrative to establish 'identification'. There is also what they call the
'frequency-factor' – that people act during a time-span that fits the frequency of
the news media (daily) better than do the actions of 'structures' that are much
harder to connect with specific events in a 24-hour cycle.

This last point is particularly interesting. Is it a 'social structural' or a
'cultural' phenomenon? In some respect, it is structural – if the media operated
monthly or annually rather than daily, perhaps they would speak more often of
social forces than of individuals. Indeed, examining journalism's 'year-end

reviews' would very likely turn up more attention to social trends and structural changes than can be found in the daily news. But, then, is the fact that the press operates on a daily basis for the most part structural or cultural? Is there some basic primacy to the daily cycle of the press, of business, of government, of sleeping and waking, that makes the institutions of journalism essentially human and person-centred in scale and inescapably so?

Or might there be some more or less universal processes of human perception that lead to an emphasis on the individual? Does this have less to do with something peculiarly American or Western or capitalistic than it does with what psychologists refer to as the 'fundamental attribution error' in human causal thinking – attributing to individuals in the foreground responsibility for causation that might better be attributed to background situations or large-scale trends or structures? That news definitions and news values differ across cultures can be demonstrated by comparative research. For instance, the Soviet media, like Western media, operate on a daily cycle, but very little of the news concerns happenings in the prior twenty-four hours (Mickiewicz 1989: 30). Soviet news organizations operate according to long-range political plans and stockpile stories and editorial to meet political needs (Remington 1988: 116). The sense of immediacy taken by Western media to be a requirement of news (and often taken by critics to be an ideologically loaded weakness of journalism) is not, the Soviet case would suggest, an invariant feature of bureaucratic organization, occupational routines, or a universal diurnal human rhythm. It is rooted instead in a nation-specific political culture.

So one need not adopt assumptions about universal properties of human nature and human interest (although I think it would be foolish to dismiss them out of hand) to acknowledge that there are aspects of news-generation that go beyond what sociological analysis of news organizations is normally prepared to handle. Richard Hoggart has written that the most important filter through which news is constructed is 'the cultural air we breathe, the whole ideological atmosphere of our society, which tells us that some things can be said and that others had best not be said' (Bennett 1982: 303). That 'cultural air' is one that in part, ruling groups and institutions create, but it is in part one in whose social context their own establishment takes place.

The cultural air has both a form and content. The content, the substance of taken-for-granted values, has often been discussed. Gans (1979) arrived at a list for American journalism that includes ethnocentrism, altruistic democracy, responsible capitalism, small-town pastoralism, individualism, and moderatism as core, unquestioned values of American news. They are the unquestioned and generally unnoticed background assumptions through which the news is gathered and within which it is framed. If these elements of content fit rather well, conventional notions of ideology or the common sense of a hegemonic system (Gans calls them 'para-ideology'), aspects of form, operate at a level more remote from ideology as generally understood.

By 'form', I refer to assumptions about narrative, storytelling, human interest, and the conventions of photographic and linguistic presentation that shape the presentation of all of the news the media produce. Weaver (1975) has shown some systematic differences between the inverted-pyramid structure of print news and the 'thematic' structure of television news; Schudson (1982) has argued that the inverted-pyramid form is a peculiar development of late nineteenth-century American journalism and one that implicitly authorized the journalist as political expert and helped redefine politics itself as a subject appropriately discussed by experts rather than partisans; Hallin and Mancini (1984) demonstrate in a comparison of television news in Italy and the United States that formal conventions of news reporting often attributed to the technology of television by analysts, or to 'the nature of things' by journalists, in fact stem from features of a country's political culture. All of this work recognizes that news is a form of literature and that one key resource journalists work with is the cultural tradition of storytelling and picture-making and sentence construction they inherit, with a number of vital assumptions about the world built in.

If there is a general cultural air journalists breathe along with others in their society, there is also a specifically journalistic cultural air tied to the occupational practices of journalists. The 'routines' of journalists are not only social, emerging out of interactions among officials, reporters, and editors, but literary, emerging out of interactions of writers with literary traditions. More than that, journalists at work operate, not only to maintain and repair their social relations with sources and colleagues, but their cultural image as journalists with a wider world. Robert Manoff shows how television news reporters deploy experts in stories not so much to provide viewers with information but to certify the journalist's 'effort, access, and superior knowledge' (1989: 69). Barbie Zelizer (1990) has carefully demonstrated the ways in which reporters in American broadcast news visually and verbally establish their own authority by suggesting their personal proximity to the events they cover. They employ visual and verbal techniques to transform a cultural value (that an eyewitness is authoritative, that proximity to an event certifies an observer's account of it) to an occupational practice. But that practice is realized not so much in the gathering of news as in its presentation to television audiences; regardless of how the news was in fact 'gathered', it is presented in a style that promotes an illusion of the journalist's adherence to the journalistic norm of proximity. The reality journalists manufacture provides not only a version and vision of 'the world' but of 'journalism' itself.

Conclusions

The approaches to the study of news I have reviewed often ignore possibilities for change in the nature of news. When William Rivers (1962) studied Washington correspondents in 1960, a generation after Leo Rosten had studied them, asking some of the same questions Rosten had asked, he found reporters more free from directives from their home offices than they had been in the 1930s. When Leon Sigal studied changes in the front pages of the *New York Times* and the *Washington Post*, he found that from the 1950s to the early 1970s, news stories were more likely to be based on more than one source and to include material gathered from (sometimes disaffected or dissident) bureaucrats lower down in the organizational hierarchy. My own research (1982) found that in the 1880s news stories of presidential addresses did not try to summarize the key points of a speech but that by 1910 a 'summary lead' was a standard form, an assertion, in a sense, of the authority of the press to *define* the key political reality of the day. Anthony Smith (1980) found major changes in the nature of newswork in British journalism in his review of changes in journalistic values and practices. Contemporary accounts of the Soviet press make it clear that Glasnost has rapidly and radically altered the content of the news; it has enabled frank reports of accidents, disasters, and political protests that would never have appeared in the past (Mickiewicz 1988; Remington 1988). In general, historical studies of the press reveal significantly different patterns of newsgathering and newswriting over time that are rarely referenced or accounted for in contemporary sociological studies of news.

All three approaches reviewed here tend to be indifferent to comparative as well as to historical studies. Comparative research is cumbersome, of course, even in the age of word processors and computer networking. More telling, I think, media studies are genuinely linked to national political issues – they are an academic meta-discourse on the daily defining of political reality. The motive for research, then, is normally conceived in isolation from comparative concerns. If this strengthens the immediate political relevance of media studies, it weakens their longer-term value as social science.

All three approaches, finally, have greatly advanced our understanding of the media by focusing on the specific institutions and the specific processes in those institutions responsible for creating the cultural product we call news. They have sought to abandon broad functionalist guidelines that understand the media by positing some general social function the media serve (although the political economy perspective is not yet free of a functionalist orientation). This, I think, has been to the good. Still, an implicit normative functionalism has been smuggled into many studies: the idea that the news media *should* serve society by informing the general population in ways that arm them for vigilant citizenship. I am sympathetic to this, as one goal the news media in a democracy should try to serve, but I do not think historically it is a very good approximation of what role the news media have played – anywhere. The most important problem with this model is that the news media have always been a more important forum for communication among elites (and some elites more than others) than with the general population. In the best of circumstances, the fact of a general audience for the news media provides a regular opportunity for elites to be effectively embarrassed, even disgraced, as Brent Fisse and John Braithwaite show in their cross-national study of the impact of publicity on corporate offenders (1983). But even here the 'audience' or the 'public' has a kind of phantom existence that the sociological study of news production has yet to consider in its theoretical formulations.

Notes

1   This is a revised version of an essay that first appeared in *Media, Culture and Society*, II, 1989.

References

BAGDIKIAN, B., 1983: *The Media Monopoly*. Boston: Beacon Press.

BENNETT, T., 1982: 'Media, 'Reality', Signification', in M. Gurevitch, T. Bennett, J. Curran, and J. Woollacott, *Culture, Society and the Media*. London: Methuen. pp. 287–308.

BREED, W., 1952, 1980: *The Newspaperman, News and Society*. New York: Arno Press.

BREED, W., 1955: 'Social Control in the Newsroom: A Functional Analysis', *Social Forces*, 33: pp. 326–355.

COHEN, B. C., 1963: *The Press and Foreign Policy*. Princeton: Princeton University Press.

COHEN, S. and J. YOUNG, (eds) 1973: *The Manufacture of News: A Reader*. Beverly Hills: Sage.

COOK, T. E., 1989: *Making Laws and Making News: Media Strategies in the U.S. House of Representatives*. Washington, DC: Brookings Institution.

CROUSE, T., 1973: *The Boys on the Bus*. New York: Ballantine.

CURRAN, J., A. DOUGLAS and G. WHANNEL, 1980: 'The Political Economy of the Human-Interest Story', pp. 288–342 in Anthony Smith (ed.), *Newspapers and Democracy*. Cambridge, MA: MIT Press.

CURRY, J. L., 1990: *Poland's Journalists: Professionalism and Politics*. Cambridge: Cambridge University Press.

DE MATEO, R., 1989: 'The Evolution of the Newspaper Industry in Spain, 1939–87', *European Journal of Communication*, 4: pp. 211–226.

DOWNING, J., 1984: Radical Media: *The Political Experience of Alternative Communication*. Boston: South End Press.

DREIER, P., 1982: 'Capitalists vs. the Media: An Analysis of an Ideological Mobilization Among Business Leaders', *Media, Culture and Society 4* (1982) pp. 111–132.

DREIER, P. and S. WEINBERG, 1979: 'Interlocking Directorates', *Columbia Journalism Review*, November/December: pp. 51–68.

DUNNE, D. D., 1969: *Public Officials and the Press*. Reading, MA: Addison-Wesley.

EPSTEIN, E. J., 1973: *News From Nowhere*. New York: Random House.

FISHMAN, M., 1980: *Manufacturing the News*. Austin: University of Texas Press.

FISS, B. and J. BRAITHWAITE, 1983: *The Impact of Publicity on Corporate Offenders*. Albany: State University of New York Press.

GALTUNG, J. and RUGE, M., 1970: 'The Structure of Foreign News: The Presentation of the Congo, Cuba and Cyprus Crises in Four Foreign Newspapers' in Tunstall, ed. pp. 259–298.

GANS, H. J., 1979: *Deciding What's News: A Study of CBS Evening News, NBC Nightly News, Newsweek and Time*. New York: Pantheon.

GANS, H. J., 1985: 'Are US Journalists Dangerously Liberal?' *Columbia Journalism Review (November/December)*, pp. 29–33.

GIEBER, W., 1964: 'News Is What Newspapermen Make It', in Dexter, L. A. and Manning, D., *White, People, Society and Mass Communications*. New York: Free Press.

GITLIN, T., 1980: *The Whole World Is Watching*. Berkeley: University of California Press.

GOLDENBERG, E., 1975: *Making the Papers*. Lexington, MA: D. C. Heath.

GUREVITCH, M., BENNETT, T., CURRAN, J., and WOOLLACOTT, J., eds, 1982: *Culture, Society and the Media*. London: Methuen.

HACHTEN, W. A. and GIFFARD, C. A., 1984: *The Press and Apartheid: Repression and Propaganda in South Africa*. Madison: University of Wisconsin Press.

HALL, S., 1973: 'The Determination of News Photographs', in Cohen, S. and Young, J., eds. *The Manufacture of News: A Reader*. Beverly Hills: Sage, pp. 176–190.

HALLIN, D. C., 1983: 'The Media Go to War – From Vietnam to Central America', *NACLA Report on the Americas*, (July/August).

HALLIN, D. C., 1985: 'The American News Media: A Critical Theory Perspective', pp. 121–46 in J. Forrester (ed.), *Critical Theory and Public Life*. Cambridge, MA: MIT Press.

HALLIN, D. C., 1986: *'The Uncensored War': The Media and Vietnam*. New York: Oxford.

HALLIN, D. C. and MANCINI, P., 1984: 'Speaking of the President: Political Structure and Representational Form in US and Italian Television News'. *Theory and Society*, 13: pp. 829–850.

HARTMANN, P. and C. HUSBAND, 1973: 'The Mass Media and Racial Conflict', pp. 270–83 in S. Cohen and J. Young (eds) *The Manufacture of News: A Reader*. Beverly Hills: Sage.

HERMAN, E. S. and N. CHOMSKY, 1988: *Manufacturing Consent*. New York: Pantheon.

HESS, S., 1981: *The Washington Reporters*. Washington: Brookings Institution.

HESS, S., 1984: *The Government/Press Connection*. Washington, DC: The Brookings Institution.

HUGHES, H. M., 1940: *News and the Human Interest Story*. Chicago: University of Chicago Press.

LAHAV, P., ed., 1985: *Press Law in Modern Democracies: A Comparative Study*. New York: Longman.

LICHTER, S. R., ROTHAM, S., and LICHTER, L. S., 1986: *The Media Elite: America's New Powerbrokers*. Bethesda, MD. Adler and Adler.

LIPSTADT, D., 1986: *Beyond Belief: The American Press and the Coming of the Holocaust 1933–1945*. New York: Free Press.

MANOFF, R. K., 1989: 'Modes of War and Modes of Social Address: The Text of SDI'. *Journal of Communication*, 39: pp. 59–84.

MICKIEWICZ, E., 1988: *Split Signals: Television and Politics in the Soviet Union*. New York: Oxford.

MILLS, R. D., 1981: 'The Soviet Journalist: A Cultural Analysis'. Ph.D. dissertation, University of Illinois. Ann Arbor: University Microfilms International.

MOLOTCH, H. and LESTER, M., 1974: 'News as Purposive Behavior: On the Strategic Use of Routine Events, Accidents, and Scandals'. *American Sociological Review*, 39: pp. 101–112.

MORTENSEN, FRANDS and SVENDSEN, E. N., 1980: 'Creativity and Control: The Journalist Betwixt His Readers and Editors'. *Media, Culture and Society*, 2: pp. 169–177.

MURDOCK, G. and GOLDING, P., 1977: 'Capitalism, Communication and Class Relations', pp. 12–43 in Curran, J., Gurevitch, M. and Woollacott, J., eds, *Mass Communication and Society*. London: Edward Arnold.

MURDOCK, G., 1982: 'Large Corporations and the Control of the Communications Industries'. In Gurevitch, M., Bennett, T., Curran, J. and Woollacott, J., *Culture, Society and the Media*. London: Methuen. pp. 118–150.

PALETZ, D., REICHERT, P. and MCINTYRE, B., 1971: 'How the Media Support Local Governmental Authority'. *Public Opinion Quarterly*, 35: pp. 80–92.

PARK, R. E., 1923: 'The Natural History of the Newspaper'. *American Journal of Sociology*, 29: pp. 273–289.

PEARCE, F., 1973: 'How To Be Immoral and Ill, Pathetic and Dangerous, All At the Same Time: Mass Media and the Homosexual', pp. 284–301 in S. Cohen and J. Young (eds) *The Manufacture of News: A Reader*. Beverly Hills: Sage.

REMINGTON, T. F., 1988: *The Truth of Authority: Ideology and Communication in the Soviet Union*. Pittsburgh: University of Pittsburgh Press.

RIVERS, W., 1962: 'The Correspondents After 25 Years', *Columbia Journalism Review*, 1: pp. 4–10.

ROBINSON, M. J. and SHEEHAN, M. A., 1983: *Over the Wire and On TV*. New York: Russell Sage Foundation.

ROSTEN, L. C., 1937: *The Washington Correspondents*. New York: Harcourt, Brace.

SAHLINS, M., 1985: *Islands of History*. Chicago: University of Chicago Press.

SCHUDSON, M., 1978: *Discovering the News: A Social History of American Newspapers*. New York: Basic Books.

SCHUDSON, M., 1982: 'The Politics of Narrative Form: The Emergence of News Conventions in Print and Television', *Daedalus*, 111: pp. 97–113.

SIGAL, L. V., 1973: *Reporters and Officials*. Lexington, MA: Lexington Books.

SMITH, A., 1980: *Newspapers and Democracy*. Cambridge, MA: MIT Press.

SPARKS, C. and SPLICHAL, S., 1989: 'Journalistic Education and Professional Socialisation', *Gazette*, 43: pp. 31–52.

TUCHMAN, G., 1972: 'Objectivity as Strategic Ritual: An Examination of Newsmen's Notions of Objectivity'. *American Journal of Sociology* 77, 660–679.

TUCHMAN, G., 1976: 'Telling Stories', *Journal of Communication*, 26 (Fall): 93–7.

TUCHMAN, G., 1978: *Making News: A Study in the Construction of Reality*. New York: Free Press.

TWUMASI, Y., 1985: 'Social Class and Newspaper Coverage in Ghana', in F. O. Ugboajah, ed., *Mass Communication, Culture and Society in West Africa*. Munchen: K. G. Saur, Hans Zell Publishers, 219–220.

WEAVER, P., 1975: 'Newspaper News and Television News', in D. Cater and R. Adler (eds), *Television as a Social Force*. New York: Praeger.

WEBER, M., 1921, 1946: 'Politics as a Vocation', in Gerth, H. and Mills, C. W., ed. From *Max Weber: Essays in Sociology*, pp. 77–128.

WHITE, D. M., 1950: 'The Gatekeeper: A Case Study in the Selection of News'. *Journalism Quarterly* 27: 383–390. Also reprinted in Dexter, L. A. and White, D. M., eds, *People, Society, and Mass Communications*. New York: Free Press, 1964.

ZELIZER, B., 1990: 'Where is the Author in American TV News? On the Construction and Presentation of Proximity, Authorship, and Journalistic Authority', *Semiotica*, 80.

8

A Mass Communication Perspective on Entertainment Industries

Joseph Turow

The aim of this chapter is to outline contemporary issues in the study of entertainment industries and describe their importance for the broad field of mass communication research. A major obstacle to accomplishing this goal, curiously enough, is marking off what is meant by entertainment industries. The great majority of studies encompassed by this overview do not even use the term. Moreover, even when writers do use it, they do not define it. A search through the mass communication literature for work that specifies the meaning of 'entertainment industries' came up empty. In fact, 'entertainment' itself has rarely been described systematically by mass communication scholars, even those who see it as their domain. A recent, widely appreciated, volume titled *Studies in Entertainment* (Modleski 1986) is typical. Nowhere do the editor or contributors try to come to grips with the word's meaning even though they stress its centrality to their intellectual interests. Academic reference books also tend to offer little guidance. Raymond Williams' (1976) *Keywords*, subtitled 'a vocabulary of culture and society', ignores the term. A couple of other recent media studies dictionaries (Conners 1982; Watson and Hill 1984) also do not list it.

The main argument of this chapter is that it is not only possible to define what is meant by an entertainment industry, it is useful. Adding the term entertainment industries to the research vocabulary is virtually required in view of the substantial changes coursing through the contemporary Western mass media system. In addition, academics who think in terms of entertainment industries when they explore mass media organizations can broaden the significance of their work for others who study the creation of mass media materials. Just as important, they can contribute fresh insights to researchers who investigate the uses and consequences of mass media.

The Need for an Organizing Term

Before specifying a meaning for 'entertainment industry', it will be helpful to explain briefly the need for such a term. It is motivated by an unhealthy fragmentation and insular focus that exists across much of the literature on

160

mass media industries. Broadly speaking, it is possible to discern two groups that contribute to this literature – a large contingent that studies journalism and a smaller number that focuses on nonjournalistic media operations such as radio plays, theatrical films, music recordings, and TV sports presentations. Over the years, the journalism researchers have taken on the characteristics of a subfield within communication, building on previous findings and theoretical discussions across news industries and tying them to larger issues of media consequences.

By contrast, researchers who have studied nonjournalistic media organizations have tended to reflect little sense of building a scholarly area that can be extended, replicated, challenged. The major problem has been conceptual. In spite of their use of terminology from such cross-disciplinary perspectives as the sociology of art and the production of culture, researchers have rarely considered organizational dynamics as transcending particular media and helping to inform our understanding of a general process called mass communication. People who have studied the book industry, for example, have tended to ignore research on the television industry while people who studied comic book publishing have ignored scholarly writings about the other two.

Interactions of media industries have also typically not been of interest in studies of nonjournalistic media, except from the standpoint of studies (e.g., Wasko, 1989) that have noted conglomerate ownership patterns. When it comes to examining organizational and interorganizational processes, the traditional form of research has been to focus on one or another of the most salient media industries in society – the TV industry, the movie industry, the cable industry, and a few others – and to leave it at that. It is a narrow focus which has weakened the ability of research on media industries to contribute to the mass communication field's dialogue about the implications of media processes across society.

The balkanized approach to studying nonjournalistic media industries has also inhibited researchers on mass media industries from studying some of the most important changes taking place in their own back yards. The media world has been undergoing transformation as a result of three interrelated phenomena – fragmentation, globalization, and conglomerization. Fragmentation refers to the increased number of new media channels that have resulted from marketers' interests in reaching increasingly narrow audience segments with technologies such as cable television, direct broadcast satellites, low power TV, and videocassette recorders. Conglomerization refers to the progressive growth of large corporations (Bertelsmann, Time Warner, Sony) holding under their wings a number of media firms that create a variety of media products in different media industries. Globalization refers to expansion of the fragmentation and conglomerization phenomena across national borders.

One hallmark of these trends is the blurring of boundaries between mass media industries. Executives realize that for many purposes it is meaningless to ascertain where, for example, the movie industry ends and the cable TV, book, broadcast television, and home video industries begin. To them, much more important than observing boundaries is the search for *windows* of media opportunity – for instance, the best moment to exhibit a film in theatres, publish it in book version, then move the movie to home video, then to cable

TV, then to network TV, then to local syndication. The need to move product across the boundaries of media industries has been spurred by the dictates of conglomeration and the economics of media fragmentation. That, together with frenzied competition, has also accelerated the promotion of media materials across a panoply of locations – from newspapers and radio talk shows, to shirts, toys, and even foods.

These and related activities raise a wide range of questions about changing levers of control over nonjournalistic mass communication, their relationship to journalistic activities, and their implications for society. The lack of vigorous cross-media theorizing and the traditional focus on individual industries have combined to make much of the field silent on these issues. Moreover, the failure to conceptualize 'mass communication' at a level that points towards generalizable processes rather than particular industries has resulted in the virtual absence of work on the roles such arenas as the toy, supermarket, and food industries play in the fast-changing media world.

This paper proposes that one way to orient research on 'nonjournalistic' mass media industries in needed new directions is through a systematic explication of the relationship between the terms mass communication and entertainment. As the following sections will show, when a mass communication perspective is linked to a definition of entertainment industry, ways to connect studies of different media industries conceptually become quite clear. Linking the terms also suggests ways to study the interrelationships between media. By entering the field through these terms, enduring issues in the field take on a special vibrancy and a gamut of new challenges becomes apparent.

A Mass Communication Perspective

A mass communication perspective on mass media industries is one that encourages thinking about mass communication as a process that transcends particular media. Two propositions that begin to inform such a perspective are shared widely by researchers in this arena. The first is that mass media organizations release materials that are important from a societal standpoint. The premise centers on the idea that mass media provide unique potential for large numbers of otherwise different and unrelated people to orient around similar depictions of the world, despite individual differences in interpreting the depictions. The second proposition, articulated by thinkers as different as Karl Marx (see Murdock, 1982), Max Weber (1976), and Robert Park (1922), is that mass communication's unique potential for the broad sharing of depictions comes not just from the technology involved. Rather, it comes from the use of those instruments by large-scale organizations as they apply standards of mass production to the creation and dissemination of a wide variety of portrayals.

The premises suggest the following definition: Mass communication is the industrialized (mass) production, reproduction, and multiple distribution of messages through technological devices. Messages are linguistic or pictorial representations that appear purposeful. The word industrialized means the process is carried out by mass media industries – that is, by conglomerations of organizations that interact in the process of producing and distributing messages. The statement that mass communication involves the creation and dissemination of messages implies, then, that the activity is part of the larger social process of creating meaning. The definition proposes, however, that unlike attempts to understand the creation of meaning among individuals and in small groups, research on the production and dissemination of mass media messages requires seeing organizations and industries as the creators of meaning.

Obviously, organizations are made up of people. They are, to quote Howard Aldrich (1979), 'goal-directed, boundary maintaining activity systems'. His characterization highlights the essential social nature of organizations, yet it also underscores that organizations are not merely the sum of the individuals that constitute them – their particular personalities and backgrounds. Rather, as he says, they are 'products of, and constraints upon, social relations'. The roles that people take on as members of one organization tilt them in directions that might well be different from the ones they take on in other contexts.

It is the industrial application of technology for the production and distribution of messages to various places that provides the potential for reaching large, separate, diverse groups of people that make up society. The industrialization of communication in Western societies can be dated from the nineteenth century, when machines powered by steam or electricity (the steam-driven printing press, the movie camera, the record player) were joined to large, hierarchical organizations for the purpose of producing and distributing messages widely and cheaply. Note, however, that the definition presented here avoids setting requirements about the number and nature of people attending to the messages. Whether and how the production process influences, or is influenced by, the size and characteristics of the audience should be (and has been) a matter of discussion and empirical examination.

Many other issues regarding the activity, content, and consequences of mass communication can cascade directly from the definitions just presented. Yet a systematic mass communication *perspective* on media industries is most likely to emerge by formulating a view on the relationship between industrial process, message sharing, and the social fabric. Clearly, no single approach is likely to satisfy every thinker on the subject. What relationship exists between industrial process, message sharing, and the social fabric is a question that researchers have answered with a rather wide continuum of arguments about the connection between Western capitalist mass media and social power. At one end, political economists with a traditional Marxist orientation have insisted on a straightforward 'base-superstructure' model of that link (see, e.g., Garnham 1983; Murdock 1982; Gitlin 1979). They have argued that the fundamental elite-governed economic relationships in a society (the base) give rise to, are reflected in, and are reinforced by, mass media materials (the superstructure). Toward the other end of the continuum, 'culturalists' with a less determinist perspective on the relationship between media materials and power have insisted that Western mass media materials reflect a vast array of ideas about the world from a variety of viewpoints. They contend the media do that as part of the complex rituals in which all segments of population engage in order to build and repair the social order constantly (Newcomb and Hirsch 1982; Carey 1975).

Between these viewpoints is a panoply of others that imply different ideas about the base-superstructure relationship as well as about ritual, culture, the limits of argument and the diversity of ideas (Williams 1980; Hall 1982). Despite the disagreements, a few more propositions can be suggested from works in cultural anthropology (Geertz 1973; Turner 1977; Powdermaker 1951), industrial sociology (Touraine 1977), and communication research (Gerbner 1969 and 1974; Adorno 1954) that can bind a broad spectrum of researchers. One is that mass communication is a key vehicle through which the various actors (individuals and organizations) that make up society try to define themselves and others. Mass media (the technological devices used in mass communication) have the capacity to present cultural models – images of the forms and structures of life – to huge numbers of people in vivid form. Those models enact conduct by individuals along with the consequences of their conduct. In the course of doing that, they also portray the activities of institutions – the sets of organizations that hold power over education, business, the law, the military, medicine, and other aspects central to the life of individuals in society. Many accept the presentations as 'common sense', or 'the way it is', for others if not for them. But for some people the media images provoke discontent over the definitions society is sharing of itself. The media images lead them to want to place their version of individuals and institutions alongside the others in the media, to call attention to themselves, and to gain legitimacy for their beliefs.

A second proposition, related to the last one, is that the presentation of cultural models takes place through performance, most often through narrative performance. Telling stories about the social order is, in other words, the most important – and potentially most socially volatile – function of the sharing of messages. In Western society, a variety of storytelling forms have developed, with their own storytelling constraints and degrees of professionalization. Documentaries, newsmaker interviews, evening news spots and other types of news performances, for example, are expected to follow certain rules of facticity which fictional presentations need not observe. The rhetoric of 'truth claims', the professionalism that surrounds journalism, the aura of democratic importance news has within Western society, and the growth of journalism school faculties have all encouraged particular scholarly attention to the creation of news (for a review, see Whitney and Ettema 1987; also see Ettema and Glaser 1985). This proposition argues, however, that other forms of societal storytelling have equal, and perhaps even more profound, implication for the assimilation of cultural models and argumentation over them. Movies, songs, and sports presentations, for example, can let people in on certain ways of life, get them angry about certain values, make them feel good about their beliefs. The mass communication perspective therefore does not privilege news or any other form of performance in encouraging research on the industrialized creation and dissemination of messages.

All this leads to a third proposition: The messages of mass media, as well as arguments about the messages, speak to issues of position and power in society. Who gets depicted, what about them gets depicted, why, with what consequences, at what time, and in what situation – these are questions creators of all cultural models answer in the course of their work. The answers may carry substantial emotional and intellectual significance for those who come into contact with them. That sometimes can be noticed by simply gauging whether viewers or readers react angrily or enthusiastically to the output. Often, though, many people might feel comfortable with the cultural models presented; for them, the materials may represent what Gerbner (1972) terms a celebration of conventional morality. Still others may see in the depictions norms that are accepted by the larger society, even if they disagree with them. They may exercise a public tolerance of shared models.

But even when there a few loud public complaints about particular media materials, the struggle to control arguments still takes place. The reason is that on a daily basis a broad gamut of organizations, from banks to advertising agencies to public relations firms to government agencies to labor unions, routinely try to guide portrayals towards their interests by placing pressures on creators and distributors. A number of studies of Western media (Gitlin 1979; Schiller 1969 and 1989; Murdock 1982; Curran 1982; Turow 1984) have noted that dominant forces within a society have often managed to ensure that only ideologically compatible media organizations get hold of mainstream channels of communication. They have done it by ensuring that the basic legal and commercial terms through which industries are allowed to operate make it likely that only organizations with certain fundamental perspectives on the world could survive.

The mass communication perspective, then, directs researchers on mass media industries to understand how the industrialized creation and distribution of performances of all sorts relates to larger issues of power and the symbolic construction of society. What cultural models get enacted in which media, how, why, and with what consequences? A raft of unexplored and underexplored topics flow out of this question.

Understanding Entertainment

The concept of entertainment can help probe many of these areas, particularly those relating to nonjournalistic activities that cross industry boundaries. The first step to illustrating the utility of the term is to induce a definition. Entertainment derives from the Latin *tenere*, which means to hold or to keep steady, busy, or amused. The notion of making money off an audience by keeping it steady and amused remains central to those in the business of entertainment, as Erik Barnouw and Catherine Kirkland (1989) note:

> When a film or television program is classified [by its creators] as entertainment, the label implies that it is intended primarily to absorb the attention and to leave agreeable feelings. Any weightier roles of communication, such as education or persuasion, are assumed to take a back seat, in contrast to other types of content such as news, political communication, or advertising. Entertainment may indeed inform or persuade, but it is generally presumed that these effects are secondary or incidental and will not interfere with the real function of pleasant diversion. This assumption is embedded in such phrases as 'mere entertainment' and 'pure entertainment', and in the idea of entertainment as an escape from reality.

The foregoing excursion into etymology and familiar usage suggests a definition: Entertainment is performance (through narrative or non-narrative means, recorded or live) organized to attract audiences for personal satisfaction or financial profit rather than for explicitly educational, journalistic, political, or advertising goals. An entertainment industry, by extension, involves the interorganizational creation and release of performances to attract audiences for financial profit rather than for explicitly educational, journalistic, political, or advertising goals. The key factor distinguishing an organization creating entertainment from one creating other forms of media material, then, lies in the tradition of performance that is being followed. The people who make up entertainment organizations understand their work as being removed from the rhetorical approaches associated with didactic or persuasive forms of communication – news, education, and advertising as well as political argumentation and propaganda. The absence of an explicit tradition of didacticism or persuasion is what people mean when they use the term 'mere entertainment'.

It ought to be stressed that this conception of entertainment does not totally exclude attempts by creators to persuade or inform. Clearly many movies called entertainment by their production firms have been written and produced with the intention of making a political point (e.g. '*Mississipi Burning*') or an educational one ('*Holocaust*'). What should be clear, however, is that the underlying values and themes entertainment companies allow in their output are typically ones executives believe would not be obnoxious to most people in the target audience. Even more important from the standpoint of defining entertainment is that the primary concern of the organizations releasing the performance (though not necessarily the individual writers or directors) is with the economic viability, audience enjoyment, and technical quality of the work itself (often in that order), not with the fate of educational, commercial or political messages attached to it.

This approach is classically embodied in Hollywood mogul Sam Goldwyn's quip that messages are for Western Union telegrams, not his movies. The organizational stance is in part a protective strategy, in part a bid for credibility. As a protective strategy, it is a way to fend off groups that insist certain depictions constitute 'propaganda'. By encouraging the view that Hollywood movies, are not for political statements, studios discourage boycotts of their products. More important, they discourage perceptions that their products are less 'amusing' or 'diverting' than they might otherwise be.

It has already been noted that advertising cannot be considered entertainment since its performances involve explicit attempts at persuasion. Still, the advertising of entertainment is an integral aspect of an entertainment industry. So is the use of public relations (PR) and promotion to spread the word about entertainment products. Public relations calls attention to entertainment products by encouraging discussion of them across a variety of media (radio, TV, magazines) and performance types (talk, action-adventure, news). Promotion activities call attention to entertainment performances by associating them with T-shirts, soft drinks, computer games, theme parks, toys, and other commercial goods and services. Both public relations and promotion rely heavily on the need producers of other materials have for their works. PR people exploit the need by people who work in news and entertainment firms to come up with novel ideas quickly and inexpensively (see Gandy 1982, 1990; Turow 1983; Cheney and Vibbert 1987). Workers engaged in promoting entertainment know that many creators of goods and services expect that their products will sell better when associated with popular shows or characters.

Inclusion of advertising, public relations, and promotion in the discussion of an entertainment industry's activities, along with the mention of news as an outlet for industry publicity, points to the broad landscape on which the study of entertainment can take place. Entertainment, it should be clear, need not always be mass communication. A juggler in a city park is typically entertainment, whether or not mass media cover or broadcast it. Still, entertainment as big business in Western societies is almost always related in one way or another to the mass communication process. Broadway shows could not exist without media coverage, for example. Moreover, successful Broadway productions get turned into records, made into movies, discussed on TV, written up in magazines. Similar cross-media activities are the rule for other expensive 'live acts', from sporting events to rock concerts.

These activities suggest that an entertainment industry is best viewed not only in terms of general entertainment products associated with a particular technology – for example, movies or TV shows. The term might often be more useful as a construct of the interorganizational activities that form around particular narratives or other performances. From this standpoint, it is possible to see entertainment industries as creating and releasing specific performances that extend beyond individual products (books, movies, records, stage plays) to encompass all the concatenations and reverberations of those performances across a variety of locations. So, for example, one can speak of the entertainment industry that forms around the rock group New Kids on the Block or the fictional pop culture hero Dick Tracy. In the Tracy case, the entertainment industry may be seen as comprising the organizations involved in creating and distributing the Dick Tracy narrative in its various manifestations over five decades – from the comic strip to the serial films to cartoons, movies, T-shirts, watches, coats, lunch boxes, and other related matter.

For some it might be interesting to follow this process simply in order to point out the dimensions of cross-media activities or to track diffusion of various types of materials across mass media boundaries. From a mass communication perspective, though, the emphasis should be on the considerations which guide the industrialized creation and distribution of entertainment toward certain cultural models, and certain displays of social power in those models, along with possible implications of these processes for the larger society. The length of this essay permits pointing to only some of the many fascinating questions that spring to mind along these lines. The remaining pages will illustrate how a mass communication perspective on entertainment industries can help researchers explore a few key issues that apply across a variety of mass media industries. Some of the issues to be discussed are enduring in the sense that they have appeared in much work on individual media, though the work has not often related them to mass media processes generally. Other issues can be described as new concerns, since they speak directly to questions that arise as a result of the cross-media dynamics built into the concept of entertainment industries.

Some Enduring Issues

The Tension Between Innovation and Control

Probably the theme that most commonly threads through writings on the considerations that shape mass media material is that they are characterized by what Paul Hirsch and Paul DiMaggio (1976) call 'the constant and pervasive tension that exists between innovation and control', or resistance to innovation. The phenomenon has been entered in different ways, at different levels of abstraction. Most commonly, researchers have pointed out how pressures associated with the tasks of creating records (Frith 1989 and 1988; Denisoff 1975 and 1985), prime time television shows (Gitlin 1983; Cantor and Pingree 1983; Turow 1978), Hollywood movies (Gomery 1986; Bordwell, et al. 1985), children's books (Turow 1981) and other media materials lead them to develop routines that set limits on what can be created and released. Much of this work stresses the predictable patterns of content that result from these controls. A number of studies, however, also point to considerations that encourage innovations – that is, departures from the ordinary (Pekurney 1982; Johnstone and Ettema 1980; Turow 1982).

A key point to be made about these scattered studies is that they are often quite different from one another in the way they see change, continuity, and the reasons for them. Most relevant to the relationships between industrial process, entertainment, and social fabric are studies that focus on the way structures of institutional power are woven into the work of mass media organizations. These 'interinstitutional' studies typically trace broad relationships between entertainment producers and the institutions that impinge on them. Studies of the links between governments and media industries, nationally and transnationally, represent one broad category of research along these lines (e.g. Mosco 1982). Another group of studies looks historically and synchronically at relationships between nongovernmental entities and media producers. Examples are works on the interactions between the banking industry and the Hollywood studios (Wasko 1982), between advocacy groups representing various institutions and the television networks (Montgomery 1989), between the medical system and producers of fictional programs about medicine (Turow 1989), between the sports system and the television industry (Rader 1984), between celebrities from different walks of life and the industries that create their images (Braudy 1986).

A strength of interinstitutional research is that it inquires into both the historical contexts and the contemporary interorganizational activities that set the stage for certain media representations and not others. At the same time, interinstitutional researchers' concentration on broad patterns have led them to neglect close examination of the way interorganizational pressures get translated to the creation and distribution of particular entertainment materials. Scrutiny of that sort typically has been carried out by academics who adopt what might be called an 'industrial' approach. Industrial researchers tend not to be interested in the issues of hierarchy, authority, and cultural power. They seem content with going no further than pointing to direct industrial demands on message creation when explaining patterns of entertainment content.

So, for example, an industrial researcher might tie trends in TV depictions to the pragmatic needs of the production executives and their network counterparts. Interinstitutional researchers, by contrast, would investigate if larger societal forces outside the industry had direct or indirect influence over those developments. The conception of 'change' or 'innovation' relevant for study is also different between the two groups. Institutional researchers tend to look for fundamental shifts in cultural models, to assert that 'real' change rarely happens, and to focus, therefore, on continuities in the exercise and depiction of power. Industrial scholars, on the other hand, tend to be interested in considerations that cause change in even the most subtle features of storytelling (see, e.g., Pekurney 1982; Hirsch 1972; Intintoli 1984; Coser, Kadushin, and Powell 1982).

Despite these differences between the two research streams, many of the findings from the 'industrial' literature can be reconceptualized to illuminate concerns about cultural power implicit in the mass communication perspective. The challenge of future research is to explore particular entertainment industries in ways that incorporate the close organizational attention of the industrial research stream with the broad societal perspective of the interinstitutional approach. The aim should be to track with increasing clarity the way broad structures of power within and across societies insinuate themselves into the particular activities of those who create and distribute specific entertainment materials. A number of approaches from industrial and organizational sociology can help inform this sort of work. Theories of resource dependence (Pfeffer and Salancik 1978; Aldrich 1979) population ecology (Hannan and Freeman 1989), bank control (Glasberg 1981), bank hegemony (Mintz and Schwartz 1983), and class hegemony (Domhoff 1978; Useem 1982) hold the potential to speak to these issues in fascinating ways. Researchers on mass media industries have only recently begun to observe their usefulness (see Dimmick and Rothenbuler 1984; Turow 1984 and 1989; Wasko 1982).

The Importance of the Individual

The theories just noted hold in common the premise that structure rather than individual personalities shapes the operation of an organization or industry. The structure of an organization is the pattern of roles (that is, of interdependent activities) that have evolved among the various people who comprise the organization. Similarly, the structure of an industry comprises the role pattern that has evolved among the organizations that regularly interact to produce a product or service. An important step toward understanding the structure of an industry or organization – or of the entire interacting system of media industries – lies in grasping the historical events that have caused various elements of the organization, industry, or system to coalesce in a certain way. Role patterns may have their roots in critical incidents, power struggles, even national philosophies, that shaped them at birth or later. Many academics agree, in fact, that the structure of a mass media system ultimately reflects the overall power relations of the society in which it emerges and develops.

Still, to say that structure rather than individual personality is what counts in shaping media material is to state an arguable premise. Some scholarly writers (see Newcomb and Alley 1983; Newcomb and Hirsch 1984) and most popular chroniclers of the entertainment business (e.g. Bedell 1981; Gabler 1988) prefer to use personality and background rather than structure to explain entertainment industry activities. For researchers and policymakers, the choice of one or the other viewpoint is quite significant. A strict corrollary of the structural contention, for example, is that investigations of the social backgrounds and personal interests of writers, producers, directors, and other creators of entertainment are irrelevant to understanding their output. Another logical outgrowth of the structural view is that attempts to 'improve' racial, ethnic, class, and gender images in entertainment material by hiring people from those backgrounds will lead nowhere unless structural changes are made in the industry to allow new employees' initiatives to take root. On the other hand, the conviction that personality and background are key determinants can lead to explanations of media output that verges on name-calling and bigotry (Turow 1989).

Clearly, the issue need not be posed in terms of either industry structure or personal background. A more realistic way to proceed is to ask about the conditions under which the backgrounds, personalities, and personal interests of people who work in entertainment organizations 'make a difference' for the cultural models that are released to target audiences. Also important to study are the conditions under which certain organizational and industrial structures set boundaries for the leeway that personality traits and backgrounds are allowed in the creation of entertainment. Different entertainment industries may allow different degrees of personal 'freedom' to their creators. Who gets hired to enjoy that freedom, and what the boundaries of that freedom are, may be determined by a combination of personal factors and structural aspects of the organizational and institutional environment.

The Role of the Audience

Ultimately, of course, the materials created by entertainment industries are exhibited to, and judged, by, consumers in the society at large. How these people ought to be viewed and what their role is in the industrialized creation and distribution of cultural models is a subject that has been near the center of almost all discussions of mass media industries. Viewpoints on the nature and power of 'the audience' vary substantially. Most of the discussion has revolved around advertiser-sponsored television. Some researchers (e.g. Bauer 1971) insist that consumers have tremendous say in what is produced. 'Feedback' through market research is terribly important to TV organizations, they argue, since, after all, company profits depend on satisfying the audience. At the other end of the spectrum are those (Symthe 1977; Ewen 1976, 1988; Schiller 1989) who argue that the audience is essentially a commodity media practitioners sell to advertisers. This argument insists that over several decades advertisers have gotten people used to certain types of material, or have transmuted ('co-opted') what most people have liked, so that it can be used with continual updating as a vehicle to sell commercial products and the lifestyles of consumption.

Between these viewpoints is a range of opinions that emerge, mostly implicitly, in a variety of studies. Muriel Cantor, one of the few industry researchers who has shown an explicit and enduring concern with the audience, pointed out in the early 1970s (Cantor 1971) that the most immediate 'audience' for television producers are the network executives, not the people 'out there'. Her point was that the most proximate constraints necessarily take precedent over far-off concerns in the daily work of making television. Espinoza (1982), Intintoli (1984), and others have, however, noted that creators do think of their viewers in working on story development. And, in recent years Cantor has also insisted on the need to take account of the new fragmented TV environment when thinking of the audience's power. Cantor and Cantor (1986) have argued that contemporary concerns by TV executives with targeting particular groups instead of a 'mass audience', so that their programs will be attractive to advertisers, give those audience members more power than before to have their interests reflected in content.

Yet another way to understand the audience (Turow, 1982, 1984, 1992) casts its alleged power in a different light. This view distinguishes between an audience and a public. A public consists of the real individuals who make decisions to use or not use certain media materials. A mass media audience, by contrast, is a construct created by mass media industries to describe the groups who are being targeted by the creators and distributors. The demographic and psychographic categories production executives use to plan media materials – they speak, for example, of reaching women eighteen to thirty four years old who are 'belongers' – reflect the interests of the organizations (usually advertisers) that pay the creative costs. Market research is a way to find out about people – but only 'the right' people from a marketing standpoint, and only through questions that the production firms and their sponsors find useful. An audience, then, has the nature of its power defined by the industry that constructs it. The most interesting questions to ask from this viewpoint are about the way organizations construct audiences, the consequences that it has for the cultural models media industries release, and the arguments that may ensue when members of the public and public advocacy groups attempt to change both the audience images of producers and their cultural models.

Each of the foregoing views on the audience deserves to be confronted explicitly in research on entertainment industries. Especially needed is work on the implications of the audience at various stages of the same mass communication phenomenon. It is important, for example, to understand how audience images at the stage where marketing executives conduct interorganizational business differ from audience images at the point where the firm's producers, directors, and writers face the challenge of actually creating materials. The cross-media activities that are becoming increasingly common in entertainment industries undoubtedly lend even more complexity than before to the way organizations generate and handle audience images. An entertainment industry focus should also be helpful in encouraging research on audiences beyond TV. Rare are scholarly consideration of audiences in arenas, such as the book industry, that are not dependent on advertising. Never asked is how audience images within an entertainment industry change when a narrative moves from trade book to mass market paperback to magazine cover to movie.

Some New Concerns

The Power of Conglomerates Over Entertainment

The preceding example, along with others presented in this chapter, illustrates how the concept of an entertainment industry can add new slants to enduring scholarly questions about the mass communication process. Beyond new slants on old issues, however, a mass communication perspective on entertainment can raise cross-media concerns that have hardly been broached by researchers on mass media industries. During the past decade and a half many large media corporations have gathered under their umbrellas firms that represent production and distribution interests in a variety of mass media. Their goal increasingly is to link various corporate operations philosophically and practically. As a Gannett executive put it in the firm's in-house magazine (*The Ganetteer*, May 1982), conglomerate leaders know that 'as audiences become fragmented, the dollars available for programming [on any one channel] will decrease, because everyone's share of the audience will be smaller'.

One way to adjust for that is to move the creative material across as many media outlets as possible to justify production. So, corporate executives strive to interconnect interests, personnel, products, and services of many parts of their conglomerates so as to cover all media opportunities as efficiently as possible. Two related strategies underlie their efforts: (1) View the various companies of a media conglomerate as parts of a unified whole that should work together to move corporate products across new and old media; and (2) improve a conglomerate's ability to exploit its strengths across media by forging joint licensing, syndication, and public relations ventures with other established companies.

In effect, these activities make the media conglomerates fulcrums or central nodes for a number of entertainment industries. The Walt Disney Company, for example, has long orchestrated the movement of its characters and narratives across properties that it owns (theme parks, record companies, broadcast TV shows, cable channels, clothing stores) as well as those with which it establishes promotion and licensing agreements or cultivates public relations connections. The activities raise important questions about the control such conglomerates can or do exercise over the cultural models millions of people share across a variety of media channels.

The Politics of Producing Cross-National Entertainment

The developments just described are not limited to American firms. Conglomerates based outside the US such as Sony (Japan), Finninvest (Italy), Bertelsmann (Germany), Hachette (France), and News Corp (Australia) have been active internationally in the creation and dissemination of entertainment since the early 1980s. Most of the narratives and other performances that define entertainment still derive from American frames of reference, partly because the US is still the most lucrative single market, partly because American notions of entertainment have colonized much of the world (Schiller 1969; Tunstall 1977). Nevertheless, the shifts in ownership along with profound changes in the structure of Europe (both Western and Eastern) portend new approaches to making and marketing theatrical films, TV shows, records, and other mainstream entertainment vehicles. Research should focus on tracking the implications of these changes for the choice of creative personnel as well as for changes and continuities in the cultural models they depict. Here is the issue of organizational innovation and control applied to cross-media and cross-national planes.

The Relationship Between Entertainment and News

Also increasingly global is the relationship between entertainment and news. This issue is likewise not new. Statements such as 'news is more and more often being turned into entertainment' have appeared in both academic and popular literature for decades. Writers have long worried that in their pursuit of certain audiences news organizations have been abandoning journalistic norms and emphasizing audience enjoyment in choosing and shaping news narratives.

The mass communication perspective proposed here places the issue in a somewhat different light, however. As noted earlier, news and entertainment both encompass powerful forms of storytelling. The storytelling forms are different from one another, with different claims to audience attention and identification. Still, the cultural models portrayed across news and entertainment may enact similar depictions of the world. As an example, consider what might happen when TV viewers share network evening news program depictions of 'the drug war' in tandem with network TV series portraying it fictionally. The various portrayals may well have the ability to spark societal discussions on the drug war and to set the terms for that discussion. For many in the audience, TV fiction's suggestion of 'behind the scenes' realism – of underlying 'truth' – may well supplement and complement truth claims in the news stories. Others may find fault with certain portrayals. Still others may dismiss both news and entertainment programming as exaggerating the entire drug problem for commercial reasons. Whatever the opinions, however, the shared images would encourage discussion on certain societal phenomena and not others. If they agree on nothing else, viewers would probably share the notion that news and entertainment producers together consider 'the drug war' important.

The ability to direct societal discussions by coordinating depictions toward (and away) from certain subjects increases when conglomerates hold both news and entertainment firms under their corporate umbrellas. Open to investigation is the extent to which conglomerates use their avowedly journalistic outlets as ways to promote their wide-ranging entertainment properties and the cultural models that go with them. Of related interest is the way in which news executives act to cultivate audience belief in the journalistic integrity of their products while pursuing a strategy of linking news and entertainment organizations for the parent firm's profit.

One of the few examples of this phenomenon to reach the public stage is Time Warner's handling of author Scott Turow and his books *Presumed Innocent* and *The Burden of Proof*. At the precise time Warner Books was releasing *Presumed Innocent* in paperback and a few weeks before Warner Brothers was to release the film version of the narrative, *Time* magazine drew up a cover story on the author that trumpeted both the first book and the film.

Rival *Newsweek* magazine's subsequent sniping at Time Warner for what appeared to be a blatant attempt of corporate aggrandizement under the guise of journalism led to solemn denials by *Time* editors.[1] They insisted the Time Warner conglomerate had granted them autonomy to preserve both their journalistic integrity and their magazine's credibility (*Time*, July 2, 1990, p. 8). Little was clear in public versions of the controversy. It seems reasonable to suggest, however, that conglomerates' synergistic approaches to their journalistic and entertainment (and perhaps even education and political) holdings will increase in coming years.

Concluding Remarks

The preceding pages have implied that the study of entertainment industries from a mass communication perspective invariably raises questions that go beyond matters of organizational process and media content to those of media uses and consequences. The fundamental proposition underlying the perspective is that entertainment industries create and disseminate cultural models that are often shared broadly within a society across a variety of media. Exploring this proposition means adopting a societal, rather than individual, unit of analysis. It involves trying to understand models of society people share through the media, trying to follow the cultural argumentation that takes place throughout society as a result of the models, trying to track ways organizations and individuals attempt to exert control over those depictions, and trying to extrapolate implications that the organizational processes, cultural models, and cultural argumentation hold for structures of dominance, and reaction to dominance, in society.

These topics are intimately interrelated. Study of societal uses and consequences of mass media must go hand in hand with the study of the industries involved in the process of mass communication. The concept of an entertainment industry provides the intellectual space that is necessary to link theoretical and practical issues across domains that mass communication researchers hardly ever connect and often do not even mention. Many research avenues are open. There is much to learn.

Notes

1   It might be noted that *Newsweek*'s owner, The Washington Post Company, has nowhere near the cross-media property of *Time*'s parent, Time Warner. *Newsweek*'s sniping at rival *Time* took place as the trade press was forecasting Newsweek's declining appeal to Madison Avenue. Observers speculated that *Newsweek* would not be able to compete with *Time*'s decision to offer deep discounts to clients who purchased advertising on several Time Warner properties at the same time. Lacking *Time*'s conglomerate power, *Newsweek* could not offer fear such deals. The magazine's instigation of this public controversy about *Time* should, perhaps, be seen in the context of this corporate jealousy, and fear.

References

ADORNO, T., 1954: 'How To Look at Television', *Quarterly of Film, Radio, and Television* 8.

ALDRICH, H., 1979: *Organizations and Environments*. Englewood Cliffs, New Jersey: Prentice Hall.

BARNOUW, E. and KIRKLAND, C., 1989: 'Entertainment', *Encyclopedia of Communication*. New York: Oxford University Press.

BAUER, R. A., 1971: 'The Obstinate Audience: The Influence Process From the Point of View of Social Communication', in Schramm, W. and Roberts, D. (eds) *The Process and Effects of Mass Communication*. Urbana, Illinois: University of Illinois Press.

BEDELL, S., 1981: *Up The Tube: Prime Time TV and the Silverman Years*. New York: Viking Press.

BORDWELL, D., THOMPSON, K., STAIGER, J., 1985: *The Classical Hollywood Cinema: Film Style and Mode of Production to 1960*. New York: Columbia University Press.

BRAUDY, L., 1986: *Frenzy of Reknown: Fame and its History*. New York: Oxford University Press.

CANTOR, M., 1971: *The Holywood TV Producer: His Work and His Audience*. New York: Basic Books.

CANTOR, M. and CANTOR, J., 1986: 'Audience Composition and Television Content: The Mass Audience Revisited', in Ball-Rokeach, S. and Cantor, M., *Media, Audience, and Social Structure*. Beverly Hills: Sage.

CANTOR, M. and PINGREE, S., 1983: *The Soap Opera*. Beverly Hills: Sage Publications.

CAREY, J., 1975: 'A Cultural Approach to Communication', *Communication* 2:1.

CHENEY, G. and VIBBERT, S., 1987: 'Corporate Discourse, PR, and Issues Management', in Jablin, F., Putnam, L., Roberts, K. and Porter, T., *Handbook of Organizational Communication*. Newbury Park, California: Sage Publications.

CONNERS, T., 1982: *Longman Dictionary of Mass Media and Communication*. New York: Longman, 1982.

COSER, L., KADUSHIN, C., and POWELL, W., 1982: *Books: The Culture and Commerce of Publishing*. New York: Basic Books.

CURRAN, J., 1982: 'Communications, Power, and Social Order', in Gurevitch, M., Bennett, T., Curran, J., and Woollacott, J. 1982: *Culture, Society, and the Media*. London: Methuen.

DENISOFF, R. S., 1975: *Solid Gold: The Popular Record Industry*. New Brunswick, N.J., Transaction Books.

DENISOFF, R. S., 1986: *Tarnished Gold: The Record Industry Revisited*. New Brunswick, N.J.: Transaction.

DIMMICK, JOHN and ROTHENBULER, ERIC, 1984: 'The Theory of Niche: Quantifying Competition Among Media Industries', *Journal of Communication* 34: 1 (Winter), pp. 103–119.

ESPINOSA, P., 1982: 'The Audience in the Text: Ethnographic Observations of a Hollywood Story Conference', *Media, Culture, and Society* 4.

ETTEMA, J. and GLASER, J., 1985: 'On the Epistemology of Investigative Journalism', *Communication* 8.

ETTEMA, J. and WHITNEY, D. C., 1987: 'Professional Mass Communicators', In Berger, C. and Chaffee, S., *Handbook of Communication Science*. Newbury Park, California: Sage Publications.

EWEN, S., 1976: *Captains of Consciousness: Advertising and the Social Roots of Commercial Culture*. New York: McGraw Hill.

EWEN, S., 1988: *All Consuming Images: The Politics of Style in Contemporary Culture*. New York: Basic Books.

FRITH, S., 1987: 'The Industrialization of Popular Music', in Lull, J. (ed.), *Popular Music and Communication*. Beverly Hills, California: Sage Publications.

FRITH, S. (ed.), 1989: *Facing the Music*. New York: Pantheon.

GABLER, N., 1988: *An Empire of their Own: How the Jews Invented Hollywood*. New York: Crown.

GANDY, O., 1981: *Beyond Agenda Setting*. Norwood, New Jersey: Ablex.

GANDY, O., 1990: 'Public Relations and Public Policy: The Structuration of Dominance in the Information Age', in Toth, E. and Heath, R. (eds), *Rhetorical and Critical Approaches to Public Relations*. Hillsdale, New Jersey, Lawrence Erlbaum Associates.

GARNHAM, N., 1983: 'Toward a Theory of Cultural Materialism', *Journal of Communication* 33.

GEERTZ, C., 1973: *The Interpretation of Cultures*. New York: Basic Books.

GERBNER, G., 1969: 'Institutional Pressures on Mass Communicators', *Sociological Review Monograph* 13.

GERBNER, G., 1972: 'Communication and Social Environment', *Scientific American* 227.

GERBNER, G., 1974: 'Teacher Image in Mass Culture: Symbolic Functions of 'Hidden Curriculum'', in Olsen, D. (ed.), *Media and Symbols, Part 1*. Chicago, National Society for the Study of Education.

GITLIN, T., 1983: *Inside Prime Time*. New York: Pantheon.

GITLIN, T., 1979: 'Prime Time Hegemony', *Social Problems* 26:3.

GOMERY, D., 1986: *The Hollywood Studio System*. New York: St. Martin's Press.

HALL, S., 1982: 'The Rediscovery of 'Ideology': Return of the Repressed in Cultural Studies', in Gurevitch, M., Bennett, T., Curran, J., and Woollacott, J., *Culture, Society, and the Media*. London: Methuen.

HANNAN, M. and FREEMAN, J., 1989: *Organizational Ecology*. Cambridge, Massachusetts: Harvard University Press.

HIRSCH, P., 1972: 'Processing Fads and Fashions', *American Journal of Sociology* 77.

HIRSCH, P. and DIMAGGIO, P., 1976: 'Production Organizations in the Arts', *American Behavioral Scientist*, 19.

INTINTOLI, J., 1984: Taking Soaps Seriously: *The World of 'The Guiding Light'*. New York: Praeger.

JOHNSTONE, J. and ETTEMA, J., 1980: *Positive Images: Breaking Stereotypes with Children's Television*. Newbury Park: Sage Publications.

MODLESKI, T. (ed.), 1986: *Studies in Entertainment*. Bloomington and Indianapolis: Indiana University Press.

MOSCO, V., 1982: *Pushbutton Fantasies: Critical Perspectives on Videotex and Information Technologies*. Norwood, New Jersey: Ablex.

MURDOCK, G., 1982: 'Large Corporations and the Control of Communication Industries', in Gurevitch, M., Bennett, T., Curran, J., and Woollacott, J., *Culture, Society, and the Media*. London: Methuen.

NEWCOMB, H. and ALLEY, R. (eds), 1983: *The Producer's Medium: Conversations with Creators of American TV*. New York: Oxford University Press.

NEWCOMB, H. and HIRSCH, P., 1984: 'Television as a Cultural Forum: Implications for Research', in Rowland, W. and Watkins, B., *Interpreting Televison*. Beverly Hills: Sage Publications.

PARK, R. E., 1922: The *Immigrant Press and its Control*. New York, Harper and Row.

PEKURNEY, R., 1982: 'Coping With Television Production', in Whitney, D. C. and Ettema, J. (eds) *Mass Communicators in Context*. Beverly Hills: Sage Publications.

POWDERMAKER, H., 1952: *Hollywood: The Dream Factory*. New York: Little, Brown.

SCHILLER, H., 1989: *Mass Communication and the American Empire*, Boston, Beacon Press.

SCHILLER, H., 1969: *Culture Inc.: The Corporate Takeover of Public Expression*. New York: Oxford University Press.

SMYTHE, D., 1977: 'Communication: Blindspot of Western Marxism', *Canadian Journal of Political and Social Theory* 1:3, pp. 1–27.

TOURAINE, A., 1977: *The Self-Production of Society* (Translated by D. Coleman), Chicago: University of Chicago Press.

TUNSTALL, J., 1977: *The Media Are American*. New York: Columbia University Press.

TURNER, V., 1977: 'Process, System, and Symbol: A New Anthropological Synthesis', *Daedalus* 106:2.

TUROW, J., 1978: 'Casting for Television: The Anatomy of Social Typing', *Journal of Communication* 28.

TUROW, J, 1979: *Getting Books to Children*, Chicago: American Library Association.

TUROW, J., 1982: 'The Role of the Audience in Publishing Children's Books', *Journal of Popular Culture* 16.

TUROW, J., 1982: 'Unconventioal Programs on Commercial Network Television', in Whitney, D. C. and Ettema, J. (eds), *Mass Communicators in Context*. Beverly Hills: Sage Publications.

TUROW, J., 1983: 'Local Television: Producing Soft News', *Journal of Communication* 33:2.

TUROW, J., 1984: *Media Industries: The Production of News and Entertainment*. New York: Longman.

TUROW, J., 1985: 'Cultural Argumentation and the Media', *Communication* 8.

TUROW, J., 1989: 'Roots and Routes' (Book review of *An Empire of their own*), *Journal of Communication* 39.

TUROW, J., 1989: *Playing Doctor: Television, Storytelling, and Medical Power*. New York: Oxford University Press.

TUROW, J., Media Systems in Society: Understanding Industries, Strategies and Power. New York: Longman

WASKO, J., 1982: *Movies and Money: Financing the American Film Industry*. Norwood, New Jersey: Ablex.

WASKO, J., 1989: 'What's So "New" About the "New" Technologies in Hollywood' in Dervin, B., Grossberg, L., O'Keefe, B. and Wartella, E. (eds), *Rethinking Communication Volume* 2. Newbury Park, California: Sage Publications.

WATSON, J. and HILL, A., 1984: *A Dictionary of Communication and Media Studies*. London: Edward Arnold.

WEBER, M., 1976: 'Towards a Sociology of the Press', *Journal of Communication* 26:3.

WILLIAMS, R., 1976: *Keywords: A Vocabulary of Culture and Society*. New York: Oxford University Press, 1986.

WILLIAMS, R., 1980: 'Base and Superstructure in Marxist Cultural Theory', in Williams, R., *Problems in Material Culture*. London: New Left Books.

9

The Globalization of Electronic Journalism

Michael Gurevitch

Introduction

The notion of globalization has become one of the more common, rather overused buzzword of our times. Often accurately, sometimes hyperbolically, all manner of events, processes, products and ideas, from political and military conflicts, to the organization of industrial production, to consumer products, to markets, to culture, both 'high' and 'popular', are endowed with a global embrace. Yet perhaps in no other field has globalization become so immediately visible as in television generally, and television news specifically. Every television viewer witnesses the process every day.

Overuse of a concept leads, inevitably, to its trivialization. Much of the discussion of the globalization of the media, both in the media themselves and often also in the academic literature, is either platitudinous, repetitive, or soaked in the aura of 'high tech'. The great 'media events' of our time, such as the live broadcasting of the landing on the moon, or of the explosion of the Challenger, or of sports events such as the Olympic games, are invoked to illustrate and dramatize the marvels of the new technologies. Less attention is paid to questions concerning the social, cultural, economic and political antecedents and consequences of this 'communication revolution'. A 'blue Skies' psychology seems to permeate the discussion, according to which this 'revolution' will bring people and nations together, shrink our world and turn it into McLuhan's prophesied 'global village'. It is a perspective based on the implicit assumption that 'communication is a good thing'; that tensions and conflicts stem from 'breakdowns in communication', and that if we could only have 'better communication' a more harmonious global order will come about.

To be sure, the other side of that coin has also been argued forcefully. The seemingly boundless optimism about the potential promises expected to emerge from the 'communication revolution' has been countered by critics who raised two related objections: first, there were those who saw in an unbridled tide of global communication genuine threats to the autonomy and the viability of the cultures of weaker and more dependent societies, primarily indigenous Third World cultures, but also the cultures of some First World societies, whose 'authenticity' and uniqueness were seen as perilously vulnerable to the products of Hollywood and US television. (Note, for example, the publication in 1989 of the European Community Green Paper, *Television without Fron-*

tiers, designed, amongst other things to create 'a trade barrier' to limit American entertainment imports – in the name of national cultural 'preservation' (Smith 1991), or the debate in France, a few years ago, about the pernicious effects of 'Dallas'. Second, questions were raised about the economic, political and ideological interests being served by an unlimited and 'free' flow of communication. Were these, the critics asked, indeed 'technologies of freedom', (in Ithiel Pool's (1983) memorable phrase), or did they actually threaten to undermine the capacity of weaker countries to structure their national media systems, and formulate their own national communication policies according to their own lights?

The challenge for students of international communication is to 'get a conceptual grip, beyond the language of gee-whizzery, on an escalating yet formless, sprawling and globe-shaking process that may be impinging on people's senses of their places in the world and on the power of regimes to effect their wills within it' (Blumler 1989). Although in this chapter we do not intend to confront this challenge fully, we wish to depart from the arguments referred to above, which for the most part date back to the heyday of the debate about 'media imperialism' in the 1970s, and instead, explore the impact of one aspect of that process, namely the globalization of television news, on the *shifting balance of relationships of dependency* in a number of areas: between notionally dominant and subordinate national media systems; between media institutions and political institutions; inside the television industries, between national and 'local' television news services; between television encoders and audience decoders. But before we embark on that discussion, a brief description of the institutional structures involved in the globalization of television news is in order.

The Institutional Structures

Claims concerning the globalization of the news media are not, of course, new or even recent (see, for example, Schramm 1959 and Hachten 1987). The printing press crossed national and cultural boundaries long before television. The international news agencies have been in the business of disseminating news materials around the world for almost a century and a half (Boyd-Barrett 1980; Fenby 1986). Radio and films were oblivious to national boundaries almost since their inception. Yet the advent of satellite technology, facilitating the instant transmission of visual materials around the world, may be argued to have ushered in a qualitatively new stage in the globalization of news.

On what grounds do we make this claim? Our reasons are two-pronged. First, we would argue that the institutional arrangements for transmitting and exchanging television news materials, spawned by the availability of satellite technology, have transformed the organizational structures engaged in the global dissemination of news materials, toward a greater decentralization of the system. Second, we argue that the differences between the flexibility and degree of 'openness' of verbal vs. visual texts (see, for example, Fiske 1987) render the dissemination of visual materials qualitatively different from the 'old' system of news transmission by the wire agencies.

The deployment of satellite technology for use in the global dissemination of television news has not only extended the reach and increased the speed with which visual news materials are transmitted around the globe, but has also led to the setting up of new institutional arrangements dedicated to the international dissemination of television news materials (Sherman and Ruby 1974; Kressley 1978; Fisher 1980; Eugster 1983; Lanispuro 1987). At least three 'arms' of that system need to be identified here:

1   The international television news agencies Visnews and WTN (Worldwide Television News), outgrowths of the 'traditional' news agencies Reuters and UPITN, distribute television news materials around the clock, both in the form of 'raw' footage and in the form of complete stories, to television news organizations around the world.

2   International satellite delivered news services, such as the US based CNN and the British-based *Super Channel* and *Sky News* provide fully-shaped television news programs via satellite. Of these three, CNN's reach is the widest, indeed nearly global. For this reason it is probably one of the most significant actors on the global news scene.

3   Systems of television news exchanges operate under the umbrellas of a number of regional broadcasting organizations, such as the European Broadcasting Union, the Asian Broadcasting Union, the Arab States Broadcasting Union and Intervision, serving the Eastern Bloc countries.

These three arms, and the US television networks, are linked in a complex interlocked system of international distribution and exchange of television news materials.

The International Television News Agencies

The international television news agencies, outgrowths of the global wire agencies – UP and Reuters – and functioning along the same lines (but replacing words with pictures) play a central role in the globalization of electronic journalism. The three major international agencies, the London-based Worldwide Television News (WTN, formerly UPITN, owned by Independent Television News and United Press International), and Visnews, (owned by Reuters, the BBC and NBC), and CBS Newsfilm provide the regional news exchange systems with news footage from around the world, and are therefore essential to the functioning of the news exchange systems. The European news exchange organization, Eurovision, whose own story sources are confined to its European member countries, looks to the agencies for the first coverage of big non-European stories; to topical hard news coverage from the third world and other areas outside of Europe, and to sports news, 'soft' stories and other off-beat stories that relieve the 'bulletin gloom factor' (Mahoney 1975; Fenby: 1985). Stories offered by Eurovision's member stations are preferred to stories matched by the news agencies, but often the news agency story serves to reassure the news coordinators and news editors that the stories supplied by the member country is complete and accurate. A news agency story is often perceived as free from 'political motivation' and hence as more objective (Mahoney 1975; Fisher 1980).

This faith in the news agencies' 'objectivity' is driven by the assumption that pictures are more 'objective' than words. The agencies themselves reinforce this faith through the 'dope sheets' they produce to accompany and 'explain' the news footage they provide. These are written in a style that aims to be as 'neutral' as a descriptive narrative can possibly be, in order to be acceptable to a diverse range of news editors in different countries and to meet the ideological sensitivities of news services in over 100 countries. This is accomplished by the avoidance of all potentially controversial terminology and adherence to a 'minimalist' language. The imperative to be non-judgemental extends even in extreme cases, as a Visnews executive tells it:

> If the PLO bomb a bus load of kids in Tel Aviv, Visnews would not describe that as an atrocity; we would not describe the PLO as terrorists, nor would we describe them as freedom fighters; nor would we, ourselves, refer to that specific event as a tragedy. We might well quote somebody else as saying it was a tragedy. The reason is quite simple. To many of our subscribers, the PLO blowing up a bus load of children anywhere might be a victory for the oppressed people of Palestine. There are no militarists in *Visnews*; there are no freedom fighters. We have to choose this very precise middle path.

Ironically, this extreme 'objectivity' can have the opposite consequences, since 'raw materials' are highly vulnerable to manipulation for different story-telling purposes. Indeed, it is easy to see how the 'raw' footage supplied by the agencies may be used for a variety of editorial purposes by television news editors around the world. Anecdotal evidence of this was related by a member of WTN's bureau in Tel Aviv. During an especially cold winter spell in Europe a few years ago, a cameraman on the bureau's staff suggested a story that could appeal to freezing European television viewers. He went to the Tel Aviv waterfront and shot some footage of bathers splashing in the sea, (thus attempting to illustrate the different, milder climate). The footage was duly sent to WTN's headquarters in London, and from there was transmitted to WTN's clients. WTN's bureau chief in Tel Aviv, who regularly monitored the news on Jordanian Television, was surprised the following evening to see their footage on Jordan Television's news broadcast, used to illustrate a story about the decline of tourism to Israel. The pictures did, indeed, show a rather sparsely populated beach.

The risk of manipulation is not the only problem inherent in the emergence of global video wire services. As Powell (1990) puts it, if news editors around the world will start building their newscasts from universally available pool pictures,

> news coverage will have evolved into a video commodity, as anonymous and bland as any product on the future exchanges. and there is another hazard: Very little foreign news footage is tagged and attributed to its source. Yet in most countries the originating agency is the government-run television network. Editors who would never approve stories filed by official propaganda writers may routinely approve the use of video shot and edited by government agencies.

The 'modus operandi' of the international news agencies is thus almost identical to that of their progenitors, the international wire agencies. The only differences may stem from the fact that the latter work with words, while the former trade in pictures.

The News Exchange System

While the first two 'arms' of the globalized news system referred to earlier constitute coherent, centralized organizations, the global news exchange system is a rather decentralized, loose grouping of regional news exchange organizations. The process of decentralization and the emergence of a supranational system can be observed in the structure and operational mode of the European news exchange system.

Internally, each of these regional organizations is based on collaboration between its constituent national broadcasting services. Through a constant flow of telex messages and daily closed circuit telephone conferences between specially designated 'news coordinators' and news liaison personnel based in the broadcasting organizations in different countries, an on-going exchange of information is maintained about the availability of, and the interest in visual materials of news events (Lantenac 1975; Lindmuller 1988). The news exchange services and agencies then provide the technical support arrangements for receiving and sending news materials via satellite to those news organizations who expressed an interest in them.

Fourteen of the 33 EBU members provide news coordinators for the daily exchange. The duties of the news coordinators are essentially those of 'gate keeping', relating to the selection and choice of stories to be sent on the exchange system and to determining questions of priority – both on selection of items and choice between different offerings on the same story. Perhaps the most sensitive part of their job involves the need to consider the needs of all the members' services and to make selection decisions that reflect supra-national considerations. They are required to transcend their own national news interests and to adopt a cross-cultural, 'global' news perspective (Lantenac 1975: 12). In the words of one news coordinator, an employee of SRG (the Swiss Radio and Television service):

> When I am coordinating for Eurovision, I just forget SRG. I do my work on a Eurovision basis and if something comes up that SRG would have liked to have they have always the means of taking the unilateral (i.e. a one member feed) to get the material.

The requirement of serving a 'global' clientele is especially significant in the first satellite feed of the day (dubbed EVN-0), which contains stories chosen solely on the judgement of the news coordinator. Later feeds reflect the needs and wants of the different broadcasting organizations, as expressed during the editorial teleconference. Usually, when a story is 'bought' by three or more members it is incorporated into the satellite feed. But it is not uncommon for the news coordinator to continue to hold on to a story with an eye on future EVNs, even if there is not enough immediate demand for it.

Despite initial pessimism that the news coordinators would be 'biased' in their pre-selection, experience and analysis have shown that they conform to the general consensus: on over ninety out of 100 items, their choices would have been the same as the outcome of a general consultation (Lantenac: 12). The similarity in news judgements reflects a remarkably high degree of shared news values in countries with highly varied political ideologies and perspectives on the functions of the media. These shared news values are reflected in the preference for hard news stories that are likely to be of interest to most, or all members, and are the outcome of a shared news culture based on mutual understanding, and born out of daily interaction (as well as at least bi-annual face-to-face meetings of all news coordinators). More generally the shared news judgement is also based on a shared vision of the EBU. As one of the news coordinators put it: 'Any agenda that the EBU has is an agenda put to it by its members . . . We are a service organization. The members decide if there is to be any agenda'. He also agreed with our judgement that the news coordinator role is not 'programmatic' but rather is one of a 'facilitator'.

Given this community of shared professional values and judgement, the task of selecting the news stories to be shared becomes highly routinized, almost as if the system was operating on automatic pilot. The global news gatekeepers and coordinators become 'traffic cops', regulating the stop-and-go of information, rather than selectors of news stories, operating their own independent judgements. In fact, as news selectors and coordinators must serve and satisfy *other news editors*, (rather than the general viewing audience) it is not surprising that their decisions tend to reflect even more loyally the journalistic consensus on news values. Thus, news is news and 'everybody' knows it. Thus, this relatively small group of 'news coordinators' and liaison personnel perform a primarily 'gate-keeping' function, albeit on a global basis. They constitute a 'global newsroom', in many ways much like the newsrooms observed by White (1950) and Breed (1955).

Toward North-South parity?

The significance of the operations of the news exchange system has to do not only with its contribution to the globalization of the flow of television news materials but also with its implications for the relationships of dependency implied in the traditional argument about 'media imperialism', according to which western media institutions and interests dominated the global media system, and served as the back door for the reintroduction of western economic and cultural influences into Third World countries (e.g. Tunstall 1977, UNESCO 1980).

Our argument is based on observations of the operations of the Eurovision News Exchange system, conducted during 1987. In the course of these we observed the relationship between the European and other regional news exchange organizations, primarily Asiavision and Intervision, and formed the impressions that the global system is becoming increasingly decentralized, and that the relationships between the various regional organizations reflect their *interdependence*, rather than dependence and domination. We noticed, for example, a considerable degree of give and take between the European and the Asian systems, more adequately characterized as peer relationships than as dominant and subordinate systems. Admittedly, our evidence is impressionistic, yet it seems that the era in which two or three global news agencies dominated the flow of world news from bases in London, Paris or New York, requiring that news stories be channelled to the centers before being disseminated again outward toward the 'periphery', is being gradually superseded by one in which Tokyo and Kuala Lumpur (the coordinating centers for Asiavision) play a role more on par with the one played by the centers of the EBU news exchange system in the various European capitals. More recently, an agreement signed in September 1990 between CBS News and the Japanese Tokyo Broadcasting System (TBS) points in the same direction. By mid-1991 CBS News and TBS expect to have merged their news bureaus and field coverage throughout the world, 'creating the world's most expensive system of satellite news-gathering' (Powell 1990). Considering CBS News' historical position as the unassailable flagship of American television news, the prospect of a combined US-Japanese newsgathering organization must provide compelling evidence of the changes that took place in the relationships of dependency between Eastern and Western news organizations over the last decade.

We should not, however, accept the evidence pointing toward greater interdependence and potential parity without considering at the same time some counter evidence. The apparent availability of CNN's transmissions in (according to latest figures) 127 countries around the world could arguably provide fresh support for the weary 'media imperialism' thesis. CNN provides, inevitably, an American perspective on domestic as well as 'foreign' (i.e. non-American) events. Its newscasts are, by definition, impervious to the process of domestication that characterizes the processing of news stories by editors working within the culture and meaning systems of their own societies. Hence the argument that CNN represents a renewed and revised instance of US influence on, if not domination of, globalized news. The 'threat' of such influence inheres not only in the dissemination of a US-centered view, but also in the impact it might have on television newspersons around the world as a professional 'role model'. But while the consequences of CNN's ubiquitous availability should not be underestimated (in fact, CNN's actual impact has not, as yet, been documented empirically and it remains the subject of speculation), it should also be noted that CNN remains, of course, an alternative (rather than the main) news service in the many countries where it is available, and that because of the language requirements its audience is necessarily confined to the elite. These factors must mitigate to some extent the potential impact of CNN's feared global reach.

Thus, the significance of the regional news exchange organizations, as well as of the international news agencies and services such as CNN, as contributors to the globalization of electronic journalism goes beyond their role as disseminators of news materials. It lies equally in the way they have institutionally sidestepped national ideological differences in favor of regional cooperation, and in the way they have elevated the professional ideology of Western journalism to supra-national status.

Television's Many Roles and Power Relationships

All discussion of the mass media are ultimately concerned with the issue of power. Although different schools of thought have conceptualized the issue in different ways, and have defined and studied the power of the media differently, the underlying rationale for their concern is the same: the media should be examined because they wield considerable power and influence in modern societies. Power, however, does not exist on its own. Rather, it is manifested only in the context of interactions and relationships, whether between individuals, institutions or societies. The power of the media can therefore be examined only in relational contexts. Our argument is that the globalization of television has enhanced the role of television in ways that had a formative impact on these relationships, and hence on the 'balance of power' between the media and other social institutions, primarily the institutions of power in society – government and other political institutions.

The enhancement of the roles, and the powers, of television can be traced to its emergence, in the era of instant global communication, as an *active participant in the events it purportedly 'covers'*. Television can no longer be regarded (if it ever was) as a mere observer and reporter of events. It is inextricably locked into these events, and has clearly become an integral part of the reality it reports. The notion that television, and the media generally, should be more properly regarded as participants in the world they report on, rather than observers has for many years, and still is, a controversial one. For it challenges one of the central tenets of western journalism, namely that the media should stand 'outside, and be detached from, the subjects of their reporting, if they are to be true to the norms of objectivity, impartiality and neutrality'. They must observe events and relate them to their audiences as if from the perspective of 'God's eye'.

But in spite of the hallowed status of this position, this 'norm of apartness' is clearly flawed, both empirically and conceptually. Journalists cannot extricate themselves from their societal context, either physically, socially or culturally, any more than other members of society can. They cannot, therefore, claim – and hence should not pretend to – be able to observe the social world as if they were not part of it, as if from a position 'floating' above it. Wherever they appear, and whichever event they 'cover', they inevitably become a part of the environment which they observe and of the event they report. There is nothing new, of course, about this argument. Yet it is worth re-stating here because the rapid globalization of television news has established the participatory nature of television news as more crucial and fraught with consequences than ever before. Nowhere is this more dramatically visible than at the international level.

The International Level

The role that television now plays in the conduct of international relations is merely an extension onto the international level of the actively participatory role that the media have always played in the lives of societies. But the dramatic expansion of the stage upon which television now performs this role – from a national/societal onto a global one – has endowed it with a qualitatively new and sharper edge. This is especially the case in times of social and political turmoil, of rapid and revolutionary social change, or in periods of international crises. The capacity of television, utilizing satellite technology, to tell the story of an event *as it happens*, simultaneously with its unfolding, can have direct consequences for the direction that the event might take. Some of more memorable examples of this recently are television's coverage of the Gulf war, its reporting of the revolutionary events in Eastern Europe in 1989, and the role played by television in the student uprising in Tiananmen Square in Beijing in 1988.

The presence of television cameras impacted on these events in some significant ways. Consider the following:

- First, in each of these cases television created a global audience for the event. Probably never before was the claim that 'the whole world is watching' so true and apt. Interestingly, the events that attract a global audience can be quite varied. They range from the obvious ones – wars (in the Persian Gulf) and acts of terrorism and other political violence, to revolutions, (such as the transformation, peaceful and otherwise, of the regimes of Eastern Europe in the late 1980s), to uprisings, (such as the Chinese students ill-fated demonstration in Tiananmen Square in 1988 or the Palestinian Intifada), to dramatic scientific/political events, such as the landing on the moon; sports events like the Olympics, or 'human interest' stories, such as the plight of three whales under the Alaskan ice. The diverse nature of these events suggests that the rationale for their global dissemination stems less from their inherent significance for a global audience (however that significance is defined) than from their 'newsworthiness', an attribute bestowed on events by media practitioners. Thus, it is television, rather than the events themselves, that transformed the city squares and other sites in which these events took place into a global stage, watching these events.

- Second, the consequent global publicity given to these events by 'live' television undoubtedly influences the behavior of the actors or the protagonists involved. Clearly, the publicity enjoyed by the demonstrating students in Tiananmen Square helped to sustain the demonstration and was probably taken into account by the Chinese authorities, perhaps first constraining their response and later hastening it. Large scale publicity probably also acts as a mobilizer, leading the yet uninvolved to get involved. For example, the call for mass demonstrations in Wenceslas Square in Prague in 1989 publicized by television, was apparently responsible for recruiting even more demonstrators and, indeed, to engulf the whole society in the process of political change. The fall of the Berlin Wall in the glare of the television cameras undoubtedly endowed this event with an even greater symbolic value than it might have had, had it not been witnessed 'live' by countless millions around the world.

- Third, global television assumes a significant role in the construction of world public opinion. As Blumler (1989) puts it:

> The news media are not only a selectively-focusing and agenda setting force in international affairs. They are also a world-opinion defining agency. For at present, they virtually have a monopoly over the construction of world opinion, its agenda of prime concerns, and its main targets of praise and blame. At present, at least, what they tell us about what world opinion apparently holds on a certain matter can rarely be double-checked by international opinion poll results.

It should, of course, be noted that the role played by the media in the construction of world opinion is an extension, onto a global scale, of the similar role they play in their own societies. However, whereas public opinion in a given society is typically tapped through surveys and polls – thus being a construct of the pollsters' work – *global* public opinion is, of course, wholly a media construction. In the absence of global polls or other similar 'hard' evidence, global public opinion is inevitably a product of media practices.

● Fourth, television acts as a 'go between', a channel of communication, especially in instances in which hostile relationships between governments tend to preclude direct contacts. One of the more celebrated examples of television's capacity to open up such channels of communication is the role imputed to US television in bringing about the visit by the Egyptian President, Anwar Sadat to Jerusalem. The news people who 'mediated' between the Egyptian President and the Israeli Prime Minister may or may not deserve credit for Sadat's trip, but at the very least they created a channel of communication where no other *public* one existed, and through which the opposing leaders appeared to communicate with each other *almost* directly.

A number of recent examples suggest that globalized television sometimes assumes not merely the role of a 'go between' but may launch reportorial initiatives that tend to blur the distinction between the roles of reporters and diplomats. The Sadat-Begin 'dialogue' is one case in point. More recently, discussing American television's coverage of the Persian Gulf crisis, a *Washington Post* columnist dubbed it 'teleplomacy'. He referred to the scramble by television reporters and news anchors to interview the Iraqi President, in the course of which the interviewers slid, almost imperceptibly, into the roles of advocates, as if representing their own government, and negotiators, exploring with their interviewee avenues for resolving the crisis.

Such 'extra-professional' behaviour raises questions and some criticism of the performance of television journalists and its consequences. It has been argued, for example, that the scramble to secure the first interview with Saddam Hussein, born of the immense competitive pressures under which reporters and networks labor, offered the interviewee a platform from which to address a global audience directly, going 'above the heads' of other governments; that the reporters tend to become advocates for their own side; their own governments and its policies, and that consequently they usurp the role of the true professional advocates, the government's own representatives.

The role journalists sometimes play as go-betweens in international crises raises other questions concerning the very nature of the journalism they profess to practise. The active participation of journalists in the events they presumably 'cover' is often achieved at the cost of sacrificing some traditional journalistic norms, such as editorial control over which actors (and perspectives) to incorporate into the story and which to ignore. Journalists reporting from Iraq during the Gulf war were, of course, aware that they were being 'used' by their Iraqi hosts to present a view of the hostilities as seen through Iraqi eyes, yet were criticized by television viewers in the West for spreading Iraqi 'propaganda'. (One conservative American Senator went as far as denouncing CNN's correspondent in Baghdad as a 'sympathizer' with the Iraqi regime). Likewise, in the wake of the American bombing of Tripoli in 1986, the Libyans assisted Western television crews in filming civilian casualties, and naturally restricted access to military areas (Wallis and Baran 1990). By facilitating the work of these journalists, both the Iraqis and the Libyans did, ironically, contribute to upholding the traditional journalistic norm of 'balance' – of showing 'the other side'. The motives impelling the journalists, however, stem, more likely, from competitive pressures than from adherence to the norm of 'balance'.

In addition to the hazards of control and manipulation that the media undergo in their new role as international political brokers, it is not entirely clear that the consequences of their interventions are always beneficial. For example, questions could be raised whether the failure of the diplomatic negotiations that preceded the Gulf war could be attributed, at least in part, to the fact that they were made part of a public discourse, and thus were framed in political and highly ideological terms that left little room for deal-making.

● Fifth, television's participation in events further blurs the line between 'social reality' and 'media reality'. It goes to the heart of the role of the media as 'definers of social reality', and beyond. The familiar approach to viewing the 'reality defining' role of the media suggests that, as Bennett (1982) for example, puts it,

> . . . *what* 'events' are 'reported' by the media and the *ways* in which they are signified have a bearing on the ways in which we perceive the world and thus, if action is at all related to thought, on the ways in we act within it'.

The presence of journalists, and especially of television cameras, in any event goes beyond selecting what to report and how to report it. It impacts on the very behavior of the actors involved in the event, and thus alters its nature. 'Reality' and its portrayal on the screen are so inextricably intertwined as to become virtually indistinguishable. In fact, the farther the event from the audience, the more likely it is that the reality of the event on television will become the only 'reality'. Instant global television thus renders the complexity of the relationship between television portrayals and 'reality' even more acute. Television's coverage of political conventions, for example, has long been acknowledged to influence all aspects of the event, from its timing, to the scheduling of speakers, to the choice of colors on the podium. In the case of more chaotic, violent and potentially controversial events such as wars and other armed conflicts television's reality assumes predominant significance.

Inside the Television Industries

Media systems around the world vary in many ways. The relationship between the press and broadcasting systems and the political system is governed, in every country, by the nature of its political system and the norms that characterize its political culture. The socio-political and the economic structure of different societies also determine the internal structure of their media systems, their modes of finance, and consequently the intra-system relationships between different media organizations. Thus, for example, the American broadcasting system, truly reflecting its economic base, has always been regarded as a 'classic' example of a privately owned, commercially driven system, claiming autonomy from government and other forms of political controls. Many European countries, on the other hand, had a 'mixed' media system, combining state controlled or public service media organizations side by side with privately owned commercial organizations. For many years these structures were fairly stable, exhibiting little propensity for change. The advent of the new communication technologies appears to have changed all that. It is not the purpose of this chapter to explore these changes. (For a discussion of some of these developments see, e.g. Blumler, in this volume). Our concern here is limited to examining the impact of the introduction of satellite technology on the relationships between different television organizations.

The US experience is most instructive in this regard. This is so partly because the American broadcasting system is the largest in the world, certainly in terms of the number of different television outlets, but especially because its specific structure, consisting of three national commercial networks, a smaller public television network, a range of affiliate local stations and a sizeable number of independent local stations, constitutes a complex system of power dependencies, which turned out to be vulnerable to the potential impact of technological change. For many years televisions news in the American context meant, by and large, network news. The global news gathering machineries constructed by the networks' news organizations required resources above and beyond those available to any single station. As a result, local stations were always dependent on the networks' resources for news materials which originated beyond their immediate home areas. News programs produced by local stations reflected this dependency in the ways in which networks' originated materials were used in those (fairly infrequent) instances when foreign or other remote news stories were inserted into 'local' news shows.

Satellite technology has altered these dependencies. It enabled local stations to receive remote stories directly, often from their own sources. The cost of sending a reporter equipped with a satellite dish to a remote location where a major news story is unfolding is becoming increasingly affordable for single stations, especially when the prestige value of having one's own correspondent on the scene is considered. Thus, by extending the news reach of local stations the same technology that contributed to the globalization of television news has, perhaps paradoxically, promoted developments in the opposite direction, namely increasing decentralization of news gathering.

The new status and prestige gained by local television news has also resulted in increased economic returns for local stations through steadily increased ratings. According to a 1985 study by Baran (quoted in Wallis and Baran 1990), local television news in some stations accounts for 40 to 60 per cent of the stations' profits. These profits, in turn, allow the local stations to buy further national and foreign news footage.

While these developments are, for the most part, evident in the commercialized and virtually deregulated American broadcasting arena, parallels are emerging in Europe. 'Even in the European context of highly regulated broadcast media, many local lobbying groups are agitating for extended regional and local broadcast media' (Wallis and Baran 1990). This is bound to affect the position, and the market share, of large scale, centralized news organizations. In the long run it might result in an increasing fragmentation of television news production. Thus far this might be primarily an American phenomenon, but it could be clearly extrapolated to the global scene. In that case, it could make smaller, less affluent television news organizations less dependent on the 'big boys' in the news business, and more capable of deploying the technology to serve their own needs. Satellite technology might prove to be the key for at least a partial liberation of television news services in smaller First World and Third World countries from dependency on the richer and more powerful news organizations. It might initiate the 'post media imperialism' era.

Encoders and Decoders

The debate about the 'balance of power' between those responsible for the production and shaping of media texts – the encoders on the one hand, and members of the media audiences – the decoders) on the other, has received renewed attention over the last decade with the formulation of 'reception theory'. According to Curran, (1990), this 'revisionist scholarship' in media studies consisted of two major shifts: first, the emergence of scholarship that emphasized the 'inconsistencies, contradictions, gaps and even internal oppositions within texts', and that thus departed from earlier theoretical formulations that regarded texts as carrying coherent and dominant meanings; and second, a shift that stressed a view of the audience as active and autonomous – 'a reconceptualization of the audience as an active producer of meaning', challenging the assumption that 'audiences responded in prescribed ways to fixed, preconstituted meanings in texts'. It is useful to speculate, in the framework of these reconceptualizations, about the position of the audience for television news in an era of global journalism. By and large, this discussion is inevitably speculative, since hardly any empirical evidence is as yet available on that issue.

First, much of the news materials disseminated globally, but especially the 'raw materials' disseminated through the regional news exchange systems and the television news agencies (Visnews and WTN) may be properly described as 'open' texts. 'Openness' here implies the extent to which different kinds of texts constrain the meanings embedded in them or, alternatively, allow for multiple decodings of their meanings. Thus, it can be argued that verbal texts (e.g. news stories in the printed press) are relatively 'closed' (i.e. they constrain the range of interpretations or meanings of the events they report) since *any account of an event necessarily defines its meaning*. On the other hand, 'pure' visuals (i.e. visuals unaccompanied by a verbal caption or text) are relatively 'open', as they are susceptible to a wider range of interpretations or 'stories' based upon them. The visual materials that are the stock in trade of the news exchange organizations and the news agencies are, indeed, sent primarily in the form of 'raw materials', that is, unedited footage, including only 'natural-sound'. The task of editing and shaping these materials into news stories remains in the hands of news editors in the different broadcasting organizations. Thus, while the same visual materials might be used by editors in different countries, the final shape of the stories they are telling, their narrative and thematic structures, and the meanings embedded in them remain in the hands of editors working with different national audiences in mind. In fact, such is the degree of 'openness' of the visuals that come down from the satellites, that they could be regarded almost as 'an empty vessel' (Barkin and Gurevitch, 1986).

The resulting diversity of meanings offers an almost unique opportunity to witness the ways in which television news construct different social realities. By comparing the similarities or differences in the meanings encoded into a variety of stories of the 'same' event, some insight may be gained of the degree of control that encoders have over the construction of meanings. In an era of increasing globalization of television news such comparative analysis may also offer an important antidote to 'naive universalism' – that is, to the assumption that events reported in the news carry their own meanings, and that the meanings embedded in news stories produced in one country can therefore be generalized to news stories told in other societies (Gurevitch and Blumler 1990).

How does this process impact on the 'autonomy of the audience' – the capacity of audience members to act as active producers of meanings? Since audience members have no access to the more 'open' texts of raw visuals and are only exposed to already fully fashioned stories, their position as news consumers may not have changed from that in the era of 'conventional' television news. It would therefore be plausible to assume that they may not have gained any greater autonomy vis-a-vis the story tellers. In fact, it might be possible to argue that, faced with a larger amount of news stories from far-away places (for that is one of the changes that the global flow of news facilitates), their dependence on the encoders to make sense of these events actually increases. Presented with stories of events for which they have no ready-made 'schemas' (Graber, 1984), or frameworks for interpretation, viewers are less able to negotiate and construct the meanings of these events for themselves, and are inevitably more dependent on the perspectives embedded in the stories. Their power position vis-a-vis the correspondents and editors who bring them these stories is thus diminished.

As suggested earlier, we have no evidence to support that conclusion. It is based on a rather simple extrapolation of current theories of media-audience relationships. However, if it were to be confirmed it might result in another swing of the theoretical pendulum, a retreat from the recent formulations of 'reception theory', back to the theories of powerful media and powerless audiences.

Concluding Remarks

The process of globalization of electronic journalism is growing apace, transforming the flow of communication around the world and impacting in myriad ways on the ways people and societies know, perceive and understand the world and conduct relationships with each other. Perhaps paradoxically, however, the defining contours of the process are not easy to discern. The difficulty we are confronted with in trying to grasp the nature and consequences of this process lie partly in the rapid development of the technology that facilitates its rapid emergence and change of the institutional structures that carry the globalization process forward, and the diverse ways in which the implications and the consequences of these developments manifest themselves. But the more significant obstacle, as was suggested earlier, lies in our uncertainty about the most appropriate and theoretically productive way to conceptualize the process. In the absence of a comprehensive theoretical framework these diverse phenomena will remain unrelated, disconnected and more difficult to make sense of.

In this chapter we attempted to offer a starting point for the construction of such conceptual framework. One starting point, we suggested, may be found in the *shifting balance of relationships of dependency* between different participants in the networks of global communication. Each 'communication revolution', from the Guttenbergian to the electronic, to the emergence of global, satellite-based communication, brought in their wake a transformation in the power relationships in society: the printing press contributed to undermining the power of the Papacy; the press facilitated the consolidation of the dominance of the middle classes in industrial societies; the electronic media, among other things, helped to legitimate counter-cultures and other stirrings against the existing social order. The globalization of television, and more specifically the emergence of television news as a truly global phenomenon may, or may not be a 'revolution' on par with these other historical revolutions. But the path to understanding it might be the same.

Notes

I wish to thank my colleague, Mark Levy, for his help in shaping the theme and the ideas in this chapter; and my research assistant, Anandam Kavoori, for his valuable contributions.

References

BARKIN, S. and GUREVITCH, M., 1987: 'Out of Work and on the Air: Television News of Unemployment', *Critical Studies in Mass Communication*, vol. 4, no. 1.
BENNETT, TONY, 1982: 'Media, 'Reality', Signification', in Gurevitch, Michael et al. (eds) *Culture, Society and the Media*. London: Methuen.
BLUMLER, JAY, 1989: 'The Internationalization of Communication', Paper presented to College of Communication, University of Texas, Austin, Texas.
BOYD-BARRETT, OLIVER, 1980: *The International News Agencies*. Beverly Hills: Sage.
BREED, W., 1955: 'Social Control in the Newsroom: A Functional Analysis', *Social Forces*, vol. 33.
CURRAN, JAMES, 1990: 'The New Revisionism in Mass Communication Research: A Reappraisal', *European Journal of Communication*, vol. 5, no. 2–3.
EUGSTER, ERNEST, 1983: *Television Programming across national boundaries: the EBU and OIRT experience*, Dedham: Artech House.
FENBY, JONATHAN, 1986: The International News Services, New York: Schoken books.
FISHER, HAROLD A., 1980: 'The EBU: Model for Regional Cooperation in Broadcasting', in Journalism Monographs, No. 68, Association for Education in Journalism.
FISKE, JOHN, 1987: *Television Culture*. London and New York: Methuen.
GRABER, DORIS, 1984: *Processing the News*. New York and London: Longman.
GUREVITCH, MICHAEL and BLUMLER, JAY, 1990: 'Comparative Research: The Extending Frontier', in Swanson, D. and Nimmo, D. (eds), *New Directions in Political Communication*, Newbury Park, California: Sage.
HACHTEN, WILLIAM A., 1987: *World News Prism: Changing Media, Clashing Ideologies*. Ames: Iowa State University Press, second edition.

KEUNE, RICHARD, 1987: '*Electronic Media and the third world: Exchange and Cooperation – or Condescension and Confrontation*', Bonn: Friedrich-Debert-Stiftung.

LANISPURO, Y., 1987: 'Asiavision News Exchange', *Media Asia*, vol. 14, no. 1.

LANTENAC, PIERRE BRUNEL, 1975: 'Live from the Eurovision newsroom in Geneva. A day like any other' in *EBU Review: Programmes, Administration, Law*, Vol. 26, No. 3, pp. 11–15.

MAHONEY, 1975:

POOL, ITHIEL DE SOLA, 1983: *Technologies of Freedom*. Cambridge, MA: Harvard University Press.

POWELL, ADAM CLAYTON III, 1990: 'The Global TV News Hour', *Gannett Center Journal*, New York: vol. 4, no. 4.

SCHRAMM, WILBUR, 1959: *One Day in the World's Press: fourteen great newspapers on a day of crises, November 2.* Stanford: Stanford University Press.

SMITH, ANTHONY, 1990: 'Media Globalism in the Age of Consumer Sovereignty', *Gannett Center Journal*, vol. 4, no. 4, Fall 1990.

WALLIS, ROGER and STANLEY BARAN, 1990: *The Known World of Broadcast News*. London and New York: Routledge.

WHITE, D. M., 1950: 'The 'Gate keeper': A case study in the selection of news', *Journalism Quarterly*, vol. 27.

10

The New Television Marketplace: Imperatives, Implications, Issues

Jay G. Blumler

This chapter examines the transformation of a major mass medium that had functioned in the same fashion for some thirty to forty years. Based on a single delivery system (broadcast air waves), television consisted of a small number of channels, programmed by a comparatively small circle of competitors for viewers' attention. The main sources of finance, lines of industry organization, and patterns of audience patronage were relatively stable. Those changes that did take place from time to time – in, for instance, the flow of revenues, distribution of audience favors, cycles of program genre fashions, and regulatory controls – were all relatively minor, more marginal than systemic. In the last decade, however, a 'gale of creative destruction' has been unleashed on electronic media systems throughout the advanced industrial world (Schumpeter 1942). An extraordinarily potent mix of technological, organizational, financial, and political factors has disrupted the prevailing, familiar patterns of such systems and forced their architects to re-examine and redeploy their resources. This chapter aims to identify some of the most influential forces driving this restructuring and to assess their consequences.

The focus here is the emerging and still evolving 'new television marketplace' in the United States. In that country the multichannel revolution is now so advanced that it offers a veritable laboratory for identifying the likely imperatives and effects of an expanding, market-driven, lightly regulated broadcasting economy. Channels have proliferated, competition has intensified, and audiences have fragmented over the course of the last decade. Cable is booming, installed in 1991, in over 60 per cent of the country's households, whereas in 1980 fewer than 20 per cent of television households subscribed. More than 70 mostly profitable cable programming services vie for acceptance in 30-plus channel systems (gradually being replaced by 50-plus channel systems). Terrestrial stations have also multiplied – with 400 'independents' in addition to all the local affiliates of ABC, CBS and NBC (some 100 each). A new fourth network (Fox Broadcasting) has successfully established itself after only a few years of operation, defying the negative odds offered by many skeptics when it was launched. To receive all of these channels, many American homes have at least two TV sets (and 30 per cent are estimated to have three), 70 per cent have videocassette records/players, and at least as many are armed with remote control devices. This plentitude of viewing options has, in audience ratings terms, sent the three formerly dominant networks into a tailspin that their pilots have not managed to reverse (down to 68 per cent in November 1988 primetime from 85 per cent in 1980).

Such developments give rise to many provocative questions. Is commercial television a quite different kind of animal in conditions of channel abundance from the one that sported standardized, lowest–common–denominator spots in conditions of scarcity? What imperatives are driving the new video market-place? How are they shaping the offerings of program providers and conse-quently the range and quality of what viewers can choose to watch? What, if anything, is being shortchanged? What directions and problems are entailed for policy makers? Such issues were central to a two-year (1986–88) inquiry into the evolution of multichannel television in the United States that was based largely on extended interviews with 150 industry figures and was funded by the John and Mary R. Markle Foundation.

The following analysis of the new television marketplace unfolds in three stages. First, the 'new and hectic' competitive environment (*Broadcasting*, January 11, 1990, p. 39) engendered by multichannel television is examined, regarding it as a source of imperatives to which all would-be significant players and providers must respond. Next, some of the main consequences of such a system are evaluated. The theme here is one of mixed outcomes. The multi-channel video marketplace incorporates numerous tensions, interleaving ben-efits with certain serious causes for concern that are not always recognized as such. This leads to a third and concluding section, in which certain core policy challenges posed by the growth of a transformed television marketplace are considered comparatively – for the United States and for Western Europe (to which some of its elements are now being diffused). The likely fate of such diffusion is intriguingly poised. Attracted by the promise of channel abund-ance, many European countries that previously protected their telecasters from competition are now giving market forces their head. Development of most new delivery systems and services is being entrusted to private concerns. Regulatory controls are being removed or relaxed. Once mighty public service broadcasting organizations are being challenged, invaded, and diminished; are contemplating new roles; and in some cases are becoming more market-minded themselves.

The new-style American television system is not bound, however, to triumph everywhere. The restructuring process should not be likened to an invincible freight train, rolling downhill, unimpeded, to its inevitable destina-tion. It should be borne in mind that this singularly American dynamic is being introduced into societies with different cultures, political systems, and broad-casting systems than those that nurtured television in the United States.

What undoubtedly does loom ahead is a confrontation between two different models of television provision – majoritarian and pluralist – which had histori-cally evolved in the New and the Old Worlds, respectively. In the majoritarian model, pride of paramount place tends to be given to satisfaction of the personal and immediate gratifications of as many individual audience members as possible. Television is a business, more or less like any other, and a broadcasting market, shaped by consumers' viewing decisions, is analogous to a popular democracy, governed by citizens' voting decisions. As channels increase, broadcasters should be transformed from public trustees to market-place competitors, and 'the public interest should be defined by the public's interest' (Fowler and Brenner, 1981). Presumed societal and cultural goods are subordinate or irrelevant in this model – at any rate they simply have to take their chances in the rough and tumble of marketplace outcomes.

In the pluralist model the nature of broadcast communication is conceived differently. It is not merely a product that may please or displease; a tool for realization of individual purposes; or a conveyor belt for the transfer of information. It is also a mental and spiritual transaction about meanings and relationships. This conception is pluralist at several levels: in the multiplicity of audience types served and audience images catered for; in respect of program making, striving to match it to the heterogeneity of the viewing public and ensuring that each program form has sufficient resources to be good of its kind; and in respect of service to society, implying that all significant sectors of the community, divided by interests, values, and identities, are entitled to have their main concerns reflected tolerably authentically in program output. It is from the pending clash and interpenetration of these opposed models of provision that the principal features of late twentieth-century television will eventually emerge.

Imperatives

The notion of competition is often applied loosely to media affairs. For multichannel television, the main impression conveyed is of an extended system, in which more providers place more programs before viewers, whose preferences then allow the better ones to survive and flourish. Scant attention is paid to competition as a more far-reaching process that guides organizational strategies, redistributes resources, and creates conditions of production that favor certain types of programs and discourage others. Yet many sources of ever tighter pressure are part and parcel of a competitively driven multichannel television system. They may be grouped as springing from: (1) an increase in the number of players and outlets competing for viewers; (2) a change in the audience problematic; (3) a resulting higher premium on strategies for gaining and keeping attention; (4) the economics of program production; and (5) a struggle for industry power.

A chaos of competitors

From a highly structured system in which three major broadcast networks competed in rather stylized and predictable patterns before the 1980s, Ameri-can telecasters find themselves caught in a maelstrom of competitors, each striving to capitalize on its own strengths and to profit from its rivals' weak-nesses. The multichannel competition for audiences has consequently become more complex and more preoccupying – more difficult to control and shot through with greater uncertainty for all engaged in it.

In their former prime, network strategists, like oligopolists in other indus-tries (cf. Picard, 1989, pp. 77–78), while keen to attract more viewers and advertising revenue than their rivals, had settled into relatively stable, even interdependent patterns of competition. Now, however, they are surrounded on all sides by newcomers who are unwilling to confine themselves to narrowcast programming for specialist tastes and to leave the networks in command of the market for mass appeal programming. These include Fox Broadcasting; syndicated programming on independent stations; TNT, a cable-operator-supported mass appeal channel; USA Network, a studio-backed (Paramount/MCA) general entertainment cable service; and ESPN, an all-sports cable channel. Competition within the cable universe is also becoming multifaceted, creating an 'internecine battle for channel space and advertising dollars' (*Channels*, March 1990, p. 33). Many movie channels are vying with each other. The national sports channel, ESPN, is being challenged by a growing number of regional services, as well as by the renewed determination of all three mainstream networks to capture rights to the most attractive events. In the news field, CNN competes with FNN and CNBC. The family audience is sought by Disney, CBN, Lifetime, and the Family Channel. The Nashville Network is pitted against country Music Television. At the time of writing, two new comedy services were competing for space on cable systems, while schemes were under consideration for two channels featuring televised court scenes. An interviewed executive of Nickelodeon (a cable service for children) said that its fare was in competition with children's programming on HBO, Showtime, the Disney Channel, the three older networks, independent stations, and cartoons on USA Network. Another cable executive maintained that, 'We're all competing with one another; we view anything that can come up on the set as a competitor'.

The Audience Problematic

Program providers not only face a more crowded field of competitors, but their relations with audiences have also been transformed in three respects. First, there is heightened uncertainty about the likely audience response to all individual program offerings. In the words of a producer for multiple markets, 'The one rule that . . . is absolutely true is, you don't know if your show's going to work or not, nobody knows'. Of course, such uncertainty has always been part and parcel of commercial television, since schedulers and programmers could never tell whether what they had fashioned would appeal to the intended audience until resources had been committed and the show aired. But it is magnified in a multichannel system by the increased number of competitors and outlets to which audience members can turn. As a CBS business affairs reporter has painted the resulting predicament:

> The audience that you think you've got, that you thought you were talking to for the last ten years, may have in the last five or six wandered off somewhere. You are not exactly sure where they have gone, and you are not exactly sure who is left, leaving you in the disconcerting position of making television and asking at the same time: Who am I talking to?
>
> Krulwich 1990, p. 7

The increased difficulty of sensing how to cater effectively for an audience encourages much tinkering with program makers' initial ideas to align them with hunches about how they might swing with viewers; a heavy reliance on prior testing of pilot versions with sample audiences (with in-built biases to the familiar and the immediately appealing); and preferences for concepts reminiscent of past successes.

Second, the competition for audience attention has become more 'relentless' (as an interviewed station manager termed this feature of the process), due to the inelasticity of consumers' available time for viewing. Year-by-year A. C. Nielsen Co. data show that, although when the number of channels started to increase, Americans viewed somewhat more television than before, thereafter the amount of time they spent watching television flattened out. In 1982, for example, when only 21 per cent of US households could receive fifteen or more channels, the average set was in use for 6 hours, 48 minutes; yet in 1988, when 64 per cent could receive fifteen or more channels, daily set use averaged only 7 more minutes at 6 hours, 55 minutes. Since the audience pie is not getting bigger, seekers of slices of it have to wrest them from each other, making the chase for audiences almost a zero-sum game. This encourages a practice of keeping popular shows on the air for as long as possible, no matter the cost to creative inspiration, and makes it more risky to nurture promising shows through initially lean patches before viewers have learned to appreciate them.

Third, the increase in channels plus the greater ease of switching with remote control devices have bred a new image of the standard viewer that is influencing how some programmers cater to such a person. This is the image of the capricious audience member, who has grown up with multichannel television, become accustomed to its style, enjoys riffling through its many offerings, and incessantly grazes across the dial in search of ever more entrancing viewing pastures. In a network executive's words: 'The audience, because of all the alternatives that are available to them, keep looking around, bouncing around, and hitting those buttons.' According to a media analyst, such a 'bounty of buttons dovetails nicely with the ever-shortening attention span of viewers', explaining 'television's current emphasis on rapid-fire pace – news updates, sports breaks, rock video clips, and a growing number of 15-second commercials'.

It should be stressed that such characterizations reflect an influential image of the typical audience member and are not necessarily an accurate account of how he/she is actually reacting to extended choice, though a 1988 survey claimed to find much evidence of 'grazing' particularly among younger people (*Channels*, September 1988). Favored by it, however, are strategies of immediate attention gaining and qualities of pace, impact, brevity, the arresting, and the dramatic; out of line is anything that needs gradually to establish itself or requires thought and reflection to absorb.

The Battle for Attention

With more channels to choose from, with viewers more likely to be actively guided by interest and preference than habit when deciding to watch, and with a need to stand out above the clutter, program providers are under greater pressure to offer something disinctive and to attract attention to their particular wares. This has implications for programming, scheduling, and promotion.

Programming for commercial television in the United States has always had two faces, imitative and innovative: 'It can involve an ability to follow one's leader, 'cloning' another network's or producer's hit, as well as an instinct for breaking away at the right moment onto a more novel path' (Blumler 1986, p. 95). Most observers agree, however, that when only three networks prevailed, much of American commercial television was 'patterned and derivative' with 'unconventional programs [being aired] only in rare instances' (Turow 1982, p. 107).

The onset of multichannel television does appear to have shifted this balance to some extent, weakening reliance on what one interviewee called the 'cookie-cutter approach' to programming. As a financial analyst pointed out, receptivity to change in the new marketplace 'has to increase because there's only a certain amount of time that the audience will keep watching the same forms of product'. In the words of the executive of a multimedia conglomerate:

> The fact that you have more ultimately leads you to try and make yourself distinctive in some manner. The question is, how distinctive are you going to be?

This informant's terms were well chosen, for very probably the operative motive in the new conditions is the desire to be distinctive. And although this may create openings for dramatically or aesthetically innovative productions that would not have been tried in the past (a *Twin Peaks*, say), to get this drive in perspective, it is important to appreciate that it can be satisfied in other ways as well. Cosmetic differences of presentation and gimmicks may serve (e.g., through animation, singing policemen, or a rap-chanting hero). Casting may help (e.g., by hiring well-known stars to play the leading roles in a production). The intensified competition among broadcast and cable networks for the rights to screen major sporting and other events is also explained by the distinctiveness it confers on those who acquire the rights to them. As the executive of a cable channel explained why it was prepared to submit high bids for such events:

> That's very important because . . . those are things that people wait for days to see, and it has a very high-profile effect. . . . There are only about forty of them out there.

Other qualifications on the receptivity to difference engendered by new marketplace conditions should also be kept in mind. As the executive of a pioneering service explained:

> In television . . . the differences tend to be marginal. They have to be 1, 3, or 5 degrees off-course rather than hard-right rudder. Otherwise, you are going too far away from what the audience has already voted for as the kinds of programs they want to watch.

Moreover, even innovative programming must eventually work in market terms, reaching the ratings targets the financial managers need and expect, which will not always be an unconventional show's own appropriate audience level (whatever that may be).

Competitive *scheduling* for multichannel television has also become more intricate, having to take account of what so many rivals are likely to be placing before the audience. In the syndication market particularly, the decisions of individual stations over what programs to buy and when to schedule them are often strongly influenced by elaborate statistical calculations and professional advice from 'rep' firms (companies that represent them in selling their spot advertising time) and from station-group executives. Such counsel tends to entrench rules of conventional wisdom about the conditions of market success, how best to schedule, and what appeals to audiences, while dampening temptations to take risks and try the exceptional. In general, the more complicated conditions of the new television marketplace increase the influence of 'middlemen' of all kinds (talent agents and syndicators as well as rep firms), whose data counter insecurity by supposedly providing more objective bases for decision making, and who often come to assume that their experience, extending beyond any factual information at their command, gives them special qualifications for judging unsentimentally what will work best.

In addition, with more outlets and more entrepreneurs seeking audiences, a more competitive marketplace puts a higher premium on program *promotion*. As a producer pointed out:

> The most difficult aspect of developing new programming is getting people to know what you're offering [because] it's so hard to cut through the clutter.

According to a studio supplier of movies for syndication:

> Promotion is specially important for the independent stations, because they do not have national stuff coming down at them in the same way that the network affiliates do.

A cable advertising executive was concerned that:

> The cable industry has been the last to focus on how to promote its programming and needs to put this right, preferably by a cooperative effort of programmers and multi-system operators.

The established networks have invested more imaginatively and heavily in promotion recently as well, both on air (lavishing more screen time and production gloss on such efforts) and off (including exclusive publicity facilities in large retail chain stores and sports grounds, posters, t-shirts, and video releases). A significant incentive for purchasing the rights to a major sporting event, even at punishing prices, has been the opportunity to familiarize viewers during the breaks with the service's other program offerings. In the fall of 1990, even public television hired Young and Rubicam to help it mount an unprecedented advertising campaign of promotion spots on commercial television (network and cable) 'to remind people that PBS is an option and to increase sampling' (*New York Times*, October 1, 1990, p. D10).

Of course, if promotion is more important, it is correspondingly more vital for programming to have promotable qualities. According to industry insiders, this favors programs based on a 'simple idea, able to be told about in something like a sentence', as well as ones with dramatic hooks, exciting action, confrontation and horror, something sensational, and generally what is already familiar to the audience.

The Economics of Program Production

During its 1980s expansive phase, the providers of US television benefited from the relative buoyancy of its two main revenue streams. Funds from individual viewers (through cable subscriptions and videocassette rentals and sales) steadily increased, while advertisers also spent more, even tolerating ever higher 'costs per thousand' to reach the shrinking mass audience delivered by ABC, CBS, and NBC. Maintenance of such levels cannot be guaranteed in the future, however, particularly as far as income from advertising is concerned, which could be threatened by the onset of an economic recession and/or the appeal of alternative ways of bringing goods and services to the attention of would-be customers.

Meanwhile, the pressures of new marketplace conditions have been more directly felt on the expenditure side of the financial equation. Programs are the center around which the multichannel marketplace revolves, and those who can provide a competitive edge in this regard have been able to set their price in the bidding wars among and within the various outlets. Those producers, writers, and directors who have worked on successful shows, for example, find themselves very much in demand and able to exact a premium for their services. As CBS's Entertainment Division president put it:

> Everybody's trying to protect their position, and the way to protect it is by buying great talent. So you're having to step up the sums that you're willing to pay for talent in order to maintain your independence and survivability

So, at the very time that audiences have been fragmenting, becoming more choosy and difficult to pin down, program-making costs have been continually increasing, as illustrated by the real dollar cost jump of made-for-television movies from an average of $670,000 per film in 1980 to $1,360,000 in 1987 (Waterman, 1989). Program cost inflation is evident, too, in the doubling of the average price of syndicated programs between 1981 and 1986; the ever more lucrative contracts for coverage rights to major sporting events that leagues and teams have been able to negotiate (e.g. rights revenues for National Football League games increased at an average rate of 98 per cent per season between 1986 and 1990 [*Electronic Media*, March 12 1990, p. 1]); and skyrocketing prices for successful theatrical movies, boosted by competitive bidding among broadcast networks and stations and many pay and basic cable services.

Such economic influences have reinforced three tendencies that had characterized US commercial television before the onset of multichannel expansion. One is the drive to maximize audiences, which affects even those services that appear designed to cater for more specifically targeted types of viewers and tastes. Indeed, there is 'more pressure than ever before to come up with hits' in the new television marketplace (*Variety*, May 2, 1990, p. 295), despite the lower viewing levels that even the most successful shows might expect to attain in the context of all-round audience fragmentation. This is not only because higher ratings translate into bigger earnings, but also because a hit scored serves as a subsidy for the producing organization, giving it more leeway to run risks, cover costs, compensate for losses on other projects, and finance future ventures. As the same *Variety* article explained, 'Fox needs one or two more hits next season to continue its momentum and to solidify its reputation with the production community', while for the older networks, 'finding hits [would be] one way to stem the slide'. Smaller independent production companies are especially keen to achieve a programming hit as a way to keep afloat and to ensure that their future offerings are seriously considered. Another factor is the increased power that accrues to holders of hits. Several interviewees stressed how the King World organization's control of a few syndication blockbusters (e.g. *Wheel of Fortune* and *Jeopardy*) enabled it to press stations to accept other programs from its stable and to schedule them in the most profitable time slots. As a studio executive confirmed:

> It is still a hits-driven business. The hits give you the leverage. And we live for the day we get leverage in any area. Everybody lives for that.

A station group official even went so far as to contend that, 'Without the hit, the system doesn't work.'

A second feature of commercial television, greatly bolstered by multi-channel proliferation, is the incentive for producers and distributors to tailor programs for acceptability in multiple markets, both domestic (network, cable, syndication, home video) and global. In the words of a media economist: 'There are tremendous forces moving in the direction of widespread distribution of whatever kind of program you're talking about.' Partly this has come about because audience success for an individual program is such a chancy business that producers are continually striving to compensate for many failures by raking in all the available jackpots whenever an audience winner comes along. Partly it is because, as average audience and revenue levels fall, it is far less likely that a show's appearance in a single outlet of the splintered marketplace will suffice to cover the ever inflating costs and expected profits. Less likely to be produced under these conditions, then, are program types and themes that have limited marketability, including those with a culture-specific appeal.

New forms of leverage for advertisers, stemming from the combination of escalating production costs and limited resources to meet them, comprise a third respect in which the new television marketplace has accentuated a characteristic of the old. Such leverage can take several forms. It can affect the ability of shows to get on the air – as in the syndication market, where, through what is called 'barter', stations with limited budgets can obtain, without payment, programs that have commercials built into them that were sold in advance by the syndicator and/or the production company. There are even indications of renewed interest on the part of advertisers in developing their own fully sponsored shows as in the early days of television. Would-be makers of special interest videos are also appealing to potentially supportive advertisers at a sufficiently early stage for the interests of the latter to be taken into account.

In the case of the broadcast networks, aware that they are engaged in greater competition for advertising than ever before, new and formerly unthinkable services and facilities have been on offer. In the words of ABC's senior vice-president of marketing:

> We realize we have a tremendous equity we haven't used before, like programs and performers and the network identification. What we're trying to do is utilize these things in marketing.

Ingenious tie-ins and product promotions have resulted, such as using a product as a prominently visible prop in a program; making a show's set available to a company for filming in its commercials; and making stars available for appearances in sponsors' promotional efforts.

Such 'value-added' extras are sometimes available from cable services as well. According to CNBC's senior vice-president for advertising sales:

> In cable, the restrictions on billboards are more lenient [than at the broadcast networks]. We offer sponsorship, in-program IDs, special tie-ins, contests and segment sponsorship – all for less of an outlay in dollars.
>
> (*Channels*, April 1990, p. 58)

As *Ad Week* (February 4, 1990) concluded: 'The economics of cable encourage participation in program content, giving advertisers opportunities to custom-create an environment for their messages.'

A likely thrust of such increased leverage is suggested in the comment of a Philip Morris advertising executive: 'Controversy isn't our objective' (*Wall Street Journal*, June 16, 1989). Probably most at risk in such circumstances are programs dealing with subjects that can polarize audience sympathies (e.g. abortion) or offend the standards adhered to by significant audience sectors (with threats of product boycotts in the background). Thus, advertisers' and agencies' 'hit lists' of programs unsuitable for commercials have been lengthening. New programs are being pitched as 'advertiser friendly' at industry conferences, to stations, and in the trade press. That leading broadcasters themselves are willing to acquiesce in the process is implied by the reported comment of a network executive to the effect that, 'Advertisers do not want to be involved, *and rightly so* [emphasis added], in controversy or controversial themes'.

The Struggle for Power

Finally, the competition bred by new marketplace conditions is no longer just a fight for bigger audience shares, higher earnings and profits, but also and increasingly a battle for control over key assets – talent, popular programming, effective ways of distributing and exhibiting it – that is, a struggle for power. As Sumner Redstone, chairman of the multi-media conglomerate, Viacom, has put it:

> In many ways we live in a world of fear, and threats, and reaction, and frequently overreaction . . . The name of the game is ego and power and leverage.
>
> *The Caucus Quarterly*, April 1990, pp. 26, 31

This feature of the competitive environment has spurred many organizational realignments, with networks investing in cable, cable services embarking on joint ventures with networks, cable operators investing in program services, station groups linking with production companies, syndicators forming production arms, studios buying stations, production companies diversifying their investments and program operations, and already huge and multifaceted entertainment complexes merging with each other (as in the 1989 case of Time-Warner). Waiting in the wings, according to some industry leaders, is even a network-studio alliance. Organizational conglomeration, concentration, and both vertical and horizontal integration are thus all on the march.

Several imperatives of new marketplace competition are undoubtedly responsible for such developments, including:

- Incentives to diversify, to hedge one's bets for an uncertain future, ensuring that if certain outlets and programs disappoint, others can make up for it.

- In the case of production companies, a need to control distribution outlets in order to guarantee at least a minimal take-up of their wares.

- In the case of distributors, a need to invest in program suppliers so as to control their competitive offerings more effectively, including what they cost.

- The greater difficulty smaller companies have in raising capital in these circumstances.

Implications

What kind of television system do these driving forces tend to fashion if they are not restrained or diluted by politics or policy? This section outlines those features that are suggested by US experience.

Greater Viewer Choice

For the viewer who is willing to pay for it, there is an extension of choice in several senses, though the monetary terms of his or her access to it may change over time. Quantitatively, of course, the number of viewing options for most Americans has increased dramatically. Qualitatively, cable subscribers can watch many programs not previously available – e.g. 24-hour news, gavel-to-gavel congressional coverage, nature documentaries, all-day sports, premium movies, and round-the-clock culture as well as rock round-the-clock! The tyranny of scheduling uniformity across channels has been weakened if not smashed, notably by cable, but also by the counter-programming strategies of Fox Broadcasting and independent stations. The new technologies (VCRs in particular) also allow viewers to decide *what* to view *when*. As a media economist summed up:

> I'm a little short with those who say all cable has done is give us all that we were seeing before. They are wrong for two reasons. One, it's not so bad that people are getting more of what they wanted. . . . And two, they are getting a lot of things that are different and new. Any fair critic of the system has to accept that the range and variety of things that are available now, at least to cable viewers, are substantially greater than what were available on the networks during the period from 1948 to 1980.

There is much justification for this emphasis on the positive contributions of cable television. During cable's period of rapid growth the industry's leaders recognized that its appeal depended on the claim to offer a sort of 'diversity'. Consequently, they subsidized and supported certain services without prospect of early reward – as with C-SPAN, Black Entertainment Television, and the

Dsicovery Channel. Cable has also given a fresh lease on life to certain programming areas, for which the networks had catered in highly standardized ways. Examples include sports (with coverage of a wider range of games and events); children's programming (where animation no longer monopolizes provision); and politics on CNN and C-SPAN (where the greater amount of time available allows expanded coverage of major events, sustained interviews and call-in programs, coverage of committee deliberations, and longer extracts from newsmakers' speeches and conferences).

How solid is the basis for such enhanced consumer choice? On the face of it, it appears durable. As MacDonald (1990, pp. 260–61) has pointed out: 'Cable has several structural checks against its becoming a streamlined operation similar to the [former] broadcast monopoly.' Because 'the promise and raison d'être of cable television is program diversity, failure to deliver what subscribers consider a sufficiency of choice will be fatally self-destructive'; it needs to 'please its audience every month or run the risk of expensive disconnections'. Moreover, such checks are supported by the availability of 'free' over-the-air video as an alternative for dissatisfied customers.

Nevertheless, certain threats to the current terms of choice cannot be entirely discounted. One arises from the monopoly power enjoyed by cable operators almost everywhere (competitive 'overbuilds' are extremely rare), including at the time of writing, a freedom to charge subscribers whatever the market will bear. After local government authority over such charges was curbed by the Cable Communications Policy act of 1984, rates increased steeply in many communities. Operators justified this on the ground that many of the resulting resources were invested in original programming, the costs of which had been inexorably rising. Jogged by constituents' complaints, however, Congress has been reconsidering the 1984 deregulation with three aims in mind: FCC regulation or oversight of charges; must-carry assurances for independent and public TV stations; and fair access to cable programming for operators of competing technologies (e.g. DBS).

At the same time, cable industry leaders have been contemplating certain changes in how they supply service to customers. So far most channels on operators' systems have been bundled for sale at a composite rate in a large 'basic' package, supplemented by premium fees for a few individual movie channels. Executives of Tele-Communications Inc., the largest US cable system operator, have pointed out, however, that offering fewer services would limit audience fragmentation and help advertisers to aggregate viewership of their commercials. Moreover, schemes for unbundling the basic package have been tried in pilot areas, breaking it down into several tiers, including, for example, a 'lifeline' service of a small number of channels at low cost, a standard offering, and a higher price for an enlarged buy. Some industry leaders have even suggested that the future might belong to a completely *a la carte* system, with customers paying separately only for those individual channels they wish to have. Such a development would, of course, eliminate scope for cross-subsidies within the basic package, and it could reduce patronage of the less popular services.

Intensified Commercialism

An increasingly bottom-line orientation, with concentration on producing only that which promises the greatest profit, tends to prevail. This is even the case with American television, which always *was* a business. Yet there were also opportunities to strive for other qualities in both factual and fictional television. Network news and documentaries aspired to a responsible journalism that would tell people what they needed to know, not merely what would shock, titillate, and hold attention. Similarly, an influential strand in Hollywood production for the networks was that of including treatments of controversial themes and social problems in entertainment programming, particularly in 'movies of the week'. The motives for this varied, with some producers seeing it as a way to keep viewers abreast of current issues, some as a stimulus to concern, some as a chance to insert prosocial messages into popular programs. These days, however, one hears less about such noncommercial concerns, which could pale and recede further as the scramble for multimarket audiences becomes yet more hectic and dominant, and profit margins, even when momentarily high, seem ever in jeopardy. Thus, some interviewed program makers reported the emergence of a more tough-minded rhetoric among those who responded to their pitches and commissioned their projects, along the lines:

> We're not interested in socially redeeming programs . . . We're not here to cure cancer. Viewers don't want to see this.

Some analysts pin much of the responsibility for this tendency on certain deregulatory steps of the 1980s, particularly the elimination of anti-trafficking restrictions (according to which stations once bought could not be sold again for five years). This encouraged short-term profit-taking, increased the amount of debt to be serviced, and brought finance-oriented (as opposed to communication-oriented) individuals into management positions.

A Hedonistic Bias

Everything in the system tends to take second place to entertainment – because there is more revenue to be earned from it, it is more readily syndicatable in multiple markets, it is easier to promote, and it fits a dominant image of how people supposedly use their television sets, looking most of the time for instant gratification, relaxation, excitement, and escape. As the president of a cable service put it:

> We see that entertainment in its broadest description remains the most popular format for TV in the US, and . . . viewership is only going to come in really large numbers in an entertainment mold.

Thus, the heavyweight cable channels are mainly those providing mass appeal entertainment rather than offerings targeted to niche audiences – USA Network, ESPN, WTBS, TNT, and the pay movie channels. Even those more specialist services that might have been immune to it have fallen under the entertainment spell. Cable's programming service for children, Nickelodeon, for example, promotes itself as the 'fun channel for kids'. The chief executive of Black Entertainment Television felt obliged to remind Afro-American producers in 1989 that its middle name was *Entertainment*. The cultural channel calls itself an Arts & *Entertainment* network. What was formerly the Christian Broadcasting Network and is now the Family Channel has switched its programming signals from religious to entertainment fare. The Discovery Channel is reportedly losing interest in more demanding documentaries. Overall, then, there is a considerable privileging of entertainment programming and related production values, with a corresponding tendency either to limit or exclude expenditure on other program types or qualities or to oblige them to conform to entertainment criteria.

Public Affairs Constrained

The civic vocation of mainstream television news, public affairs, and political coverage comes under increasing pressure. It is true that certain branches of factual television have advanced and flourished in recent years. CNN has achieved respectable viewing levels, has been a critical and financial success, and is establishing a global as well as a domestic presence. Broadcast local news is booming in both late afternoon and late-night slots. Cable operators in different parts of the country are pioneering regional and local news programs, some on a 24-hour basis.

Nevertheless, heightened competition tempts national network news (still the most heavily viewed programs of their kind and the air time most sought by political leaders wanting to reach a mass audience) to avoid complexity and hit only those highlights that will gain and keep viewers' attention. As a retired CBS reporter told a House of Representatives committee in 1988 about the shifting priorities of that former bastion of journalistic solidity:

> We were ordered to add glitz. We were told to feature a celebrity interviewed at least every half-hour and if we did offer issue-oriented segments, the watchword was to give more heat and less light, the idea being that a noisy shouting match was a much better ratings draw than any reasoned debate.

Feature material tends to drive out 'hard' stories. Thus, a recent analysis not only showed that in the first half of 1990 the three networks' nightly news bulletins had doubled the amount of time they devoted to stories about showbusiness personalities and events (compared with the whole of 1989 and 1988), but when asked to comment on this pattern, their executives justified it on the ground that entertainment was what people tended to talk about most often. Further, they predicted that 1991's survey would be showing them doing more of the same. Another study of 36 local stations' evening news found only four minutes per hour devoted to local and state politics or public policy (Entman, 1989).

Moreover, while certain forms of news prosper, analysis and discussion tend to flag. Although the networks have included a few more public affairs shows in their primetime schedules than in the past, they all take the form of magazines, carving up material into short segments, often featuring dramatized re-enactments, celebrities, nostalgia, and other entertainment appeals. Relatively shortchanged in such a climate, then, are exercises in sustained journalistic analysis, issues that cannot readily be dramatized, and passages of speech beyond the 10-second soundbite limit. At best, this yields a flawed process of public accountability, with few forums in which issues can be regularly explored from multiple perspectives, bringing together in some dialogue and interchange the views of decision takers, their opponents, informed journalists, experts, and spokespersons of concerned interest and advocacy groups.

Programs beyond the Pale

A regime of increased channels and competition does not only extend choice; it also redefines choice, closing or narrowing doors on certain kinds of programs. Most at risk in the new television marketplace are productions that are relatively expensive to make but are unlikely to recoup their costs in viewer and revenue terms. Less favored, then, are:

- Original television plays that cannot be extended into widely marketable series.

- Major documentary projects.

- 'Critical and controversial programmes covering everything from the appraisal of commercial products, to ideology, philosophy, and religion' (Peacock Committee Report 1986, p. 127).

- Critical examinations of the role of television and other mass media in society, including deliberate exercises of viewer challenge and accountability.

- Anything that seems preachy, pedantic, or measured in pace and materials requiring active and not passive attention.

- Educative fare intended to inform, stimulate, and broaden the horizons of children.

In fact, overcommercialization and trivialization are not unfair characterizations of television for American children, even in the abundance of new marketplace conditions. There is no network-provided regular weekday series for children. Broadcaster-provided children's programming is full of commercials, taking up 22 per cent of available air time according to one survey. The principle of separating program content from advertising has gone by the board, with some productions, based on characters sold as toys in the shops, being veritable program-length commercials.

Standards Under Pressure

There is an increasing tendency to tailor programming to an image of the kind of medium that television is presumed to be: fast moving and emotional, not deliberate, cognitive, or logical. Thus, in American television, there has been a decline in an assured sense of standards and a marked loss of respect for boundaries within which the competitive chase for audiences might be contained. There has been a striking explosion of the so-called 'reality' genre of programming, giving center stage in a mushrooming number of talk shows, audience participation shows, 'infotainment' magazines, and crime and trial reconstruction shows, to shock, scandal, prurience, and combative confrontation. A philosophy of programming for the 'video generation' has developed among certain more recently arrived producers, to the effect that television should never be didactic, rationalistic, open to complexity ('Subtlety is out', said one) or sensitive to privacy concerns ('An advantage of television is that you get a sense that you are a voyeur', said another). Even the three big networks, originally more careful in these matters, have given in from time to time, reducing the staffs and powers of their previously formidable Standards and Practices Divisions, and screening sensationalist programs that would not have been aired in earlier times. In the justifying and revealing words of an NBC executive:

A network cannot hew to higher standards if its competitors all round adopt lower ones. It becomes a greyer issue when it's all around you, and you're the last person crying, 'Wait a minute'.

In a highly commercialized system, the main bulwark against this tendency is, somewhat ironically, the occasional refusal of advertisers to place their commercials in what is sometimes termed 'tabloid' material.

Mixed Prospects for Creativity

According to the more than fifty producers, writers, and directors with experience of working for two or more program-commissioning markets who were interviewed at length, the modern video marketplace has, at one and the same time, opened up more places to which they can take their wares *and* it has generated pressures to limit receptivity to imaginative and original production.

On the plus side, it is a boon to program makers that their ideas can now be taken to more than 'three candy stores' and that their projects that were not accepted, failed, or faltered in one market may have a second or third chance in another. There is more work overall, and they can sometimes negotiate various trade-offs with the new outlets that compensate for failure to land a network contract, such as larger orders and more relaxed production schedules. Many reported a greater readiness among the new outlets to consider, at least initially, program ideas that would never have got onto broadcast network schedules in the old days, like *Brothers*, *It's Garry Shandling's Show*, and *Max Headroom*. Pay cable channels especially, advertising-free and supported by more adventuresome subscribers, have allowed program makers to exercise greater freedom in choice of subject, format, treatment, and language.

These same program makers, however, pointed out that this expanded marketplace still includes only a limited number of outlets that can afford to be creatively more freewheeling as a matter of policy. Furthermore, whereas initial receptivity to new ideas is one thing, willingness to persevere with them is another, and they cited instances of how buyers of initially accepted innovative concepts had managed to water them down before they reached the screen (or not long after). They had also felt the effects of an encroaching bottom-line mentality that could reduce creative priorities to near vanishing point ('What it boils down to is higher numbers, that's all . . . It's very depressing to the creative process if you pay attention to it'). It favored shows that are economic to produce (game shows, talk shows, 'reality' shows) over programs that require 'wonderful scripting, fine acting, good direction, time in production'. It encouraged a factory approach to production (among several examples of treadmill-like schedules mentioned by informants, one team had managed to turn out 45 reality-based shows in 2.5 months!). Also privileged in such a competitive environment are immediate-appeal shows, formats and production styles, including reruns and remakes of past successes (e.g. *Star Trek*, *The Munsters*, *Charlie's Angels*). One producer excoriated this trend as 'regurgitation television', calling it 'bad for TV and bad for us as producers because it takes away slots for . . . original programming, which is what we pride ourselves on. When the creative community writes someone else's scripts they are turned into a bunch of androids.'

Not surprisingly, most program makers find multichannel television preferable to the oligopolistic system it has replaced, but when the interviewees were asked to which outlet they would most prefer to take their *next* ideas, the great majority unhesitatingly cited the major broadcast networks. Not only do they provide larger audiences, they said, but they can make your reputation ('It's good for your career'), they are more likely to provide the resources enabling you to translate your concept into a good program, and they offer the best gateway to lucrative ancillary markets. Their response suggests that, despite the recent problems of the networks and the impressive rise of cable, much of the system's incentive structure is still skewed toward scale and grandeur of effort, a longer mass audience reach, bigger monetary rewards and prospects (through back-end earnings), and network-based credits and prestige.

Overall, it does appear that new market proliferation has pushed back the boundaries of the permissible and relaxed formerly rigid notions of what might work on US television generally, but some informants expressed reservations about even these creative gains. A producer-writer put his finger on a significant distinction:

> It's true that because the new marketplace is so competitive, everybody's got a motivation to be a bit different. But what about being a bit better? I see little of that.

In part, such a disparity reflects the conflict between a ratings-driven concern to be popular and a quality-driven concern to give the less predictable pleasures of stretched imaginations and horizons. As Warnock (1990, p. 18) argues:

> If broadcasters are compelled to give people what they think they want rather than what they will actually enjoy, if they have to offer what people will choose if asked, rather than what they might have chosen if they had known about it, then they will have to forget about . . . quality.

It also reflects the fact, however, that quality concerns are always vulnerable in a fully commercial television system because they have no assured place at its decision-taking tables.

Policy Issues

The significant policy challenges associated with the emergence of the new television marketplace are more problematic for Americans, more profound for Europeans. For the former, the changes in train, however traumatic for particular stakeholders, generate in essence more of what has always fuelled US broadcasting: more competition, more revenue chasing, more players competing more intensively for the attentions of a more fragmented audience. For the latter, the new order introduces change in the rules of the communication game itself.

East of the Atlantic

How Europeans have conceived and organized television will be fundamentally challenged in at least four ways in the future. First, the relationship between money and programming could shift from that of servant to that of master (as the US record on television advertising unequivocally shows). Even in advance of implementation of the British government's 1990 Broadcasting Act, leading Independent Television (ITV) company executives were exploring new ways of raising program finance, including sponsorship, because, as one put it: 'The new competition for audiences will call for money in large and growing quantities, as expectations rise and the competition for talent inflates costs' (Plowright 1990, p. 3).

Second, as the hedonistic bias gains ever more ground, news, public affairs, and political programming could be downgraded from its hitherto honored to a second- or even third-class status. In the past, British broadcasters aimed to steer a course between their responsibility for the welfare of the political system and an awareness of the limited political appetite of the ordinary viewer (Blumler et al. 1986; 1989). During national election campaigns, for example, schedules were rearranged, special programs introduced, political staffs redeployed, and the length of flagship news bulletins doubled to accommodate much extra coverage, including special steps to strengthen its analytical dimension. In the 1987 General Election there was no pulling back from such extraordinary measures even when ratings for the news programs declined. Such commitments could be more difficult to sustain in the forthcoming period.

Third, as fear grows that the fickle viewer may readily wander off elsewhere, the purposes of programming could shift, increasingly subordinating the communication of meaningful experience to the mere holding of attention. Interviews with British broadcasters in the period before multichannel expansion was imminent suggest that the public service framework did provide a congenial home for communication aspirations of the former kind (Nossiter, 1986). There was the current affairs producer who described British broadcasting as 'the principal forum which enables the whole nation to talk to itself'. There was a concern to communicate something intelligibly about culture, arts, and science to an audience reaching well beyond the cognoscenti and the already involved, illustrated by the arts programmer who proclaimed: 'Never before has there been the opportunity to speak to all the people or to make available to them the whole of British culture.' There were producers in the regional ITV companies who saw their work partly in terms of nourishing networks of geographical identities and ties – 'sustaining community in parts of Britain that are sparsely populated and remote from London', as one put it. There was the soap opera producer who said: 'We are trying through our serial to make people think about relationships and the problems around us – whether it's race or teenagers and their parents or caring for the elderly.' In the new television marketplace, however, such aims could increasingly seem naively utopian.

Fourth, the very philosophy of public service broadcasting could suffer a deepening crisis of confidence, identity, and legitimacy (Syvertsen 1991): uncertain of its mission; unclear whether, and, if so, how far, to compete with commercial swashbucklers on their more pragmatic terrain; fearful of long-term anachronistic irrelevance. Whatever the eventual outcome, the long-standing commitments of European public service providers to broadcasting quality, range, and standards will face threats from new marketplace impera-tives. Range requires a readiness to commit resources to less popular program-ming areas in some disregard of the audience levels that are likely to be reached. Quality requires an avoidance of formulae, a readiness to take creative risks, a commitment to provide shelters against overwhelming produc-tion demands, and (as a US writer-producer put it), 'people with courage all along the line to put good ideas into development, then give them a go, and then stay with them when at first they are slow in the ratings'. Maintenance of standards requires some confidence in the integrity of ground rules that are more or less shared among all leading competitors (Blumler 1989a). All these preconditions will be challenged by new marketplace forces.

That is why policy makers in most West European societies have been pursuing, in different ways, a twin-track approach: on the one hand, opening the doors to more competition, commercialism, and channel abundance; on the other hand, devising safeguards to protect societal and broadcasting values thought vulnerable to the pressures these will unleash. This is not the place for detail about such measures, but, in general, varying greatly and unevenly from country to country, they tend to take four forms:

- Continuing designation of the original broadcasting bodies as 'cornerstone' providers of public service television with their own public source of income, typically an annual licence fee exacted from each set-owning household.

- Licencing requirements, stipulating certain 'quality' criteria for commer-cial franchise applicants.

- Imposition of obligations on franchise holders to include certain forms of programming in significant amounts in their services (e.g. news, regional programs, children's television, etc.).

- In some places, the creation of new authorities with a watching brief over standards.

In the last decade of the twentieth century, then, many European societies may try to have it both ways, embodying the majoritarian model of television provision in commercially run enterprises and the pluralist model in slimmed-down and beleaguered but still sizable public service organizations. Whether such coexistence will prove viable could turn, first, on how the viewing audience distributes its favors to the old and new competitors and, second, on the integrity and imagination shown by the embattled public service broad-casters in pursuit of their far more difficult tasks.

West of the Atlantic

The debate on the appropriate role of public policy for television under conditions of channel abundance is far different in the United States than it is in the countries of Western Europe. Europeans at least know what their central problem is, despite much uncertainty over the likely effectiveness of the solutions being contemplated to meet it. In contrast, the American debate tends to lack a coherent focus.

It is not that US policy makers' plates are empty. On the contrary, they face a scatter of many specific problems, the discussion of which is often reduced either to level-playing-field conflicts of interest (e.g. over the financial interest and syndication rules, cable reregulation, must carry requirements, compulsory copyright, syndicated exclusivity, etc.) or to the intricacies of technological midwifery (e.g. over fiber-optic cable, high-definition television, and related issues of spectrum allocation). Although certain more principled concerns have surfaced at times in congressional committee deliberations – including a determination to protect 'free', over-the-air TV; child viewers from blatantly commercial exploitation; and cable consumers against excessive subscription charges – these do not add up to an elaborated, overall policy perspective.

The core obstacle to progress in these terms is basically ideological. The ingrained free market ethos of the American culture fosters a presumption that all consequences of increased competition in the television marketplace will be beneficial. Silence smothers any 'downsides' that might flow from the intensification of competition. Disinclined to seek out such dangers and disadvantages, policy makers are then hamstrung for ways of identifying and coping with any that might emerge.

Yet there are many programming needs that the competitive marketplace cannot meet, or will not meet well, because it privileges:

- Citizens with higher incomes, and the interests for which they are prepared to pay.

- Large resource providers, such as advertisers.

- Large audience-pullers, as in the incentive to score hits.

- What is most likely to be acceptable in multiple markets – the common denominator in new form.

- What has most immediate and arresting appeal.

- What large conglomerates and middlemen of all kinds expect to be most profitable (Blumler, 1989b).

In such a marketplace, suppliers who are disinclined to follow these imperatives court the triple risk of having to make do with skimpy resources; being assigned to lower rungs on the industry's ladders of reputation and prestige; and being sucked back into the dominant system at some cost to their integrity.

The outcome is a television system in which communication-dependent public goods are continually vulnerable to shrinkage and neglect as a result of commercial pressures. These include diversity; a free, wide-ranging, and robust marketplace of ideas; provision of a national political forum with high standards of responsible journalism in its support; multicultural interchange and understanding; full and fair access for those with something to say to those who might wish to hear it; the educative needs of children; and impulses of producer creativity, originality, and desire to provide materials worthy of viewers' involvement, reflection, and use in the circumstances of their lives. Although all these values do have some place in US multichannel television, they are always in danger of being marginalized and sacrificed for the sake of a short-term financial fix.

In principle, there are two broad strategic avenues along which policies of reform could proceed. One is a regulatory approach, which would specify, as obligations on licence and franchise holders, certain contributions to society's communication goals in return for the publicly conferred privileges they enjoy. Although not to be ruled out in certain cases (e.g. children's programming), in US conditions, such an approach is liable to be thwarted by running afoul of First Amendment principles, lack of a strong tradition of broadcast regulatory administration, or the difficulty of imposing regulatory requirements on entrepreneurs that run strongly against the economic grain.

An alternative approach would aim to build up a substantial public sector with the mission to serve those values that commercial television cannot pursue for their own sake. Although, as organized at present, US public television has the principles, it lacks the resources to perform such a role at all effectively. It has been kept on short funding rations throughout its history. Even the $245 million that Congress appropriated for public radio and television for fiscal year 1991 was regarded as relatively generous. Public broadcasting is rarely able to compete with commercial provision in production-value terms. It tends to concentrate almost entirely on worthy fare that the commercial vendors for the most part ignore – documentaries, children's programs, science, history, the arts, BBC drama, and so on – unleavened with domestically produced entertainment. It relies heavily on a small number of production teams working within relatively unvarying series formats. Not surprisingly, its audience share has been persistently low and its status sometimes little better than marginal. Provoked by the challenges and problems of multichannel expansion in the commercial sector, a determination to rethink strategies for programming, scheduling, promotion, and audience holding, and to utilize the available resources more effectively, has latterly been spreading throughout the ranks of public television (PBS/CPB 1990). Short of a significant increase in those resources, however, it will rarely be able to do more than provide occasional oases for viewers suffering from a cultural thirst in the commercial desert and will lack a system-influencing capability.

Perhaps the most fundamental policy challenge that faces US policy makers today lies, then, not in the maze of conflicting intra- and inter-industrial interests on which many marketplace developments tend to force their gaze, but in finding ways to realize the constructive potential of the country's public television system. The long-term objective might be one of building a mixed television economy in the United States, including both a principled and an amply and securely funded public sector and a marketplace that thrives and flourishes according to its own dynamics.

References

BLUMLER, JAY G., 1986: 'Television in the United States: Funding Sources and Programming Consequences', *Research on the Range and Quality of Broadcasting Services*. A Report for the Committee on Financing the BBC, London: Her Majesty's Stationery Office.

BLUMLER, JAY G., 'New Television Industry Developments in the United States: Some Policy Implications', paper presented to the 17th Annual Telecommunications Policy Research Conference, Airlie House, Airlie, Va., October, 1989.

BLUMLER, JAY G., 1986b: *The Role of Public Policy in the New Television Marketplace*. Washington, DC: Benton Foundation.

BLUMLER, JAY G., GUREVITCH, MICHAEL, and NOSSITER, T. J., 1986: 'Setting the Television News Agenda: Campaign Observation at the BBC', in Crewe Ivor, and Martin Harrop (eds), *Political Communications: The General Election Campaign of 1983*. Cambridge: Cambridge University Press.

BLUMLER, JAY G., GUREVITCH, MICHAEL and NOSSITER, T. J., 1989: 'The Earnest Versus the Determined: Election Newsmaking at the BBC, 1987', in Crewe, Ivor and Martin Harrop (eds), *Political Communications: The General Election Campaign of 1987*. Cambridge: Cambridge University Press.

ENTMAN, ROBERT M., 1989: *Democracy without Citizens: Media and the Decay of American Politics*, New York and Oxford: Oxford University Press.

FOWLER, MARK S. and BRENNER, DAVID L., 'A Marketplace Approach to Broadcast Regulation', *Texas Law Review*, Vol. 60, 1982, pp. 207–257.

Home Office, 1986: *Report of the Peacock Committee on Financing the BBC*. London: Her Majesty's Stationery Office.

KRULWICH, ROBERT, 1990: 'The Television Environment in the 1990s', keynote address to conference on Exploring Primetime, Public Broadcasting Service and Corporation for Public Broadcasting, Washington, DC.

MACDONALD, J. FRED, 1990: *One Nation under Television*, New York: Pantheon Books.

NOSSITER, T. J., 1986: 'British Television: A Mixed Economy', in *Research on the Range and Quality of Broadcasting Services*, A Report for the Committee on Financing the BBC. London: Her Majesty's Stationery Office.

PICARD, ROBERT G., 1989: *Media Economics: Concepts and Issues*. Newbury Park, London, and New Delhi: Sage.

PLOWRIGHT, DAVID, 'A Welcome Intruder', *Airwaves*, No. 23, Summer 1990, pp. 2–3.

PUBLIC BROADCASTING SERVICE AND CORPORATION FOR PUBLIC BROADCASTING, proceedings of a conference, Exploring Primetime, Washington, DC, 1990.

REDSTONE, SUMNER, 'A Speech to the Caucus', *The Caucus Quarterly*, April 1990.

SCHUMPETER, JOSEPH A., 1942: *Capitalism, Socialism and Democracy*, New York: Harper.

TUROW, JOSEPH, 1982: 'Unconventional Programming on Commercial Television: An Organizational Perspective', in Ettema, James S. and Whitney, D. Charles, (eds), *Individuals in Mass Media Organizations: Creativity and Constraints*. Beverly Hills and London: Sage.

SYVERTSEN, TRINE, 1991: 'Public Television in Crisis: Debate and Critique in Britain and Norway', *European Journal of Communication*, Vol. 6, No. 1, pp. 95–114.

WARNOCK BARONESS, 1990: 'Quality and Standards in Broadcasting', in Miller, Nod, Cresta Norris and Janice Hughes (eds), *Broadcasting Standards: Quality or Control?*, Manchester Monographs, pp. 7–25, University of Manchester Department of Extramural Studies.

11

In Defense of Objectivity

Judith Lichtenberg

Introduction

American journalists embrace the ideal of objectivity as one of the fundamental norms of their profession. The distinction between news, where objectivity is thought possible and desirable, and opinion, where objectivity is thought impossible, is deeply entrenched in the journalistic culture. Inextricably intertwined with truth, fairness, balance, neutrality, the absence of value judgements – in short, with the most fundamental journalistic values – objectivity is a cornerstone of the professional ideology of journalists in liberal democracies.

Yet the objectivity of journalism has come increasingly under fire in recent years. The criticisms come from a variety of quarters and take several different forms. We are told by some that journalism *isn't* objective; by others that it *cannot* be objective; and by still others that it *shouldn't* be objective. Sometimes the same critic seems to be making more than one of these charges.

One challenge comes from critics of varying political stripes who claim that the media have not represented their views adequately or reported their activities impartially. We hear accusations that the media have a 'liberal bias', that they overemphasize unrest or look too hard for muck to rake. Other critics contend that, on the contrary, the press serves the conservative interests of government and big business. Aggrieved individuals and groups of all kinds charge that news coverage of this or that issue is unfair, biased, or sensational.

Those who attack journalism on these grounds seem to share one crucial assumption with those they criticize. Charges of bias or unfairness suggest at least that objectivity is possible – why complain of bias unless a contrast can be imagined? But many contemporary critics of journalism reject this assumption. Not only is journalism not objective, they say; it couldn't be. As one recent journalism textbook puts it, objectivity 'is a false and impossible ideal', and although all media writers claim it in some way, 'they are all wrong' (Kessler and McDonald 1989, pp. 24, 28).

This view has its roots in the sociology of knowledge and today finds its fullest expression in postmodernism; it is shared by many sociologists, humanists, legal scholars, and other social critics. They believe that the most common understanding of objectivity rests on an outmoded and untenable theory of knowledge, according to which objective knowledge consists in correspondence between some idea or statement and a reality 'out there' in the world.

'Objectivity', in the words of a former journalism school dean, 'is an essential correspondence between knowledge of a thing and the thing itself' (McDonald 1975, p. 69). But according to the critics, reality is not 'out there'; it is 'a vast production, a staged creation – something humanly produced and humanly maintained' (Carey 1989, p. 26). Reality, on this view, is 'socially constructed', and so there are as many realities as there are social perspectives of the world. There is no 'true reality' to which objective knowledge can be faithful.

One might expect these critics to reach the conclusion that objectivity is impossible with a certain sense of regret or disappointment: we had hoped true, real knowledge was possible, but alas we find it is not. But those who believe objectivity is impossible often hold it to be an undesirable and even dangerous ideal. Objectivity is a strategy of hegemony used by some members of society to dominate others (MacKinnon 1982, p. 537); a 'strategic ritual' enabling professionals to 'defend themselves from critical onslaught' (Tuchman 1972); even 'the most insidious bias of all' (Schudson 1978, p. 160).[1] At best, objectivity 'is a cultural form with its own set of conventions' (Schiller 1981, p. 5).

The Compound Assault on Objectivity

There's a certain oddness in this compound assault on objectivity – that journalism isn't objective, that it couldn't be, that it shouldn't be – for the charges are essentially incompatible. Thus, although often a single critic makes more than one of these accusations, no two of them taken together makes sense. Why not?

1   The sincere complaint that a piece of journalism isn't objective makes sense only against the background assumption that objectivity is possible (why bother complaining about the inevitable?).

2   The insistence that journalism cannot be objective makes superfluous the view that objectivity is undesirable (why bother denouncing the impossible?).

3   The assertion that objectivity isn't desirable makes senseless the complaint that journalism isn't objective (what's the complaint?).

But these apparent confusions do not result from simple muddle-headedness; they embody a logic of sorts. Let us try to reconstruct roughly the chain of reasoning to the all-encompassing conclusion that objectivity in journalism doesn't, couldn't, and shouldn't exist:

• Experience continually confronts us with examples of clashes of belief (between individuals, between cultures) that we cannot resolve – we don't know how to decide who is right.

• No one can totally escape his or her biases; no one can be completely objective.

• Therefore, the idea that there could be an objective, true account of things is a fiction.

• Therefore, anyone who sincerely thinks there can be such an account is deluded by a faulty understanding of the relation between mind and the world.

- This faulty understanding has significant practical consequences; belief in objectivity and adherence to practices thought to be implied by it reinforces existing power relations and cultural and political chauvinism.

- Therefore, the aspiration to objectivity, whether innocent or not, serves as a prop in an ideological agenda.

- So, in other words, real objectivity is impossible and its attempted manifestations are either naive or insidious or both.

Who is this enemy that makes such strange bedfellows, uniting critics from left and right and bringing together the most theoretical of academic scholars with worldly practitioners of journalism? There is no single enemy; there are several. In elevating objectivity to an ideal one may be endorsing several different ends or the supposed means of attaining them. And so the attack on objectivity can represent a variety of different complaints. Since the values captured by the term 'objectivity' vary greatly – in the extent to which they are possible, probable, actual, or desirable – the legitimacy of the complaints varies as well.

My fundamental aim is to show that in its core meaning we cannot coherently abandon objectivity, and that insofar as the critics of objectivity make sense – which often they do – they themselves do not abandon it, whatever they may think. How is this possible? Those who purport to reject objectivity are really doing one or more of the following: rejecting objectivity explicitly while covertly relying on it; confusing objectivity with something else, i.e. denouncing values, like neutrality, often associated with but distinct from objectivity; criticizing practices or methods commonly but perhaps mistakenly thought to attain objectivity.

Metaphysical Questions

Our most fundamental interest in objectivity is an interest in truth. We want to know how things stand in the world, or what happens, and why. In this sense, to claim that a particular piece of journalism is not objective is to claim that it falls short of providing the truth or the whole truth. And to deny that objectivity is possible is at least to deny that there is any way of getting at the truth, because (according to this view) all accounts of things are accounts from a particular social, psychological, cultural, or historical perspective and we have no way of adjudicating between conflicting accounts, no neutral standpoint from which to evaluate them. To deny that objectivity is possible is often also to insist, not only that we can never get at the truth, but that for precisely this reason it makes no sense to think there is any such thing. Even to speak of 'truth' or 'the facts', these critics strongly suggest, demonstrates a certain naiveté.

To doubt that objectivity is possible, then, is to doubt that we can know how things *really* are or what *really* happens, where 'really' means something like 'independently of our own perspective'. But there is a crucial ambiguity in the phrase 'our own perspective'. One way to doubt the objectivity of a story or an account of things is to challenge the particular perspective from which it is told. So, for example, one might doubt that American news accounts of the United States' bombing of Libya in 1986 told an objective story. When our worries take this form, we may be doubting that a particular account is objective – i.e. true or complete – but we need not be denying that it is possible to tell an objective, or at least a more objective, story. Indeed, we typically have specific ideas about how to go about getting one. We seek out foreign press accounts of these events, compare them to each other and to American news accounts, and evaluate inconsistencies within and between stories in light of a variety of standards. We inquire into a news organization's sources of information, likely obstacles to the reliability of its judgements, whether it has interested motives that might give it reason to distort the story, and so forth. We have, in short, a multitude of standards and practices for evaluating the reliability of information. It is rare, in the quick-and-messy world that journalists cover, that these standards and practices enable us to determine the whole truth and nothing but the truth in a particular case. But it is equally rare that we have no guidance whatever.

Often, however, the challenge to objectivity connects to deeper philosophical worries, to the centuries-old debate between realists and idealists. The metaphysical realist says that there is a world or a way things are 'out there' – i.e. independently of our perspective. Traditionally, 'our' perspective meant not yours or mine or our culture's, but the human perspective, or even the perspective of any possible consciousness. The ideal of knowledge presupposed by this view holds that objects or states of affairs in the world are 'intrinsically' or 'independently' a certain way, and that knowledge consists in somehow 'mirroring' the way they are.

The metaphysical idealist denies that we can know what the world is like intrinsically, apart from a perspective. The world is our construction in the sense that we inevitably encounter it through our concepts and our categories; we cannot see the world concept- or category-free. Kant, from whom the contemporary idealist critique derives, described universal categories shaping our perception of the world that are necessary for human beings to experience the world at all. The sense for Kant in which we cannot get outside our perspective is unthreatening, because by 'our' perspective Kant means not that of our clan or culture but that of all human consciousness. So understood, idealism poses no threat to objectivity. The idealist can make all the distinctions the realist can make: between the real and the illusory, what is 'out there' and what is 'in here', the objective and the subjective. Lions are real and unicorns mythical; trees and sky are 'out there' and stomach-aches and beliefs are 'in here'. Idealism leaves everything as it is (Luban 1986, pp. 708–11).

But Kant opened the door to a more threatening relativism. For having admitted that our knowledge of the world is relative to a framework, it was a natural step to the view that the categories moulding our experience depend partly on concrete and particular conditions that vary from culture to culture, community to community, even person to person. When twentieth-century thinkers took this step, arguing not simply that reality is constructed but that it is socially constructed – constructed differently, therefore, by different groups and cultures – they repudiated Kant's consolation that we could accept idealism while preserving objective, because universal, knowledge.

Global Doubts and Local Doubts

When critics tell us that reality is socially constructed by way of explaining that our news accounts of events are not objective, what are they saying? That our culture, our political and other interests do much to structure and determine the way we (whoever 'we' may be) look at the world, and that our news reports reflect, reinforce, and even create these biases? Of course this is true. Yet some of the sharpest critics of the press make this latter argument without calling into question the possibility of objectivity; indeed they rely on it, as I would argue they must (Chomsky 1969). But the assertion that reality is socially constructed means something more than this. There is a finality and inevitability about it: we believe what we believe because of our gender or class or cultural attachments; others with other attachments believe differently, and there is no adjudicating between our beliefs and theirs, for there is no neutral standpoint.

Yet surely the critics do not mean that we can never get outside our perspective in this sense, outside the particular world-view in which we have been raised, that we can never look at it, criticize it, judge it. They have, after all. How do they know that the American news accounts of the Libyan bombing are partial, except by comparison with some other actual or possible accounts? Their judgement rests partly on other sources of information, which taken separately or taken together have, they believe, proved more consistent or coherent.

The point is that it makes no sense to criticize a statement or description as biased or unobjective except against the background of some actual or possible contrast, some more accurate statement or better description. We have a variety of means to settle differences between conflicting beliefs or to establish one view as superior to another. We get more evidence, seek out other sides of the story, check our instruments, duplicate our experiments, re-examine our chain of reasoning. These methods don't settle all questions, but they settle many. In showing us how, say, British news stories construct reality, critics of necessity depend on the possibility of seeing and understanding alternative versions of the same events. And if no means existed to compare these alternative 'realities', the charges would have no bite. For the critics' point is not that these alternative 'realities' are like so many flavors of ice cream about which *de gustibus non disputandum est* but that those who see things in one way are missing something important, or getting only a partial view, or even getting things wrong.

Typically, the social constructionist critique vacillates between two incompatible claims: the general and 'global' assertion that objectivity is impossible because different people and cultures employ different categories and there is no way of deciding which framework better fits the world; and the charge that particular news stories or mass media organizations serve an ideological function or represent the world in a partial or distorted or otherwise inadequate way. It is crucial to see that these charges are incompatible. Insofar as objectivity is impossible there can be no sense in the claim – certainly none in the rebuke – that the media are ideological or partial, for these concepts imply the possibility of a contrast. And conversely insofar as we agree that the media serve an ideological function or bias our vision, we implicitly accept the view that other, better, more objective ways are possible.

Transcultural Communication

Lurking in the assault on objectivity is the assumption that different cultures possess radically different and impermeable worldviews. But this claim is overstated. Two points are important. First, despite all the talk about differences in worldview we share a great deal even with those from very different cultures. Second, even where we see things differently from those of other cultures we can see *that* we see things differently and we can see *how* we see things differently. So our worldviews are not hermetic: others can get in and we can get out. As we shall see, the two points are not wholly separable: the distinction between sharing a perspective and being able to understand another's perspective is not sharp.

It is easy to fall under the sway of the doctrine of cultural relativism, and probably every undergraduate who has encountered the work of Whorf or Sapir (or many others) has been struck with the vivid realization of the crucial role of language in shaping one's experience and worldview. But the truth in this insight has been exaggerated. For one thing, what impresses us here depends partly on the premise that different 'worldviews' take the same underlying stuff, the same data of experience, and shape it differently. So, ironically, the 'aha experience' of relativism rests on the commonsense recognition of one world out there – something that the relativist is often at pains to deny.

For another, the differences between worldviews can be exaggerated. Even those from very different cultures can agree, despite their deeply different conceptions of time, to meet at ten and to come together at what all recognize as the negotiating table. Intractable disputes between cultures and segments of a society arise sometimes because their values diverge; equally often, however, intractable disputes arise precisely because their values coincide. Both the Israelis and the Palestinians invest Jerusalem with sacred and irreplaceable value. In what sense do their worldviews clash? As Francis I is supposed to have said about Henry VIII: 'Henry and I agree about everything: we both want Calais.' Even where our points of view clearly differ, what should we make of this fact? As Donald Davidson puts it (Davidson, 1984, p. 184):

> Whorf, wanting to demonstrate that Hopi incorporates a metaphysics so alien to ours that Hopi and English cannot, as he puts it, 'be calibrated', uses English to convey the contents of sample Hopi sentences. Kuhn is brilliant at saying what things were like before the revolution using – what else? – our postrevolutionary idiom.[2]

Our worldviews, then, are not unalterable and hermetic. We can and do come to see things as others see them – not just others from our culture but from radically different ones. Thucydides brings the agony of the Athenians' war to life; Ruth Benedict gets us to see 'the uses of cannibalism'; Faulkner shows us how things look to an adult with the mind of a child. The possibility of communication between cultures is perhaps inseparable from the first point: from the outset different cultures possess points of commonality and contact, and these enable us to travel back and forth. Could there be a point to history, anthropology, literature, journalism, biography if this were not so?

Of course, some people and some cultures are easier to understand than others. Sometimes, at the limit, we remain after all in the dark. But mostly we can succeed more or less in overcoming the barriers. We can see the world as others see it.

Deconstructing 'The Social Construction of Reality'

But if other 'realities' aren't hermetic and impermeable, that takes much of the wind out of the assertion that reality is socially constructed. For the usual connotations of the word 'reality' are exhaustive and exclusive: reality is all, and all there is. If instead there are many possible realities, and ways to get from one to the other, then we can see into each other's worlds, and our realities can thereby be altered.

Perhaps it will be argued that even when we seem to escape the determination of our vision by a particular social construction, even when we seem to see things in a new light, that new vision is also socially constructed. Suppose, for example, that, partly as a result of changes in American news accounts, over the last several years Americans have begun to understand the Palestinian point of view in the Middle East conflict better than they had before.[3] It might be said that these changes result from differences in the American political establishment's view of its own geopolitical interests; the changes, then, are themselves socially constructed out of the web of American ideology.

No doubt changing American interests partly explain the changes in perception. But to insist that apparently divergent views *always and only* derive from the push of the dominant culture's interests amounts to an unfalsifiable conspiracy theory. Here the claim that reality is socially constructed verges on the empty. But if there are other possible sources of our changed view apart from the dominant ideological forces, then we must ask what work the concept of social construction is doing. Is the point simply that ways of looking at the world don't come into being *ex nihilo*, but are rather the product of . . . of *something* – the total social-political-economic-cultural-psychological-biological environment? And is this no more than the claim that everything has a cause? Beyond these extremely general assertions the view that reality is socially constructed seems to add nothing. For if every view is socially constructed but there is no view that can *not* be socially constructed we learn nothing of substance when we know that reality is socially constructed.

None of this is to say that the media do not sometimes (even often) present events in a distorted, biased, or ideological way. On the contrary, we can only explain this fact on the assumption that there are better and worse, more and less faithful renderings of events, and that, despite our own biases, preconceptions, 'conceptual schemes', we can escape our own point of view sufficiently to recognize the extent to which it imposes a structure or slant on events that could be seen differently.

The word 'reality' is to blame for some of the confusion.[4] By her own account, one crucial theme of Gaye Tuchman's book *Making News* is that 'the act of making news is the act of constructing reality itself rather than a picture of reality' (Tuchman 1978, p. 12). Tuchman's point trades on ambiguities in the term 'reality'.

News can illuminatingly be said to construct reality rather than a picture of it in two senses. First, some events are genuine media creations. When *Newsweek* proclaims on its cover that 'Nixon Is Back', then in a crucial sense Nixon *is* back. To have arrived on *Newsweek*'s cover is to be back from whatever realm of nonbeing one used to inhabit. But this kind of news story, although highly significant, represents no more than a fraction of the total news product.

Second, the act of making news is an act of constructing reality in the sense captured by the sociological commonplace that 'if a situation is defined as real it's real in its consequences'. If people believe that news stories of an event are accurate, they will behave accordingly, and for certain purposes those stories, however inaccurate they might be, function as 'reality'. But news stories purport to represent an independent reality, and although they often fall short, if we abandon the concept of a reality independent of news stories we undermine the very basis on which to criticize the media's constructions.

The Existence and Meaning of Facts

Most people have a crude picture of what objectivity means, and this partly explains its bad name. Belief in objectivity does not mean that every question that can be posed or about which people might disagree has a single determinate right answer. If objectivity meant this we would be wise to reject it.

What, then, does belief in objectivity commit us to? At the very least it means that some questions have determinate, right answers – and that all questions have wrong answers. So, for example, it is a fact that George Bush is currently the President of the United States, and that in March 1989 the tanker Exxon Valdez spilled more than 10 million gallons of oil into Alaska's Prince William Sound.

Do the relativists and postmodernists deny that George Bush is President or that the Exxon Valdez spilled millions of gallons of oil into the sound? Let us hope not. How, then, do they reconcile these unassailable facts with their repudiation of objectivity? We find several strategies.

1 One is to insist that nevertheless such facts are socially constructed. But what does this mean? No reasonable person would deny that for there to be such a thing as a President of such a thing as the United States, a wide variety of complex social institutions must be in place. If that is all it means to say this fact is socially constructed, nothing significant turns on admitting it. But typically the point of emphasizing the constructedness of a fact is to undermine its truth or credibility. Yet however constructed 'George Bush is President' may be, it is no less true or credible for that.

A variation on the theme that all facts are socially constructed is the claim that they are all 'theory-laden'. Certainly every factual statement can be understood to imply decisions about the usefulness or appropriateness of categorizing things in one way rather than another. If we want to dignify even the most commonsensical of such categorizations with the label 'theory', who's to stop us? But then we must keep in mind that there are theories and theories. 'The human fetus is a person' and 'The PLO is a terrorist organization' are laden with controversial theories; 'The earth revolves around the sun' and 'The lion is a mammal' are laden with theories not seriously contestable in modern times. Facts, then, may be theory-laden; but whether they therefore lack objectivity depends on the particular theories they carry as freight. 'George Bush is President' may in some sense rest on a theory or conceptual framework, but it is one so widely shared and innocuous that the label 'theory-laden', usually brought as an accusation, loses its bite. Without an account of the faulty theory embedded therein, we can rest content: when our theories are good, theory-ladenness is nothing to be afraid of.

The facts used here as illustrations are, of course, quite trivial ones, and that might seem to weaken the point they are used to illustrate. But it is crucial to recognize that the most radical social constructionists and postmodernists exempt no facts, however humdrum, from the realm of the constructed (and to-be-deconstructed). So the burden falls on them to answer the argument even for trivial cases.

2   An alternative strategy for the relativist is to exempt such facts from the realm of the socially constructed, but to insist that they are trivial and that all nontrivial 'facts' of the kind prominent in news stories are socially constructed in an interesting sense. Yet to admit this is more significant than it looks. First of all, there will be *lots* of these trivial facts, perhaps an infinite number of them. Second, they will serve as a check that any viable conceptual scheme must meet; they will, in other words, ground or constrain worldviews in something beyond themselves. In this sense it is hard to see how such facts can be trivial, even if taken one by one they seem to lack a certain cosmic weightiness. Finally, having admitted the existence of some non-socially-constructed facts, it will prove difficult to draw the line between these and the socially constructed ones, especially given the constraints the former place on the latter. So the camel of objectivity gets its nose in the tent.

3   A third strategy is to admit the independence of some facts from socially produced theories but to insist that nevertheless these facts will be interpreted differently by members of different groups or cultures, and that these interpretations, themselves social constructions, will invest the same facts with different meanings. This claim can be understood in at least two ways. Let us consider them in turn.
(a)   In one sense there is no disputing that these facts will be interpreted differently by different people. We all agree that the Exxon Valdez spilled millions of gallons of oil, but we disagree about its causes and the agents responsible for it, its consequences, its implications for public policy, its symbolic significance (or lack of it).

Yet our disagreements about these matters of 'interpretation' will in turn depend partly on facts, such as the captain's alcohol level at the time of the accident, whether he left the bridge and if so when, as well as other questions not so clearly resolvable. The constraint of facts will rule out some interpretations as unacceptable; even if it typically leaves room for disagreement, sometimes the evidence compels a particular conclusion. Not just our legal system but the web of expectations on which everyday life depends rests on the possibility of knowing all sorts of things 'beyond a reasonable doubt'. So the insistence that an interpretation of the facts is beyond the reach of objective evaluation is simply overstated. There may generally be room for disagreement, but not all the room in the world. Some interpretations are better than others, and some are simply wrong.

(b) A second sense in which it may be said that different people and groups will invest the same facts with different meanings can be illustrated by a study of British, American, and Belgian coverage of elections in Ireland. The study found that the BBC story focused on the potential consequences of the vote for British-Irish relations; the CBS story used the election as a peg to talk about Irish unemployment and its potential consequences for immigration to the United States; and the Belgian account focused on the role of the Catholic Church in Irish politics, the relation between church and state being an important issue in Belgium (Gurevitch and Roeh 1989). It makes sense to say that each story took the same set of facts but interpreted them differently; each invested the facts with different meanings.

The point is important, and we should not underestimate the significance of this 'meaning construction' function of the mass media; it bears extensive examination. But those who stress this point tend to conflate the distinction between meaning and reference. The British, American, and Belgian news reports invest the Irish election with different meanings – they see it as signifying different things – but they all refer to the same events and will presumably agree about certain crucial facts, such as who won the elections. Indeed, the three stories may be perfectly compatible with each other. We are not surprised to find that the same events have different significance for people of varying histories, cultures, or interests. We might put this point by saying that the issues raised here go *beyond* the question of objectivity, but they do not subvert objectivity. I conclude that these challenges pose no threat to the existence of objective facts.

Objectivity and Beyond

But belief in objectivity does not mean that about every question we might ask (or everything that reporters report) there is a single right answer. The interesting question is how extensive the realm of objective facts is; and here objectivity's critics make an important contribution. Imagine a continuum of objectivity along which to locate the variety of subjects and statements news reporters investigate. At one end we find the relatively straightforward and uncontroversial facts of the kind we have just been discussing. In the middle we find statements about which clearly there is a truth, a 'right answer', but where to a greater or lesser extent the answer is difficult to discover. How did the dinosaurs go extinct? Who were the high-ranking Communists in MI5? Did Jeffrey MacDonald murder his wife and daughters? The answers to some of these questions may depend partly on what we mean by certain terms (like 'murder'), but even assuming consistent usage we may reasonably disagree about the answers. Still, we do not doubt that there are definite answers.

The line is sometimes thin between cases where clearly there is a truth about the matter although we have difficulty finding out what it is, and those where it cannot be said that there is a truth about the matter. Did Rasheeda Moore entrap Washington, DC Mayor Marion Barry in the Vista Hotel on January 18, 1990 during a sting operation designed to catch Barry in the act of taking cocaine? Although their encounter is preserved on videotape, the conversation between them is ambiguous. Uncertainty might depend simply on insufficient evidence and on alternative possible understandings of the meaning of entrapment. But disagreements may also depend on what assumptions we make about the meaning of certain gestures, expressions, and interactions. Depending on the framework in which we embed the bits of evidence, the gestures and utterances, we will get different answers. And the question 'Which framework is the appropriate one?' may not always have a determinate answer. On the other hand, often it does. Once we know the context of a given utterance or action, the ambiguous often becomes unambiguous. Did she or didn't she? The answer is yes or the answer is no.[5]

For many of the complex goings-on between people, both at the 'macro' political level and at the 'micro' interpersonal level, the language of truth and objectivity may be thin and inadequate. When, for example, we have heard in detail 'both sides of the story' from two quarrelling lovers or friends, we may sort out some clear truths about what happened, but in the end we may still be left with a residue of indestructible ambiguity, where we want to say not simply that we can't be sure what happened but that at the appropriate level of description there is no single determinate thing that happened. Now it seems clear that examples of this kind of ambiguity and indeterminacy abound for the most interesting and important subjects covered in the news. Where we have not only conflicting or insufficient evidence but also competing frameworks within which to situate ambiguous information and no clear way of choosing among them, if often makes little sense to speak of 'the' truth about the matter.

I must leave for another place the important task of elaborating this realm as it affects journalism. Here I want to make two points. First, however significant and extensive this realm is, it still forms a limited part of the object of journalistic investigation. Second, and more important, the journalist (and indeed anyone who hopes to understand the world) must arrive at the conclusion of indestructible ambiguity only reluctantly, after arduously searching to find out what really happened. We must, in other words, proceed under the assumption that there is objective truth, even if sometimes in the end we conclude that within a particular realm the concept of truth does not apply, or that in any case we will never discover it. The concepts of objectivity and truth function for us as 'regulative principles': ideals that we must suppose to apply, even if at the limit they do not, if we are to possess the will and the ways to understand the world.[6] And we do possess, even if to an imperfect degree, the will and the ways.

The Politics of Objectivity

I hope to have shown in the foregoing discussion not only why we must make the assumption that objectivity is possible, but also why critics have thought otherwise. But we still do not have a complete answer to the question (although hints are strewn along the way) why many of these critics not only deny that objectivity is possible but express hostility toward the idea. Why are they angry rather than sorry?

The main reason is that they see the claim of objectivity as the expression of an authoritarian, power-conserving point of view. Michael Schudson (1978, p. 160) describes this attitude as it arose in the 1960s:

> . . . 'objective' reporting reproduced a vision of social reality which refused to examine the basic structures of power and privilege. It was not just incomplete, as critics of the thirties had contended, it was distorted. It represented collusion with institutions whose legitimacy was in dispute.[7]

Is this view right? I think in many ways it is. But there are a variety of accusations implicit here that need to be sorted out.

First, the assertion of objectivity seems to heighten the status of claims to which it attaches. To insist not only that the enemy is winning the war, but that this statement is objective seems to elevate it to a higher plane of truth or credibility. The assertion of objectivity then appears to involve a certain arrogance, a setting up of oneself as an authority. Now in one sense this is silly. Ordinarily when we say 'The sky is blue' we imply 'It's an objective fact (for all to see) that the sky is blue.' My belief that what I say is true or objective adds nothing to the belief itself. At the same time, to the extent that we are convinced of our own objectivity or that of others, we are less likely to be open to other points of view. Belief in one's own objectivity is a form of smugness, and may lead to a dangerous self-deception. Belief in the objectivity of others (such as the news media) enhances their credibility, often unjustifiably.

So acceptance of the ideology of objectivity – the view that institutions like the news media are generally objective and are sincerely committed to objectivity – has significant political consequences, as the critics suggest. Your belief that a newspaper always and only publishes true and objective information will serve as an impediment to your political and intellectual enlightenment, whether you are a consumer or a producer of news. But for the ideology of objectivity to have the political consequences the critics suggest, we must add a further premise: not only that people believe the press is objective, but also that the news provided favors established powers. (We can imagine an alternative: an opposition press with a great deal of authority and credibility.)

Is the press biased in favor of the powers that be? One reason to think so is that mass media organizations are vast corporate entities; they are *among* the powers that be, and so have interests in common with them. I am interested here in a different question, however. Does the commitment to objectivity *itself* create biases in favor of the conservation of political power? This is the implicit claim of some of objectivity's critics: that the methods associated with the ideal of objectivity contain an inherent bias toward established power.

One reason for thinking that objectivity is inherently conservative in this way has to do with the reporter's reliance on sources. Among the canons of objective journalism is the idea that the reporter does not make claims based on her own personal observation, but instead, attributes them to sources.[8] Yet sources must seem credible to perform the required role, and official, government sources – as well as other important decisionmakers in the society – come with ready-made credentials for the job. In addition, they often have the skills and the resources to use the news media to their advantage. Yet such sources are not typically disinterested observers motivated only by a love of truth.

Journalists therefore confront a dilemma. If they provide to such sources an unfiltered mouthpiece, they serve the sources' interests. In order not to provide an unfiltered mouthpiece, journalists must make choices about which of the sources' statements are sufficiently controversial to call for 'balancing' with another point of view, and they must choose the balancing points of view. And if, in cases where the official view is doubtful, they merely balance the official source's view without even hinting at the probable truth, they mislead the audience. Each of these policies raises troubling questions about objectivity.

The first alternative, simply to provide an unfiltered mouthpiece, characterizes the press's response to Joseph McCarthy in the 1950s. But although we can see why journalists might have worried about challenging McCarthy's accusations, it is just as clear that leaving them unanswered does not satisfy any intelligent conception of objectivity. We care about objectivity because we care about truth; giving credibility to baseless charges – whether by commission or omission – cannot count as objective.[9]

It follows that journalists must make judgements about the credibility of sources and what they say. Objectivity does not mean passivity. But when does a source's statement invite challenge? The obvious answer is: when it seems controversial. But what seems controversial depends on the consensus existing in the culture at a given time. And that consensus derives partly from powerful ideological assumptions that, while unchallenged in the culture, are by no means unchallengeable. So it is that I. F. Stone argues that 'most of the time objectivity is just the rationale for regurgitating the conventional wisdom of the day' (quoted in Hertsgaard 1989, pp. 65–6). What goes without saying may be dogma rather than truth.

Supposing, however, that the journalist does recognize that an official view is sufficiently controversial to invite challenge, she must choose which opposing sources to cite and how to frame the debate between the opposing points of view. Is the dispute taken to span a fairly narrow range of the political spectrum? If so, the press may be criticized for being overly mainstream. Is the opposing point of view chosen an 'extreme' one?[10] In that case the press may sensationalize the matter at hand or marginalize the opposition by making them seem like crazies. Either way, the journalist cannot avoid exercising judgement.

These dilemmas explain another of the standard criticisms of journalism's commitment to objectivity: not that it necessarily favors established power, but that it leads to a destructive agnosticism and skepticism.[11] Objectivity must be 'operationalized', and this is done through the idea of balance. In exploring controversial issues, the journalist does not himself commit to a view, but instead gives voice to different sides of the story. The reader is left to judge the truth. But if the journalist truly balances the views, there may be no rational way for the reader to decide between them. And so she comes to the conclusion that 'there's truth on both sides' – or neither. Every view is as good as every other. Rather than connecting with truth, objectivity, according to this way of thinking, leads to cynicism and skepticism.

Yet both these criticisms – that objectivity favors established power, and that it leads to skepticism and indecision – suffer from too mechanical a conception of objectivity. It is easy to see how the problems they address arise in the transition from objectivity-as-an-ideal to objectivity-as-a-method. In part, they stem from a confusion between objectivity and the appearance of objectivity. Questioning the remarks of an important public figure may look partisan, while leaving them unchallenged does not; but the appearance is misleading and only skin deep. Similarly, leaving two opposing points of view to look equally plausible where one has the preponderance of reason and evidence on its side is a charade of objectivity. It reflects the common mistake of confusing objectivity and neutrality. The objective investigator may *start out* neutral (more likely, she is simply good at keeping her prior beliefs from distorting her inquiry), but she does not necessarily *end up* neutral. She aims, after all, to find out what happened, why, who did it. Between truth and falsehood the objective investigator is not neutral.

The confusion between objectivity and neutrality arises, I think, because of the widespread belief that 'values' are not objective, true, part of the 'fabric of the universe'. According to the positivist outlook of which this is part, the objective investigator will therefore remain 'value-neutral' and his inquiry will be 'value-free'. But the identification of neutrality and objectivity within a given realm depends on the assumption that there is no truth within that realm. I have not here addressed the question whether values are objective; but having argued that facts are, it follows that the objective investigator will not be neutral with respect to them.

As a journalistic virtue, then, objectivity requires that reporters do not let their preconceptions cloud their vision. It doesn't mean they see nothing, or that their findings may not be significant and controversial. Nevertheless, it is easy to see why many people confuse objectivity and neutrality. Often the outsider cannot easily tell the difference between a reporter who has come to a conclusion based on a reasoned evaluation of the evidence, and one who was biased toward that conclusion from the start. The safest way to seem objective, then, may be to look neutral.

The Inevitability of Objectivity

We have good reasons, then, to suspect claims to objectivity. People who insist on their own objectivity protest too much; they are likely to be arrogant, overconfident, or self-deceived. In fact, those who acknowledge their own biases and limitations probably have a better chance of overcoming them than those who insist they are objective. Those who have faith in the objectivity of others may be complacent or dangerously naive. They fail to see the many obstacles – inborn and acquired, innocent and insidious, inevitable and avoidable – on the way to truth.

My defense of objectivity, moreover, in no way amounts to the claim that the press (in general or in any particular manifestation) is in fact objective or free of ideological or other bias. Sometimes the biases of the press result from overt economic or political purposes, as when news organizations suppress damaging information about corporations to which they belong; sometimes from structural or technological features of media institutions, such as television's reliance on good pictures. But it is also true that, paradoxically, the aspiration to objectivity can contain biases of its own, by advantaging established sources or by encouraging an artificial arithmetic balance between views and tempting reporters to maintain the appearance of neutrality even in the face of overwhelming 'nonneutral' evidence. These tendencies are genuine, although not, I have been arguing, insuperable.

To believe in objectivity is not, then, to believe that anyone *is* objective. My main purpose has been to show that, nevertheless, insofar as we aim to understand the world we cannot get along without assuming both the possibility and value of objectivity. That the questions reporters ask have answers to which people of good will and good sense would, after adequate investigation, agree is the presupposition that we make, and must make, in taking journalism seriously. The problems of objectivity are political, not metaphysical.

Notes

1   I should add that although Schudson is sympathetic to this view, in this passage he is characterizing it rather than espousing it.

2   Whorf's views can be found in Whorf, 1956. For a clear critique of Whorfian relativism, see Devitt and Sterelny, 1987, pp. 172–84.

3   For evidence of this change, see Schmidt, 1990, A1, reporting a New York Times/ CBS News Poll on changes in American attitudes toward Israel and the Palestinians.

4   Indeed it is tempting to think that much tedious disagreement and many pointless disputes could be avoided if only we could ban from conversation, for at least a few decades, a few central terms – reality, truth, objectivity, facts.

5   So an objectivist can perfectly well agree with Stanley Fish – perhaps to his dismay – that 'no degree of explicitness will ever be sufficient to disambiguate the sentence if by disambiguate we understand *render it impossible to conceive of a set of circumstances in which its plain meaning would be other than it now appears to be*' (Fish 1980, pp. 282–3). As long as we can know what context, framework, or set of conventions actually governed the circumstances – which often we can – we will be entitled to conclude that in *these* circumstances she meant *x* or did *y*.

6   The idea of a regulative principle or ideal comes from Kant: 'the ideal in such a case serves as the *archetype* for the complete determination of the copy . . . Although we cannot concede to these ideals objective reality (existence), they are not therefore to be regarded as figments of the brain; they supply reason with a standard which is indispensable to it, providing it, as they do, with a concept of that which is entirely complete in its kind, and thereby enabling it to estimate and to measure the degree and the defects of the incomplete' (Kant 1965, p. 486 [A569 B597]).

7   See also Hallin, 1986, pp. 63–75. For a good discussion see West, 1990.

8   This is not strictly speaking true: as an eyewitness to events, the reporter often enunciates facts directly; even when not an eyewitness, he does not attribute every statement made to a source. The reporter couldn't get his stories off the ground if every statement had to be attributed to a source. The question when a statement is seen as sufficiently important and controversial to require attribution goes to the heart of disputes about objectivity and the appearance of objectivity, as the quote from I. F. Stone below illustrates.

9   Note in this connection Schudson's discussion of Bob Woodward and Carl Bernstein's approach in the Watergate investigation. Schudson believes that the ideal of objectivity implies the conventional, passive model of journalism associated with the press's response to McCarthy. Yet he remarks that Woodward and Bernstein 'insisted that they did nothing exceptional. They denied that their manner of reporting was distinctive; to them, "investigative reporting" is just plain reporting . . . They make a case for a journalism true to an ideal of objectivity and false to the counterfeit

conventions justified in its name' (Schudson 1978, pp. 188–9). Even Schudson, one of objectivity's influential detractors, here acknowledges (what Woodward and Bernstein have no trouble seeing) that much of what goes under the name of objectivity reflects a shallow understanding of it. The distinction often manifests itself in the use of quotation marks; sometimes critics talk of objectivity, at other times of 'objectivity'.

10   Obviously what we characterize as extreme depends again on the prevailing consensus at the time, and may therefore involve controversial political judgements. The dilemmas – and journalists' common capitulation to the prevailing political consensus – are hilariously illustrated in Cockburn, 1987.

11   The criticisms are not unconnected. Nature's abhorrence of a vacuum may mean that given a precise balancing between two opposing views, the prestige of the view associated with established power will cause it to dominate.

References

CAREY, J. W., 1989: *Communication as Culture: Essays on Media and Society*. Boston: Unwin Hyman.

CHOMSKY, N., 1969: 'Objectivity and Liberal Scholarship', in *American Power and the New Mandarins*. Harmondsworth: Penguin.

COCKBURN, A., 1987: 'The Tedium Twins', in *Corruptions of Empire*. London: Verso.

DAVIDSON, D., 1984: 'The Very Idea of a Conceptual Scheme', in *Inquiries into Truth and Interpretation*. New York: Oxford University Press.

DEVITT, M. and STERELNY, K., 1987: *Language and Reality*. Cambridge: MIT Press.

FISH, S., 1980: *Is There a Text in This Class?* Cambridge: Harvard University Press.

GUREVITCH, M., LEVY, M. and ROEH, I., 1991: 'The Global Newsroom', in P. Dahlgren and C. Sparks (eds.), *Communication and Citizenship: Journalism and the Public Sphere in the New Media Age*. London: Routledge.

HALLIN, D., 1986: *The 'Uncensored War': The Media and Vietnam*. New York: Oxford University Press.

HERTSGAARD, M., 1989: *On Bended Knee: The Press and the Reagan Presidency*. New York: Schocken Books.

KANT, I., 1965: *Critique of Pure Reason*. New York: St. Martin's Press.

KESSLER, L. and MCDONALD, D., 1989: *Mastering the Message: Media Writing with Substance and Style*. Belmont, California: Wadsworth.

LUBAN, D., 1986: 'Fish v. Fish or, Some Realism About Idealism', *Cardozo Law Review* 7.

MACKINNON, C., 1982: 'Feminism, Marxism, Method, and the State: An Agenda for Theory', *Signs* 7.

MCDONALD, D., 1975: 'Is Objectivity Possible?', in Merrill, J. C. and Barney, R. D. (eds.), *Ethics and the Press: Readings in Mass Media Morality*. New York: Hastings House.

SCHILLER, D., 1981: *Objectivity and the News*. Philadelphia: University of Pennsylvania Press.

SCHMIDT, W. E., 1990: 'Americans' Support for Israel: Solid, But Not the Rock It Was', *New York Times*, July 9.

SCHUDSON, M., 1978: *Discovering the News: A Social History of American Newspapers*. New York: Basic Books.

TUCHMAN, G., 1972: 'Objectivity as Strategic Ritual', *American Journal of Sociology* 77.

WEST, R., 1990: 'Relativism, Objectivity, and the Law', *Yale Law Journal* 99.

WHORF, B. L., 1956: *Language, Thought, and Reality*. Cambridge: MIT Press.

SECTION III

Mediation of Cultural Meanings

12

On Understanding and Misunderstanding Media Effects

Jack M. McLeod, Gerald M. Kosicki and Zhongdang Pan

Viewing the landscape of media studies or its alternative title, mass communication research, is apt to leave the observer in a confused state. One might 'read' the scene as a very strange war; armed camps wearing ill-fitting uniforms with odd labels (e.g. 'media effects', 'critical', 'cultural') ostensibly engaged in a common enterprise yet each warring with other camps and even bickering among themselves. Viewed more optimistically, the acrimony might be interpreted merely as symptoms of enthusiasm and energy in a growing and dynamic intellectual field.

The disarray means that a scholar wishing to enter the field and make sense of the enterprise will need a map that provides a reasonably accurate and undistorted picture of the location and activity of the various intellectual camps. Our purpose here is to examine how the media effects approach, sometimes called the 'dominant paradigm' of the field, can be understood and sometimes misunderstood by observers of the media studies field. We will begin by trying to identify what seems to be common to that which could be called the media effects research perspective.

Definition of the media effects perspective is a task made difficult by the great diversity in theoretical styles, research questions and methods of gathering evidence and making inferences. Our definition of the approach will capture within it the work of many scholars who would be uncomfortable with the label, and many more for whom it would not fit as their primary identification. As will be discussed later, part of the discomfort may stem from the pejorative meaning that has been assigned to the label by its critics working from other perspectives. Our goal is to clarify contemporary approaches to media effects, not to provide an exhaustive literature review of the area. More extensive reviews are available (e.g. Roberts and Maccoby 1985; Bryant and Zillmann 1986).

What is the Media Effects Approach?

The most obvious common characteristic is that the primary focus is on *audiences*. The term audiences is to be understood at various levels, as individuals, in their social surroundings, and as part of societal or cultural institutions. Audiences may be viewed as collective masses or publics, but the focus also may be on the reactions of audience members as incumbents in certain specialized roles; e.g. economic and political elite decision makers.

The second characteristic is the specification of *influence*, either in terms of changes or prevention of changes in the audiences among the units of analysis at varying levels of abstraction. This influence may take many forms, as variation in physiological response, as changes in attitudes, cognition and behavior of individual audience members, or as various types of collective change (e.g. increased homogeneity in a community, political instability in a society). Not all changes at the various social system levels have their direct counterparts in changes at the level of the individual audience member (e.g. homogeneity). Media effects researchers attempt to build theory at various levels of analysis from macrosocietal to individual and even to the level of physiological responses. It may also include research seeking to establish connections between these levels (i.e. cross-level influences).

The third characteristic is the attribution of the source of influence or effect to a particular aspect, form or content, of a *media* message system, medium, type of content, or individual message. The media of concern may be mass (e.g. broadcast, newspapers) but also more specialized media such as direct mail and the new technology. There is a clear theoretical commitment, symbolized by the term 'effect' itself, to a predominant flow of influence from the media and its messages to the audience. This does *not* imply, however, a unidirectional flow of influence leaving the audience as a passive recipient. The term 'effect', particularly in recent theorizing, by no means denies and in fact accentuates the contributions of prior orientations of the audience in directing the form and extent of media influences (e.g. Bauer 1964; Kline, Miller and Morrison 1974; Rosengren, Wenner and Palmgreen 1985; Levy and Windhal 1985; Hawkins and Pingree 1986).

Two other tendencies are common to this approach. The terminology of *variables* (e.g. independent, dependent, intervening) with varying notions of causality is used to describe the process and conditions under which such effects are most likely. Finally, there is a tendency to formulate propositions about effects in ways accessible to *empirical testing*, broadly conceived. Empirical is used in two senses: the key variables can be observed (not necessarily quantified, although quantification and statistical analyses are seen as strong forms of evidence) and the propositions are capable of being tested, that is, they can be shown to be wrong.

Media effects research is quite heterogeneous in both theoretical concerns and methods and has limited common characteristics. It is therefore presumptuous to declare it a 'paradigm'. The minority position of mass media research in the field of 'communication science' (Berger and Chaffee 1987) raises further doubts as to whether it could be called dominant over other perspectives.

Images of Media Effects as Seen by its Critics

In contrast to our view of its diversity, media effects research is viewed as much more homogeneous by its critics. At the risk of over-simplification, we will summarize three of these images. Later, in evaluating these critiques, we will argue that many of their features have considerable merit in illustrating the problems and limitations of media effects research. We will also contend, however, that in certain essential ways these images are oversimplified and distorted, particularly in being dated and overly narrow.

The Critical Studies Critique

The critique emanating from the various branches of the critical studies perspective most often assumes that media effects research is based on a stimulus-response learning theory that is confined to two variables (media stimulus and effect) without mediation. Further, effects research is seen as overly individualistic in orientation and as flawed in its methodological reductionism that implicitly places blame on individuals for their lack of knowledge and participation (Golding 1974). These and other effects research tendencies are viewed as ideological biases revealing the falsity of the claim of objectivity and ethical neutrality (Gitlin 1978).

Media effects research is said to be overly restrictive in studying only one type of effect: persuasion. Other types of effects are said to be largely ignored. Further, effects are confined to those intended by the 'sender' i.e. the manipulative intent of the administrator. The media effects perspective thus lacks theoretical ties to the production of messages as embedded in the power relations of society. Media effects research is said to take messages as neutral and as non-problematic givens whose limited variations are the only source of causality and to be overly simplistic in dimensions of messages selected for study (Althusser 1971; Golding and Murdock 1978; Golding 1981).

Most fundamentally, media effects research is seen as exclusively administrative in character and intent (Gitlin 1978). That is, its practitioners are highly dependent upon corporate media and the government establishment for their funding and, consequently, for the legitimacy of research questions to be tied to the marketplace and government policy. Lost is a commitment to either theoretical development or to the improvement of the human condition.

Ironically, according to the critical critique, the media effects approach belies its name in understating effects of the mass media. As a consequence of its limitations, media effects research fails to explore the cumulative, delayed, long-term and unintended effects including those which stabilize the status quo (Golding and Murdock 1978). Consideration of these variants of effects would revise upward estimates of the strength of media impact.

The Cultural Studies Critique

The critique by cultural studies adds more objections of its own to the above list. The most fundamental of these is the charge that the media effects approach uses inappropriate terminology and causal apparatus in speaking of variables and effects (Hall 1980, 1982; Carey 1989). Media effects research is said to reflect the 'behavioral mainstream hegemony' (Hall 1982), in being constrained by an outmoded positivist philosophy. The alleged focus on physical observable properties, invariant relationships and empirical science verification are seen as fatal flaws of effects research and social science more generally.

The effects tradition, by focusing on limited variations in isolated individuals, is said to segment and dehumanize the audience and to separate persons from their cultures. By attempting to formulate general laws of human behavior, effects research overlooks important cultural variation in the way people respond to the media (Hall 1982). According to the cultural critique, the media effects approach understates the activity of the audience in constructing meaning from messages. At worst, it is charged with treating audience members as dupes. Effects research is seen as overly message-driven and implicitly overstates media effects to the extent we can speak of effects. What is ignored is the constructive process of meaning production within the fabric of culture (Hall 1980; Carey 1989). In simplifying media messages by treating them as concrete psychological stimuli and by focusing on their manifest easily-manipulated features, effects research is as reductionistic towards content as it is to the audience. The quantification used in effects research ignores important qualitative differences in messages and meaning in audience reception.

The Behavioral Science Critique

Some of the strongest criticism of the media effects approach comes from those who might be presumed to be more hospitable among behavioral scientists. The argument is that the empirical results of effects research do not support its claims of powerful media effects. According to a leading proponent of this critique (McGuire 1986), this tacit acceptance of media power results from a kind of silent conspiracy of media effects researchers with two quite different types of bed-fellows: critical theorists and applied practitioners in advertising and public relations who justify their existence and salaries by claiming strong effects. Also contributing to this alleged overstatement of media effects, according to this argument, is the commitment among academic researchers to finding effects – journals seldom publish null findings and young scholars are required to publish.

A second point of this 'friendly fire' attack is the attribution of cause to the media. In some cases, the medium may have been acting simply as a vehicle carrying the message of some other source, the advertiser or the newsmaker, and yet this is termed a media effect. Added to this is the problem with nonexperimental effects research where the causal direction is ambiguous – the 'effect' actually may be selectively seeking out the media 'cause'. More generally, the result of attributing influence to media by effects researchers is seen as being scientifically imprecise and atheoretical in moving away from specifying what particular features of a message have what particular effects.

The 'media-centric' conceptions of effects researchers, according to the behavioral critique, also results in theoretical incoherence by mixing macro conceptions of the production process with micro concepts of effect (cf., Reeves 1989). According to this view, such vague concerns with media are lacking in specification of the stimulus which leads us away from the fundamental objective of building a behavioral science of human behavior.

Various methodological criticisms are added to the critique in the form of complaints about weaknesses in research design, the lack of national samples and non-optimal statistical procedures. These disconfirm further the claims to legitimacy of effects research in the eyes of some behavioral scientists and affirm its marginality.

Some Notes on the History of Media Effects Research

Although space limits preclude an extensive historical treatment, it may be useful to summarize five points of apparent and common misunderstanding of media effects research history.

First, we should note that the history of concern with media effects began long before Paul Lazarsfeld and the Columbia University voting and campaign studies in the 1940s, as it is often assumed. In the pre-empirical era of the late 19th and early 20th centuries, there was considerable concern about the effects of the press among the theorists and observers of society. Notable among these were Max Weber (1910), Walter Lippmann (1922), John Dewey (1927), and Robert Ezra Park (1940). Weber in particular had plans, unfortunately never fulfilled, of a study of press impact, very much empirical as we define it. A founder of American journalism education, Willard Bleyer (1924), included questions of press effects among his concerns. It is important to note that these observers tended to approach the press as *reformers* of journalism and of the larger society, not as proponents of administrative views.

Second, empirical work on media effects extending to the decade before Lazarsfeld shows no sign of using a simple stimulus-response model of universal effects as supposed by its critics. Simple models and assumptions of powerful effects may (Lowery and DeFleur 1983) or may not (Chaffee and Hochheimer 1985; Wartella and Reeves 1985) have characterized public fears, practitioners claims and some research of the 1930s, but these were certainly not reflected in the research sponsored by the Payne Fund studies of the effects of motion pictures on children (Charters 1933). Their research design and results indicate the impact of personal and contextual factors altering the effects of messages and their summation of these complex effects did not add up to being called powerful. Similarly, findings from the best example of strong media effects, the Orson Welles' 'War of the Worlds' radio play, showed that some groups were more likely than others to believe and react to the broadcast (Cantril 1940). The research on attitude change by Carl Hovland and his associates begun in World War II (Hovland, Lumsdaine and Sheffield 1949) and continued at Yale University also used relatively complex models, examining a host of psychological conditions altering media effects.

Third, the phrase administrative research coined by Lazarsfeld (1941) is quite inadequate as a description of the history of media effects. This is especially so when 'administrative' is taken to mean research devoted to the financial gain of commercial media or to maintaining the status-quo of government policy. As mentioned, early concern with effects of the press was reformist in potentially changing rather than defending media practices.

Concern over the effectiveness of Hitler's propaganda machine in the 1930s was very much an applied concern, but the development of materials devoted to teaching young Americans how to recognize the techniques of propagandists (e.g. glittering generalities, card-stacking) (Lee and Lee 1939) was motivated by reformist democratic ideals not by an attempt to make propaganda more effective. The thirties also marked the start of applied research on the size and composition of radio and magazine audiences. It was clearly administrative and often used academics as experts. With the advent of television 20 years later, however, audience research became highly profitable and commercial and academic ties were largely severed.

The term administrative, used broadly in terms of its connection with applied research, does fairly characterize much of American media effects research of the forties through the sixties. Lazarsfeld's Bureau did carry the title of 'Applied' and Hovland's wartime work was devoted to persuasion (e.g. messages to sell the importance of the war to the armed forces) although it soon shifted from narrowly applied concerns to general principles. After the war, some media researchers sought funding from military, security and other governmental agencies with sometimes questionable goals. Even during this period, however, the bulk of published effects studies were still reformist and at least by implication critical of media practices. Then, and even more today, media managers see effects research along with other media research as irrelevant or at most harmful to their purposes.

Fourth, it appears that various observers have focused too much on Paul Lazarsfeld in making him almost synonymous with their problems with media effects research. His work and that of his associates can be considered the most notable in the history of the effects tradition: the voting studies of the 1940 and 1948 election campaigns (Lazarsfeld, Berelson and Gaudet 1948; Berelson, Lazarsfeld and McPhee 1954); commentaries on media campaigns (Hyman and Sheatsley 1947; Star and Hughes 1950); and the study of personal influence (Katz and Lazarsfeld 1955) most notably. These studies asserted: that the most likely effect of the mass media was to reinforce pre-existing views and secondarily to mobilize the undecided to move toward their demographic 'predispositions'; that media persuasive campaigns are ineffective and reach mainly those already reached; and that personal influence predominates over media influence via a two-step flow where opinion leaders use media information to influence other people.

One might see a hegemonic thrust to minimizing effects in such conclusions, but a close reading of the Columbia research reveals ample numbers of cautionary notes about the limitations of their findings and recommendations for future research and a host of interesting findings actually showing media effects. In fact, the highly negative reactions of Todd Gitlin (1978) might well have been directed instead to Lazarsfeld's colleague Bernard Berelson (1959) for prematurely burying communication research and to Lazarsfeld's student, Joseph Klapper (1960) for his greatly exaggerating the weakness of media impact into the 'limited effects' model which in the ensuing years has been taken as the heart of the 'dominant paradigm'.

Although Klapper's view of limited media effects influenced how such effects were regarded for more than a decade, this minimalist view of media influence was never universally accepted. At least five researchers – Lang and

Lang (1959), Key (1961), Blumler (1964) and Halloran (1964) – during this period viewed media as having stronger effects (McQuail 1987). Research on media and national development (Lerner 1958; Rogers 1962; Schramm 1964) was also optimistic and naively so about the possibilities of media to play an interactive role as multiplier in social change.

Finally, there is a history of media effects research after Lazarsfeld. From about 1970 onward, there has been a marked growth in media studies in the US, Western Europe and in parts of Asia manifested in terms of numbers of students, amount of research, and general visibility in academic and public circles. Doubtless much of the rise in popularity stems from the growth of television as the dominant entertainment and news medium. A possible consequence of this was the sudden increase in congressional interest in the effects of televised violence on children. This translated into substantial support for research under the auspices of the US Surgeon General (Comstock and Rubinstein 1972). The studies in the Surgeon General's report constituted a mixture of administrative mandate (i.e. did violence cause aggression?) and basic theoretical work.

As the field grew, stronger trans-Atlantic connections emerged including growing American awareness of Western European work including critical and cultural scholarship. Unfortunately, on all sides this was framed less as an opportunity and more as a war as witnessed by *Ferment in the Field* (Gerbner 1983). Along with influences of the European concerns with macrosocial and production processes, media effects research has changed in many other ways in recent years.

With the exception of the Surgeon General's research funding of 20 years ago, opportunities for funding from either government or media institutions has been largely lacking for academic researchers. Although this has restricted temptation to do narrow administrative research, it has also lead to localized and scattered independent research. Applied media research goes its own way via Los Angeles *Times* and CBS-New York *Times* polls. Vast amounts are spent on proprietary research evaluating effects of advertising and public relations campaigns largely independent of academic research. Most media managers see academic media research as too abstract to be useful and too negative to be considered seriously for its policy implications. Certain concepts, e.g. agenda-setting do seep through and achieve managerial legitimacy, not as useful ideas but rather as iron laws.

Among the most noticeable trends of contemporary media effects research is the heightened concern with theory rather than simply with empirical findings. There is particular attention paid to building theories of media effects that deal with specific communication phenomena not subsumable under concepts from behavioral social psychology and other fields of human behavior (e.g. Tichenor, Donohue and Olien 1970; McCombs and Shaw 1972; McLeod and Chaffee 1972; Ball-Rokeach and DeFleur 1976; Noelle-Neumann 1984). Further, more complex models of media effects and more sophisticated statistical methods are being explored and used to connect previously isolated communication processes.

Contemporary Views of Media Effects

The past twenty years have seen a considerable evolution in the study of mass media effects. Rather than attempting to summarize recent literature in the short space allotted, we can suggest five distinctive directions effects research has taken in recent years: expansion of effects; elaboration of media content; formulations of media production; conceptions of audience activity; and process models and levels of analysis. Taken together, they reveal an understanding of media effects as a multi-level process connecting media production with outcomes of active reception by audiences.

Expansion of Effects

A dramatic expansion of the range of effects investigated is one the most distinctive features of recent media effects research. These proposed effects go well beyond persuasion and attitude change that so dominated as criteria thirty years ago. This expansion is the direct result of the infusion into communication research of diverse theoretical perspectives ranging from psychophysiological (e.g. Zillmann 1982; Reeves, Thorson and Schleuder 1986) to cognitive social psychological (e.g. Reeves, Chaffee and Tims 1982; Iyengar and Kinder 1987; Graber 1988) to cultural anthropological (e.g. Dayan, Katz and Kerns 1984; Liebes and Katz 1986).

McLeod and Reeves (1980) suggested seven dimensions that might be used to conceptualize media effects. The first four listed below are forms of media effects, the fifth represents content domains of effect, the sixth reflects the locus of media influence responsible for effects, while the final dimension concerns conceptual and methodological distinctions among such effects. We will examine the first five dimensions in this section; the last two dimensions will be dealt with later in the paper.

1 micro vs. macro
2 alteration vs. stabilization
3 cumulative vs. non-cumulative
4 long-term vs. short-term
5 attitudinal vs. cognitive vs. behavioral
6 diffuse-general vs. content-specific
7 direct vs. conditional

Taken in combination, these seven dimensions used as simple dichotomies (or as a trichotomy in the case of the fifth dimension) would form a matrix of 192 different conceptual types of media effects. Chaffee (1977) has made a similar point about the diverse possibilities for effects. Of course, other dimensions are possible. The point is nonetheless that media effects may take different forms, have distinctive processes, and require assessment in varied ways. As will be seen, progress has been made in broadening the study of media effects, but there is more to be done in expanding the reach of effects while at the same time integrating what is learned in a more comprehensive fashion. One thing that the history of the field makes clear is that neither the search for universal generalizations about media effects nor their repudiation on the basis of a limited set of effects is apt to lead to fruitful research and understanding the relationship between media and their audiences.

Micro vs. Macro
Individual audience members have been the predominant unit of analysis for the past half century of media effects research. The choice of such 'micro' units reflects the social psychological theories of attitude and the experimental methods that were most salient in the postwar era. Quite often, however, the theoretical and policy issues require generalization to more macro units of analysis. As a result, macro inferences about the larger society are frequently made on the basis of simple summation of micro data gathered from individual audience members (e.g. Gerbner et al. 1986). There are problems with moving across levels of analysis by such simple aggregation procedures (Pan and McLeod 1991). Societal consequences cannot be inferred solely from the estimates of averaged individual change. What is functional for individuals may be problematic for the society and vice-versa. The knowledge gap hypothesis, for example, asserts that although the media may succeed in conveying information to a population, they may do so in differing degrees to various status groups (Tichenor et al. 1970; Robinson 1972). The media may thus contribute to a 'knowledge gap' between the more advantaged and less advantaged groups depending on the relative gain in information at each status level.

Scholars interested in media effects in recent years have become more sensitive to impact on various types of social systems – on families, communities, social movements, organizations, societies and the international community (e.g. Tichenor et al. 1980; Gitlin 1980; Blumler, Dayan and Wolton 1990). Effects are today conceived of and studied at each of these levels, although the most common unit is still the micro individual. Conversely, conceptions of the production of media content are largely formulated at the macro level (e.g. Donohue, Tichenor and Olien 1972; Gerbner 1973; Turow 1984; Herman and Chomsky 1988). Our point is not that any of these units is inherently a 'correct' choice and that research at other levels should be abandoned. Rather, the point is that understanding of media not only needs theory and research at various micro and macro levels but also that it requires connections between production and audiences as well as cross-level conceptual connections (Pan and McLeod 1991).

Alteration vs. Stabilization
Another variation in the form of media effects is that they may either facilitate change in the audience or they may prevent change or stabilize an existing situation. Most effects research has dealt with change, largely because change attributable to media influence is easier to observe than is lack of change. Charges that the media act to enhance the status quo are more common as suppositions than as research findings. Research on stabilization is by no means absent, however. In the 1960s, there was a substantial amount of experimental work on immunizing against persuasive messages (McGuire 1964; Tannenbaum 1967). One of strongest conclusions of the Columbia voting studies noted earlier was that the dominant effect of the media is to 'reinforce' preexisting attitudes among voters (Lazarsfeld et al. 1948; Berelson et al. 1954). Unfor-

tunately, their measurement of reinforcement was highly questionable; a voter was said to have been reinforced if her/his voting preference was the same near election day as it had been early in the campaign. There is some evidence that during the Watergate scandal the media may have deflected change in the political system by emphasizing that 'the system works' and attributing blame to Richard Nixon as the 'bad apple in the barrel' (McLeod et al. 1977). But more destabilizing changes (e.g. voter volatility) also have been identified (Becker, McCombs and McLeod 1975; Blumler and McLeod 1974).

Cumulative vs. Non-cumulative

Another difference in the form of effects is between changes which accumulate over long periods of time from multiple messages and those which are the result of exposure to a single media message. Although both types of effects are likely, the two imply rather different processes to achieve their impact. In the Gerbner et al. (1986) cultivation research, the impact of television on the heavy viewers' social reality judgements is conceptualized as the product of the entirety of messages on prime-time entertainment television, not from any one television program or message. Cultivation effects thus are cumulative with repeated exposure over time. Messages have their effects in part because they appear as a natural part of television culture rather than from their unusual qualities.

Non-cumulative messages, on the other hand, achieve their effects from their ability to capture attention from the distinctive features of the message, whether the feature has visual, thematic or verbal appeal (e.g. Anderson, Levin and Lorch 1977; Iyengar and Kinder 1987). This form of media effect is most likely to be studied in experimental situations where the content features of specific messages are varied (but see Ball-Rokeach, Rokeach and Grube 1984). Non-cumulative effects are not incompatible with cumulative effects, but they are not likely to be examined within the same research designs.

Long-term vs. Short-term

Most experimental studies of media effects deal with immediate relatively short-term effects following exposure to a message. Most such designs do not include another form of effect, the long-term consequences of such exposure. Ordinarily, we might expect short-term reactions to media to dissipate after a period of time (e.g. excitation effects, Zillmann 1982; and priming effects, Berkowitz and Rogers 1986 and Iyengar and Kinder 1987). This does not mean that immediate responses are unimportant; for example, an aggressive act immediately triggered by a sadistic sexual episode on television may have as serious consequences as an identical act somewhat delayed after media exposure.

Long-term effects may be manifested in a variety of ways. First, the response generated by exposure may simply persist over time. Alternatively, the appearance of the effect may depend on a number of other conditions: additional exposure to similar media messages (the cumulative effect discussed above), appropriate environmental conditions conducive to enacting the effect, or strengthening of the response from social support of the effect. In these cases, the effect is likely to be evidenced only after a lapse of time following exposure and may be missed by research designs measuring only short-term reactions.

For example, decisions about who won televised presidential debates in 1976 seemed to have been delayed until impressions could be confirmed later by media 'experts' and discussions with other people (Sears and Chaffee 1979) and their most important influences on vote turnout and knowledge were indirect through increased interpersonal discussion and interest in the campaign (McLeod, Bybee and Durall 1979).

Attitudinal vs. Cognitive vs. Behavioral
Although the traditional distinction between attitudinal, cognitive and behavioral (conative) effects is appropriate only to the individual as the unit of analysis, this distinction does serve to capture much of media effects research and to provide an organizational scheme for examining it.

Attitudinal Effects
For much of its early period, it could almost be said that the history of media effects research was the history of attitude change research. After a brief period of decline reflecting the disenchantment of social psychology with attitude research, considerable new research has appeared that emphasizes persuasive outcomes. Two models have particularly helped revitalize this area: the cognitive Elaboration Likelihood model of persuasion (Petty and Cocioppo 1986) and the Reasoned Action model linking attitudes, perceived social norms and behavior (Fishbein and Ajzen 1975). But these models so far have generated only limited applications in voting and communication campaign effect studies (e.g. O'Keefe 1985; Fazio and Williams 1986; Krosnick 1988; Granberg and Brown 1989; Rice and Atkin 1989). Although most of the work tends to be short-term, non-cumulative and micro, some has focused on macro effects, such as the effects of advertising on the aggregate demand for certain products (e.g. Warner, 1977; Weinberg and Weiss 1982).

Cognitive Learning Effects
Increasingly, attention has been directed towards 'learning' effects from the media, emphasizing the role of the media as a source of information. There have been a spate of recent volumes on learning and memory for facts as dependent variable, in the areas of advertising messages, news and political information, as well as recall of television characters (e.g. Robinson and Levy 1986; Bradac 1989; Becker et al. 1975; Drew and Reeves 1980; Neuman 1986; Ferrejohn and Kuklinski 1990). Other research reminds us that not only is the amount of learning important, but also *when* it was learned (Chaffee and Choe 1980; Bartels 1988) as well as what is *not* remembered (Gunter 1987). Although most of this work too tends to be relatively short-term, non-cumulative and micro, there are notable exceptions in the comparisons of communities (Tichenor, Donohue and Olien 1980); multiple data sets over time (Neuman 1986); and a year-long panel study (Graber 1988).

Cognitive Construction Effects
More subtle effects of media that have been examined go well beyond learning discrete facts to consider the news media as an interpreter of events and public policies (Gamson and Modigliani 1989; Iyengar 1987, 1989; Crigler et al. 1988; McLeod, et al. 1987). The media, through choice of language and repetition of

certain story schemas, organizes and frames reality in distinctive ways. Furthermore, these frames may go beyond raising the salience of the problem or issue in question (agenda-setting as in McCombs and Shaw 1972; Iyengar and Kinder 1987), but also, stemming from their formulation of the isue, suggest approaches or solutions to the problem. For example, framing the issue of drug abuse in the United States by using the 'drug war' metaphor implies a strong application of law enforcement and even military intervention into the problem (McLeod et al. 1990). Alternative frames could focus either on health effects or on the economic implications of the problem. The former might make treatment solutions more likely while the latter might steer solutions away from military technology to the legal arena, where issues of legalization, personal responsibility and creating negative tax and price incentives would come to the fore. This line of research opens up a new domain of media effects while also connecting to the dynamics of the public policy process.

Cognitive Social Reality Effects

The power of mass media to create our symbolic environment is referred to as social reality effects. Evidence has at least partially supported the hypotheses that the media provide cues about the nature of social reality (Gerbner et al. 1986; Wober and Gunter 1988), for the agendas of our concerns (Downs 1972; McCombs and Gilbert 1986; Iyengar and Kinder 1987) and for the climate of public opinion (Noelle-Neumann 1984; Davison 1984).

Behavioral Effects

The mass media have been looked upon as a major source for behavioral modelling and for excitation (Bandura 1977; Malamuth and Check 1981; Zillmann 1982; Huesman et al. 1984), for relaxation (Kubey and Csikszentmihalyi 1990), as well as for various types of behavioral intentions such as voting (Himmelweit, Humphreys and Jaeger 1986; Patterson 1980; Dunleavy and Husbands 1985; Miller et al. 1990). Attention to behavioral effects has led to examination of both antisocial and prosocial behaviors (see Hearold 1986).

Research on behavioral effects of media may be traced as far back as the Payne Fund studies. Several areas have received sustained attention over the years: adolescents' socialization; public information and commercial advertising campaigns; political campaigns and citizen participation; and development communication and the adoption of innovation. Most research on behavior effects has been micro-oriented, message-specific and short-term in focus. There are exceptions, however, where long-term as well as macro-level behavioral effects are identified. For examples, consider the 22-year study of the effect of televised violence on aggressive behavior (Huesman et al. 1984) and the long-term comparative research on the introduction of television in three nations (Centerwall 1989).

Recently, mass media influences on social relationships have been examined, including media images affecting the functioning of organizations and other institutions (Diamond and Bates 1988; Patterson 1980; Cook 1989; Ginsberg and Shefter 1989; Blumler et al. 1990). Effects of media are thus extended well beyond their impact on the general audience.

Elaboration of Media Content and Use

All media effects research carries implicit or explicit assumptions about media content and the roles of audience members. The expansion of effects has been accompanied by further elaborations of how the input of media is viewed. A major distinction pertinent to media input is that between diffuse-general and content-specific influences (the sixth dimension above). Diffuse-general effects are those stemming largely from the activity of media use. One example of this is the time spent watching television displacing other things persons might be doing such as reading books or participating in community life (Parker 1963; Brown, Cramond and Wilde 1974).

Another type of diffuse-general effect centers on the *form* rather than the content of the medium. McLuhan (1964) was a major proponent of this view when he insisted that the medium was the message, not its content. While some content-specific approaches imply 'we become what we see', diffuse-general approaches make less of a connection between the specifics of content and the outcomes manifested. As examples, aggressive behavior can be predicted from the unpredictability of formal features of entertainment television as well its violent content (Watt and Krull 1977), and that both aggressive and erotic film content could enhance similar physiological excitations (Zillmann 1971, 1982).

Content-specific formulations continue to dominate conceptions of media effects. The ways of looking at content, however, have changed considerably. Expanding beyond the confines of quantifiable manifest content analysis of Berelson (1952), researchers have conceived content as a holistic message system (Gerbner 1973), as a textual structure (van Dijk 1988), as a symbolic representation of reality with various embodiments of meanings (Hartley 1982), and as a system of organized conceptual frames which shape how audiences understand and interpret reality (McLeod et al. 1987). The wide range of conceptual work on media content moves much beyond the simple dichotomy of diffuse-general vs. content-specific to allow for a much wider range of possible content-related media effects and for a much closer fit between the subtle content characteristics analyzed and the effects examined. The net effect is to broaden conceptions of content to consider units ranging from discrete *stimuli* to larger sets or messages or message *systems*.

Formulations of Media Production and Content

Broader conceptions of media content bring with them the need for stating traditionally implicit theories of media production and content as more explicit theoretical propositions. Of common concern to all media scholars are the production forces that account for the variance in the media content. For effects researchers, this is further extended to include what differences variation in media content make in audiences' understandings and reactions to such media content.

Both sociological studies of communicators and media organizations (e.g. Tuchman 1978; Gans 1979; Ettema and Whitney 1982; Turow 1984) and psychological studies of cognitive heuristics (e.g. Nisbet and Ross 1980; Stocking and Gross 1989) have contributed to our understanding of the processes and flaws of media operations and content. We have chosen three very different examples each having implications particularly for news content and effects.

The first example is the macro-structural political economy approach of Herman and Chomsky (1988). They specify a propaganda model operating at the institutional level to constrain through five filters the news content of the media in the US and in other capitalist countries: the financial integration of media with the rest of the economic community; advertising as the financial base of media operations; reliance on official sources of information; orchestrated flak campaigns as a means of disciplining media; and anti-communism/ pro-capitalism as the dominant ideology. To test their formulation, they attempt to show how stories similar in other ways receive differential treatment according to their fit into these filters (e.g. whether a massacre takes place in a friendly-capitalist or unfriendly-communist country). There are untested, if reasonable, assumptions about audience effects underlying their examples of different story content. Effects research might test such assumptions by comparing the effects, say, of a story that omits American battle casualties with one that contains such figures.

A second example is the micro-social approach of Bennett (1988) who specifies four information problems in the news that combine to prevent the audience from developing a real understanding or a basis for political participation: personalization, dramatization, fragmentation and normalization. The first of these problems, *personalization*, is a tendency for the news media to concentrate on people engaged in political struggles rather than on the power structures and processes behind the issues. *Dramatization*, the second information problem, refers to the tendency for journalists to select those events which are most easily portrayed in short, capsule stories with actors at their center. The third tendency, *fragmentation*, fed by the first two tendencies, isolates stories and facts such that events become 'self-contained happenings' but have no past or future. Finally, journalists tend to use official sources who provide soothing *normalized* interpretations of crises and problems without going into their deeper meanings.

Each of Bennett's information problems in news content contains explicit or implicit hypotheses about various audience outcomes. For example, together these information problems would lead audiences to adopt passive attitudes, to blame individuals rather than the system for problems, and to lack understandings characterized by complexity, historicity and connectedness.

Our third example comes from cognitive psychological studies of heuristic strategies and short-cuts people use in information processing that arise naturally from the limited personal capacities of all persons and from a host of cultural and situational factors (e.g. Nisbett and Ross 1980). For example, research shows that even professionals schooled in statistical inferences are susceptible to 'illogical' reasoning similar to that of the average person (Tversky and Kahneman 1974; Nisbett and Ross 1980). Journalists, no less than others, thus should exhibit faulty reasoning by carrying their own cognitive biases and inference-making inadequacies over to the news they write (Stocking and Gross 1989). The term 'bias' as used here is much broader than the traditional journalistic definition as the intrusion of partisan opinions or slant into the story.

At the risk of over-simplification, we might divide processing problems roughly into three groupings: *categorization* of the stimulus or issue; *selection* of information regarding the event; and *integration* of the information as the basis of inference making and behavior.

Categorization, a basic process of human thinking (Wyer and Srull 1981), may be best seen in the journalist's selection of terms, concepts, metaphors and headlines. Journalists have a great deal of discretion in how they frame stories, at least in certain situations. It matters whether an open-ended US military commitment is discussed as 'another Vietnam' or as a battle against 'another Hitler', or in some other, more accurate terms. It is clear that certain journalistic workways, bureaucratic arrangements, training, social standing and values may result in certain categorizations being favored by journalists (e.g. Tuchman 1978; Gitlin 1980).

Selection of information by journalists is an important channel for possible cognitive bias. Selection may be heavily influenced by 'off the top of the head' notions or in support of journalists' naive theories about a given situation (Taylor and Fiske 1978; Stocking and Gross 1989). Journalists' workways also encourage selecting vivid instead of dull information, unusual dramatic cases rather than more representative baseline data.

A final class of biases involve errors of integration that are referred to by psychologists as illusory correlation and fundamental attribution error. *Illusory correlation* refers to the tendency to form an inappropriate causal linkage based on skimpy information. Is a political candidate who forgets to attribute a quote one time in a speech he has given dozens of times guilty of plagiarism? Are several cases of a rare disease found in one area conclusive proof of an environmental hazard? *Fundamental attribution errors* involve a systematic bias toward holding individuals rather than systemic structures responsible for a situation. This suggests that problems are more likely to be seen in media accounts as the result of 'a few bad apples' in the barrel instead of bad management practices that allowed the fruit to spoil due to lack of proper inventory control. These and other cognitive shortcomings are shared by journalists and their audiences. But we should not equate the two sets of biases. Journalists' biases reflected in news stories may act to accentuate, modify or multiply the biases of those attending to those stories.

Conceptions of Audience Activity

For several decades, media effects theorists have struggled to specify properly the sense in which audiences are active. Failing to do so would be to leave an image of the audience as passive dupes or victims of media content. There is doubt in the broader media studies field, however, regarding the desirability of proposing strong audience activity in media theory. Gitlin (1978) seems to regard the conception of an active audience as a diversion from understanding real media effects, while Gerbner et al. (1986) argue that people watch *television* not its content. Others add that viewing is done mainly at low levels of involvement (Krugman 1983, Darwise and Ehrenberg 1988). Similarly, Kubey and Csikszentmihalyi (1990) conclude that television is essentially a passive, relaxing, mindless activity. Balanced against these views are the majority of media scholars who see audiences as being in some sense more active in the construction of meaning. Although there is no easy resolution of the activity issue, it is possible to examine several approaches to audience activity and to see how each is related to media effects.

Gratifications

The idea that indviduals are motivated to use media in various ways to meet their needs, often called the 'uses and gratifications' approach, began at Columbia University in the 1940s (cf., Herzog 1944; Wolfe and Fiske 1949; Berelson 1949). Gratifications research activity languished during the 50s and 60s, but has seen a resurgence in the past two decades (cf. Blumler and Katz 1974; Rosengren et al. 1985). Traditionally, uses and gratifications has been seen as an *alternative* to media effects research rather than as a complement to it, replacing message-driven effects ('what media do to people') with an audience-driven perspective ('what people do with media'). This view has been criticized as implying that audiences are seen as obtaining any desired gratification (any chosen effect) from any type of content and as having a conservative functionalist bias that justifies any sort of media content and absolves it of any harmful effects (Elliott 1974).

It is possible to see uses and gratifications research as an important complement to media effects research. Blumler and McQuail (1969) found that, in the British General Election of 1964, strength of motivation to watch party broadcasts interacted with viewing such broadcasts to enhance political information gain. McLeod and Becker (1974) identified four dimensions of gratifications sought from political information and showed effects above and beyond controls for media exposure and other variables. While gratifications sought may enhance learning, they may also act to deter agenda-setting effects. Readers strongest in motivation to seek campaign information, unlike those with lesser motivation, did not adjust their rankings of salience according to the emphasis placed on certain issues in the newspapers they read (McLeod, Becker and Byrnes 1974).

Selectivity

The idea of selectivity goes back at least to the early Columbia University campaign studies. The idea is that people selectively seek out information which is consonant with their preexisting attitudes and beliefs and avoid information which is discrepant with their views. Hyman and Sheatsley (1947) concluded that selectivity operates at various junctures in the reception process: exposure, attention, perception or interpretation, and retention. Selectivity would thus interact with media messages enhancing effects of consonant material and reducing or eliminating the impact of discrepant content.

After a half-century of research, it appears that the first half of the proposition is secure insofar as people do seem to prefer and seek out supportive over neutral or irrelevant information (Frey 1986; McGuire 1986; Katz 1987). The other half of the selectivity proposition, the avoidance of discrepant materials, is much less secure considered in the light of more recent research. By logic alone, total avoidance of conflicting information would seem to be more 'costly' a strategy for a person to pursue than to deal with whatever discrepant information comes from media. Further, evidence points out certain conditions when discrepant material is actually preferred to other information (e.g. Berlyne 1960; Kleinhesselink and Edwards 1975; Frey and Wicklund 1978; Streufert and Streufert 1978).

The efficacy of selectivity, in the exposure and attention phases at least, depends on the ability of the audience member to anticipate which messages are consonant and which are discrepant. Although pre-selection of print media content seems feasible enough, electronic media are less well indexed and often attended to without planning thus making selectivity a more questionable description of activity. Unfortunately, selectivity is almost always used as a dependent variable rather than as a variable mediating the effects of messages. Selectivity of consonant material, at least, is likely to be operating at all phases of media reception but its role in processing messages and shaping their effects is not well understood at present.

Attention
Perhaps the most obvious form of audience activity is attention, the focusing of increased mental effort. Common-sense assumptions tell us that learning from media should be enhanced at higher levels of attention (Chaffee and Schleuder 1986). Attention should be particularly important for the use of television. Whereas print media use virtually demands attention, television users are more free to vary their mental effort and to pursue other activities at the same time. Attention is complicated by being measured in a variety of ways. Attention considered by physiological measurement has a short time-span of milliseconds and is largely below the person's awareness and control (Reeves et al. 1986). When examined at a more conscious level from self-report, it represents a statement of generalized and purposive focus applied to a particular type of media content with a much longer time-span. It is likely that attention so considered is largely content-specific with little overlap in the levels of attention accorded to public affairs news content, entertainment content and to advertising, and is correlated across television and newspapers (McLeod and Kosicki 1986).

Attention has effects independent of the level of exposure. Chaffee and Choe (1980) found that attention paid to television news accounted for much more of the gains in campaign knowledge than did the frequency of news viewing, although much stronger effects were found for newspaper exposure to hard news content. In certain situations, the influences of news exposure and attention may interact to produce a combined effect beyond their additive effects (McLeod and McDonald 1985). Self-reports of attention to entertainment and to advertising have been less thoroughly examined; although a limited attempt to validate self-reports of attention to advertising produced largely null results, experiments on attention conceived and measured physiologically have demonstrated effects of advertising (Reeves et al. 1986).

Media Images
Media scholars have developed theories specifying some of the various flaws in media content (see Media Production section above). It is likely that audiences too have such conceptions, or 'common-sense theories' about the media (McQuail 1987). To the extent that people do have such lay theories or images, it is reasonable to consider them as a form of audience activity potentially affecting how people use media and what they get from their content. Media

managers and public relations practitioners too may have their own media theories; at least from the vast sums of money they spend researching and promoting it, they appear to assume that one dimension of image, *credibility*, is vital to media effects. They may be wrong with respect to one type of effect, learning from news media content (Whitney 1985). Audience members with the most favorable evaluations of *news information quality* – those who think news is quite accurate, complete, thoughtful and responsible – have been shown to learn *less* from news than other readers and viewers (McLeod et al. 1986; Kosicki and McLeod 1990).

Perceptions of news quality, however, is by no means the only and likely not the most important dimension of media images. Audiences seem to have both clear and diverse, if not necessarily informed, ideas of how media work. McLeod et al. (1986) identified four other dimensions of audience media images that have been replicated several times: *patterning of news*, the idea that news adds up to a comprehensive picture of the world; *negative aspects of content*, the view that news is dull, sensational, dominated by bad news, and by reporters' biases; *dependency and control*, a tendency to see media institutions as hegemonic in being consonant, controlling and that people rely on them too much; and *special interests*, a tendency to see media as representing special interests and being special interests themselves. Even after controlling for a host of social structural and media use variables, patterning of news has shown a consistent pattern of enhancing learning from news. Beyond learning of factual information, all five dimensions of media images are implicated in various ways to other effects: media use, choice of strategies for processing information; community involvement, cognitive complexity, and the framing of major news stories (McLeod et al. 1987; Kosicki and McLeod 1990).

Information Processing Strategies

Audience activity also has been seen in the strategies people use to cope with the 'flood of information' that threatens to overwhelm them (Graber 1988). Our ability to identify such strategies depends on two key assumptions: that individuals are able to monitor and to verbalize in providing self-report data about their processes; and that these strategies are relatively stable over time. Levy and Windahl (1984) conceive of strategies as *pre-activity* selectivity in scheduling and time-budgeting, *dur-activity* interpretation at the time of exposure, and *post-activity* as a 'coin of exchange' in subsequent interpersonal communication. All three forms of activity were related to enhancing gratifications obtained from news programs.

Another approach to strategic activity identified three dimensions of audience news information processing (Kosicki, McLeod and Amor 1987). The first, *Selective Scanning*, involves skimming and tuning out items as a response to the volume of news and limited time available. *Active Processing* reflects audience 'processing difficulties' (Graber 1988) by going beyond a given story to interpret or reinterpret the information according to the person's needs. Finally, *Reflective Integration* represents the often fragmented nature of news and the salience of certain information such that it is replayed in the person's mind and becomes the topic of discussion with other people.

Each of the dimensions has been shown to have a connection to various types of political effects (Kosicki et al. 1987, 1988; Kosicki and McLeod 1990). The extent of learning political information, political interest and participation are all restricted by Selective Scanning and enhanced by Reflective Integration. Although Active Processing does not appear to influence learning significantly, it does have a positive impact on both interest and political participation.

All three processing strategies are related to different conceptual frames that people used to interpret and understand media messages (McLeod et al. 1987). Processing strategies not only vary across individuals and over different phases of media exposure, but also are associated with variations in cognitive responses. As conceived within this framework, information processing refers to individually varying processes of meaning construction and understanding rather than a uniformly programmed input-output process (as criticized by Livingstone 1990).

Other Types of Activity
Many other conceptions of audience activity have implications for media effects. Interpersonal relations, once seen as an alternative to media diminishing its effects (Katz and Lazarsfeld 1955; Katz 1987), are now viewed as varying patterns potentially either enhancing or limiting effects. For example, presidential debates increased interpersonal discussion which in turn influenced outcomes such as information gain and vote turnout (McLeod et al. 1979). Media reliance, the preference for or dependence on a particular medium for a given type of content, is another form of audience activity with implications for media effects (Becker and Whitney 1980). Reliance also has been shown to be a contingent condition limiting effects to the medium relied on most in studies of the effects of gratifications sought from television news (McLeod and Becker 1974) and agenda-setting by newspapers (McLeod et al. 1974).

Audience activity in various forms does seem to add to our knowledge by specifying conditions of news media effects. Activity does not imply rationally calculated decisions about media use, however. Instead, activity places media as only one element in peoples' busy lives. People are 'active' in various ways largely to cope with the flood of media information that must be balanced with other commitments. The antecedents of these forms of activity and their effects, we should note, are not reducible to social status or any other set of variables. They tend to reflect a combination of modest influences of many structural, cultural and political variables.

Processes, Models and Levels of Analysis

As should be clear already, most contemporary research is informed by the notion that media do not have universal across-the-board effects. Rather, research attempts to identify conditions under which media exposure may lead to effects for certain members of the audience. McLeod and Reeves' (1980) seventh dimension, direct vs. conditional effects, captures this development. Whereas Klapper (1960) saw such conditions as indicating that media effects were limited and minimal, present day researchers see them as showing where and how effects take place. They have no commitment as to overall strength of effects and indeed averaging strength across audiences with differential effects may be misleading.

One set of conditions influencing media effects are those originating prior to exposure. If the control for the third variable identifies some subgroup of the audience (potentially a group as large as a nation or culture) in which the media effect is found and another in which it does not take place, we can say that this conditional third variable has revealed a *contingent* condition. For example, both newspaper reliance and low motivation to seek political information acted as contingent conditions for the newspaper agenda-setting effect (McLeod et al. 1974). Another type of pre-exposure condition is where the third variable acts as a *contributory* condition making the effect more likely. Prior angering of a viewer, for example, can make aggressive behavior more likely (Berkowitz 1962). As discussed earlier, the knowledge-gap hypothesis suggests social status as a conditional variable where the media may inform status groups at uneven rates (Tichenor et al. 1970).

Conditional variables may also intervene during and after media exposure representing either an internal cognitive or social process set off by exposure. As mentioned earlier, research indicates that exposure to presidential debates stimulated interpersonal political discussion which, in turn, had much greater impact on the political process than did the initial exposure (McLeod et al. 1979). Other debate research also indicates that perceptions of who won the debates were not well formulated until several days afterward when debate viewers had a chance to read press evaluations and to discuss the verdict with others (Lang and Lang 1979; Morrison, Steeper and Greendale 1977).

Interactions of media use and conditional variables may take many forms. In certain situations where the effects of exposure are *opposite* in direction, we can identify a transverse interaction with potentially significant relationships; without examination of the third variable, the conclusion might have been that media had no effect whatsoever (McLeod and Reeves 1980). It is vitally important to identify conditional effects and to incorporate them into media theory. They require systematic investigation of more complex models. In recent years, there has been increasing recognition of models taking the form O-S-O-R. The addition of the two Os represents a profound difference. The first O represents the totality of structural, cultural and cognitive influences the media audiences bring to the reception situation. As we have seen, the S is no longer confined to discrete micro-stimuli of a message but alternatively may be conceptualized in terms of units ranging up to macro-message systems. It is possible that the term 'stimuli' is misleading in its implied narrowness and that some other concept should be substituted for it. The second O denotes what happens in the viewing situation between the reception of the message and the response of the audience member. It too may be conceptualized at various levels ranging from a short-term physiological response to the social context of the reception situations to a complex set of interpersonal interactions that may occur after reception. Finally, the R term of response, as we have seen has been broadened to include a longer time span and social consequences as well as individual change.

The O-S-O-R model is meant to emphasize the strong role of cognitive processes both in receiving and interpreting the message and in formulating responses. Cognitive processes function not only as mediating factors but also as vital components of the entire process. The mass media are considered an important source of influence in that they supply our frames of references, define and locate important public issues, and provide data for our cognitive activities. Cognitive processes are also a part of the message production process influencing journalists and their sources. None of the cognitive processes focus denies the importance of more macro social structures on both the media production and audience reception processes. Creative message production and diverse audience readings should not blind us to various organizational and social structural influences on these individual cognitive performances. The theoretical problem is to develop cross-level linkages that lose neither media production or the audience (Pan and McLeod 1991).

Conclusions

The critical and cultural studies critiques have been shown to be both historically limited and overly narrow in their conceptions of contemporary media effects research. A close examination of media effects research demonstrates that a simple S-R model inaccurately describes the effects perspective from its early empirical phases to the present day. Further, the term 'administrative' may have been appropriate to the Lazarsfeld era, but is very misleading when applied either to empirical work before Lazarsfeld or to the past 20 years of media effects research. Rather than serving the narrow applied needs of media managers, effects research has been predominantly reformist in examining potential problems with existing media content. The problems are largely those which adversely affect some vulnerable segment of the public (e.g. children, lower status persons), although a sizeable minority of effects researchers do study ways to make advertising messages and publicity more effective. Reform as a research goal, of course, remains unsatisfactory to critical scholars in that its concern is with changes within the existing system and thus lacking in an a priori commitment to fundamental transformation of that system. Whatever their private views on the ultimate necessities of redistributing wealth and power etc., advocacy of changes effects researchers state as implications from their evidence, are more likely to be confined to changes compatible with public service and social responsibility conceptions of media. The policy implications of recent research have broadened from earlier remedies (e.g. making messages simpler, balanced between political parties) to solutions that imply more basic changes linked to message systems and the production process.

Contrary to the assertions of these critiques, media effects research has long since gone beyond persuasion as the sole effect of concern. Equating of media effects with persuasion is an historic remnant of the control of the research agenda by Berelson (1959) and Klapper (1960) for more than a decade. Similarly, the charge that media effects research is confined to a positivist atheoretical desire to discover 'natural' concepts to build universal laws of human communication has characterized little since the Project Revere search for an invariant diffusion curve (DeFleur and Larsen 1948). If there is a dominant trend in contemporary effects research, it is the broadening of outlook on effects and the conditions of media production and messages. It is now relatively common to see social structural and cultural conditions included among theoretical considerations.

Media effects research is vulnerable, however, to several serious charges by critical and cultural studies. The first is the potential for an individualistic bias in media effects theory. The bulk of research in this tradition uses the individual as the primary unit of observation. Conceptions of social system effects are less clearly developed than those of individuals and appear mostly, but not exclusively (e.g. Tichenor et al. 1980), as social implications in the conclusions sections of research primarily dealing with individual effects. Individualistic bias will remain a threat until more adequate cross-level (i.e. macro-social to micro-individual and vice-versa) influences are dealt with theoretically (Pan and McLeod 1991).

Another weakness of effects research identified by its critics is the lack of systematic ties to message production. There has been increasing attention to 'horizontalizing' media effects theory in recent years (e.g. Neuman 1989), but the tendency to separate production, message system and audience effects research is apt to continue in the immediate future. Linking audience reception with media production is easier said than done; the existing concepts in each domain are lacking in 'goodness of fit' – concepts used to analyze media production and audiences were developed independently without concern for their connection. Examples bridging these separate parts, however, can be seen in research examining power relationships in information control and dissemination (Donohue et al. 1972; Tichenor et al. 1980; Blumler and Gurevitch 1975, 1981; Turow 1984).

A third persisting challenge from its critics is to represent adequately variations in media content in effects research. Most effects research deals with actual content variations only by implication or by assumption. The charge that it inappropriately reduces media content to psychological stimuli devoid of cultural context applies to much of effects research, but we can also point out that increasing attention is being paid to broader connections of media content. This is an area where media effects research potentially can benefit from cultural studies as well as from discourse analysis (e.g. van Dijk 1988; Gamson and Modigliani 1989).

Media effects research will continue to struggle with understanding the various conceptions of audience activity. It is clear that audiences should be regarded neither as passive dupes nor as active rationalists, but there is considerable territory in between. Activity has been programmatically examined from motivation (e.g. gratifications sought) to attention to processing strategies used to deal with media. But the social structural and other antecedents of the various forms of activity are only partly identified, although it is clear none are simple outcomes of a single type of influence. Conceptual disputes continue over the meaning of attention and other concepts and work on media images and processing strategies is at an early stage.

The behavioral science critique of media effects research appears to have overstated the extent to which strong and powerful effects are claimed. Although it is true that Noelle-Neumann (1973) raised the question of whether research has justified a return to the notion of powerful media effects, most researchers seem content to identify statistically significant proportions of variance that can be attributed to mass media without making claims as to power. Certain issues frustrate a simple assessment of the power of media effects in nonexperimental research: what social structural and demographic controls are appropriate; whether controls should be applied simultaneously or one at a time; whether the forms of activity should be added to exposure effects; whether interactive effects and indirect effects are included in the total effect; and whether corrections for measurement error have been made. Obviously, the lowest estimates of media influence will be obtained where many controls are applied simultaneously and where only direct effects of time spent or exposure to content are considered without correction for measurement error. Although media effects researchers probably should be more straightforward in stating that their effects are not powerful but *important nonetheless*, it is not them but others (e.g. popular writers, public officials and the public generally) who make the boldest claims of media power. To the extent public acceptance of powerful media effects may be used by unscrupulous officials to launch assaults on media and other institutions (e.g. attacks on media and the arts in America), media researchers may have to make clear the non-massive strength of media effects. Many theories of media effects are stated without disclaimers of their great strength and contingent nature; it is quite possible that these theories would be quite different and very likely more interesting if these modifications were made clear. Contributions to theory and public policy are most likely to come through identification of contingent and contributory media effects, not through futile arguments about averaged effects.

The behavioral criticism of mis-attribution of causality to media in effects research will remain as a warning to media researchers. Undoubtedly, asserting 'television' without further specification as a cause of anything is potentially misleading. If television covers an event dominated by a source (e.g. a press conference by political leaders), is it fair to say changes in the viewing audience are a media effect? It would be better if we could separate what portions of the event (or an agenda) are attributable to sources and which can be said to have been contributed by journalistic practices. This requires a more firm theoretical connection to the production process, including conceptions of how messages might have been constructed differently (e.g. the research programs of the Glasgow Media Group 1976; Robinson and Levy 1986). The implied 'horizontalizing' in this 'media-centric' strategy is in tension with the approaches of other 'effects-centric' researchers who believe theoretical development is most likely to come from concepts emanating from social psychology and other social science fields.

The 'vertical' connections of the various micro- and macro-levels of analysis will remain a challenge to media effects and other research traditions. There is, admittedly, tension within media effects research as to 'boundary conditions' of concepts (i.e. their domain in terms of implications for other levels of intellectual discourse) and which levels might be crossed in theorizing. One area of communication research makes connection to the 'floor' of physiological processes (e.g. brain-waves associated with messages) while another reaches to the 'ceiling' of social processes (e.g. interpersonal communication enacted by messages). They address quite different research questions and are not easily connected. There is nothing inherently wrong in two (or many) separate research domains if both acknowledge that *all* theoretical systems and research traditions have limited explanatory power. If notions of research as a zero-sum game (i.e. certain research must be denigrated to appreciate other research) can be rejected, the damaging outcomes of intellectual warfare might be avoided.

The media effects perspective outlined in this chapter is so diverse as to make the label 'dominant paradigm' very misleading and any quest for a 'correct' approach quite fruitless. Warfare involving methods and standards of evidence, levels of analysis, and different emphases on production and audience are likely to continue. This is both the burden and the challenge of media studies as a 'variable field' (Paisley 1980). We are advocating neither a total war of natural selection of the 'correct' approach nor a simple merger of theoretical perspectives and research strategy into some kind of intellectual shepherd's pie.

We do believe that communication and intellectual stimulation is possible both within and between perspectives and that there is evidence that such has already taken place. There is, for example, a growing interest in media audiences and their reactions within the various media studies perspectives. Our study of media effects research reaches three general conclusions: (1) that variations in theoretical perspectives and research strategies help generate complex and rich data of media production and audiences' media consumption; (2) that both horizontal connections across productions and audience outcomes as well as vertical connections between various levels of analysis will enrich our understanding of media processes and effects; and (3) that progress in the media studies areas will be more likely if the varying perspectives gain some measure of mutual respect and abandon total war against each other while identifying the real 'enemy' in ignorance, inequality, political repression and abuses of power.

References

ALTHUSSER, L., 1971: Ideology and ideological state apparatuses. In Lenin and Philosophy and Other Essays. London: New Left Books.

ANDERSON, D. R., LEVIN, S. R., and LORCH, E. P., 1977: The effects of TV program pacing on the behavior of preschool children. AV Communication Review, 25, pp. 159–166.

BALL-ROKEACH, S. and DEFLEUR, M. L., 1976: A dependency model of mass media effects. Communication Research, 3, pp. 3–21.

BALL-ROKEACH, S., ROKEACH, M., and GRUBE, J. W., 1984: The Great American Values Test. New York: Free Press.

BANDURA, A., 1977: Social Learning Theory. Englewood Cliffs, NJ: Prentice-Hall.

BARTELS, L., 1988: Presidential Primaries and the Dynamics of Public Choice. Princeton University Press.

BARWISE, P. and EHRENBERG, A., 1988: Television and its Audience. London: Sage.

BAUER, R. A., 1964: The obstinate audience. American Psychologist, 19, pp. 319–328.

BECKER, L. B., MCCOMBS, M. E., and MCLEOD, J. M., 1975: The development of political cognitions. In S. H. Chaffee, (ed.), Political Communication. Beverly Hills, CA: Sage.

BECKER, L. B. and WHITNEY, D. C., 1980: Effects of media dependencies on audience assessment of government. Communication Research, 7, pp. 95–120.

BENNETT, W. L., 1988: News: The Politics of Illusion (2nd Ed.), New York: Longman.

BERELSON, B., 1949: What 'missing the newspaper' means. In P. F. Lazarsfeld and F. Stanton, (eds), Communication Research 1948–49. New York: Duell, Sloane and Pearce.

BERELSON, B., 1952: Content Analysis as a Tool of Communication Research. New York: Free Press.

BERELSON, B., 1959: The state of communication research. Public Opinion Quarterly, 23, pp. 1–6.

BERELSON, B., LAZARSFELD, P. F., and MCPHEE, W. N., 1954: Voting: A Study of Opinion Formation in a Presidential Campaign. Chicago, IL: University of Chicago Press.

BERGER, C. R. and CHAFFEE, S. H. (eds), 1987: Handbook of Communication Science. Newbury Park, CA: Sage.

BERKOWITZ, L., 1962: Aggression: A Social Psychological Analysis. New York: McGraw-Hill.

BERKOWITZ, L. and ROGERS, K. H., 1986: A priming effect analysis of media influences. In J. Bryant and D. Zillman (eds), Perspectives on Media Effects. Hillsdale, NJ: Lawrence Erlbaum.

BERLYNE, D. E., 1960: Conflict, Arousal and Curiosity. New York: McGraw-Hill.

BLEYER, W., 1924: Research problems and newspaper analysis. Journalism Quarterly, 1, pp. 17–22.

BLUMLER, J., 1964: British television: The outlines of a research strategy. British Journal of Sociology, 15, 223–233.

BLUMLER, J. G., DAYAN, D., and WOLTON, D., 1990: West European perspectives on political communication: Structures and dynamics. European Journal of Communication, 5, 261–284.

BLUMLER, J. G. and GUREVITCH, M., 1975: Toward a comparative framework for political communication research. In S. H. Chaffee (ed.), Political Communication. Beverly Hills, CA: Sage.

BLUMLER, J. G. and GUREVITCH, M., 1981: Politicians and the press: An essay in role relationships. In D. D. Nimmo and K. R. Sanders (eds), Handbook of Political Communication. Beverly Hills, CA: Sage.

BLUMLER, J. G. and KATZ, E. (eds), 1974: The Uses of Mass Communications: Current Perspectives on Gratifications Research. Beverly Hills, CA: Sage.

BLUMLER, J. G. and MCLEOD, J. M., 1974: Communication and voter turnout in Britain. In T. Legatt (ed.) Sociological Theory and Survey Research. Beverly Hills, CA: Sage.

BLUMLER, J. G. and MCQUAIL, D., 1969: Television in Politics. Chicago: University of Chicago Press.

BRADAC, J. J., 1989: Message Effects in Communication Science. Newbury Park, CA: Sage.

BROWN, J. R., CRAMOND, J. K., and WILDE, R. J., 1974: Displacement effects of television and child's functional orientation to media. In J. G. Blumler and E. Katz (eds), The Uses of Mass Communications: Current Perspectives on Gratification Research. Beverly Hills, CA: Sage.

BRYANT, J. and ZILLMANN, D. (eds), 1986: Perspectives on Media Effects. Hillsdale, NJ: Erlbaum

CANTRIL, H., 1940: The Invasion from Mars: A Study in the Psychology of Panic. Princeton, NJ: Princeton University Press.

CAREY, J. W., 1989: Communication as Culture: Essays on Media and Society. Boston, MA: Unwin Hyman.

CENTERWALL, B. S., 1989: Exposure to television as a cause of violence. In G. Comstock (ed.), Public Communication and Behavior (Vol. 2). New York: Academic Press.

CHAFFEE, S. H., 1977: Mass media effects: New research perspectives. In D. Lerner and L. M. Nelson (eds), Communication Research – A Half Century Appraisal. Honolulu: East-West Center.

CHAFFEE, S. H. and CHOE, S. Y., 1980: Time of decision and media use during the Ford-Carter campaign. Public Opinion Quarterly, 44, 53–59.

CHAFFEE, S. H. and HOCHHEIMER, J. L., 1982: The beginnings of political communication research in the United States: Origins of the 'limited effects' model. In E. M. Rogers and F. Balle (eds), The Media Revolution in America and Western Europe. Norwood, NJ: Ablex. Reprinted in M. Gurevitch and M. R. Levy (eds), Mass Communication Review Yearbook (Vol. 5). Beverly Hills, CA: Sage. 1985.

CHAFFEE, S. H. and SCHLEUDER J., 1986: Measurement and effects of attention to news media. Human Communication Research, 13, pp. 76–107.

CHARTERS, W. W., 1933: Motion Pictures and Youth: A Summary. New York: The Macmillan Company.

COMSTOCK, G. and RUBINSTEIN, E. A. (eds), 1972: Television and Behavior: Reports and Papers III: Television and Adolescent Aggressiveness. Rockville, MD: National Institute of Mental Health.

COOK, T. E., 1989: Making Laws and Making News: Media Strategies in the U.S. House of Representatives. Washington, DC: Brookings Institution.

CRIGLER, A. N., JUST, M. R., NEUMAN, W. R., CAMPBELL, D. C., and O'CONNELL, J., 1988: Understanding Issues in the News: 'I Don't Know Much About This But . . .' Paper presented at American Association for Public Opinion Research, Toronto, Canada.

DAVISON, W. P., 1984: The third-person effect in communication. Public Opinion Quarterly, 47, pp. 1–15.

DAYAN, D., KATZ, E., and KERNS, P., 1984: Armchair pilgrimages – the trips of John Paul II and their television public: An anthropological view. On Film, 30, pp. 25–34. Reprinted in M. Gurevitch and M. R. Levy (eds), Mass Communication Review Yearbook (Vol. 5). Beverly Hills, CA: Sage. 1985.

DEFLEUR, M. L. and LARSEN, O. N., 1948: The Flow of Information: An Experiment in Mass Communication. New York: Harper and Brothers.

DEWEY, J., 1927: The Public and its Problems. New York: Holt, Rinehart and Winston.

DIAMOND, E. and BATES, S., 1988: The Spot: The Rise of Political Advertising on Television (Rev. Ed.). Cambridge, MA: The MIT Press.

DONOHUE, G. A., TICHENOR, P. J., and OLIEN, C. N., 1972: Gatekeeping: Mass media systems and information control. In F. G. Kline and P. J. Tichenor (eds), Current Perspectives in Mass Communication Research. Beverly Hills, CA: Sage.

DOWNS, A., 1972: Up and down with ecology: The issue-attention cycle. Public Interest, 28, pp. 38–50.

DREW, D. and REEVES, B., 1980: Learning from a television news story. Communication Research, 7, pp. 121–135.

DUNLEAVY, P. and HUSBANDS, C. T., 1985: British Democracy at the Crossroads: Voting and Party Competition in the 1980s. London: George Allen & Unwin.

ELLIOTT, P., 1974: Uses and gratifications research: A critique and a sociological alternative. In J. G. Blumler and E. Katz (eds), The Uses of Mass Communications: Current Perspectives on Gratifications Research. Beverly Hills, CA: Sage.

ETTEMA, J. S. and WHITNEY, D. C. (eds), 1982: Individuals in Mass Media Organizations: Creativity and Constraint. Beverly Hills, CA: Sage.

FAZIO, R. H. and WILLIAMS, C. J., 1986: Attitude accessibility as a moderator of the attitude-perception and attitude-behavior relations: An investigation of the 1984 presidential election. Journal of Personality and Social Psychology, 51, pp. 505–514.

FERREJOHN, J. A. and KUKLINSKI, J. H. (eds), 1990: Information and Democratic Processes. Urbana, IL: U. of Illinois Pr.

FISHBEIN, M. and AJZEN, I., 1975: Belief, Attitude, Intention, and Behavior: An Introduction to Theory and Research. Reading, MA: Addison-Wesley.

FREY, D., 1986: Recent research on selective exposure to information. In L. Berkowitz (ed.), Advances in Experimental Social Psychology (Vol. 19). New York: Academic Press.

FREY, D. and WICKLUND, R. A., 1978: A clarification of selective exposure: The impact of choice. Journal of Experimental Social Psychology, 14, pp. 132–139.

GAMSON, W. A. and MODIGLIANI, A., 1989: Media discourse and public opinion on nuclear power: A constructivist approach. American Journal of Sociology, 95, pp. 1–37.

GANS, H. J., 1979: Deciding What's News: A Study of CBS Evening News and NBC Nightly News, Newsweek, and Time. New York: Vintage Books.

GERBNER, G., 1973: Cultural indicators: the third voice. In G. Gerbner, L. Gross, and W. H. Melody (eds), Communication Technology and Social Policy: Understanding the New 'Cultural Revolution'. New York: Wiley and Sons.

GERBNER, G. (ed.), 1983: Ferment in the Field (special issue). Journal of Communication, 33.

GERBNER, G., GROSS, L., MORGAN, M and SIGNORIELLI, N., 1986: Living with television: The dynamics of the cultivation process. In J. Bryant and D. Zillmann (eds), Perspectives on Media Effects. Hillsdale, NJ: Lawrence Erlbaum.

GINSBERG, B. and SHEFTER, M., 1989: Politics By Other Means: The Declining Importance of Elections in America. New York: Basic Books.

GITLIN, T., 1978: Media sociology: The dominant paradigm. Theory and Society, 6, pp. 205–253. Reprinted in G. C. Wilhoit, H. de Bock (eds), Mass Communication Review Yearbook (Vol. 2). Beverly Hills, CA: Sage.

GITLIN, T., 1980: The Whole World Is Watching: Mass Media in the Making and Unmaking of the New Left. Berkeley, CA: University of California Press.

GLASGOW MEDIA GROUP, 1976: Bad News. London: Routledge and Kegan Paul.

GOLDING, P., 1974: Media role in national development: Critique of a theoretical orthodoxy. Journal of Communication, 24, pp. 39–53.

GOLDING, P., 1981: The missing dimension – News media and management of social change. In E. Katz and T. Szecko (eds), Mass Media and Social Change. Beverly Hills, CA: Sage.

GOLDING, P. and MURDOCK, G., 1978: Theories of communication and theories of society. Communication Research, 5, pp. 339–356.

GRABER, D., 1988: Processing the News: How People Tame the Information Tide (2nd Ed.), New York: Longman.

GRANBERG, D. and BROWN, T. A., 1989: On affect and cognition in politics. Social Psychology Quarterly, 52, pp. 171–182.

GUNTER, B., 1987: Poor Reception: Misunderstanding and Forgetting Broadcast News. Hillsdale, NJ: Lawrence Erlbaum.

HALL, S., 1980: Cultural studies: Two paradigms. Media, Culture, and Society, 2, pp. 57–72.

HALL, S., 1982: The rediscovery of 'ideology': Return of the repressed in media studies. In M. Gurevitch et al. (eds), Culture, Society and the Media. London: Methuen.

HALLORAN, J. D., 1964: The Effects of Mass Communication, with Special Reference to Television (Working Paper No. 1). Leicester: Leicester University Press.

HARTLEY, J., 1982: Understanding News. New York: Routledge.

HAWKINS, R. P. and PINGREE, S., 1986: Activity in the effects of television on children. In J. Bryan and D. Zillmann (eds), Perspectives on Media Effects. Hillsdale, NJ: Lawrence Erlbaum.

HEAROLD, S., 1986: A synthesis of 1043 effects of television on social behavior. In G. Comstock (ed.), Public Communication and Behavior (Vol. 1). New York: Academic Press.

HERMAN, E. S. and CHOMSKY, N., 1988: Manufacturing Consent: The Political Economy of the Mass Media. New York: Pantheon.

HERZOG, H., 1944: What do we really know about daytime serial listeners? In P. F. Lazarsfeld (ed.), Radio Research 1942–1943. New York: Duell, Sloane and Pearce.

HIMMELWEIT, H. T., HUMPHREYS, P., and JAEGER, M., 1986: How Voters Decide: A Longitudinal Study of Political Attitudes and Voting Extending Over Fifteen Years and the British Election Surveys of 1970–1983. (Rev. Ed.), Milton Keynes: Open University Press.

HOVLAND, C. I., LUMSDAINE, A. A., and SHEFFIELD, F. D., 1949: Experiments on Mass Communication. Princeton, NJ: Princeton University Press.

HUESMANN, L. R., ERON, L. D., LEFKOWITZ, M. M., and WALDER, L. O., 1984: The stability of aggression over time and generations. Developmental Psychology, 20, pp. 1120–1134.

HYMAN, H. H. and SHEATSLEY, P. B., 1947: Some reasons why information campaigns fail. Public Opinion Quarterly, 11, pp. 412–423.

IYENGAR, S., 1987: Television news and citizens' explanations of national affairs. American Political Science Review, 81, pp. 815–831.

IYENGAR, S., 1989: How citizens think about national issues: A matter of responsibility. American Journal of Political Science, 33, pp. 878–900.

IYENGAR, S. and KINDER, D. R., 1987: News that Matters: Television and American Opinion. Chicago: University of Chicago Press.

KATZ, E., 1987: On conceptualizing media effects: Another look. In S. Oskamp (ed.) Applied Social Psychology Annual, (Vol. 8), Beverly Hills, CA: Sage.

KATZ, E. and LAZARSFELD, P. F., 1955: Personal Influence. New York: Free Press.

KEY, V. O., 1961: Public Opinion and American Democracy. New York: Knopf.

KLAPPER, J., 1960: The Effects of Mass Communication. New York: Free Press.

KLEINHESSELINK, R. R. and EDWARDS, R. E., 1975: Seeking and avoiding belief-discrepant information as a function of its refutability. Journal of Personality and Social Psychology, 31, pp. 787–790.

KLINE, F. G., MILLER, P. V., and MORRISON, A. J., 1974: Adolescents and family planning information: An exploration of audience needs and media effects. In J. G. Blumler and E. Katz (eds), The Uses of Mass Communications: Current Perspectives on Gratifications Research. Beverly Hills, CA: Sage.

KOSICKI, G. M. and MCLEOD, J. M., 1990: Learning from political news: Effects of media images and information processing strategies. In S. Kraus, (Ed.), Mass Communication and Political Information Processing. Hillsdale, NJ: Lawrence Erlbaum.

KOSICKI, G. M., MCLEOD, J. M., and AMOR, D. L., 1987. Processing the News: Some Individual Strategies for Selecting, Sense-making and Integrating. Paper presented at the International Communication Association, Montreal, Canada.

KOSICKI, G. M., MCLEOD, J. M., and AMOR, D. L., 1988: Processing Strategies for Mass Media Information: Selecting, Integrating and Making Sense of Political News. Paper presented at the Midwest Political Science Association, Chicago.

KROSNICK, J. A., 1988: The role of attitude importance in social evaluation: A study of policy preference, presidential candidate evaluations, and voting behavior. Journal of Personality and Social Psychology, 55, pp. 196–210.

KRUGMAN, H. E., 1983: Television program interest and commercial interruption. Journal of Advertising Research, 23(1), pp. 21–23.

KUBEY, R. W. and CSIKSZENTMIHALYI, M., 1990: Television and the Quality of Life: How Viewing Shapes Everyday Experiences. Hillsdale, NJ: Lawrence Erlbaum.

LANG, K. and LANG, G. E., 1959: The mass media and voting. In E. J. Burdick and A. J. Brodbeck (eds), American Voting Behavior. New York: Free Press.

LANG, K. and LANG, G. E., 1979: Immediate and mediated responses: First debates. In S. Kraus (ed.) The Great Debates: Carter vs. Ford 1976. Bloomington, IN: Indiana University Press.

LAZARSFELD, P. F., 1941: Remarks on administrative and critical communication research. Studies in Philosophy and Social Science 9, pp. 2–16.

LAZARSFELD, P. F., BERELSON, B., and GAUDET, H., 1948: The People's Choice. New York: Columbia University Press.

LEE, A. M., and LEE, E. B., 1939: The Fine Art of Propaganda: A Study of Father Coughlin's Speeches. New York: Harcourt Brace Jovanovich.

LERNER, D., 1958: The Passing of Traditional Society. Glencoe, IL: Free Press.

LEVY, M. R. and WINDAHL, S., 1985: The concept of audience activity. In K. E. Rosengren, L. A. Wenner, and P. Palmgreen (eds), Media Gratifications Research: Current Perspectives. Newbury Park, CA: Sage.

LIEBES, T. and KATZ, E., 1986: Patterns of involvement in television fiction. European Journal of Communication, 1, pp. 151–171.

LIPPMANN, W., 1922: Public Opinion. New York: Harcourt Brace.

LIVINGSTONE, S. M., 1990: Making Sense of Television: The Psychology of Audience Interpretation. Oxford: Pergamon Press.

LOWERY, S. and DEFLEUR, M. L., 1983: Milestones in Mass Communication Research. New York: Longman.

MALAMUTH, N. M. and CHECK, J. V. P., 1981: The effects of mass media exposure on acceptance of violence against women: A field experiment. Journal of Research in Personality, 15, pp. 436–446.

MCCOMBS, M. E. and GILBERT, S., 1986: News influence on our pictures of the world. In J. Bryant and D. Zillmann (eds), Perspectives on Media Effects. Hillsdale, NJ: Lawrence Erlbaum.

MCCOMBS, M. E. and SHAW, D, 1972: The agenda-setting function of the mass media. Public Opinion Quarterly, 36, pp. 176–187.

MCGUIRE, W. J., 1964: Inducing resistance to change. In L. Berkowitz (ed.), Advances in Experimental Social Psychology (Vol. 1) New York: Academic Press.

MCGUIRE, W. J., 1986: The myth of massive media impact: Savagings and salvagings. In G. Comstock (ed.), Public Communication and Behavior (Vol. 1). New York: Academic Press.

MCLEOD, J. M. and BECKER, L. B. 1974: Testing the validity of gratification measures through political effects analysis. In J. G. Blumler and E. Katz (eds), The Uses of Mass Communications: Current Perspectives on Gratifications Research. Beverly Hills, CA: Sage.

MCLEOD, J. M., BECKER, L. B., and BYRNES, J. E., 1974: Another look at the agenda-setting function of the press. Communication Research, 1, pp. 131–165.

MCLEOD, J. M., BROWN, J. D., BECKER, L. B., and ZIEMKE, D. A., 1977: Decline and fall at the White House: A longitudinal analysis of communication effects. Communication Research, 4, pp. 3–22.

MCLEOD, J. M., BYBEE, C. R., and DURALL, J. A., 1979: Equivalence of informed political participation – The 1976 Presidential debates as a source of influence. Communication Research, 6, pp. 463–487.

MCLEOD, J. M. and CHAFFEE, S. H., 1972: The construction of social reality. In J. Tedeschi (ed.), The Social Influence Processes. Chicago, IL: Aldine.

MCLEOD, J. M. and KOSICKI, G. M., 1986: Paying Attention to the Concept of Attention in Mass Media Research. Paper presented at the Midwest Association for Public Opinion Research, Chicago, IL.

MCLEOD, J. M., KOSICKI, G. M., AMOR, D. L., ALLEN, S. G., and PHILPS, D. M., 1986: Public Images of Mass Media News: What are They and Does it Matter? Paper

presented at the Association for Education in Journalism and Mass
Communication, Norman, OK.

MCLEOD, J. M., KOSICKI, G. M., PAN, Z., and ALLEN, S. G., 1987: Audience Perspectives
on the News: Assessing Their Complexity and Conceptual Frames. Paper
presented at the Association for Education in Journalism and Mass
Communication, San Antonio, TX.

MCLEOD, J. M. and MCDONALD, D. G., 1985: Beyond simple exposure. Communication
Research, 12, pp. 3–33.

MCLEOD, J. M. and REEVES, B., 1980: On the nature of mass media effects. In S.
Withey and R. Abeles (eds), Television and Social Behavior: Beyond Violence
and Children. Hillsdale, NJ: Lawrence Erlbaum. Reprinted in G. C. Wilhoit and
H. de Bock (eds), Mass Communication Review Yearbook (Vol. 2). Beverly Hills,
CA: Sage.

MCLEOD, J. M., SUN, S. W., CHI, H. H., and PAN, Z., 1990: Metaphor and the Media:
What Shapes Public Understanding of the 'War' Against Drugs? Paper presented
at the Association for Education in Journalism and Mass Communication.
Minneapolis, MN.

MCLUHAN, M., 1964: Understanding Media. London: Routledge and Kegan Paul.

MCQUAIL, D., 1987: Mass Communication Theory: An Introduction (2nd Ed.).
Newbury Park, CA: Sage.

MILLER, W. L., CLARKE, H. D., HARROP, M., LEDUC, L., and WHITELEY, P. F., 1990: How
Voters Change: The 1987 British Election Campaign in Perspective. Oxford:
Oxford University Press.

MORRISON, A. J., STEEPER, F. and GREENDALE, S., 1977: The First Presidential Debate:
The Voters Win. Paper presented at the American Association for Public Opinion
Research. Buck Hills Falls, PA.

NEUMAN, W. R., 1986: The Paradox of Mass Politics: Knowledge and Opinion in the
American Electorate. Cambridge, MA: Harvard University Press.

NEUMAN, W. R., 1989: Parallel content analysis: Old paradigms and new proposals. In
G. Comstock (ed.) Public Communication and Behavior. (Vol. 2). San Diego,
CA: Academic Press.

NISBETT, R. and ROSS, L., 1980: Human Inference: Strategies and Shortcomings of
Social Judgment. Englewood Cliffs, NJ: Prentice-Hall.

NOELLE-NEUMANN, E., 1973: Return to the concept of powerful mass media. Studies
of Broadcasting, 9, pp. 67–112.

NOELLE-NEUMANN, E., 1984: The Spiral of Silence: Public Opinion – Our Social Skin.
Chicago, IL: University of Chicago Press.

O'KEEFE, G., 1985: 'Taking a bite out of crime': The impact of a public information
campaign. Communication Research, 12, pp. 147–178.

PAISLEY, W., 1980: Communication in the communication sciences. In B. Dervin and
M. Voigt (eds), Progress in the Communication Sciences (Vol. 6). Norwood, NJ:
Ablex.

PAN, Z. and MCLEOD, J. M., 1991: Multi level analysis in mass communication
research. Communication Research, 18, pp. 140–173.

PARK, R. E., 1940: News as a form of knowledge: A chapter in the sociology of
knowledge. American Journal of Sociology, 45, pp. 669–686.

PARKER, E. B., 1963: The effects of television on public library circulation. Public
Opinion Quarterly, 27, pp. 578–589.

PATTERSON, T. E., 1980: The Mass Media Election: How Americans Choose Their
President. New York: Praeger.

PETTY, R. E. and CACIOPPO, J. T., 1986: Communication and Persuasion: Central and
Peripheral Routes to Attitude Change. New York: Springer-Verlag.

REEVES, B., 1989: Theories about news and theories about cognition: Arguments for a
more radical separation. American Behavioral Scientist, 33, pp. 191–198.

REEVES, B., CHAFFEE, S. H., and TIMS, A., 1982: Social cognition and mass communication research. In M. E. Roloff and C. R. Berger (eds), Social Cognition and Communication. Beverly Hills, CA: Sage.

REEVES, B., THORSON, E., and SCHLEUDER, J., 1986: Attention to television: Psychological theories and chronometric measures. In J. Bryant and D. Zillman (eds), Perspectives on Media Effects. Hillsdale, NJ: Lawrence Erlbaum.

RICE, R. E. and ATKIN, C. K. (eds), 1989: Public Communication Campaigns (2nd ed.). Beverly Hills, CA: Sage.

ROBERTS, D. F. and MACCOBY, N., 1985: Effects of mass communication. In G. Lindzey and E. Aronson (eds), The Handbook of Social Psychology (3rd ed., Vol. 2). New York: Random House.

ROBINSON, J. P., 1972: Mass communication and information diffusion. In F. G. Kline and P. J. Tichenor (eds), Current Perspectives in Mass Communication Research. Beverly Hills, CA: Sage.

ROBINSON, J. P. and LEVY, M. R., 1986: The Main Source: Learning from Television News. Beverly Hills, CA: Sage.

ROGERS, E. M., 1962: The Diffusion of Innovations. New York: Free Press.

ROSENGREN, K., E. WENNER, L. A. and PALMGREEN, P. (eds), 1985: Media Gratifications Research: Current Perspectives. Newbury Park, CA: Sage.

SCHRAMM, W. L., 1964: Mass Media and National Development. Stanford, CA: Stanford U. Press.

SEARS, D. O. and CHAFFEE, 1979: Uses and effects of the 1976 debates: An overview of empirical studies. In S. Kraus (ed.), The Great Debates: Carter vs. Ford, 1976. Bloomington, IN: Indiana University Press.

STAR, S. A. and HUGHES, H. M., 1950: Report on an education campaign: The Cincinnati plan for the UN. American Journal of Sociology, 55, pp. 389–400.

STOCKING, S. H. and GROSS, P. H., 1989: How Do Journalists Think? Bloomington, IN: ERIC Clearinghouse on Reading and Communication Skills.

STREUFERT, S. and STREUFERT, S. C., 1978: Behavior in the Complex Environment. New York: Halstead.

TANNENBAUM, P. H., 1967: The congruity principle revisited: Studies in the reduction, induction and generalization of persuasion. In L. Berkowitz (ed.), Advances in Experimental Social Psychology (Vol. 3). New York: Academic Press.

TAYLOR, S. E. and FISKE, S. T., 1978: Salience, attention, and attribution: Top of the head phenomena. In L. Berkowitz (ed.), Advances in Experimental Social Psychology (Vol. 11). New York: Academic Press.

TICHENOR, P. J., DONOHUE, G. A., and OLIEN, C. N., 1970: Mass media flow and differential growth in knowledge. Public Opinion Quarterly, 34, pp. 159–170.

TICHENOR, P. J., DONOHUE, G. A., and OLIEN, C. N., 1980: Community Conflict and the Press. Beverly Hills, CA: Sage.

TUCHMAN, G., 1978: Making News: A Study in the Construction of Reality. New York: Free Press.

TUROW, J., 1984: Media Industries: The Production of News and Entertainment. New York, NY: Longman.

TVERSKY, A. and KAHNEMAN, D., 1974: Judgment under uncertainty; Heuristics and biases. Science, 185, pp. 1124–1131.

VAN DIJK, T. A., 1988: News As Discourse. Hillsdale, NJ: Lawrence Erlbaum.

WARNER, K. E., 1977: The effects of the anti-smoking campaign on cigarette consumption. American Journal of Public Health, 73, pp. 672–677.

WARTELLA, E. and REEVES, B., 1985: Historical trends in research on children and the media: 1900–1960. Journal of Communication, 35, pp. 118–133.

WATT, J. H. and KRULL, R., 1977: An examination of three models of television viewing and aggression. Human Communication Review, 3, pp. 99–112.

WEBER, M., 1910: Zeitungwesen. Report to the first meeting of the German

Sociological Society, Deutsche Gesellschaft fur Soziologie, 39–62.

WEINBERG, C. B. and WIESS, D. L., 1982: On the econometric measurement of the duration of advertising effects on sales. Journal of Marketing Research, 19, pp. 585–591.

WHITNEY, D. C., 1985: The Media and the People: Americans' Experience with the News Media: A Fifty-one Year Review. New York: Gannett Center for Media Studies.

WOBER, M. and GUNTER., B., 1988: Television and Social Control. New York: St. Martin's Press.

WOLFE, K. M. and FISKE, M., 1949: The children talk about comics. In P. Lazarsfeld and F. Stanton (eds) Communication Research, 1948–49. New York: Harper.

WYER, R. S., and SRULL, T. K., 1981: Category accessibility: Some theoretical and empirical issues concerning the processing of social information. In E. T. Higgins, C. P. Herman, and M. P. Zanna (eds), Social Cognition: The Ontario Symposium (Vol. 1). Hillsdale, NJ: Lawrence Erlbaum.

ZILLMANN, D., 1971: Excitation transfer in communication-mediated aggressive behavior. Journal of Experimental Social Psychology, 7, pp. 419–434.

ZILLMANN, D., 1982: Television viewing and arousal. In D. Pearl, L. Bouthilet, and J. Lazar (eds), Television and Behavior: Ten Years of Scientific Progress and Implications for the Eighties: Vol. 2. Technical Reviews. Washington, DC: Government Printing Office.

13

Meaning, Genre and Context: The Problematics of 'Public Knowledge' in the New Audience Studies

John Corner

As other articles in this collection will variously indicate (see particularly the overview provided by Sonia Livingstone) one of the most striking points of development in the media research of the last decade has centred upon questions of 'reception'. These questions have essentially been ones about *what* meanings audiences make of what they see, hear and read, *why* these meanings rather than others are produced by specific audiences from the range of interpretative possibilities, and *how* these activities of meaning-making, located as they usually are in the settings of everyday domestic life, might relate to ideas about the power of the media and about the constitution of public knowledge, sentiment and values.

Such a development – in many ways a return to the empirical study of audiences with a new and sharper agenda concerning the nature of meaning as social action – has rightly been seen (Curran 1990) to have exerted a 'revisionary' pull on those theories about media power which were grounded in structuralist accounts of ideology and which were so highly influential in British research in the 1970s (see, for instance, Hall 1977 for a critical review from within the perspective). So much so that in some 'new paradigm' work concerned with reception, the question of an ideological level of media processes, or indeed of media power as a political issue *at all*, has slipped almost entirely off the main research agenda, if not from framing commentary. In what *might* turn out finally to be a temporary phase of 'high swing' on the pendulum, so much conceptual effort has been centred on audiences' interpretative activity that even the preliminary theorization of influence has become *awkward*. There have been a number of useful overviews of 'reception' studies recently (for instance, Schroder 1987, Morley 1989, Ang 1990, Jensen 1990a, Moores 1990) along with a consideration of their ethnographic methods (see the special issues of the *Journal of Communication Inquiry* 13.2. 1989 and *Cultural Studies* 4.1.1990).

My interest in this chapter is not in offering a further synoptic account but in bringing as pointedly into focus as I can what I see to be three key areas both of conceptual emphasis and of conceptual difficulty for the new enterprise. These point outwards towards more general problems for the theorizing and analysis of cultural power. Since my own interests are focused on the relationship between broadcast journalism and public knowledge, I shall pursue my argument with this primarily in mind, in the awareness that other aspects of the 'new wave' audience study to which I shall occasionally refer, most prominently those concerned with popular drama series, are dealt with in detail elsewhere in the present volume.

The three broad areas which I have selected are best indicated by the terms 'meaning', 'genre', and 'context'. Around each one, it seems to me, there has clustered not only a number of conflicting accounts but also confusions. One of the results of this is that although overviewing commentators may talk boldly of a thriving new 'ethnographic' tradition (in a not uncontested reference to the conventions of 'in-depth' anthropological data gathering), there is in fact a good deal of deconstructive work to be done if significant further progress is to be made. It also seems to me that the three terms are now employed in two rather distinct kinds of project, posing the 'influence/interpretation' question in different ways.

One project is concerned primarily with the media as an agency of public knowledge and 'definitional' power, with a focus on news and current affairs output and a direct connection with the politics of information and the viewer as citizen (illustrative examples here would be Morley 1980, Lewis 1985, Jensen 1986, Dahlgren 1988 Hoijer 1989, Corner, Richardson and Fenton 1990a and 1990b). The recent researches of Danish, Swedish and Norwegian scholars in the area now constitute a highly-focused and intensively theorized strand of this line of enquiry, which can conveniently be called the *public knowledge* project.

The other project is concerned primarily with the implications for social consciousness of the media as a source of entertainment and is thereby connected with the social problematics of 'taste' and of pleasure (for instance, those concerning class and gender) within industrialized popular culture. This we can call the *popular culture* project (illustrative examples would be Ang 1985, parts of Morley 1986, and Seiter et al. 1989, with Radway 1984 offering a pioneering and influential study of the reading of popular literature).

I do not mean to suggest that the two projects have no interconnection. Clearly, to fail to recognize the aesthetic character, narrative organization and broad cultural embedding of news and current affairs exposition or the social knowledges and classificatory systems at work in popular drama, would be to work with a crassly simplistic idea of what is going on. Researchers have shown themselves to be fully aware of this (see for instance Liebes and Katz 1990, and Livingstone 1988 and in this volume on the cognitive dimension of popular series drama). Yet a divergence along the lines suggested, in research problematics and the terms thought appropriate to addressing them (variously weighted towards aesthetic, psychological, sociological or directly political theorization) seems not only to be clearly discernible but to be increasing. One sign of this is the extent to which recent overviews of the area reference a different literature, allowing for a number of common, 'core' texts, according to their chosen perspective. Under my three headings I shall comment further on the nature and consequence of this divergence.

Some questions might also be asked about the general *political* relations at work (by default or otherwise) in the sudden bourgeoning of 'demand-side' research (both on fictional and non-fictional forms) from the mid 1980s onwards. In certain versions of the reception perspective, this seems to have amounted to a form of sociological quietism, or loss of critical energy, in which increasing emphasis on the micro-processes of viewing relations displaces (though rarely explicitly so) an engagement with the macro-structures of media and society. In other versions, mostly within the 'popular culture' project, a celebratory tone has sometimes appeared, the academic critic enthusiastically validating the choices of entertainment made by 'ordinary viewers' in a way which then prompts fundamental questions about the aims both of aesthetic and of social inquiry. (The hugely influential Fiske 1987 carries some of these tones, though he is a good deal more circumspect about the macro framings of economic and cultural power than many commentators have given credit for). A Norwegian scholar, Jostein Gripsrud, has noted some further possible consequences of the tendency:

> By pretending that the academic critic's pleasure is the same as anybody else's, s/he not only erases the socio-cultural differences between the academic and the genre's core audiences, but also avoids analyzing the specificities of, for instance, the film scholar's pleasures in soap-watching.
>
> (Gripsrud 1989, p. 198)

At a more general level, the widespread interest in reception issues seems to connect closely, and not co-incidentally, with certain aspects of the turn towards Postmodernism which several arts and social science disciplines have recently taken. This turn, too complex in character to summarize here, has often signalled what might be judged, according to viewpoint, as either as a 'sophistication' or a 'softening' of the terms of cultural critique. A heightened sense of ambivalence towards the artefacts and pleasures produced by the resources and market inventiveness of the Late Capitalist culture industries has been displayed at the very same time as it has become fashionable to be elaborately nervous about ideas of truth, reason and power (see the excellent synoptic account of these matters in Harvey 1989).

Under my chosen headings, I shall open out discussion on these and other points as well as on those more specifically to do with the significatory and social relations of sense-making, with the *pragmatics* of mediation.[1]

First of all, however, it might be useful, before looking in detail at its *problems*, if I were to state as succinctly as possible the broad terms of 'reception research' as I perceive them within the perspective of my own interest in the production of public knowledge. Though much of what I say has relevance for work on other than TV audiences, it is upon TV that most studies have focused and, as a result, my own discussion is often pulled into having a medium-specific character.

There is no doubt that David Morley's *The 'Nationwide' Audience* (1980) represents the single most significant publication in the emergence of the reception perspective in British research. Based on group-discussions following the video screening of an early evening news magazine, it set up an agenda about 'text-viewer' relations, interpretative variation and 'knowing through television' which has been a major influence. It is also the case that his *Family*

Television (1986), in which a number of families are interviewed in depth about their viewing habits and pleasures, was a further, important contribution. This second book showed a shift of emphasis from the plotting of specific, social correlations of text/viewer/meaning to a broad study of domestic settings and patterns of use. As I shall argue later, such a shift is not without its problems, particularly if regarded straightforwardly as a 'development' out of the earlier work.

The first of these studies, and those by other researchers which are indebted to it (few of those published over the last decade are not), can be seen as partly a reaction against two aspects of the contemporary state of theory and research. First of all, a reaction against the (often structuralist) 'textualism' of cultural studies in Britain. There had been an attempt within this strand of work to develop semiotics into a 'science of the text' whereby not only could a precise and 'deep' textual meaning be discerned by close reading, but also the 'ideological effect' a text would promote in viewers could be predicted by assessment of the positioning force it exerted upon receptive acts (see Corner 1985 for an historical tracing of these ideas in Cultural Studies). Morley's work was an attempt to break out from the formalism of this position into a more open engagement with the variables and complexities of 'meaning-in-process'.

Secondly, the relative neglect of 'meaning' in favour of 'function' and 'use' in contemporary empirical audience research was identified and reacted to (though the 'naivety' of early research on this score can be exaggerated. See Curran 1990). The form which 're-conceptualization' took here involved an attempt to carry over cultural studies' alertness to discursive and symbolic processes into an analysis of the organization and forms of viewing activities rather than those of media texts themselves. 'Influence', whatever its strength and direction, had to work through meaning, and it was to the formal and social complexity of meaning-production that the new research addressed itself. Meaning was seen as *intra-textual* (requiring analysis of textual structures), *inter-textual* (requiring analysis, among other things, of genres and relations between them) but also finally and decisively *interpretative* (requiring research into the situated practice of 'receptive' understanding).

The method, both in *The 'Nationwide' Audience* and in the sizeable number of research projects to follow Morley's lead, was quite directly to generate group talk about television following specially arranged screenings. Through such data, 'readings' (for ethnography, despite its interest in viewers' accounts, could not dispense with the need for analyst interpretation) might be made of the way in which the talk indicated patterns of variation in the meanings-for-the-viewer. These patterns might then be connected with other factors differentiating the individual viewers or viewing groups questioned. In other words, not only *variation* but also *the reasons for it and the consequences of it* might, if only in part, be accessible.

The overall general significance attributed to this work within media studies (a matter not without 'reception research' possibilities itself!) was towards seeing the variations in response as indicating a revision *downwards* in hypotheses about media power (to some extent, replicating the shifts in emphasis of an earlier chapter in media research history. See Curran 1990). Forms of interpretative 'resistance', as this was indicated in Morley's use of the terms 'negotiated' and 'oppositional' to classify types of non-aligned reading position, were seen to be more widespread than 'subordination' (the reproduction of 'dominant' meanings) and, as I have indicated earlier, a number of commentators welcomed the newly-recognized degree of viewer and reader 'independence' which this was presumed to document. It should be noted here, however, that Morley himself has never failed to emphasize in his work the extent to which cultural power and ideological reproduction work as much, if not more, through the social factors bearing upon interpretative action as they do through that which might be thought to be 'carried' by, or 'inscribed' within, media texts themselves. Failure to attend properly to this has often lead to a situation in which an overly simplistic play-off between textual power and reader freedom, with a variety of possible 'truce' positions mooted, has been implicit in debate (see the extensive and polemical treatment by a number of authors in *Critical Studies in Mass Communication 5* (1988) pp. 217–254.

I want now to turn to the first of the three areas which I have suggested merit closer, critical attention.

1 Meaning

Quite what a given critic or researcher wishes to include within the term 'meaning' in now-familiar phrases like 'the viewer constructs the meaning of the programme' or 'the text is capable of producing many different meanings', or 'this is the meaning to which you are guided by the text' is nowhere near as clear as it might be. This lack of clarity has hindered the development of productive critical dialogue between researchers and it has made for a situation in which, whilst there are a lot of (rather repetitive) profundities around concerning meaning and the media, there is a chronically under-theorized sense of what precisely is at issue.

Although spatial metaphors have to be used cautiously in investigating semantic and pragmatic processes, the notion of 'levels' can, I believe, offer some preliminary differentiations here and thereby help to highlight some of the pitfalls of too casual a usage. In many uses of 'meaning', three different levels of meaning can be seen to be indicated, often collapsed together. These are:

1 A level at which a word, image or sequence's primary signification is recognized and comprehended (e.g. the written word 'typewriter', the spoken word 'violence', a shot of a baby in a pushchair, a TV car chase). This recognition and comprehension will, of course, take account of, or be responsive to, those surrounding and concurrent factors which add up to a *context of use* (the theoretical establishment of which in any research design presents a major problem – see below). With due regard for problems of category borderlines, for many purposes this level can still be usefully thought of, following classic early semiotics, as relating to the level of 'denotation'.

2 A level at which a word, image or sequences' secondary, implicatory, or associative signification is recognized and comprehended. This level will vary according to the character either of the signifier or the signified or a combination of both (i.e. named or visually depicted entities will vary in their degree of symbolic/metaphoric resonance – a shot of a chair may have less than a shot

of a cruise missile – and so will named abstractions like 'politeness' or 'death'). Clearly, the secondary signifying force of each verbal phrasing or articulation of image will be dependant in part not only on its local elements but on their organization within the larger textual unit which is being attended to. At this secondary level, the effect of variations in the resources upon which viewers draw to make sense of and to evaluate their viewing will be greater than at the primary level, where the grounding of interpretative work is in more broadly consensual sign-forms and conventions. A *biographical* as well as a *social* variable may start to figure more strongly in the organizing of perceptual, cognitive and significance-according activity. The term 'connotation' continues to be useful to indicate the level of signification involved here, though it has too often been thought of exclusively in terms either of the 'emotive' or of the associations generated by visual images. Moreover, many applications of the denotation/connotation distinction are woefully simplistic and rigid.[2]

3   A level at which viewers and readers attach a generalized significance to what they have seen and heard, evaluating it (perhaps in relation to its perceived presuppositions and entailments if it has propositional force) and locating it within a negotiated place in their knowledge or memory, where it may continue to do modifying work on other constituents of their consciousness (and, indeed, of their unconscious). When some researchers talk of the 'response' or of 'the reading' which a particular media artefact elicited, it is clearly to this level which they are most often referring. The widely-used idea of 'preferred reading' to indicated a weighting of significations in a text towards one ideologically-aligned understanding of it also relates most directly to this level (Morley 1980 is a seminal application). Although the concept of 'preferred reading' signalled a welcome move away from 'hard' notions of textual power (the general significance 'encoded' need not be the one 'decoded') and towards the influence/interpretation interface, its use really remained limited to news and current affairs texts, particularly those in which declaredly neutral discourses were in fact organized in terms of systematically 'weighted' categories and relationships. Even here, in addressing the long-standing problematics of journalism's professed objectivity, slippage across different levels of meaning is evident. In a study of the cultural political and consequences of the popular press, James Curran and Colin Sparks develop a useful discussion of just how obstructive this slippage can be to a conceptualization of media power (Curran and Sparks, 1991), a point I return to below.

In engaging with this level of 'response', a general distinction between factual and fictional or entertainment-based texts needs to be retained. In the former, the viewer is often drawn quite directly into a 'response' which involves relations of belief and disbelief, agreement and disagreement. The kinds of text-processing which viewers perform in the two cases are likely to be quite distinctive. Morley (1980) is, again, the seminal instance of agreement/disagreement variation being plotted in respondent talk.

For the purposes of an investigation into the interaction between media forms and audiences, it seems a good idea to keep some such three-tier differentiation in mind, perhaps theorizing it more tightly and with a less impressionistic vocabulary, in relation *both* to significatory forms and their interpretative processing (see the useful attempt in Lewis 1985). This might act not only against the terminology of mechanistic unity ('decoding') but also against loose generalization. In a recent and shrewd account of current research issues, Peter Dahlgren (1988) appears to fall temporary victim to this tendency when he notes:

> By 'meaning' I refer here to the processes of making sense of the world around us. It has to do with creating a general coherence in our lives, of establishing an order in which to anchor our existence.
>
> (p. 287)

This is certainly true but by no means is it enough.

To illustrate the clear need for differentiation in analytic practice, we can take the example of two people who meet at work the morning after the broadcasting of a television play which both saw. They discuss the play and quite soon a difference of judgement emerges about the ending, which one person thought moving and the other silly. How far is this difference actually one of assessments being made of the same set of meanings? How far are evaluative criteria and their application really at issue? It might well be that further debate uncovers the fact that they have divergent notions of what was actually 'going on' in the ending. We could even imagine a situation where, after one of them has persuasively put the case to the other about just what *was* happening in the last scene, there is now agreement that, indeed, it was a moving and apt conclusion. There is a further twist we can give to this imaginary circumstance. Let us say that right from start the two agree that the play and its ending were impressive. Does this guarantee that they have a shared version of its meaning? No. It is perfectly possible (though perhaps less likely than the first scenario) that there are radical divergences in their sense of what it all meant or what key parts of it meant. And if the conversation gets intense enough for detailed appraisals to be offered, such divergence may become apparent and put a halt to their mutual appreciation, shifting it into debate and dispute.

Having suggested that a 'levels' model of meaning may be useful to hang on to and refine, despite problems if the typology becomes over-rigid, I want now to note two particular difficulties which then immediately arise and require attention (since they are usually 'disguised' by the failure, right from the start, to register differentiation). We can call one of them the *linearity problem*, the other the *part-whole* problem.

The linearity problem follows from regarding the different levels of meaning (either in my crude typology or any refined variant) as somehow activated *in a sequence of separate moments* (the spatial metaphor tends to slide analysts into thinking this way). Thus, the viewer accords primary meaning, then secondary meaning, then significance, in a phased process. Clearly, this will not do. Anticipations of significance work to guide the registration of secondary and the organization of primary meaning right from the start of a stretch of viewing or reading activity. As a programme or article unfolds within transmission-time or reading-time, a developing structure of anticipation and possibilities, together with the specific inter-textual connections and evaluations made by readers or viewers, bears 'downwards' on the reading at the same time as there is also a generative process 'upwards' from primary signification through into a generalized significance. This inter-articulation of sense-making practices, ranging from the basic construing of words and images through to the making of propositional, thematic and/or fictive-imaginary understandings and assessments, is a continuous, self-modifying 'loop' process rather than anything working through distinct and separate phases. It is also, thereby, a process which is saturated *culturally* throughout,though to rather different degrees and effect at different points. (On the 'incremental' character of this process see Lewis 1983 and the social psychology perspective of Hoijer 1990. Reception research as a whole could benefit from a firmer engagement with the kind of issues raised in recent 'text comprehension' literature, despite its behavioural orientation. See, for instance, Bradac (ed.) 1989).

The part-whole problem is a related issue. For as well as meaning-making requiring a movement 'upwards' from the recognition of, for instance, colours, shapes and sounds to the attributing of significance, there is also a movement 'outwards' from the interpretation of localized signifiers to an ongoing entity which is seen finally to be the expressive whole (the advert, the play, the news item, etc). And just as the 'upward' movement is accompanied by the 'downward' process of realizing new primary meanings within generalized framings, so this movement 'outwards' is accompanied by an 'inwards' movement locating elements, perhaps retrospectively, within the emerging organization of the programme/text and its broader inter-textuality. This duality presents a challenge to researchers, who require to engage with its dynamics, not slip into using established categories and divisions.

Although I have done little more than raise some questions and perhaps suggest both the necessity and the awkwardness of coming to closer terms with the phenomena under study, I want to leave this account of meaning by drawing out some of its principal implications for current theorizing around texts and readers.

The main implication concerns the extent to which, and the manner in which, 'openness' and variation in meaning are regarded as aspects of text-reader relations. For the extensive use of the term 'polysemy' (see Fiske 1987) to indicate the richness of meaning possibilities in media texts has tended to suggest an indeterminacy *only* closed down by interpretative action (even if this action *is* seen to be one shaped within the terms of the cultural system rather than being an act of 'free choice'). In part, this may be the result of theoretical observations about the polysemy of individual signs when considered in abstract being transferred over to observations about their use within textual structures. In the latter situation the signs, whether they be visual or verbal, are clearly narrowed in their activated significatory range through their combination with other signs (Morley 1981 discusses this point usefully).

Whatever the reason for this assumption of general textual 'openness', such a perspective neglects among other things the considerable degree of *determinacy* possessed by texts. This determinacy is simply a result of their using, among other things, systems of signification based on widespread social/national acceptance and having relatively low levels of ambiguity. Terry Eagleton (1983) brings this out very well in discussing aspects of the argument about text-reader relations within literary studies:

You can say that perceiving eleven black marks as the word 'nightingale' is an interpretation, or that perceiving something as black or eleven or a word is an interpretation, and you would be right; but if in most circumstances you read those marks to mean 'nightgown' you would be wrong. An interpretation on which everyone is likely to agree is one way of defining a fact . . . Interpreting these marks is a constrained affair, because the marks are often used by people in their social practices of communication in certain ways, and these practical social uses *are* the various meanings of the word.

(p. 86)

Eagleton's example could easily be exchanged for one from a newspaper article or from the speech of a television documentary. It is less easy to transfer it across directly to the use of images since the system of image signification (still or moving) is nowhere near as tightly codified as writing and speech, but the basic point about textually-exerted constraints on meaning still obtains. It clearly remains true, as the new interpretative perspective is keen to point out, that 'meaning' does *not* inhere within texts, and is far better seen as a property of interpretative production (and therefore, as essentially 'unstable') even where the most uncomplicated and familiar of routine significations are concerned (e.g. NO ENTRY, 'Hello, David'). But the effect of determinate *signification* upon this production is something which the use of the term 'polysemy' has not always recognized and, at its worst, has dismissed (see Jensen 1990a and Curran and Sparks on some of the political implications here).

One reason for this is the continued dominance in film and media studies of a literary perspective on meaning. In this perspective, 'meaning' (often seen as synonymous with that completed entity 'the reading') nearly always implies what I have indicated above as 'third-level' activity – the considered attribution of significance, socio-cultural relevance and value – and does so principally in relation to the various 'imaginary' satisfactions to be derived from attending to fictional narratives. Valuable and, indeed, now 'classic' examples here would be the work of Ian Ang on regular viewers of *Dallas* and Janice Radway on the readers of romantic fiction (Ang 1985 and Radway 1984). However, if this usage (meaning equals imaginative response) becomes general then a disastrous degree of slippage around the question of textual openess and closure is almost guaranteed. Over the last decade, lack of adequate differentiation here has trapped a number of reflections upon text-audience relations within a fundamental banality of approach from which not even the most ingenious theoretical elaborations can release them (see the critique in Morris 1988). On occasion, assertions of the fact of 'polysemy' have come dangerously close to precluding any real investigative interest either in the social causes and consequences of interpreting things differently or in the operation of cultural power through the media.

By contrast, I would want to argue that the researching *together* of interpretative action and textual signification is still the most important thing for audience research to focus upon. It is clear that investigations at what I have termed the 'secondary' level of activity, conventionally the 'connotative' must be central to this inquiry. For, with non-fictional forms, this is an important level in the operations whereby both textual mechanisms and readerly frames of reference work to generate thematic understandings and evaluations from specific significatory elements. Attention to differences of interpretation here cuts directly into the practices of cultural reproduction. This level has, of course, been the one at which the most interesting text-analytic work in Cultural Studies has operated – connecting 'outwards' both into specific rules of discursive organization and also, more ambitiously and speculatively, into the thematics of popular consciousness and the movements and conflicts which are observable therein. As I noted above, reception studies have clearly problematized that diagnostic project, with its confident projections straight into viewers' heads, but some of the questions on the earlier agenda are still worthy of the asking, as I shall suggest in my conclusions.

2   Genre

Genre is a principal factor in the directing of audience choice and of audience expectations ('shall I watch X?, what might it be like'?) and in the organizing of the subsets of cultural competences and dispositions appropriate for watching, listening to and reading different kinds of thing. Once again, Morley himself has made some useful connections in a postscript essay on the 'Nationwide' project (Morley 1981) but these were sketchy and have received little if any sustained development (though see Jensen 1986 p. 119 for useful comment). Genre is the second area where I believe increased critical attention is required. For without recognition by the researcher that 'television', both as a formal system and as a social process, is constituted from often very different communicative forms and activities, the danger is that an essentialistic tendency will, by default, assert itself. Textual analysis of the media has already suffered from this tendency, particularly so analysis of television, where the range of forms and uses is extremely broad yet closure down to medium unification (e.g. 'television is . . .'; 'television portrays . . .'; television cannot . . .') is common (Ellis 1982 provides an influential example). Though the search for characteristics of television-audience relations in respect of communicational and 'epistemic' properties of the medium itself (see Dahlgren 1988) is well worth pursuing, too urgent an approach to a general theory here is bound to reproduce this essentialism.

The most consequential division across the television genres is the most obvious one and one I have referred to already – that between fictional and non-fictional programming. Although this is not always a clean division in formal systems – certain principles of television 'grammar', for instance, apply to both – the levels of referentiality, modes of address, forms of propositional or more associative, symbolic discourse and the presence or otherwise of television's own representatives (e.g. presenter, host, reporter) serve to mark the two areas out into distinctive communicative realms.

The characteristic properties of text-viewer relations in most non-fiction television are primarily to do with kinds of *knowledge*, usually regulated and framed by direct address speech. This is so even if the programme is devised as an entertainment (for instance, a gardening programme, a popular music review, a sports broadcast).

The characteristic properties of text-viewer relations in fictional television are primarily to do with *imaginative pleasure*, particularly the pleasures of dramatic circumstance and of character. In the last few years, there has been a shift away from news and current affairs as the 'paradigm' form for British and American reception studies and towards popular domestic drama series or 'Soaps', particularly the more successful US series. The result of this emphasis has been an intensive linking of work on reception with questions of realism, pleasure, gender and viewing context (see Sonia Livingstone's article in this volume for citation and discussion). The resulting studies and the closely inter-referenced debate which has followed have been productive, but along with the steady institutionalization of this particular version of the reception agenda has gone a relative lack of interest in questions of perception, comprehension and understanding. In some discussions of reception processes, journalistic genres have been seen as irredeemably *male* and 'closed' in contrast to the progressive *female* 'openess' of the viewing relations typically obtaining in popular drama (see Fiske 1987). This view is rooted in highly speculative ideas about the gendered character of 'polysemy' in relation both to programme intentions and formats and the typical viewing relations encouraged. One consequence of it seems to have been further to reinforce that division between 'public knowl-edge' and 'popular culture' perspectives to which I referred at the start of this essay. It is sometimes implied that journalism's drive towards the facts, towards a truth, is naively and obsessively empiricist, and neglectful of the nature of all public communication as creative play, as necessarily 'invention'. However question-begging such a position is, its connection with aspects of postmodernist commentary has given it a surprising degree of influence in one form or another.

In the first problem area outlined above, around 'meaning', I noted how confusions and complacencies had begun to hinder the development of audi-ence studies. My argument about genre is that too little attention has been paid to how its specificities affect viewing behaviour (including its degrees of intensity and of concurrent room activity) and that, increasingly often, re-search and arguments focused on 'soap' series have been put into service as indicative of television-in-general. These separate issues of meaning and of genre are, of course, interconnected in a number of ways, so that conceptual problems with one may well affect clarity of theorization in dealing with the other. For instance, as I also noted earlier, to talk of the 'meaning' of a fictional text can be to move straight away to a quite generalized level of response. 'Meaning' here is immediately something to do with imaginative relations – something to do with the cultural satisfactions involved in relating to characters and to dramatic situations. The noting of differences at *this* level may be vulnerably close to the everyday observation that, first of all, different people like different things and, secondly, that people often like the same things for different reasons. If unconnected to a sociological programme of inquiry, research topples backwards into the relativities of 'taste' and any generalized theories of cultural power within which the research may appear to be conducted are, in fact, merely a speculative appendage.

Questions both of meaning and of genre are implicated in the third problem area I have chosen to examine – that of context. For revised notions of what constitutes the operative and researchable 'context' or 'setting' for media audience activity have been among the most important points of re-assessment in recent research.

3   Context

Across a number of different areas of humanities and social science inquiry a shift away from 'formalism' in the analysis of meaning (this being regarded as an exclusive concern with matters of discursive form or 'message structure') has entailed a more direct engagement not only with processes of interpretation but also with contexts and settings. This has occurred in different ways within the disciplines of literary studies, musicology, art history and sociology, to take notable instances, as well as in media and cultural studies. However, perhaps the most intensive theorization of the issue has occurred in linguistics (see Levinson 1983). The aim has been to analyze meaning (across all 'levels', though as I have pointed out this is not usually made explicit) as socially situated.

Immediately, this broadening out of attention from forms to what are seen as constitutive settings of use poses a problem, though it may not be one immediately addressed by the researcher. Put simply, the problem is this – 'what do you include in context and where does context stop?' Or, put the other way round and more dramatically, 'what *don't* we have to consider?', 'what *doesn't* contribute to the construction of meaning here?'

In the case of television studies, I think it is helpful to see the attempt to 'situate' acts of viewing as an attempt to relate analysis to *two* contextual realms not simply one – *the social relations* of viewing and the *space/time settings* of viewing. These are not usefully conflated and I want to explore a little further what is entailed in researching them in the light of the two basic questions posed above. Investigation into the social relations of viewing carries the reception researcher into the multiple and complex structures and processes which might bear on the *sociality* of interpretative action. Among these are the 'objective' demographic variables – class, gender and age being clearly prominent – but also those less easily plottable yet often highly significant variations in disposition and 'cultural competence' (including familiarity with particular linguistic and aesthetic conventions) which occur *within* as well as between the conventional sociological categorizations. It was part of the conclusion of *The 'Nationwide' Audience* that these latter variables, conceptualized by Morley as the positioning of audience members in varying kinds of 'discursive space', giving a different resourcing to individual practical consciousness, were more significant than his initial hypotheses had suggested. They frequently 'over-rode' or confounded the broad system of socio-economic sampling which had been central to his research design. Further development here has been slow, despite wide discussion of the issues involved (see for instance Brunt and Jordin 1986 for an excellent account of demographic issues in reception surveys). Clearly, classificatory schemes which can work at an 'intermediate' level are necessary, however tentatively projected, if research is not to be caught between unhelpfully broad social typologies on the one hand and banal and unproductive truisms about individual uniqueness on the other. As I shall suggest later, such schemes might involve theme-specific categories (viewer interpretations of economic accounts, for instance, being likely to produce a different pattern of variation from that generated by directly political accounts). They might also explore viewers' occupational variables (types, conditions and experiences of work) more thoroughly and sensitively.

It is in the second, albeit connected realm – that of inquiry into the space/ time settings of viewing – that major development has occurred recently. The most ambitious work here at the time of writing is the ongoing project of Morley and Silverstone at Brunel University (see Morley and Silverstone 1990), a project which not only engages with television viewing but with the full range of use of information technology in the home. An emphasis on the situating of viewing in its space and time contexts does not give up on the analysis of general social relations but tries to trace these through the daily routines and rituals of a domestic life within which television may be watched with varying degrees of attention and disattention and concurrently with a number of other household activities and chores (influential earlier studies here were Collett and Lamb 1986 and Morley 1986). Such an emphasis places reception analysis within a 'micro-sociology of everyday life', the better to catch at the constituent moods, motives and 'rituals' of viewing.

One of the problems which seems to follow from working within this perspective is that it then becomes difficult if not impossible to research around single text-viewer relations. Indeed, these become conceptually displaced by the more general relationship obtaining between television and home-life. Moreover, the preferred research methodology itself, in its concern for obtaining situated enthnographic data, tends to be wary of even such limited 'experimental' procedures as the special screening of video material to generate discussion. Thus, insofar as the specific significatory work of television is registered in such research, it is most often at the level of the favourite series or genre of programme. Such information is often richly informative, and it opens television research to perspectives on *use* under-explored within earlier conceptualizations of text-viewer interaction. For instance, it shows *how* in general the flow of meanings from programmes is rhythmically absorbed and made active within daily conversations, the conduct of hobbies and enthusiasms and the organization of daily life. Nevertheless, localized moments of signification, turning the elements and structures of programmes into sense, are still the nodal points around which the social dynamics of television operate. An understanding of the scale and subtlety of the 'life-worlds' within which acts of viewing are set must inform but cannot replace attention to these. This is particularly so where the medium's *more direct* public knowledge functions, rather than its breadth of culturally reproductive entertainments, are under scrutiny. Displacement here reinforces the displacement which I noted earlier in the shift in attention towards fictional genres.

Given the current promise of 'situated' studies, it is also quite easy to *over*-state the extent to which the removal of acts of viewing from the naturalized and fragmented flow of mundane use – such as occurs in the case of researcher-organized screenings – creates an unacceptable degree of distortion in viewers' responses. As well as the relativities of situation, there are the continuities and carry-overs of formed personal identity, preferences and attitudes to take account of here as well as the significatory stabilities of the texts themselves. These are all partial and interdependent constituents of 'meaning-for-the-viewer' but exclusive emphasis on the former within a strong theory of context-dependency risks a situation in which the research forever circles inquisitively around an object which it has, theoretically, abolished. As Charlotte Brunsdon has recently put it:

> The fact that the text is only and always realized in historically and contextually situated practices of reading does not demand that we collapse these categories into each other.
>
> Brunsdon 1989 (p. 126)

I suggested earlier that a basic problem presented to all contextually-focused communications research concerns where the 'edges' of relevant context are to be drawn. As well as deciding on an order of significance among all those things which can be designated as 'contextual' in relation to the main object of study (an order which can, of course, be modified in the course of the research), reception analysts also have to decide on those *methods* which will register significant things with appropriate detail and precision. This is by no means a novel situation for social research, but what may be remarkable is the degree to which the significant is not directly accessible to the researcher. For many things which make up the experiential fabric within which situated acts of reading occur are only registerable at all via speculation from data variously and perhaps obliquely held to be indexical of them. The size of this gap between the 'relevant context' and the 'researchable context' may be peculiar to work in the sociology of meanings. The study of attitudes and opinions, for example, though it also works with the unobservable, has conventionally been able to place a good deal of evidential weight (however critically framed) on the recorded statements of respondents *directly* engaging with and articulating the topic under research.

Given the presence of such a gap, there seems to me to be almost a strain of self-destructiveness at work in some of the current enthusiasm for extending contexts of analysis ever broader at the same time as holding out for an increased ethnographic depth. In a recent and generally very perceptive article, even Ien Ang, one of the most prominent and theoretically alert of recent researchers, talked of the need for a 'globalization' of the ethnographic pursuit' (Ang 1990, p. 244) without registering as much as might be deemed necessary the problems involved in pushing one, albeit sensitive, method of data collection that far out. Peter Dahlgren speculates with equivalent ambition, but with a resoluteness of tone that suggests a stronger sense of the formidable tasks that may lay ahead:

> It may well be that our only methodological option is to seriously launch ourselves on the path of anthropological 'thick descriptions' of the interface of everyday life's many settings with the media environment. (Dahlgren 1987, p. 298).

In its intellectually honourable bid to reject the grand theoreticist generalizations so disabling of media studies in the 70s, such a project is at risk of being confounded by its own empirical ambition. Just as confusions about meaning and insufficient attention to genre have exerted a limiting effect, so will an under-theorized and imprudently comprehensive notion of the contextual.

Viewers-Consumers-Citizens: Where to from Here?

Having discussed some of the problems which I believe the new emphasis on interpretation has run into but not always addressed, I want to end positively by indicating very briefly those areas where it seems to me the 'promise' of the new paradigm is considerable. My emphasis here on non-fictional output does not blind me to the great interest and importance of further reception work on TV's dramatic forms, particularly its forms of comedy, which certainly deserve far more attention than has so far been given them. The possibilities I have in mind reject the complacent relativism by which the interpretative contribution of the audience is perceived to be of such a scale and range as to render the very idea of media power naive. They also reject a rather different, if equally influential view – the radical populist presumption that popular audiences can be trusted to exercise an almost instinctive capacity to 'resist'[3] most of what they attend to via the media, apparently through mechanisms of cognition, thought process and overall social motivation not thought to require any further, closer attention.

These possibilities offer the chance to connect ideas of interpretative variation and its social determinants with the continuing debate about the media's function in organizing and disseminating public knowledge. They therefore engage with the 'influence' agenda. However much that agenda has had to be modified since the (mythical?) period when it was researched in terms of direct, monocausal processes of mental or behavioural change, the consequences of media systems for the consciousness and actions of the audience/public remain the most important goal of media inquiry. In a recent overview of research in Western Europe, Jay Blumler *et al.* called for more attention to 'citizen-readers' and for inquiry into:

> questions about how major political institutions and processes, including their symbolic meanings or claims, are 'read' and interpreted by those who follow reports about them in the mass media.
>
> Blumler, et al. 1990 (p. 275/276)

Peter Golding has also made a claim for 'the resurrection of the concept of citizenship as a critical bench-mark of enquiry in communications research' (Golding 1990, p. 100). To a degree, such an essentially public concept might act as a corrective complement to the rhetoric of the privatized 'consumer', which has undergone such opportunistic expansion in recent policy debate and which has sometimes achieved an odd and facile alignment with research emphases on 'pleasure'. How might a re-focused reception studies converge with the kind of enquiry looked for by Golding?

First of all, I think, by attempting to connect back to some quite old questions about the 'everyday' forms of comprehension of the social and political realm which are variously constitutive of civic disposition and opinion. How *is* public knowledge around particular nodal themes like 'the economy', 'defence', 'energy', 'health' and 'education' actually resourced from the variety of images, concepts, explanations and testimonies differentially available through media channels, as one set of agencies among others but ones central to the interconnecting of private and public realms?

Address to this question will require the interconnecting of cultural studies and sociological perspectives with those of social psychology and linguistics. The to and fro movements which I referred to earlier, between the different levels of activity constitutive of 'making sense', will only yield to analysis of such an interdisciplinary kind. So the sort of project I am outlining, though it can certainly find some guidance from previous attempts to plot and theorize 'attitudes and opinions', is distinctive in its address both to the detail of communicative form *and* to those factors of interpretative activity which recent work on reception has so indelibly placed on the research agenda. To turn to the conceptual apparatus which such research could employ, patterns of variation in the distribution, uptake and use of 'public knowledge' might productively be addressed by applying a range of interest group, occupational and political affiliation categories in addition to the main socio-demographic factors. Jensen (1990a) indicates how the modes of viewing of informational television might be differentiated in relation to use-values and, in an innovative attempt at bridging empirical research foci, in relation to the actual patterns of channel selection (1990b). Dahlghren (1988) has offered an account of how TV-initiated talk about public affairs can, itself, be generically defined.

Projects primarily designed not by reference to specific groups, settings or genres but to specific public issues receiving media treatment within different generic conventions could be particularly illuminating. A splendid example, which stopped short of a reception study, is Schlesinger, Murdock and Elliott (1983) on 'terrorism'. By holding the topic and its constituent themes constant, a sharper address to multi-levelled (including visual) meaning can be achieved whilst at the same time the 'edges' of researchable, relevant context can be more explicitly addressed. The goal here lies well beyond some further demonstrating of 'variation' among the 'active audience'. It lies in the closest possible engagement with the resources, terms and (to use a Stuart Hall phrase) the 'logics-in-use' out of which the forms of public, practical consciousness are made. Philo (1990) on public perceptions of the terms of the news coverage around the British Coal Strike and Corner, Richardson and Fenton (1990a and 1990b) on responses to TV depictions of Nuclear Energy policy have recently shown some of the possibilities. More importantly, they have also shown that close attention to 'interpretation' can, far from displacing the idea of 'influence', bring research on the formation of public and political knowledge back to it with sharper focus and renewed theoretical confidence.

Notes

1   I believe that reception research can profit from an understanding of how the debate between 'semantic' and 'pragmatic' perspectives has developed in linguistics. This debate, sometimes conducted from positions close to mutual exclusion, has not only encouraged close attention to the significatory factors involved in the production of meaning, it has brought analysis to bear on the idea of 'relevant context' and the problems of researching this. See Levinson (1983) for an excellent and lively discussion.

2   Hjlemslev (1953) offers some detailed discussion of this distinction at a date prior to its being taken up within cultural analysis through the various writings of Barthes and Eco. Eco (1976) is one of the clearest accounts I have come across though it is certainly not without its problems. It contains this interesting comment:

> The difference between denotation and connotation is not (as many authors maintain) the difference between 'univocal' and 'vague' signification, or between 'referential' and 'emotional' communication, and so on. What constitutes a connotation as such is the connotative code which establishes it; the characteristic of a connotative code is the fact that the further signification conventionally relies on a primary one . . . (p. 55/56).

Clearly, this idea of a stage of 'higher' signification being built upon the codes of lower ones is behind Barthes' hugely influential, 'three-decker' theory of myth (Barthes 1972). I am using a three-level schema less grandly and less evaluatively, as a way into differentiating more finely the processes of mundane meaning-making.

3   It is perhaps worth noting how ideas of the 'resisting' viewer are frequently linked to theories of 'polysemy', when logic would suggest quite the reverse. A viewer interpreting 'resistively' is consciously working *against* a set of meanings and values which they have (a) attributed to a programme item and (b) assumed to have been intended by the programme makers. Unless one advances a theory in which viewers 'resist' in a variety of different directions with no significant pattern of convergence, this seems to be more an argument for the (social) determinateness of texts than one for their polysemic character.

References

ANG, I., 1985: *Watching 'Dallas': Soap opera and the melodramatic imagination*. New York: Methuen.

ANG, I., 1990: 'Culture and Communication: Towards an Ethnographic Critique of Media Consumption in the Transnational Media System' in *European Journal of Communication* 5, 2–3, pp. 239–260.

BARTHES, R., 1972: *Mythologies* (trans. A. Lavers). London: Jonathan Cape.

BLUMLER, J. G., DAYAN, D. and WOLTON, D., 1990: 'West European Perspectives on Political Communication: Structures and Dynamics', in *European Journal of Communication*, 5, 2–3, pp. 261–284.

BRADAC, J. (ed.), 1989: *Message effects in communication science*, London: Sage.

BRUNSDON, C., 1989: 'Text and Audience' in Ellen Seiter et al. (eds) *Remote control: Television, audiences and cultural power*. London: Routledge, pp. 116–129.

BRUNT, R. and JORDIN, M., 1988: 'Constituting the Television Audience: A Problem of Method' in P. Drummond and R. Paterson (eds) *Television and its audience*. London: B.F.I. pp. 231–249.

COLLET, P. and LAMB, R., 1986: *Watching families watching TV*. Report to Independent Broadcasting Authority, London.

CORNER, J., 1985: 'Criticism as Sociology: Reading the Media' in J. Hawthorn (ed.) *Criticism and critical theory*. London: Edward Arnold, pp. 29–41.

CORNER, J., RICHARDSON, K. and FENTON, O., 1990a: 'Textualizing Risk: TV Discourse and the Issue of Nuclear Energy', in *Media, Culture and Society* 12, 1, pp. 105–124.

CORNER, J., RICHARDSON, K. and FENTON, N., 1990b: *Nuclear reactions: Form and response in 'public issue' television*. London: John Libbey.

CURRAN, J., 1990: 'The New Revisionism in Mass Communication Research: A Reappraisal' in *European Journal of Communication* 5, 2–3, pp. 135–164.

CURRAN, J. and SPARKS, C., 1991. 'Press and Popular Culture' in *Media, Culture and Society*, 13.2, pp. 215–237.

DAHLGREN, P., 1988: 'What's the Meaning of This?: Viewers' Plural Sense-Making of TV News' in *Media, Culture and Society* 10, 3, pp. 285–301.

EAGLETON, T., 1983: *Literary theory*. Oxford: Blackwell.

ECO, V., 1977: *A theory of semiotics*. London: Macmillan.

ELLIS, J., 1983: *Visible fictions*. London: Routledge.

FISKE, J., 1987: *Television culture*. London: Methuen.

GOLDING, P., 1990: 'Political Communication and Citizenship: The Media and Democracy in an Inegalitarian Social Order' in M. Ferguson (ed.) *Public communication: The new imperative*. London: Sage.

284   *John Corner*

GRIPSRUD, J.; 1989: "High Culture' Revisited' in *Cultural Studies* 3, 2, pp. 194–207.
HALL, S., 1977: 'Culture, the Media and the 'Ideological Effect'' in J. Curran, M. Gurevitch and J. Woollacott (eds) *Mass communication and society*. London: Edward Arnold.
HARVEY, D., 1989: *The condition of postmodernity*. Oxford: Blackwell.
HJELMSLEV, L., 1953: 'Prolegomena To A Theory of Language', Memoir 7 to *International Journal of American Linguistics*. Baltimore: Waverly Press, pp. 1–92.
HOIJER, B., 1990: 'Studying Viewers' Reception of Television Programmes: Theoretical and Methodological Considerations' in *European Journal of Communication* 5, 1, pp. 29–56.
JENSEN, K., 1986: *Making sense of the news*. Aarhus: The University Press.
JENSEN, K., 1990a: 'The Politics of Polysemy: Television News, Everyday Consciousness and Political Action' in *Media, Culture and Society* 12, 1, 1990, pp. 57–77.
JENSEN, K., 1990b: 'Reception as Flow: The "New Television Viewer" Revisited'. Paper to 17th Conference of the IAMCR, Bled, Jugoslavia, August 1990.
JENSEN, K. and ROSENGREN, E., 1990: 'Five Traditions in Search of the Audience' in *European Journal of Communication* 5, 2–3, pp. 207–238.
LEIBES, T. and E. KATZ, 1990: *The export of meaning*. Oxford: OUP.
LEVINSON, S., 1983: *Pragmatics*, Cambridge: CUP.
LEWIS, J., 1983: 'The Encoding-Decoding Model: Criticisms and Redevelopments for Research on Decoding' in *Media, Culture and Society* 5, 2, pp. 179–97.
LEWIS, J., 1985: 'Decoding Television News' in P. Drummond and R. Paterson (eds) *Television in transition*. London: BFI.
LIVINGSTONE, S. M., 1988: 'Viewers' Interpretations of Soap Opera: The Role of Gender, Power and Morality' in P. Drummond and R. Paterson *Television and its audience*. London: BFI.
MOORES, S., 1990: 'Texts, Readers and Contexts of Reading: Developments in the Study of Media Audiences' in *Media, Culture and Society* 12, 1, pp. 9–29.
MORLEY, D, 1980: *The 'Nationwide' audience: structure and decoding*, London: BFI.
MORLEY, D., 1981: 'The Nationwide Audience: A Critical Postscript' in *Screen Education* 39, pp. 3–14.
MORLEY, D., 1986: *Family Television*. London: Comedia.
MORLEY, D., 1989: 'Changing Paradigms in Audience Studies' in E. Seiter et al. (eds) *Remote control: Television, audiences and cultural power*. London: Routledge.
MORLEY, D. and SILVERSTONE, R., 1990: 'Domestic Communication – Technologies and Meanings' in *Media, Culture and Society* 12, 1, pp. 31–55.
MORRIS, M., 1988: 'Banality in Cultural Studies' in *Block* 14, pp. 15–26.
PHILO, G., 1990: *Seeing and believing*. London: Routledge.
RADWAY, J., 1984: *Reading the romance. Women, patriarchy and popular literature*. Chapel Hill: University of North Carolina Press.
RICHARDSON, K. and J. CORNER, 1986: 'Reading Reception: Mediation and Transparency in Viewers' Accounts of a TV Programme' in *Media, Culture and Society* 8, 4, pp. 485–508.
SEITER, E., BORCHERS, H. KREUTZNER, G. and WARTH, E-M., 1989: 'Don't Treat Us Like We're So Stupid and Naive': Towards an Ethnography of Soap Opera Viewers' in E. Seiter et al. (eds) *Remote Control*. London: Routledge, pp. 223–244.
SCHLESINGER, P., MURDOCK, G. and ELLIOTT, P., 1983: *Televising 'terrorism': Political violence in popular culture*. London: Comedia.
SCHRODER, K., 1987: 'Convergence of Antagonistic Traditions? The Case of Audience Research' in *European Journal of Communication* 2, 1, pp. 7–31.

14

Audience Reception: The Role of the Viewer in Retelling Romantic Drama

Sonia M. Livingstone

Rethinking the Audience

There are many ways of conceptualizing the television audience, from the populist view of a discriminating, heterogenous audience to the elitist view of a mindless, passive mass. Each approach carries particular implications for conceptualizing the role of the viewer, the nature of programmes, and the consequences of viewing television. Each raises different issues to be studied and suggests appropriate methodologies. Consider the following quotations:

> The power of the media [is] to define normal and abnormal social and political activity, to say what is politically real and legitimate and what is not.
> Gitlin 1978 (p. 205)

> In its role as central cultural medium it [television] presents a multiplicity of meanings rather than a monolithic dominant point of view . . . the raising of questions is as important as the answering of them.
> Newcomb and Hirsch 1984 (pp. 62–3)

> The longer we live with television, the more invisible it becomes . . . The mass ritual that is television shows no signs of weakening its hold over the common symbolic environment into which our children are born and in which we all live out our lives.
> Gerbner, Morgan and Signorielli 1986 (p. 17)

> Television viewing is constructed by family members; it doesn't just happen. Viewers not only make their own interpretations of shows, they also construct the situations in which viewing takes place and the ways in which acts of viewing, and program content, are put to use. . . . It is through talk about television that the audience is constituted in certain ways.
> Lull 1988 (p. 17)

> Effects [of television viewing] occur in each one of the various fields, but not to such a degree that the children would have been fundamentally changed. Television, then, is not as black as it is painted, but neither is it the great harbinger of culture and enlightenment which its enthusiasts tend to claim for it.
> Himmelweit, Oppenheim and Vince 1958 (p. 40)

> Audience members confront their experience actively, taking from it in accordance with the particular gratifications they pursue and the perceived abilities of the various media sources to satisfy these gratifications.
> Palmgreen, Wenner and Rosengren 1985 (p. 23)

These writers generally agree on the importance of television in our daily lives. Yet they disagree markedly on most or all of the major dimensions of audience analysis: in their conceptions of the audience (either active or passive, vulnerable or resistant), of the programme (as a resource from diverse motivations or a normative pressure on all, as comprised of literal or hidden meanings – moral, symbolic, behavioural, or referential), of the processes of effects (either audience selectivity or 'hypodermic' imposition, as mediated by motivation or cognition, imitation or questioning), of the nature of effects (ideological, symbolic, belief-based, or behavioural), of the level of effects (individual, familial, social mainstreaming, or political), and of the appropriate methods for study (ethnography, survey, experiment, text analysis, or social commentary). Any similarly *ad hoc* selection of quotations from influential mass media researchers would have revealed just such a diversity of approaches.

In this chapter, I will consider a recent approach to the television audience – empirical reception research – and its implications for conceptualizing the text, viewing context, and effects. Informed by a long history of theoretical debates, and taking on board some of the contradictions between active audiences and dominant messages, or directive texts and resourceful readers, empirical reception research offers an integrating, convergent approach to the television audience.

This approach focuses on the viewers' active interpretation – or meaning negotiation – of television programmes, where these are increasingly analyzed within their everyday context. Empirical reception research regards viewers' interpretations as primary, seeking to relate these to ethnographic and to effects-related concerns at a later stage. The omission of interpretative issues is seen to have impoverished other approaches to the audience, and yet the study of such issues itself raises numerous problems.

As Katz notes, following his discussion of effects research, we must still ask ourselves:

> What is the text? Where do values inhere? Who is the viewer addressed by the text? Who is the viewer in fact? What role is he or she playing? What is the immediate viewing context? What is the nature of the society within which the viewer is decoding the message?
>
> Katz 1988 (p. 367)

The approach which informs these questions seeks to apply a literary critical, reader-reception orientation to traditional problems of the television audience, recasting these problems into the new framework. Not only should we ask what readers do to texts or how texts direct readers but also the dynamic between text and reader should be addressed. How do both reader and text embody a set of expectations of the other which inform this dynamic? How do actual, empirical readers differ from researchers' expectations of the ideal or model reader? How can theories of audience and text analysis be integrated without underestimating either the role of the reader or the complexity of programme meanings, as has traditionally occurred when text and reader (or, roughly, critical and administrative mass communications research) are separated (Katz 1988)?

Reader-oriented Approaches to Audience Reception

To regard television programmes as texts and television viewers as readers is to draw on literary critical developments termed 'reception-aesthetics' in Europe (Hohendahl 1974; Holub 1984) and 'reader-response theory' in America (Suleiman and Crosman 1980; Tompkins 1980). One main proponent of reception theory outlines the central proposition:

> The work itself cannot be identical with the text or with its actualization but must be situated somewhere between the two. It must inevitably be virtual in character, as it cannot be reduced to the reality of the text or to the subjectivity of the reader, and it is from this virtuality that it derives its dynamism. As the reader passes through the various perspectives offered by the text, and relates the different views and patterns to one another, he sets the work in motion, and so sets himself in motion too.
>
> Iser 1980 (p. 106)

Eco (1979) uses the concept of code to analyze the 'role of the reader', arguing that the existence of this role itself undermines structuralist theories of what he terms the 'crystalline text':

> The existence of various codes and subcodes, the variety of sociocultural circumstances in which a message is emitted (where the codes of the addressee can be different from those of the sender) and the rate of initiative displayed by the addressee in making presuppositions and abductions – all result in making a message . . . an empty form to which various possible senses can be attributed.
>
> (p. 5)

He too emphasizes the dialectic between text and reader:

> A well-organised text on the one hand presupposes a model of competence coming, so to speak, from outside the text, but on the other hand works to build up, by merely textual means, such a competence.
>
> (p. 8)

Emphasis is shifted from an analysis of the meanings 'in' the text, central to the text-based approaches to television programmes, to an analysis of the process of reading a text. Thus the meanings which are activated on reading depend on the interaction between text and reader. Reception theory has developed within literary criticism as an alternative means of analyzing literature (or 'high culture'), to the elitist and static analyses of structural approaches. Applying reception theory to the television audience involves two key theoretical moves, that from high to popular culture, and that from ideal or model readers to actual, empirical readers. The former move is moderately uncontentious, although some literary critics would argue that analytic concepts are overstretched in the extension to popular texts, tending to exaggerate their literary merits. The latter move is more radical, as it demands empirical research, with all the epistemological and methodological problems which are thereby introduced.

Certainly model or ideal readers (Eco 1979; Iser 1980; see also Holub 1984) were originally conceived as analytic devices, ways of accommodating the polysemic, open, and context-dependent aspects of meaning within a text, and ways of recognizing the particular inscription of a reader (or subject position) within a text as central to its meaning. The advocates of empirical reception

research would, however, argue that while the readers and readings of literature may be known and available, thus obviating the need for empirical
research (Culler 1981) those of popular culture are largely unknown and
require investigation. Implicitly if not explicitly, we are still tackling the thorny
question of effects. Having argued that texts are dynamic, that meanings are
context-dependent, and that readings may be divergent, we must study the
activities of actual audiences in order to know how they interpret programmes,
within what contexts and with what interpretative resources they view television, and how and why they diverge in their readings. The direct link between
the meanings inherent in the text and the consequent effects of those meanings
on the audience has been broken, not only because viewers may choose which
programmes or programme segments to watch or because texts may target
different audiences, but also because the same 'virtual' text may mean different
things to different audiences. As this is not a wholly variable or random
process, but is constrained in important ways by cognitive, motivational,
ideological, textual and contextual factors, empirical research is needed.

Convergence in Audience Research

Empirical reception research – 'a new and exciting phase in so-called audience
research' (Hall 1980, p. 131) – has opened the way for communication between
traditional or administrative researchers and those from the critical or cultural
studies school. There is no doubt that the traditional approach can offer a range
of methods for the empirical study of television audiences (Schroder 1987),
despite some limitations in dealing with complex interpretative and ideological
issues (Carey 1985). These methods are much needed by critical scholars
feeling their way into empirical audience research. On the other hand, traditional audience researchers have tended to underestimate the complexity and,
especially, the polysemic, open and conventional aspects of programmes
considered as texts rather than stimuli (van Dijk 1987). Although critical
research has tended to ignore, presume, or underestimate the interpretative
activity of the audience (see Fejes' 1984, 'disappearing audience' in critical
mass communications), the text, too, must not be allowed to disappear
(Blumler, et al. 1985). These hitherto opposed approaches may instead be seen
as complementary and mutually challenging, each provoking the other to face
neglected problems.

   In the 'export of meaning' project, Liebes and Katz (1986, 1990) examined
the issue of cultural imperialism through empirical research on the reception of
the popular primetime drama, *Dallas*, by diverse cultural groups. They analyzed focus group discussions held during and after viewing an episode of
Dallas in people's own homes. Analysis of *Dallas* reveals basic cultural themes
which structure the programme (such as lineage, inheritance, sibling rivalry,
property, sex and marriage) which may account for the programme's popularity. While these may have suggested a common reception by the audience,
the empirical audience study found that viewers of different social and cultural
backgrounds generated very divergent interpretations of the 'same' episode.
For example, Russian Jews were found to make ideological readings centred
on the moral and political messages underlying the narratives, while Ameri-

cans focused on personalities and motivations to make their readings coherent, and Moroccan Arabs were concerned with event sequencing and narrative continuity (Katz and Liebes 1986). Each group's reading was clearly based upon and constrained by the text, and yet the interaction between cultural resources and textual openness permitted the negotiation of quite different readings on viewing the episode.

Morley's study (1980, 1981) of audience readings or decodings of the current affairs magazine, *Nationwide*, revealed how audiences diverged along political lines in their interpretations as a function of their socio-economic or labour position (see Corner, this volume, for a discussion of the importance of this work for the reception project). These readings were more or less legitimated or 'preferred' by the text (Hall 1980), with the dominant or normative readings of, for example, bank managers or schoolboys, being most consistent with the major assumptions and frameworks of the text, while the positions of the trainee teachers or trade union officials were somewhat inconsistent or negotiated. Still other groups, for example shop stewards, took a clearly oppositional position, using the resources of the text to construct a reading quite unintended by the text, though nonetheless reasonable in terms of both text and reader. Only a few viewers could not connect with the text at all (for example, black further education students) and remained alienated from it as the text did not afford them a reading congruent with their own cultural position-in the Export of Meaning project, it was the Japanese who occupied this position (Katz, Iwao and Liebes 1988). While Liebes and Katz examined the role of cultural variation in decoding (see also Silj 1988, for a comparison of audience decodings of popular dramas in different European countries), and Morley considered socioeconomic or class factors (see also Buckingham 1987, for an analysis of the readings of *EastEnders* viewers of different classes and race), other researchers have focused on the role of gender as a source of codes which inform the active 'role of the reader' (for example, Ang 1985; Hobson 1982; Seiter et al. 1987).

Viewers may diverge not only from each other but also from critics' expectations when interpreting popular culture. This strengthens the case for empirical research, and necessitates caution in making purely textual analyses. For example, Radway (1984, 1985) contrasts the readings of popular romance novels made by ordinary women readers compared to those of literary critics. She notes that 'different readers read differently because they belong to what are known as various interpretive communities, each of which acts upon print differently and for different purposes' (Radway 1985, p. 341). For example, she shows how the women emphasize literal meaning and the factual nature of language in preference to narrative consistency (preferred by the critics) when the two conflict. Although the heroine, initially described as strong and independent, ultimately is shown to submit to her hero's demands, the feminist criticism is resisted by readers in favour of an alternative (also feminist?) reading in which the heroine subtly manages to win over her hero unbeknownst to him, thus revealing her true strength, as stated at the outset.

There are various ways, analytically, of integrating text and reader. If we examine empirical reception research to date, much of it adopts an implicitly content analytic approach which undermines its explicit emphasis on semiotic or textual rather than stimulus-bound conceptions of television programmes.

In other words, text and reader are considered together by prioritizing the text and then asking how readers fit into this structure – asking, for example, whether readers match or conflict with textual meanings or, which aspects of the text, analyzed *a priori*, are reflected in audience readings. The 'texts of experience' may contribute to interpretation mainly in a 'slot-filling' capacity, where gaps to be filled are specified by the 'skeletal' structure of the text (Iser 1980) rather than by the reader's concerns. The reader or viewer tends to become fragmented by such analysis, with coherence in the reading sacrificed in favour of textual coherence. Interestingly, the psychology of textual interpretation reverses this bias. The reader's resources are conceived in terms of schemata which provide integrative, knowledge-based frameworks for active interpretation and which leave gaps or slots to be filled according to the particularities of the text. As I have argued elsewhere (Livingstone 1991), this opens the way for an analysis of the reader's sociocognitive resources which frame and direct the processes of reading a text. Such sociocognitive resources (Fiske and Taylor 1984) might involve narrative knowledge such as story grammars (Mandler 1984), character knowledge such as stereotypes or person prototypes (Cantor and Mischel 1979), and explanatory or attributional knowledge (Kelley 1972). Theorizing the role of the viewer in this way precludes being able to predict audience readings from an analysis of the text alone, without implying that these readings are entirely unpredictable or idiosyncratic. However, a truly dynamic and mutually defining conception of text and reader still seems to be lacking in this area.

A Case Study in Narrative Interpretation

We will now consider some of the ways in which viewers take an active, interpretative role in making sense of television drama, and the importance of recognizing the coherent and structured nature of audience readings will be illustrated. Regular viewers of the enormously popular, long-running British soap opera, *Coronation Street*, were asked to tell, in their own words, the story in which, as rumour had it, 'Ken was becoming too interested in Sally as a woman, instead of simply his secretary' (Livingstone 1990a, 1991). In fact, the affair between Ken and Sally was never consummated, and Ken, a central character and a middle-aged journalist, returned to his wife, Deirdre. The text is analyzed in Livingstone (1990a). The method of retelling has been variously used in audience research. Bartlett's (1932) early studies on remembering used the game of 'Chinese whispers', or serial retellings of a narrative, to examine the selection, framing and organization of material in accordance with memorial (or perceptual) principles. The principles which he identified derive from Gestalt psychology – for example, emphasis on the gist rather than the trivial, completion of gaps, omission of the unfamiliar, or insertion of connecting inferences (Kohler 1930). A similar concern with the holistic and dynamic operation of schemata lead to the development of reception-aesthetics in literary criticism. The ways in which people relate a narrative reveals the implicit operation of their interpretative processes. Only a few analyses of actual audience interpretations have been conducted within the empirical reception framework. We may still ask what viewers' readings look like, how they relate their own experiences and knowledge to the structures of the text or genre, how programmes constrain their readings, what, in short, is the 'role of the viewer'? In the present case, while most viewers wrote rather shorter stories than that presented below, this one story raises many important points for discussion. The other stories or retellings will be referred to subsequently (see also Liebes 1986, and Livingstone 1991). All viewers had watched the episodes at the time of transmission and before any knowledge of the interview. They then recalled their stories when they met the researcher, over a year after they had watched the episodes. We might note here that the very fact that people remember stories over so long a period is evidence of the importance of the programme in people's lives and, most significant from the viewpoint of reception research, it suggests the substantial fund of memories surrounding each character upon which viewers must surely draw when interpreting a current episode. Indeed, in a previous study (Livingstone 1990a), viewers could recall stories reaching back over the twenty five year history of *Coronation Street*. Here then is one viewer's account, that of a twenty five year old woman:

As far as the relationship between Ken and Sally was concerned, not a lot really happened. We had weeks of Ken being worried about his feelings for Sally changing from those of a boss to those of a potential lover, and it eventually culminated in him kissing her and embracing her in the office. Prior to this he had taken her to the Rovers several times for a drink/meal etc. supposedly to discuss a story. He told her how he felt about her. His feelings for her were obviously much stronger than hers for him and she seemed rather taken aback that he could feel so strongly for her, but also rather flattered. She seemed to have been flirting with a number of the characters in the Rovers and Ken was just one more. Nothing much more happened between Ken and Sally as they decided to take things no further. I think Ken was afraid to go further and Sally wasn't really that interested in Ken. Also, I think Ken really didn't want to split up with Deirdre, and break up yet another marriage, and face all the rumour and gossip.

Deirdre was too suspicious from the start. She began to suspect Sally and Ken long before anything was actually going on between them and she misinterpreted a number of quite innocent occurrences. Things were not going too well between her and Ken at home as he was busy working to get his newspaper established was not giving her as much time and attention as she demanded and she did not seem 100% certain that running the newspaper was a good job for him. Then she began listening to rumours and gossip and instead of confronting Ken and asking straight out what was happening bottled up all her feelings inside her.

At this time Billy Walker had returned to (visit his mother?) and help with the pub for a while. He was an old boyfriend of Deirdre's and started paying her compliments, buying her drinks, etc. and I think she was flattered by this attention. He was also drinking a lot and gambling a lot at this time, particularly with Mike Baldwin. He was going through some sort of financial crisis back in Jersey and was in a very unhappy and uncertain frame of mind. Mike and Billy became rivals in the gambling and also over Deirdre because Mike, too, started paying Deirdre a lot of attention. In the end, Billy lost out because he was drinking too much and getting himself in a dreadful state. The field was left open for Mike, Deirdre being very upset about what she heard about Sally and Ken.

Mike took Deirdre out and wined and dined her. She had told Ken that she was seeing an old girlfriend. As they sat in the car late at night at the end of the evening at the end of the street away from the Barlow's house they were spotted by Hilda Ogden. Then a few nights later Mike turned up on Deirdre's doorstep asking her to go away with him. The episode ended and we waited with baited breath until the following Monday to see what would happen. The popular press had a field day.

It was all an anti-climax she and Ken did not split up. There was a showdown with Mike in the Barlow's house. Ken and Deirdre ended up going away for a holiday to patch things up. Later, Sally was written out of the series when she wrote a story for another newspaper when Ken had refused to print it in his own – so honour was satisfied!

Let us consider this narrative. Consistent with the conventions of the soap opera genre, the beginning is very open, with a gradual development of events and no clear starting point. The romantic frame is then introduced with a description of the key event, the kiss, which drives subsequent events. The focus is on feelings rather than actions, with a readiness to speculate about each character's emotions so as to provide coherence and purpose to otherwise mundane events ('not a lot really happened . . . I think Ken was afraid to go further . . . I think Ken really didn't want to split up with Deirdre', and so forth). The account recognizes two simultaneous levels: first, visible actions and actual events and second, hidden feelings and beliefs about events (as in Deirdre's 'misinterpretation' of innocent events, her bottled up feelings, or the lies which both Ken and Deirdre tell each other).

The viewer draws on knowledge of (much) earlier episodes to provide background explanations for present motives. This knowledge may concern both general representations (Livingstone 1989) and specific knowledge, for example that Billy was Deirdre's old boyfriend. On this basis, each key action can be accounted for: Sally's generally flirtatious personality explains her actions, Deirdre and Ken's 'shaky' marriage is invoked to account for their present troubles, Billy's business crises are drawn in, and so on. The apparent contradiction between 'not much happening' and 'waiting with bated breath' which characterizes the peculiar tension of soap opera is captured in the retelling. The many inferences about motivation and personality play a central role here not only in generating coherence but also in creating multiple narrative possibilities despite the predictable nature of actual events. These inferences not only create coherence for the present narrative, but also they maintain coherence with past narratives and they generate expectations for the future. As more characters are drawn into the picture, a complex set of interconnecting links – retrospective, inferential, and predictive – is established in the mind of the viewer (Iser 1980).

In this retelling, the focus moves from Deirdre's suspicions and misinterpretations to her vulnerability and distress, our sympathies switch from Ken to Deirdre, thus altering our interpretative frame on subsequent events (Livingstone 1990b). This sets the scene for the morally satisfying return to justice represented by the second affair of the narrative, that between Deirdre and Mike, which balances the relationship between Ken and Sally. Again typical of soap opera, this affair is unproblematic until brought into the public domain by Hilda, the community gossip. The resulting tension, culminating when Mike turns up on Deirdre's doorstep to take her away (happily ever after?), is such that the referential frame is broken (Liebes and Katz 1986, 1990), and the viewer inserts both her own response and that of the nation as a whole (viewing figures for this episode, as she was aware, exceeded half of the British population).

Once again, having hooked its audience the genre offers an anticlimax, although as the cursory nature of this viewer's concluding paragraph reveals, this is unimportant. The build-up of tension and the viewers' involvement, not the events, is what counts. In contrast to the openness of the beginning, possible because the focus was on the rather dull Ken/Sally story, the dramatic tension of the retelling generated from the Deirdre/Mike story is resolved by the imposition of closure onto the ending of the narrative. Although 'Ken and Deirdre ended up going away for a holiday to patch things up' sounds plausible, in the programme, the holiday actually occurred in the middle of the narrative. This was during the lack of communication between Ken and Deirdre, being intended to establish that nothing was really wrong, and was, of course, a dismal failure, barely interrupting the continued marital crisis. Further, the events in the programme tailed away as vaguely as they had begun, satisfying genre conventions if not viewer expectations.

Structurally, this retelling falls neatly into the categories of a traditional, romantic or heroic, folk tale (van Dijk 1987; Propp 1968). The first paragraph outlines the setting, location and characters, and generally orients us towards the romantic concerns of the narrative. Paragraph two elaborates the problem, or challenge to the status quo, namely the difficulties of a shaky marriage. Next, we have the complications resulting from the community context within which events are located, as other characters with their own problems become involved, adding different perspectives on the central events. Fourthly, a resolution attempt is made, as Mike and Deirdre begin their affair. This, it is hoped, redresses the inequity of Deirdre's rejection by rewarding her (and us, the viewers) with true love and allowing her to escape an unsatisfactory marriage and create a new, happier marriage. Finally, the resolution attempt fails, the original marriage is restored, the 'other woman' is removed, and the reestablishment of order is celebrated: 'honour was satisfied'.

In fact, for 'facts' have their place in analyzing viewers' interpretations, Deirdre and Mike's affair pre-dated that of Ken and Sally by several years in *Coronation Street*! Plausible and morally satisfying though the above account is, it would be more true to say that Ken considered his affair with Sally as a result of Deirdre's famous affair with Mike, possibly from revenge or hurt pride. Not, of course, that this is more true for our viewer. For her, the affairs occurred in reverse sequence, and thus Deirdre's affair was justifiable rather than reprehensible: the misused wife gets her own back. The moral force of a retelling, with its implications for justice, victims, and social conventions, has a logic of its own.

Genre, Romance, and the Soap Opera

The analysis of audience reception has typically focused on two main genres, the news or current affairs programmes and the romance or soap opera. Corner (this volume) argues that, as different issues are addressed in analyzing these two genres, two separate, though related, projects may be said to exist, a 'public knowledge' project and a 'popular culture' project respectively.

Both the fictional and nonfictional forms have been seen, initially at least, to exemplify textual closure. In the case of the news genre, a traditional focus for research, this closure may be construed as either ideological or didactic in motive, and so reception issues concern whether or not people's readings match those intended, and if not, how the different readings are to be explained. In the case of romance and soap opera, the main subject of this paper and a relatively recent research topic, the importance of textual (and ideological closure) is much debated. Traditionally, this genre (or cluster of related genres) has been seen as ideologically closed, in that it is concerned to indulge fantasy, to redirect attention from the political to the personal, to legitimate normative or conservative judgements and expectations, and so forth. More recently, however, in order to account for its immense appeal, especially to women, some authors have argued for the openness of the genre and, additionally, for the subversive or alternative feminist subtext of the genre (Allen 1985; Fiske 1987; Livingstone 1990a; Seiter 1981). As Corner (this volume) notes, this reevaluation of popular culture brings advantages in reconceptualizing the text which could fruitfully be applied also to the public knowledge project, but it introduces an uncertainty regarding the long-standing problem of influence, for this issue becomes confused when texts become more open and viewers more active, a point to which I return in my conclusions.

The soap opera genre has been considered open insofar as its narratives are unbounded, weaving in and out of each other over time, its narratives are multiple, with no single hero and hence no prioritized moral perspective. Consequently a diversity of readings are legitimized and the interplay and contradictions between them form part of the appeal. More broadly, both the romance and the soap opera have been considered as countering or undermining the 'masculine' ethos of most popular culture, especially primetime television with its certainties, consistencies and plot linearity, by providing a female voice and a feminine or feminist form (Ang 1985; Curtis 1988; Fiske 1987). For Kuhn (1984), soap operas construct a 'gendered spectatorship' which may transcend patriarchal modes of subjectivity in a way compatible with a feminist aesthetic. As a consequence, reception research in both the news and romance genres has been concerned with revealing multiple or alternative readings of supposedly normative texts. The research has focused on issues of narrative structure, openness and closure, identification and the subject position, active and passive constructions of meaning, realist and romantic conventions, social contexts of viewing, pleasure and, implicitly at least, effects.

We should note at this point that the genre of soap opera is itself a complex hybrid of several older forms. Feuer (1984) stresses the similarities between the genre of melodrama and that of soap opera, noting the role in both of such features as moral polarization, strong emotions, the personalization of ideological conflict, interiorization, female-orientation, and excess. Consideration of the literary romance reveals a further origin, as this emphasizes 'the themes of love and adventure, a certain withdrawal from their own societies on the part of both reader and romance hero, profuse sensuous detail, simplified characters (often with a suggestion of allegorical significance), a serene intermingling of the unexpected and the everyday, a complex and prolonged succession of incidents usually without a single climax, a happy ending, amplitude of proportions, a strongly enforced code of conduct to which all the characters must comply' (Beer 1970, p. 10). Some, although not all, of this can be applied to the television drama, including the soap opera. However, Beer also notes that 'all fiction contains two primary impulses: the impulse to imitate daily life and the impulse to transcend it' (p. 10). These are often confused, so that, for example, the ways in which soap opera conforms to the romance genre, transcending everyday life, are often misinterpreted as biases when using content analysis to reveal programme meanings, for this method focuses solely on the realist or referential aims of soap opera. These latter aims are nonetheless important. The ways in which soap opera represents everyday life, frequently perceived and appreciated by its audience (Livingstone 1988), support Jordan's analysis of the soap opera as importantly influenced by the British social realist tradition. The influence of the 'kitchen sink' dramas of the 1950s and 1960s, which originated at the same time as the long-running British soap operas, helps to account for the differences between the British and American soap operas (Livingstone 1988; Liebes and Livingstone, in press). This social realist influence also accounts for the differences between soap opera and present-day continuations of the popular romance tradition, for example the Mills and Boon or Harlequin romance novels (Radway 1984), for in soap operas there are no knight in shining armour, or happy ever after endings and there is, instead, a heavy emphasis on contemporary social problems, particularly in the British soap operas.

The issue of genre is an important one for reception theory (see Corner's discussion of genre, this volume). Grant (1970) discusses realism in terms of the contract established between the writer and reality. One might also consider the contract established with the reader. For Dubrow, genre 'functions much like a code of behaviour established between the author and his reader' (1982, p. 2). It sets up expectations, it bears complex and possibly contradictory relations to other genres or codes, its conventions are historically and socially located. Dubrow argues that reader-response criticism may profitably reveal the expectations which specific, located readers apply to different genres, thus undermining the critic's tendency to see genres as absolute, consistent and deterministic. The analysis of readers' expectations of genres is important not only for our understanding of genre, but also for understanding the role of the reader in interpreting texts. Genre knowledge is one resource on which readers draw. It frames their general approach to the text, determines the types of inferential connections to be made, and establishes the paradigms of possibilities at each narrative choice point. Viewers' retelling of the soap opera narrative discussed above reveal the use of genre knowledge. For example, viewers drew inferences about the characters' motivations to lend coherence to their narratives, using frameworks which, whether construed as romantic or cynical (Livingstone 1990b), are typical of this genre and which provide an account of characters' actions, intentions and moral position:

> There's nothing like another man on the scene [Billy] to make the first man [Ken] suddenly realise what he's missing

> Maybe she [Deirdre] thought Ken was trying to get back at her (Deirdre) for having had a scene with Billy

> She [Deirdre] was determined to end the incipient affair [Ken/Sally] but was still feeling guilty over her own with Mike Baldwin

Not only may genre expectations help account for the approach which audiences take to texts from particular genres, and indeed, for the different approaches they take to different genres, but they also account for discrepancies between actual readings and predicted or 'correct' readings, as identified by text analysis. Central to the method of retelling is the assumption that genre-consistent false intrusions in viewers' readings can reveal the genre knowledge and expectations which guide their interpretations. In the case of the soap opera narrative analyzed above, the viewer who recalled the two 'affairs' in reverse order in adhering to the female voice of the genre, redressing the moral balance in favour of the misused wife. Two examples from other viewers also illustrate this point, for neither event described actually happened, but both are consistent with the genre:

> Deirdre found out [about Ken and Sally] and confronted Ken. He broke down as Deirdre was about to leave (for her mother's home no doubt)

> Ken managed to get close emotionally to Sally, and this developed into a lusty affair!!

Such 'inaccuracies' in the retellings may result from a desire to add to the dramatic excitement of the narrative. Others may result from a kind of teasing by the text in which paradigmatic choices are manipulated so as to heighten dramatic tension (Barthes 1975). When in the programme, Ken and Sally kiss or discuss an affair in the office, and when on other occasions, Deirdre enters the office unannounced yet without any compromising discovery, it is not surprising that a tension surrounding the notion of interruption and interruptability is set up such that one viewer, at least, 'remembers' how 'Deirdre walked in on them in the middle of an embrace'.

Of course, viewers may not always respect the conventions of a genre, but may instead rework the material according to different concerns, for example by heightening the drama, as above, or by closing down on areas of openness. In the first of the following retellings, the open beginning of a soap opera narrative is mirrored in the beginning of the viewer's own account. In the second, closure is imposed by the viewer:

> Ken and Billy have had a rivalry between them for quite a while. As the affair developed between Billy and Sally, Ken started to take more and more notice of Sally as a woman . . .

> It started with a kiss in the office

Similarly, viewers may accept or rework the open ending of the narrative. Compare an open account, which leaves unresolved the state of Ken and Deirdre's marriage and permits gradual change for the better (or worse) in the background of other events, with a closed, resolved, 'happy ever after' ending:

> In the end I think Billy Walker left and Sally moved on to another job. This made things easier for all concerned, especially Ken and Deirdre

> However, it ends with them both agreeing to forget, and make a go at their marriage, so everything is back to how it was before; you know, boring, lovey dovey, blah blah. Oh, and Billy leaves I think!

Such reworkings of the text, while not text-led, are nonetheless plausible, and do not actually contradict any actual happenings. These readings reflect the extent to which the text is amenable to the insertion of audience concerns or desires. Other such readings may involve reading 'against the grain', as in the oppositional readings of Morley's viewers. However, as I have argued elsewhere (Livingstone 1990a), divergent readings need not be oppositional in the sense of rejecting the normative or ideological frameworks of the text: viewers may make different interpretations from each other while retaining a generally normative perspective. For example, in one study (Livingstone 1990b), viewers made either romantic or cynical interpretations of a soap opera narrative, seeing a father's opposition to his daughter's marriage as either an expression of stubborn jealousy standing in the way of true love, or as mature wisdom seeing through an ill-fated infatuation. What the viewer does to the text here is active in the sense of requiring interpretative work and knowledge resources, but not active in the sense of negotiating any ideological distance from the text or generating any critical appraisal of it.

The analysis of genre inevitably draws upon psychological assumptions about the reader or viewer. Beer (1970) writes of the romance: 'it absorbs the reader into experience which is otherwise unattainable. It frees us from our inhibitions and preoccupations by drawing us entirely into its own world – a world which is never fully equivalent to our own although it must remind us of it if we are to understand it at all' (p. 3). Romance 'expresses the lost or repressed emotional forces of the imagination' (Beer 1970, pp. 59–60). As romance 'depends considerably upon a certain set *distance* in the relationship between its audience and its subject-matter' (p. 5), in order to understand the success of the romance, an account is required of the audience in addition to one of the text. This audience account must surely be an empirical one: we must discover the actual cognitions and circumstances of the viewer if we are to understand the relationship between reader and text. Similarly, the form of the romance, or of the soap opera, bears a close relation to the forms of everyday life: 'the rhythms of the interwoven stories in the typical romance construction correspond to the way we interpret our own experiences as multiple, endlessly interpenetrating stories, rather than simply as a procession of banal happenings' (Beer 1970, p. 9). As Modleski has argued in relation to the structure of the housewife's day, it is this parallel which accounts for the popularity of the genre, as well as explaining the lack of appeal, or perceived banality, of the soap opera or romance for those whose days are spent in the linear, goal-oriented, public world. This parallel is revealed through analysis both of the viewers' lives and the structure of the genre. As I have argued, the former analysis requires empirical investigation. In the case of the latter, we may note, for example, the traditional narrative techniques of romantic prose, all of which are seen in the soap opera, such as 'the apparent prolixity, the easy way of calling back into activity episodes and characters long abandoned, the burgeoning of story out of story . , the infinitely supple tension, the prolific and apparently disorderly inclusiveness, the way in which events engender a whole range of disconnected happenings whose connections are yet felt though never pointed . . . these narrative methods make the experience of reading the romances close to the experiencing of life' (Beer 1970, p. 76–77).

Some of the interpretative processes required to respond to these narrative methods or textual devices were illustrated by the retellings of a soap opera narrative. For example, apparently disconnected happenings may be connected through retrospective or 'retention' processes (Iser 1980). Thus viewers draw selectively on their memories of past events, which are themselves constructions, in order to infer motives which will integrate present events:

It seemed that Ken was a little unsettled in his marriage at the time

Ken was interested in Sally before her affair with Billy

As far as I can remember Sally had 'liked' Ken for quite a while (secretly so)

Similarly, viewers draw upon prior knowledge or expectations of the characters in order to make present events meaningful:

When Deirdre told Ken [about the holiday] he didn't exactly jump about with joy (but does he ever!)

This made Ken jealous, as his wife Deirdre was associated with Billy Walker some years ago. Sally also had an association with Mike Baldwin, who Deirdre had had an affair with during their marriage (Ken and Deirdre's)

Bet got a bit peeved – she was always jealous of Sally

Billy's male ego was hurt (serve him right!)

In order to make these connecting inferences, viewers may have to adopt a position of involvement in the narrative happenings – they cannot always stand at a distance. This notion of involvement may take different forms, such as identification or empathetic recognition (Horton and Wohl's 1956, 'parasocial interaction'). In other words, viewers may interpret events from the perspective either of a character perceived to be similar to themselves or from that of a character recognizable and familiar, as if one of their acquaintance. Empathetic or identification-based inferences are themselves associated with emotional responses. While noting the difficulty of interpreting the viewer's interpretations, we can suggest that inferences such as the following imply particular empathetic stances on the part of the viewers:

Sally and Ken's affair did not get off the ground as he did not want to wreck his marriage

Sally's interest in Billy was on the rebound – and he was also 'fun'

Mike thought it quite amusing, but was upset that it was hurting Deirdre, who he still had a soft spot for

In the study which revealed viewers' romantic and cynical readings (Livingstone 1990b), I show that identification with, liking of, and sympathy for key characters in a narrative may all determine the interpretative stance which viewers take. This affected the inferences they made to connect the soap opera events and resulted in the adoption of, in this case, a broadly romantic or cynical perspective.

If viewers sometimes become involved in soap opera events, they may also stand back and observe from a critical distance. In Liebes and Katz' sense of critical (1986), this involves an awareness of the constructed nature of drama as a product, focusing on the conventions, intentions or constraints according to which the programme was produced. In this sense, viewers' genre expectations are not simply used implicitly to frame the reading, but also allow the viewer to reflect upon the mechanisms of the genre. This position too is illustrated in the retellings:

> This incident became a focal point for the gossip-artistes for several weeks, mostly centering around the public house whenever any two of the parties involved were present
>
> I think things were mentioned about Deirdre's 'fling' with Mike Baldwin, at the time, which was perhaps designed to even things out between them
>
> Mainly a study of a conniving younger woman (Sally); a rather wishy-washy acceptance of admiration by Ken and a means to cement marriage between Ken and Deirdre when Sally departed. That's it, folks!

Audience Involvement and Pleasure

The complex relationship between genre, involvement, interpretation and pleasure is illustrated in the reception study referred to above (in which romantic and cynical viewers diverged in their readings of a *Coronation Street* narrative where a father opposes his daughter's marriage to the local 'baddie'). One might argue that the viewers who make the more extreme readings, one romantic and the other cynical, have in some sense missed the point of the narrative, for soap opera works to undermine simple, polarized readings through recognizing the ambivalent and contradictory meanings of events. Eco (1979) goes further, arguing that open texts play on the meanings which emerge from the relation between different readings, for example irony and allegory. Other viewers in this study adopted intermediate positions ('negotiated romantics' and 'negotiated cynics'). These readings would seem closer to the 'feminine' conventions of the genre, resisting clear and extreme moral positions, seeing the point of both sides of a debate, negotiating a compromise reading. That this process of negotiation is part of the text structure can be seen by comparison with narratives in the action-adventure genre. For example, Fiske (1987) maps out the different ideologies represented by the central characters in the crime series, *Hart to Hart*. Here, the contrast between the hero and heroine and the villain and villainess is marked by the former being more educated, more family oriented, of higher social class, happier and, of course, 'better' people. The text thereby constructs a unified subject position for the viewers, so that viewers may unambivalently identify with the hero/ine and view the events from their perspective. As Fiske notes, by making identification so easy and, hence, invisible, the genre mystifies any contradictions which in fact exist between these different social categories.

In *Coronation Street* narratives, as in soap opera generally, no such unified position is offered. Contradictions between different positions are central to the genre, to the viewing experience, and to the sense of soap operas being 'realistic' rather than fantastic idealizations. When Ken contemplated an affair with his secretary, Sally, viewers were faced with aligning their sympathies with either Sally or with Ken's wife, Deirdre. Studies of viewers' representations of television characters show that, in this instance, viewers see Sally as young and sexy, yet immoral and cold, while they see Deirdre as moral and warm, yet as rather older, staid and less sexy (Livingstone 1989). Hence, they are posed with a real conflict. The viewers' decision not only frames their interpretation of subsequent events, but also reinforces more generally their particular choice or resolution adopted. A similar conflict exists for my other example from *Coronation Street*: viewers' romantic or cynical readings result, in part, from the choice to interpret events from the perspective either of Ken or of Mike and Susan. When Ken opposed his daughter Susan's marriage to Mike, Mike was typically perceived as dominant, sexy, modern, masculine and immoral, while Ken was weak, traditional, moral and intellectual (Livingstone 1989). These characteristics are clearly evaluative, so viewers had to decide, for example, if power was more important to them than intelligence, since Mike personified the former and Ken the latter. Other choices depended on preferences in outlook in the viewers' own daily lives. For example, should one side with a modern or traditional approach to life, again as personified in the characters of Mike and Ken respectively. Still other choices depend on one's motives for viewing – does one empathize with the excitingly sexy and immoral Mike, or prefer the good but staid Ken?

As the text demands choices and involvement from the viewer, the interpretative process may involve acknowledging some of the contradictions between the different discourses, for example that of power and intelligence, or of attraction and morality. Identification, in the sense of losing oneself in a character, of being taken over, rarely happens with soap opera. Rather viewers talk of recognizing the realism of characters, considering them 'just like us', empathizing with their circumstances so that they may play with the contrasts and choices offered. Further, no harmonious resolutions or simple perspectives are offered by the text, particularly as the narratives never end, but merely merge into further narratives. In this genre, unlike action-adventure, one character never remains consistently happier or more valued than another. While in this story, Ken banished Sally and returned to Deirdre, months later he started another affair with his next secretary and left Deirdre. But is this forever? In any case, maybe Deirdre is happier without him . . .

Both involvement and critical distance require active choices and the use of knowledge resources on the part of the viewer – knowledge of the genre, the programme, the world referred to in the text, and so forth. Different genres can be seen as specifying particular text-reader relationships, thus implicating these resources in different ways – compare the soap opera to the action-adventure drama or to the documentary. Genre thus constitutes one of the determinants of audience involvement (Katz 1988), where involvement describes the experiences and roles taken by the viewer in relation to the text which then mediates television effects. The complex relation between genre, involvement and effects is suggested by the work of, for example, Himmelweit et al. (1958), which showed how television has most influence on children when the text is perceived to be realistic and the children feel involved with the events portrayed. One might note here that soap opera in particular is seen as realistic by viewers and is watched with considerable involvement (Livingstone 1988). In general, we must be careful to discriminate between reception studies carried out on different genres. The meanings of such aspects of the text as, for example, critical distance, textual openness, subject position, and divergent or oppositional readings, will vary across genres, as will the role of the viewer, the viewing context and the audience's knowledge and motivations.

The concept of pleasure, like that of involvement, serves to discriminate between genres and an analysis of pleasure is thus also central to our understanding of the viewer's role. Traditionally, it has been argued that realism and pleasure are oppositional, as pleasure is seen as associated with being escapism. In this context, the romance (and the soap opera) may be criticized because: 'it drowns the voice of reason, it offers a dangerously misleading guide to everyday life, it rouses false expectations and stirs up passions best held in check . . . [it has a] lack of intellectual power' (Beer 1970, p. 14–5). However, the pleasure of soap opera is problematic, for it includes not only the pleasures of escapism and vicarious emotional experience, but also the pleasures of recognition and validation of one's own everyday experiences (see Fiske 1987). This dilemma regarding the apparently contradictory pleasures of the soap opera may be understood when we identify the dual origins of the genre in both the romantic and realist literary traditions, fostering the pleasures of escapism and of recognition and validation respectively. Audience reception, then, need not depend on a straightforward relation between text and reader: viewers may seek different pleasures from the soap opera. Indeed, the movement between romantic and realist conventions may itself account for the genre's appeal. Viewers may find pleasure in the 'realistic illusion' (MacCabe 1974), the pleasure of denying textuality, of 'letting it flow over you', or they may enjoy becoming 'soap experts', learning the textual manipulations and conventions (Barthes 1975) and becoming critically aware of the text as product.

Ang (1985) discusses the emphasis which viewers place on the perceived genuineness of the characters. She shows how perceptions of realism in *Dallas* concern not a statistical correspondence with the viewers' world (indeed, for escapism, it must not show this correspondence) but rather an 'emotional realism', a recognition of the 'tragic structure of feeling' in *Dallas*, where feelings fluctuate between the opposed poles of happy and sad, and where happiness is always transitory. The drama provides not only an interpretative role for the viewer but also an empathetic, emotive role. Analysis of the reception of soap opera shows that the genre gives rise to ambiguous, contradictory, and varied experiences. In accounting for their pleasures in watching soap opera, viewers distinguish between fantasy and escapism (Livingstone 1988), where the former involves the release of one's imagination – a part of one's own experience. For example, in *Dallas* and *Dynasty*, one may find a pleasure in 'seeing how the other half lives', thus enjoying the glamour of a rich world. On the other hand, escapism involves the avoidance of one's present experience, with its worries, doubts and problems. Maybe also escapism does not so much reflect a desire to avoid everyday realities as a pleasure in playing with the boundaries between reality and fiction where within the safe limits of the viewing experience, one may explore the tension between real-world constraints and possible fantasy worlds. In this connection, Liebes and Katz (1990) compare the referential and lucid or playful keyings within which viewers discuss soap opera happenings.

As mentioned above, Modleski (1982) discusses the parallels between the structure of soap opera (particularly the daytime programmes) and the routine of the housewife's day. The pleasures of the daytime soap operas are, she argues, participatory in a way that primetime programmes are not. They depend not on action but on reaction and interaction. The characters are not superior in skills or glamour, but are on an equal footing with the viewer ('just like us'), and the visual pleasure is not the masculine one of fragmentation and fetishization of the female body but a holistic one of reading the person and being sensitive to unspoken feelings. Just as women must, in their role as housewife and mother, be ready to drop things, to be interrupted, to juggle multiple tasks and to enter into the problems of others, so too does the soap opera involve multiple plots, plot switching, mood changes, and invited intimacy. These pleasures are not, however, without their costs. Modleski argues that soap opera habituates women to interruption and fragmentation: through narrative redundancy and repetition they make it easy, through dramatic tension and delayed gratification, they make it pleasurable.

The Role of the Viewer

The viewers of television drama continually surprise us in their interpretations of programmes. As no corpus exists of programme interpretations made by ordinary viewers under everyday circumstances, empirical research is required to understand the role of the viewer in making sense of television. I have tried in this paper to consider what these readings look like and to point to some of the issues they raise about audience reception.

Jensen and Rosengren (1990; see also Curran 1990) compare reception analysis to other major traditions of audience analysis – effects research, uses and gratifications research, literary criticism and cultural studies – along the broad dimensions of history, theory, methodology and problems. Elsewhere (Livingstone 1990a) I have argued that research on audience reception could be taken to include both issues of interpretation and of comprehension. By comprehension I mean, for example, whether viewers receive specific programme information or whether specific textual biases are mirrored by the viewers. These are the concerns of both cognitive psychologists asking, for example, whether children can decode a narrative to discover 'who done it' or which was the baddie and which was the goodie (e.g. Collins 1983; Reeves et al. 1982), and also with researchers checking the validity or 'psychological reality' of content analyses, asking whether particular content patterns are accurately received by viewers. However, a focus on comprehension remains within the information-processing approach, conceiving of meaning within the text and only giving viewers the power to agree or disagree with this meaning. This match/mismatch conception of the role of the viewer, which often re-emerges in the guise of interpretative research, conflicts with the reception approach (see for example the debate in Cohen 1989). As Mancini (1990) outlined recently, in reception work the message is seen as fundamentally polysemic and open, interpretation is seen as organized through superthemes or schemas, rather than fragmented, as motivated by identification processes rather than disinterested, and in which meanings are actively constructed by viewers rather than passively received or misperceived (although Corner, this volume, identifies some confusions about meaning in recent writings).

Of course, a range of criticisms can be made of the reception approach, and further theoretical development is called for. Firstly, an often lauded eclecticism in methods masks real epistemological differences (familiar from many social science versus humanities debates). Secondly, the concept of interpretation tends to be reduced to a singular and untheorized process, masking the many diverse modes of text-reader interaction (critical, involved, oppositional, parasocial, etc). There has been a related tendency towards pluralism, seeing all viewers as equally powerful, although the role of social and cultural divisions among audiences is increasingly recognized. Finally, there is a problem of locating the text-reader interaction in a wider political context (Curran 1990), a problem which is increasingly avoided as researchers home in on the specificities of audience interpretations in local viewing contexts. Without this political context which would place audiences within broader social and economic processes, there is a tendency to romanticize the audience, celebrating the supposed autonomy of the viewer to the neglect of issues of power and social structure.

We can only speculate about the possible role of audience interpretations even as regards processes of media influence or effects. For some, the point of reception analysis has been to critique the assumption of strong effects, by emphasizing instead the power of the viewer to construct meanings. Others would still argue for media effects, although not necessarily conceiving of effects simply as the imposition of textual meanings on an audience. For example, Modleski emphasizes the role of form, suggesting that the fragmented interrupted nature of the soap opera genre, and hence, of the viewing experience, has an ultimately reactionary effect: 'daytime television plays a part in habituating women to distraction, interruption, and spasmodic toil' (1982, p. 100). Liebes and Katz see the different cultural readings not as evidence for null effects, but rather likely to validate or reinforce the different perspectives of the viewers: the Russians who perceive and reject the capitalist ideology behind *Dallas* may be confirmed in their criticism of Americans after watching the programme, while the Americans who focus instead on the intricacies of unfolding personalities and motivations may be reinforced in finding pleasure in a problem-solving approach – 'why did she do that?' – which they can also apply to decoding real-life events. Maybe we can conceive of television effects broadly as the ways in which television constructs, prioritizes, undermines, or elaborates the interpretative frameworks with which the viewer makes sense, not only of television, but also of everyday life. According to this approach, theorizing the role of the reader takes centre stage and as it is empirical readers, unpredictable and multiply determined as they are, rather than ideal readers who constitute a key moment in the production of meanings (Hall 1980), researching the role of the reader demands continued empirical work.

Notes

I thank Michael Argyle, Rodney Livingstone and Peter Lunt for their helpful comments on earlier versions of this paper.

References

ALLEN, R. C., 1985: *Speaking of soap operas.* Chapel Hill: University of North Carolina Press.

ANG, I., 1975: *Watching DALLAS: Soap opera and the melodramatic imagination.* New York: Methuen.

BARTHES, R., 1975: *The pleasure of the text.* New York: Hill and Wang.

BARTLETT, F. C., 1932: *Remembering: A study in experimental and social psychology.* Cambridge: Cambridge University Press.

BEER, G., 1970: *The romance.* London: Methuen.

BLUMLER, J. G., GUREVITCH, M., and KATZ, E., 1985: REACHING OUT: A future for gratifications research. In K. E. Rosengren, L. A. Wenner, and P. Palmgreen (Eds), *Media gratifications research: Current perspectives.* Beverly Hills, California: Sage.

BUCKINGHAM, D., 1987: *Public secrets: EastEnders and its audience.* London: British Film Institute.

CANTOR, N., and MISCHEL, W., 1979: Prototypes in person perception. In L. Berkowitz (Ed.), *Advances in Experimental Social Psychology, 12.* New York: Academic Press.

CAREY, J. W., 1985: Overcoming resistance to Cultural Studies. In M. Gurevitch, and M. R. Levy, (Eds), *Mass Communication Review Yearbook, 5.* Beverly Hills, California: Sage.

COHEN, A. A. (Ed.), 1989: Future directions in television news research. Special Issue of *American Behavioral Scientist, 33(2).*

COLLINS, W. A., 1983: Interpretation and inference in children's television viewing. In J. Bryant and D. A. Anderson (Eds), *Children's understanding of televison.* New York: Academic Press.

CULLER, J., 1981: *The pursuit of signs.* London: Routledge and Kegan Paul.

CURRAN, J., 1990: The new revisionism in mass communication research. *European Journal of Communication, 5(2–3),* pp. 135–164.

CURTI, L., 1988: Genre and gender. *Cultural Studies, 12(2),* pp. 152–167.

VAN DIJK, T. A., 1987: *Communicating racism: Ethnic prejudice in thought and talk.* Newbury Park, California: Sage.

DUBROW, H., 1982: *Genre.* London: Methuen.

ECO, U., 1979: Introduction: The role of the reader. *The role of the reader: Explorations in the semiotics of texts.* Bloomington: Indiana University Press.

FEJES, F., 1984: Critical mass communications research and media effects: The problem of the disappearing audience. *Media, Culture and Society, 6(3),* pp. 219–232.

FEUER, J., 1984: Melodrama, serial form and television today. *Screen, 25(1),* pp. 4–17.

FISKE, J., 1987: *Television culture.* London: Methuen.

FISKE, S. T., and TAYLOR, S. E., 1984: *Social cognition.* New York: Random House.

GERBNER, G., GROSS, L., MORGAN, M., and SIGNORIELLI, N., 1986: Living with television: The dynamics of the cultivation process. In J. Bryant and D. Zillman (Eds), *Perspectives on media effects.* Hillsdale, N. J.: Erlbaum.

GITLIN, T., 1978: Media sociology: The dominant paradigm. *Theory and Society, 6,* 205–253.

GRANT, D., 1970: *Realism.* London: Methuen.

HALL, S., 1980: Encoding/Decoding. In S. Hall, D. Hobson, A. Lowe, and P. Willis (Eds), *Culture, Media, Language.* London: Hutchinson.

HIMMELWEIT, H. T., OPPENHEIM, A. N., and VINCE, P., 1958: *Television and the child: An empirical study of the effect of television on the young.* London: Oxford University Press.

HOBSON, D., 1982: *Crossroads: The drama of a soap opera.* London: Methuen.

HOHENDAHL, P. U., 1974: Introduction to reception aesthetics. *New German Critique, 3(Fall),* pp. 29–63.

HOLUB, R. C., 1984: *Reception theory: A critical introduction.* London: Methuen.

HORTON, D., and WOHL, R. R., 1956: Mass communication and para-social interaction. *Psychiatry*, *19*, pp. 215–229.

ISER, W., 1980: The reading process: a phenomenological approach. In J. P. Tompkins, (Ed.). *Reader-response criticism: from formalism to post-structuralism.* Baltimore: Johns Hopkins University Press.

JENSEN, K. J., and ROSENGREN, K. E., 1990: Five traditions in search of the audience. *European Journal of Communication*, *5(2–3)*, pp. 207–238.

KATZ, E., 1988: On conceptualizing media effects: Another look. In S. Oskamp, (Ed.), *Television as a social issue.* Newbury Park, California: Sage.

KATZ, E., and LIEBES, T., 1986: Mutual aid in the decoding of *Dallas*: Preliminary notes from a cross-cultural study. In P. Drummond and R. Paterson (Eds), *Television in transition.* London: British film Institute.

KATZ, E., IWAO, S., and LIEBES, T., 1988: On the limits of diffusion of American television: a study of the critical abilities of Japanese, Israeli and American viewers. A report to the Hoso Bunka Foundation, Tokyo.

KELLEY, H. H., 1972: Attribution in social interaction. In E. E. Jones, D. E. Kanouse, H. H. Kelley, R. E. Nisbett, S. Valins, and B. Weiner, (Eds), *Attribution: Perceiving the causes of behaviour.* Morristown, N. J.: General Learning Press.

KOHLER, W., 1930: *Gestalt psychology.* London: Bell and Sons.

KUHN, A., 1984: Women's genres. *Screen*, *25(1)*, pp. 18–29.

LIEBES, T., 1986: Cultural differences in the retelling of television fiction. Paper presented at the International Communications Association Annual Conference, Chicago, May, 1986.

LIEBES, T., and KATZ, E., 1986: Patterns of involvement in television fiction: A comparative analysis. *European Journal of Communication*, *1*, pp. 151–171.

LIEBES, T., and KATZ, E., 1990: *The export of meaning.* Oxford: Oxford University Press.

LIEBES, T., and LIVINGSTONE, S. M., (in press). Mothers and lovers: Managing women's role conflicts in American and British soap operas. *Communication and Culture across Space and Time: Prospects of Comparative Analysis*, edited by Blumler, J., McLeod, J. M., and Rosengren, K. E. Newbury Park, California: Sage.

LIVINGSTONE, S. M., 1988: Why people watch soap opera: An analysis of the explanations of British viewers. *European Journal of Communication*, *3*, pp. 55–80.

LIVINGSTONE, S. M., 1989: Interpretive viewers and structured programs: the implicit representation of soap opera characters. *Communication Research*, *16(1)*, pp. 25–57.

LIVINGSTONE, S. M., 1990a: *Making sense of television: The psychology of audience interpretation.* Oxford: Pergamon.

LIVINGSTONE, S. M., 1990b: Divergent interpretations of a television narrative. *Journal of Communication*, *16(1)*, pp. 25–57.

LIVINGSTONE, S. M., 1991: The resourceful reader: Interpreting television characters and narratives. *Communication Yearbook*, *15*, forthcoming.

LOVELL, T., 1983: *Pictures of reality: Aesthetics, politics, pleasure.* London: British Film Institute.

LULL, J., 1988: (Ed.). *World families watch television.* Newbury Park, California: Sage.

MACCABE, C., 1974: Realism and the cinema. *Screen*, *15(2)*.

MANCINI, P., 1990: Paper presented to the Annual Conference of the *International Communications Association*, Dublin, June, 1990.

MANDLER, J. M., 1984: *Stories, scripts, and scenes: Aspects of schema theory.* Hillsdale, N. J.: Erlbaum.

MODLESKI, T., 1982: *Loving with a vengeance: mass-produced fantasies for women.* New York: Methuen.

MORLEY, D., 1980: *The Nationwide audience: Structure and decoding.* British Film Institute Television Monograph No. 11. London: British Film Institute.

MORLEY, D., 1981: The Nationwide audience: A critical postscript. *Screen Education,* *39*, pp. 3–14.

NEWCOMB, H. M., and HIRSCH, P. M., 1984: Television as a cultural forum: Implications for research. In W. D. Rowland and B. Watkins (Eds), *Interpreting television: Current research perspectives,* 58–73. Beverly Hills, California: Sage.

PALMGREEN, P., WENNER, L. A., and ROSENGREN, K. E., 1985: Uses and gratifications research: The past ten years. In K. E. Rosengren, L. A. Wenner, and Palmgreen, P. (Eds), *Media gratifications research: current perspectives.* Beverly Hills, California: Sage.

PROPP, V., 1968: *The morphology of the folktale.* Austin: University of Texas Press.

RADWAY, J., 1984: *Reading the romance: Women, partriarchy and popular literature.* Chapel Hill: University of North Carolina Press.

RADWAY, J., 1985: Interpretive communities and variable literacies: The functions of romance reading. In M. Gurevitch, and M. R. Levy (Eds), *Mass Communication Review Yearbook,* *5.* Beverly Hills, California: Sage.

REEVES, B., CHAFFEE, S. H., and TIMS, A., 1982: Social cognition and mass communication research. In M. E. Roloff and C. R. Berger (Eds), *Social cognition and communication.* London: Sage.

SCHRODER, K. C., 1987: Convergence of antagonistic traditions? The case of audience research. *European Journal of Communication,* *2,* pp. 7–31.

SEITER, E., 1981: The role of the woman reader: Eco's narrative theory and soap operas. *Tabloid,* *6.*

SEITER, E., KRENTZER, G., WORTH, E. M., and BORCHERS, H., 1987: Don't treat us like we're so stupid and naive: towards an ethnography of soap opera viewers. Paper presented at the Seminar on Rethinking the Audience, University of Tubingen, February, 1987.

SILJ, A., 1988: *East of Dallas: The European challenge to American television.* London: British Film Institute.

SULEIMAN, S., and CROSMAN, I. (Eds), 1980: *The reader in the text.* Princeton: Princeton University Press.

TOMPKINS, J. P., 1980: (Ed.). *Reader-response criticism: From formalism to post-structuralism.* Baltimore: John Hopkins University Press.

15

Gender and/in Media Consumption

Ien Ang and Joke Hermes

Introduction

In the evening [Mr Meier] gets involved in conversation, otherwise he would at least have watched the regional news; so he does not see the results again until after the news. In a way he wanted to go to bed early, and that is what he told his wife. But now he has a faint hope of being able to see the Mueller goal on the Second Channel sports programme. However he would have to switch channels. He tells his wife she looks tired. She is surprised he cares, but she does go up to bed. He fetches a beer from the kitchen. Unfortunately his wife comes back to get a drink. Suddenly the penny drops. 'My God! The sports programme! That's why you sent me to bed!' He doesn't want to get invovled, and quickly goes to the toilet. In the meantime it happens. His wife shouts, 'Hey Max Schmeling is on!' He doesn't react. He can't stand Schmeling because he has something to do with Coca-Cola. He deliberately doesn't hurry. When he comes back United's game is in progress. He is just in time to see the second, rather third-rate, goal. (. . .) In the afternoon (the next day) a neighbour tells him that his club has lost again, which is what he thought anyway, because when there is no wind he can hear the crowd in the stadium from the balcony and there has been no shouting. He goes for a walk with his wife and their younger children; some aquaintances delay him. When he comes home his elder son is watching the sports review after having slept till midday. Meier gets angry because he has wasted the day, and even more so when his son asks, 'Have you heard, United won 2–0!' As if he was an idiot! He gives his son the Bild, and the son says, 'I thought you didn't read that.' Offended, the father goes to his room, while the mother sits down next to her eldest son and watches the sports programme with him. It does not interest her, but it is an attempt at making contact.

(Bausinger 1984: 348–9)

This fascinating ethnographic account of the Meier family's dealings with the weekend sports coverage clarifies the thoroughly convoluted and circumstantial way in which concrete practices of media consumption are related to gender. Mr Meier, the male football fan, ends up not watching his favourite team's game on television, while his wife, who doesn't care for sports, finds herself seating herself in front of the TV set the very moment the sports programme is on. Gender is obviously not a reliable predictor of viewing behaviour here. The scene illuminates the fact that media consumption is a thoroughly precarious practice, structured not by psychological or sociological predispositions of individual audience members but by the dynamic and contradictory goings-on of everyday life. The way gender is implicated in this practice is consequently equally undecided, at least outside of the context in which the practice takes concrete shape.

How gender is related to media consumption is one of the most under-theorized questions in mass communication research. In this article, we hope to offer some theoretical clarification about this important question. As Liesbet van Zoonen (in this volume) has pointed out, work in this area has until now almost exclusively concentrated on women, not men, and media consumption. This bias unwittingly reflects a more general bias in society, in which women are defined as the problematic sex (Coward 1983). This is a pity, since not only femininity but also masculinity has recently been subject of increasing critical inquiry (Kaufman 1987; Seidler 1989). More importantly, we will argue here that limiting ourselves to women audiences as empirical starting point for analysis would risk reproducing static and essentialist conceptions of gender identity. While much work in this area, most of it feministically inspired, has provided us with extremely useful insights into women's media uses and interpretations, we would argue that it is now time to develop a mode of understanding that does more justice to variability and precariousness in the ways in which gender identities – feminine and masculine subjectivities – are constructed in the practices of everyday life in which media consumption is subsumed. In our view, recent poststructuralist feminist theory can help us conceptualize more properly how gender might be *articulated* in practices of media consumption. In other words, this article's main argument is that the subject of gender *and* media consumption should be rephrased in gender *in* media consumption.

The Academic Emancipation of Female Audiences

Feminist critics have displayed continuous concern about the relation of gender and media consumption. The concern has often focused upon the supposedly detrimental effects of popular media forms on women's consciousness. More specifically, the popularity among women of specifically 'feminine' genres such as soap operas and romance novels has often been explained in terms of their 'fit' with women's subordinate position in society. Early feminist accounts of women's media consumption are full of renditions reminiscent of the crude, hypodermic needle model of media effects. In *The Female Eunuch*, for example, Germaine Greer (1971) bitingly criticizes romance novels for re-inforcing a kind of 'false consciousness' among their women readers:

> It is a male commonplace that women love rotters but in fact women are hypnotized by the successful man who appears to master his fate; they long to give their responsibility for themselves into the keeping of one who can administer it in their best interests. Such creatures do not exist, but very young women in the astigmatism of sexual fantasy are apt to recognize them where they do not exist . . . Although romance is essentially vicarious the potency of the actual fantasy distorts actual behaviour. The strength of the belief that a man should be stronger and older than his woman can hardly be exaggerated.
>
> (Greer 1971: 180)

In a similar but more earnest fashion, Sue Sharpe (1974) and Gaye Tuchman et al. (1978) see the mass media as a major cause of the general reproduction of patriarchal sexual relationships. Sharpe (1974: 119) posits that '[t]hroughout the media, girls are presented in ways which are consistent with aspects of their stereotyped images, and which are as equally unrealistic and unsatisfactory', while Tuchman (1978: 6) proposes that since mass media images are full of traditionalist and outmoded sex-role stereotypes, they will inevitably socialize girls into becoming mothers and housewives, because 'girls in the television audience "model" their behavior on that of "television women"'.

Sustaining such early accounts are two related, unwarranted assumptions: first, that mass media imagery consists of transparent, unrealistic messages about women whose meanings are clearcut and straightforward; second, that girls and women passively and indiscriminately absorb these messages and meanings as (wrong) lessons about 'real life'. These assumptions have been considerably surmounted in later work, whose development can be characterized as gradually eroding the linear and monolithic view of women as unconditional victims of sexist media. This happened first of all through more theoretically sophisticated forms of textual analysis. Rather than seeing media images as reflecting 'unrealistic' pictures of women, feminist scholars working within structuralist, semiotic and psychoanalytic frameworks have begun to emphasize the ways in which media representations and narratives *construct* a multiplicity of sometimes contradicting cultural definitions of feminity and masculinity, which serve as subject positions that spectators might take up in order to enter into a meaningful relationship with the texts concerned (see e.g. Mulvey 1975 and 1990; Kuhn 1982; Modleski 1982; Coward 1984; De Lauretis 1984; Moi 1985; Doane 1987; Baehr and Dyer 1987; Pribam 1988; Gamman and Marshment 1988; and many others). These studies are important because they pay more detailed attention to the particular *textual mechanisms* that are responsible for engendering spectator identifications.

For example, in her influential analysis of American daytime soap operas, Tania Modleski (1982) concludes that the soap opera's narrative characteristics construct a textual position for viewers that can be described as follows:

> The subject/spectator of soap operas . . . is constituted as a sort of ideal mother, a person who possesses greater wisdom than all her children, whose sympathy is large enough to encompass the conflicting claims of her family (she identifies with them all), and who has no demands or claims of her own (she identifies with no one character exclusively . . . The spectator/mother, identifying with each character in turn, is made to see 'the large picture' and extend her sympathy to both the sinner and the victim . . . By constantly presenting her with the many-sidedness of any question, by never reaching a permanent conclusion, soap operas undermine her capacity to form unambiguous judgments.
>
> (Modleski 1982: pp. 92–3)

Here, a much more intricate and complex analysis is given of the textual operations of a popular genre such as the soap opera. Soap operas do not simply reflect already existing stereotypical images of women, but actively produce a symbolic form of feminine identity by inscribing a specific subject position – that of the 'ideal mother' – in its textual fabric.

· However, while such analyses of gendered spectatorship have provided us with better insight into the way in which media texts address and interpellate their viewers/readers, they generally do not problematize the way in which concrete viewers actually confront such interpellations. In fact, Modleski seems to imply that the 'ideal mother' position is an inescapable point of identification for soap opera viewers in their sensemaking of the genre. Indeed, as Robert C. Allen (1984: 94) has suggested, 'although Modleski seems to present the mother/reader as a textually inscribed position to be taken up by whoever the actual reader happens to be, she comes close at times to conflating the two'. In other words, text-oriented feminist analysis have often run the risk of being reductionist in their theoretical generalizations about gender and media consumption, a reductionism that stems from insufficiently distinguishing semiological and sociological levels of analysis. In the useful terminology of Annette Kuhn (1984), what is conflated here is the analysis of *spectatorship*, conceived as a set of subject positions constructed in and through texts, and the analysis of *social audiences* understood as the empirical social subjects actually engaged in watching television, filmgoing, reading novels and magazines, and so on.

Janice Radway (1984) has been one of the first to recognize the pitfalls of textual reductionism. In her well-known study *Reading the Romance*, she claims that 'the analytic focus must shift from the text itself, taken in isolation, to the complex social event of reading . . . in the context of . . . ordinary life' (1984: 8). In her view, then, textual analysis needs to be complemented by inquiry into how female audiences 'read' texts. In such a perspective, socially-situated women are given some maneouvre space in their dealings with media texts; their responses cannot be deduced from textual positionings. 'Reading' is itself an active, though not free, process of construction of meanings and pleasures, a 'negotiation' between texts and readers whose outcome cannot be dictated by the text (Hall 1982; Gledhill 1988). This line of argument foregrounds the relevance of 'ethnographic' work with and among empirical audiences.

A more extensive review of this ethnographic move in the study of media audiences is given elsewhere in this volume (e.g. the chapters by Livingstone, Corner, Fiske). In this context, it is sufficient to highlight the value of what is now commonly called 'reception analysis' by pointing at a recent study by Ellen Seiter et al. (1989). Through extensive interviews with female soap opera viewers in Oregon, Seiter et al. have unearthed a much more ambiguous relationship of viewers with the position of the 'ideal mother' which Modleski deems essential to the soap opera's textual operations. While the taking up of this position could indeed be recognized in the responses of some of Seiter et al.'s middle-class, college educated informants, it was consciously resisted and vehemently rejected by most of the working-class women interviewees. Their findings have led Seiter et al. to draw the following conclusion:

> The 'successful' production of the (abstract and 'ideal') feminine subject is restricted and altered by the contradictions of women's own experiences. Class, among other factors, plays a major role in how our respondents make sense of the text. The experience of working-class women clearly conflicts in substantial ways with the soap opera's representation of a woman's problems, problems some women identified as upper or middle-class. (. . .) One of the problems with the spectator position described by Modleski is that the 'ideal mother' implies a specific social identity – that of a middle-class woman, most likely with a husband

who earns a family wage. This textual position is not easily accessible to working-class women, who often formulate criticism of the soap opera on these grounds.
(Seiter et al. 1989: 241)

This insightful juxtaposition of textual analysis and reception analysis makes clear that textually-inscribed feminine subject positions are not uniformly and mechanistically adopted by socially-situated women viewers/readers. Textual generalizations about 'the female spectator' turn out to foreclose prematurely the possibility of empirical variation and heterogeneity within actual women's responses. Reception analysis makes clear however that women audiences do indeed actively negotiate with textual constructions and interpellations in such a way that the meanings given to texts – and consequently the positions eventually taken up by viewers/readers – are brought in accordance with the women's social and subjective experiences. As a result, differences in readings between women with different social positions are brought to the surface.

In summary, then, feminist work addressing issues of gender and media consumption has evolved considerably from the early emphasis on 'unrealistic' images of women and their inevitably conservative effects on female audiences. The assumption of *a priori*, monolithic reproduction of sexism and patriarchy has gradually made way to a view in which the media's effectivity is seen as much more conditional, contingent upon specific – and often contradictory – textual mechanisms and operations on the one hand,[1] and upon the active and productive part played by female audiences in constructing textual meanings and pleasures on the other. The latter trend, especially, has solicited a more optimistic stance towards women's role as media consumers: they are no longer seen as 'cultural dupes', as passive victims of inexorably sexist media; on the contrary, media consumption can even be considered as empowering (although never unproblematically), in so far as it offers audiences an opportunity for symbolic resistance to dominant meanings and discourses and for implicit acknowledgement of their own social subordination (cf. Brown 1990).

If early feminist criticism felt comfortable to speak authoritatively for the 'silent majority' of women, the more recent work is characterized by an awareness of the necessity to let 'other' women speak. If anything, this development signals a growing awareness among feminists of the problematic relationship between feminism and women (Ang 1988). As a political discourse, feminism in whatever form (see Van Zoonen, in this volume) has generally postulated an ideal of the feminist subject, fully committed to the cause of social change and 'women's liberation'. However, in the face of the tenacious resistance displayed by large groups of women against feminist politics (think only of the pro-life movement in the United States) it is clear that feminism cannot presume to possess the one and only truth about women. Indeed, as Angela McRobbie has pointed out, 'to make such a claim is to uncritically overload the potential of the women's movement and to underestimate the resources and capacities of 'ordinary' women (. . .) to participate in their own struggles as women but quite autonomously' (McRobbie 1982: 52). It is recognition of this that has led to the increasing popularity of validating – and sometimes celebrating – 'ordinary' women's experiences through research, including their experiences as audiences for media and popular culture.

We do not wish to enter into the debate whether this move towards emphasis on audience creativity, which has been a more general recent trend within contemporary cultural studies, should be seen as 'encouraging cultural democracy at work' (Fiske 1987: 286) or as researchers' wish fulfilment (Gitlin, in this volume; see also Morris 1988). Instead, we would like to take a step back and look more dispassionately at some of the theoretical absences in the trajectory that work on gender and media consumption has taken so far. In doing this, we do not aim to retreat from politics; rather, we intend to complicate the political dilemma invoked here – a dilemma framed by Van Zoonen [in this volume] in terms of the dangers of relativism and populism – through a radical denaturalization of the ways that 'gender' and 'media consumption' have commonly been coupled together in research practice. We will come back to the political issue in our postscript, in which we will defend our commitment to a radically postmodern approach to (feminist) politics, and the role of particularistic ethnographic work therein.

The Dispersion of 'Women'

Let us return, for the sake of argument, to Seiter *et al.*'s project on women soap opera viewers. In this project, working-class women emerge as being more critical or resistant to the preferred meanings proposed by soap opera narratives than middle-class women (although they were found to express their criticisms in limited and apologetic ways, e.g. in terms of lack of realism and escapism) (Seiter et al. 1989: 241/2). In other words, the project shows that at the empirical level, women cannot be considered as a homogeneous category: class makes a difference.

However, one could cast doubt on the interpretive validity of the differentiations made by Seiter et al., based as they are on macro-structural, sociological criteria (i.e. social class). Although these authors are careful in not overgeneralizing their data, there are problems with their correlating different types of reading with the different class backgrounds of their informants. For example, in another account of differences between working-class and middle-class women watching soap operas, Andrea Press (1989) seems to contradict Seiter et al.'s interpretations. Drawing her conclusions from interviews with female viewers of the prime-time soap opera *Dynasty*, Press finds that it is middle-class women who are the more critical viewers. While working-class women speak very little to differences between the *Dynasty* characters and themselves – which in Press' view indicates their acceptance of the realism of the *Dynasty* text – middle-class viewers 'consciously refuse to be taken in by the conventions of realism which characterise this, like virtually all, prime-time television shows' (Press 1990: 178). Although Press too is reluctant to overgeneralize, she does in her conclusions emphasize 'the difference between middle-class women, who invoke [ideologies of femininity and the family] in order to criticize the show's characters in their discussions, and working-class women, who invoke them only to affirm the depictions they view' (Press 1990: 179/80). This conclusion is at odds with Seiter et al.'s, who contrary found their working-class informants to be very critical of the discrepancy between textual representation and their personal experience.

In this context, it is impossible to explain satisfactorily the apparently contradictory conclusions of these two research projects, although several considerations present themselves as possible factors: differences in operationalization of social class; differences in locality (Press conducted her interviews in the San Francisco Bay Area), representational differences between day-time and prime-time soap operas, differences in interview guidelines, differences in theoretical preoccupations in interpreting the transcripts, and so on.

At the very least, however, the contradiction highlights the liability of too easily connecting particular instances of meaning attribution to texts with socio-demographic background variables. Particular accounts as dug up in reception analysis are typically produced through researchers' staged conversations with a limited number of women, each of them marked by idiosyncratic life histories and personal experiences. Filtering their responses – the transcripts of what they said during the interviews – through the pregiven categories of 'working-class' or 'middle-class' would necessarily mean a reductionist abstraction from the underdoubtedly much more complex and contradictory nature of these women's reception of soap operas. An abstraction which is produced by the sociologizing perspective of the researchers, for whom sociological categorizations such as working-class and middle-class serve as facilitating devices for handling the enormous amount of interview material this kind of research generally generates.

What we are objecting to here is *not* the lack of generalizability that is so often levelled at qualitative empirical research conducted with small samples. If anything, the richness of data produced in this kind of research only clarifies the difficulty, if not senselessness of the search for generalizations that has long been an absolute dogma in positivist social research.[2] Nor do we object to these researchers' endeavours to understand the way in which class position inflects women's reception of media texts. On the contrary, we greatly welcome such attempts to place practices of media consumption firmly within their complex and contradictory social contexts (we will return to this issue below).

What we do want to point to however is the creeping essentialism that lurks behind the classificatory move in interpreting certain types of response as originating from either working-class or middle-class experience. Such a move runs the danger of reifying and absolutizing the differences found, resulting – in the long run – in the construction of a simple opposition between two discrete class and cultural formations. Consequently, as John Frow (1987) has commented in relation to Pierre Bourdieu's (1984) important contribution to the sociology of taste distinctions, class experience comes to be considered as 'inevitably and inexorably entrapped within the cultural limits imposed on it' (Frow 1987: 71).[3]

Pushed to its logical extreme, this would not only lead to the positing of fixed differences between working-class women and middle-class women, but also the projection of unity and coherence in the responses of the two groups (although neither Seiter et al. nor Press make any explicit gestures in this direction). In our view, this form of social determinism implies a premature explanatory closure, which precludes recognition of multiplicity and transgression in the way women belonging to both groups can make sense of media. Thus, inconsistencies and variances within informants' accounts – familiar to *any* researcher who has worked with depth-interview transcripts – remain unaccounted, or are even actively repressed.[4] But differences between women are not so neatly categorizable as the sociological picture would suggest. On the contrary, the closer we look, the more likely are we going to find complexity and contradiction in any one response.

Again, our critique is not meant to imply a denial of the existence of class differences. What we do want to question, however, is 'our ability to decide ahead of time the pertinence of such differences within the study of the effectivity of cultural practices' (Grossberg 1988b: 388). Thus, rather than treating class position as an isolatable 'independent variable' predetermining cultural responses, it could best be seen as a factor (or vector) whose impact as a structuring principle for experience can only be conceptualized within the concrete historical context in which it is articulated. Class never fully contains a social subject's identity. Otherwise we can never account for either variety or change and disruption in the social experience and consciousness of people, as well as for the possibility of experiences that cut across class-specific lines, in which class is of secondary, if not negligible relevance.

As for class (or, for that matter, race or ethnicity), so for gender, as we have noted earlier, most research that sets out to examine gender and media consumption has concentrated exclusively on *women* audiences. What is implicitly taken for granted here is that gender is a given category, that people are always-already fully in possession of an obvious gender identity: women are women and men are men. Even the tentative but laudable attempts to do justice to differences between women (as in terms of class) do not go as far problematizing the category of 'women' itself. As a result, as Virginia Nightingale has remarked, studies of women as audiences are undergirded by the basic assumption of women as 'objectifiable, somehow a unified whole, a group. The qualities that divide women, like class, ethnicity, age, education, are always of less significant than the unifying qualities attributed to women, such as the inability to know or say what they want, the preoccupation with romance and relationships, the ability to care for, to nurture, others' (Nightingale 1990: 25). Or as Annette Kuhn has put it, 'the notion of a female social audience (. . .) presupposes a group of individuals already formed as female' (Kuhn 1984: 24).

Such a presumption is troublesome for both political and theoretical reasons. Not only does exclusive concentration on women as audiences unwittingly reproduce the patriarchal treatment of Woman as the defined (and thus deviant) sex and Man as the invisible (and thus normal) sex – in this sense, Andrew Ross' (1989) call for a properly audience-oriented study of pornography as a traditional 'men's genre' is long overdue;[5] more fundamentally, the a priori assumption that there is a continuous field of experience shared by all women and only by women tends to naturalize sexual difference and to universalize culturally constructed and historically specific definitions of femininity and masculinity.

The common-sense equation that women are women because they are women is in fact an empiricist illusion. As Denise Riley has forcefully argued:

> '[W]omen' is historically, discursively constructed, and always relatively to other categories which themselves change; 'women' is a volatile collection in which female persons can be very differently positioned, so that the apparent continuity

of the subject of 'women' isn't to be relied on; 'women' is both synchronically and diachronically erratic as a collectivity, while for the individual, 'being a woman' is also inconstant, and can't provide an ontological foundation.

Riley 1988: 1/2

The pertinence of this argument asserts itself rather exemplarily in the continuing trouble posed by the category of 'women' for marketers, those whose business it is to address, reach and 'catch' women as consumers. It is well-known that any marketing strategy aimed at women is less than perfect; marketers have learned to live with the fact that the dream of guaranteed successful communication – which amounts to knowning exactly how to identify 'women' – can never be fulfilled. Indeed, as one commentator has observed, 'marketers lurch from one stereotype to another as they try to focus in on the elusive female consumer' (Canape 1984: 38). Market researchers' ongoing attempts notwithstanding to come up with new categorical typifications of women – happy housewife, superwoman, romantic feminist – , 'women' remains a 'moving target' for marketers and advertisers (cf. Bartos 1982).

What we can learn from the pragmatic wisdom of marketers is that we cannot afford taking 'women' as a straightforward, natural collectivity with a constant identity, its meaning inherent in the (biological) category of the female sex. In social and cultural terms, 'women', as much as 'class', is not an immutable fact, but an inescapably indeterminate, ever-shifting category (Haraway 1985; Riley 1988; Scott 1988).

Against this background, we would argue against a continued research emphasis on women's experience, women's culture, women's media consumption as if these were self-contained entities, no matter how internally differentiated. This is not to deny that there are gender differences or gender-specific experiences and practices, it is however to suggest that their meanings are always relative to particular constructions in specified contexts. For example, in examining the consumption of a ubiquitous genre such as women's magazines, we should not only attend to both female and male self-identified readers (and arguably non-readers as well), but also pay attention to the multiple feminine and masculine identifications involved. We would argue then that the theoretical question that should guide our research practice is how gender – along with other major social axes such as class and ethnicity – is *articulated* in concrete practices of media consumption. We will elaborate on this question in the next section.

The Prison House of Gender and Beyond

Recent poststructuralist feminist theory has powerfully questioned the essentialist and reductionist view of sexual difference underlying the assumption of fixity of gender identity (male or female).[6] Poststructuralism asserts first of all that subjectivity is non-unitary, produced in and through the intersection of a multitude of social discourses and practices which position the individual subject in heterogeneous, overlaying and competing ways. A person's subjectivity can thus be described in terms of the multiplicity of subject positions taken up by the person in question. Moreover, poststructuralism claims that an individual's subjectivity is never finished, constantly in re-production as it were as s/he lives out her/his day-to-day life and engages herself/himself with a variety of discourses and practices encountering and positioning her/him. In this sense, a female person cannot be presumed to have a pregiven and fixed gender identity as a woman. Rather, an individual's gendered subjectivity is constantly in process of reproduction and transformation. Being a woman can mean many different things, at different times and in different circumstances. The en-gendering of the subject, in other words, goes on continuously through what Teresa de Lauretis has called 'the various technologies of gender (. . .) and institutional discourses (. . .) with power to control the field of social meaning and thus produce, promote, and 'implant' representations of gender' (De Lauretis 1987: 18).

To describe this process more concretely, we can make a distinction between gender definitions, gender positionings and gender identifications. Gender definitions, produced within specific social discourses and practices in which gender is made into a meaningful category (what De Lauretis calls 'technologies of gender'), articulate what is considered to be feminine or masculine in culture and society. Different discourses produce different definitions within specific contexts. For instance, Catholic religious discourse defines woman as virgin, mother or whore. It is contradicted, by radical feminist discourse that defines women as oppressed human beings, victims of male exploitation. Such discourses, and the gender definitions they produce, are never innocent; nor are they all equally powerful, coexisting in a happy plurality. They rather often contradict and compete with each other. In our societies, dominant gender discourses work to maintain relations of power between males and females in that they assign different roles, opportunities, ideals, duties and vulnerabilities to 'men' and 'women' that are classified as normal and are very difficult to break out of. This, of course, relates to the concept of gender positionings. It is at this level that work in textual analysis, as described in the first section of this chapter, has made its valuable contribution. How and to which extent discursively constructed gender-differentiated positions are taken up by concrete females and males, however, depends on the gender identifications made by actual subjects. It should be pointed out that this is not a mechanical and passive process: assuming this would imply a discourse determinism analogous to the textual determinism criticized above. How processes of gender identifications should be theorized and examined, however, is one of the most underdeveloped aspects of the poststructuralist theory of subjectivity. When, how and why, in other words, do male and female persons keep identifying with positions that are defined as properly masculine or feminine in dominant discourses?

Unfortunately, as must have become clear from our summary of developments in the field above, it is especially the passage from gender positionings to gender identifications that is theoretically relevant for work on gender and media consumption. To comprehend better the mechanisms of this process, it is useful to take up the suggestion made by Henriques et al. (1984; see also Hollway 1989) that there must be an 'investment', loosely speaking, an emotional commitment, involved in the taking up of certain subject positions by concrete subjects. As Henriques et al. put it:

By claiming that people have investments (. . .) in taking up certain positions in discourses, and consequently in relation to each other, I mean that there will be some satisfaction or pay-off or reward (these terms involve the same problems) for that person. The satisfaction may well be in contradiction with other resultant feelings. It is not necessarily conscious or rational. But there is a reason. . . . I theorize the reason for this investment in terms of power and the way it is historically inserted into individuals' subjectivity.

(Henriques et al. 1984: 238)

The term 'investment', which Henriques et al. derived from the Freudian term *Besetzung* (cathexis), is adequate because it avoids both biological or psychological connotations such as 'motivation' or 'need', and rationalistic ones such as 'choice'.[7] The term also gives some depth to the notion of 'negotiation' that was put forward earlier to conceptualize text/reader relationships. Investment suggests that people have an – often unconscious – stake in identifying with certain subject positions, including gender positions, and that the stake in these investments, and it should be stressed that each individual subject makes many such, sometimes conflicting investments all the time, should be sought in the management of social relations. People invest in positions which confer them relative power, although an empowering position in one context (say, in the family) can be quite dispowering in another (say, in the workplace), while in any one context a person can take up both empowering and dispowering positions at the same time.

Furthermore, given the social dominance of gender discourses based upon the naturalness of sexual difference there is considerable social and cultural pressure on female and male persons, to invest in feminine and masculine subject positions respectively. This leads to what Hollway (1989) calls the recursive production of social relations between men and women, which is not the same as mechanical reproduction because successful gender identifications are not automatic nor free of conflicts, dependent as they are on the life histories of individual people and the concrete practices they enter into, such as practices of media consumption. In other words, what this theoretical perspective suggests is that the construction of gender identity and gender relations is a constant achievement to which subjects themselves are complicit. In the words of De Lauretis (1987: 9), '[t]he construction of gender is the product and the process of both representation and self-representation'.

A number of audience studies that have focused on the issue of gender and media consumption can usefully be recounted in the light of this theoretical perspective. For example, Janice Radway's (1984) interpretation of romance reading provides a good example of how some female persons inadvertently reproduce their gendered subjectivity through all sorts of positions they take up and identify with in the course of their lives. Radway concluded that the women she interviewed used the act of reading romances as a 'declaration of independence' from one position accorded them by dominant patriarchal discourse: the position of ever-available and nurturing housewife and mother. At the same time, however, they submit to patriarchal discourse in their very reading, by investing so much energy in the imaginary (and wishful) reconstruction of masculinity as they interpret romances as stories about male transformation from hard and insensitive machos to loving and caring human beings. Such an analysis highlights how one and the same practice – reading romances – can contain contradictory positionings and investments, although ultimately ending up in reproducing a woman's gendered subjectivity (as Radway would have it).

However, there is still a sense of overgeneralization in Radway's interpretation, in that she has not sufficiently specified the social circumstances in which her informants performed their romance reading. In this sense James Curran (1990: 154) is right in his observation that 'Radway's *tour de force* offers an account of romance addicts' relationship to patriarchy but not to their flesh and blood husbands'. This does not invalidate Radway's analysis, since patriarchal discourses are effective in more encompassing ways than solely through direct face to face encounters, but her account does acquire a somewhat functionalist, adynamic quality the moment she transposes the analysis of how gender identifications are implicated in romance *reading* (a practice) to an explanation of individual romance *readers* (concrete historical subjects).

Ann Gray (1987; forthcoming), who studied how women relate to television and popular culture in the home, has pointed to similar contradictions in women's gender identifications, but she places them more concretely in their particular life histories. Not having had many opportunities in education and the job market, the women of Gray's study got married in order to leave their parents' homes and get settled on their own. By the time their children had grown up and they had a little more room to reflect on their lives, the patterns had been edged in. Marriage and motherhood seemed an escape at first but turned out to be a trap that was inescapable for most, despite their awareness of inequalities between men and women. The books and television programmes they prefer are tailored to female escapism and this, according to Gay, is how these women use them.[8] Gray's account makes clear how the apparent inevitability of the reproduction of femininity is in fact a result of the sedimented history of previous positionings and identifications in which these women find themselves caught, although they keep struggling against it through new investments that *are* available to them, such as consuming 'feminine' media genres and using the VCR to tape their favourite soap operas in order to be able to watch alone or with their women friends, thereby evading the derogatory comments of their husbands (Gray 1987).

One can also account for many women's gendered use of the telephone – for maintaining household activities, maintaining family relationships, for 'gossip' and 'chatter' – along these lines (Rakow 1988). Sherry Turkle's (1988) analysis of the 'masculinization' of the computer and the concommitant 'computer reticence' among some of the girls she studied, provides another example. Although all these studies did limit themselves empirically to women's responses, they can most usefully be seen as illustrating that gender does not simply predetermine media consumption and use; on the contrary, what they illuminate is that it is in and through the very practices of media consumption – and the positionings and identifications they solicit – that gender identities are recursively shaped, while those practices themselves in turn undergo a process of gendering along the way.

This, then, is what we mean by the *articulation* of gender in practices of media consumption. The concept of articulation refers to the process 'establishing a relation among elements such that their identity is modified as a result of the articulatory practice' (Laclau and Mouffe 1985: 105). In concrete terms, the concept can theorize how neither gender nor media consumption have necessary or inherent meanings; only through their articulation in concrete historical situations do media consumption practices acquire meanings that are gender-specific. Furthermore, the concept is more accurate than 'construction' or 'production' because it connotes a dynamic process of fixing or fitting together, which is however never total nor final. The concept of articulation emphasizes the impossibility of fixing ultimate meanings (Laclau and Mouffe 1985; see also Hall 1986).

To clarify the importance of seeing gender and media consumption in terms of their articulations, let us give just one more example, derived from David Morley's study of the gendering of television viewing habits in a number of working-class families in London. What sets Morley's study apart from the examples above is that he does not take individual women (and men) as empirical units of analysis, but a structured relational context, namely the modern nuclear family (see also e.g. Lull 1988; Morley and Silverstone 1990). One of the observations he makes is that there is nothing inherently masculine about the wish to watch television with full concentration (as some of the men he interviewed reported), and that there is nothing inherently feminine in the tendency of the women in the study to watch distractedly. Instead, Morley interprets this empirical gender difference as resulting from 'the dominant model of gender relations within this society' which 'is one in which the home is primarily defined for men as a site of leisure – in distinction to the "industrial time" of their employment – while the home is primarily defined for women as a sphere of work (whether or not they also work outside the home). [As a result] . . . men are better placed to do [television viewing] wholeheartedly, and . . . women seem only to be able to do [it] distractedly and guiltily, because of their continuing sense of their domestic responsibilities' (Morley 1986: 147).

However, put this way Morley's argument still sounds too mechanical, in that he tends to collapse gender positionings and gender identifications together. After all, it is not likely that the gendered pattern will be found in all (London working-class) families all the time, despite the force of the dominant discourse. (To assume this would only reproduce the objectification of working-class culture that we criticized above.) Thus, the articulation of concentration/masculine and distraction/feminine in some family homes only comes about in concrete situations, in which personal investments, social circumstances and available discourses are interconnected in specific ways within the families concerned. Articulations, in other words, are inexorably contextual.

Moreover, such articulations have to be made again and again, day after day, and the fact that the same articulations are so often repeated – and thus lead to the successful reproduction of established gender meanings, gender relations and gender identities – is not a matter of course; it is, rather, a matter of active re-production, continual re-articulation.[9] But in each family, there may be moments in which the woman becomes a much more involved television viewer, whereas her husband would lose interest in the set. No articulation is ever definitive or absolute. Under certain conditions, existing articulations can be disarticulated, leading to altered patterns of media consumption, in which women and men take up very different positions. For example, experiences such as illness, children leaving the home, extramarital affairs, political upheavals and so on may disrupt daily life in such a way to break down existing patterns. This is how change comes about.

The concept of articulation, then, can account for what Laclau and Mouffe (1985: 114) call 'the presence of the contingent in the necessary'. Moreover, the unfinished and overdetermined nature of articulations also helps to explain what Riley (1988: 103) calls 'the temporality and malleability of gendered existence'. She points out, rather ironically, that it's not possible to live twenty-four hours a day soaked in the immediate awareness of one's sex, which is another way of saying that women are only sometimes 'women', female persons steeped in an overwhelming feminine subjectivity. In other words, even though, according to De Lauretis (1987: 2), the social subject is 'constituted in gender', in everyday life gender is not always relevant to what one experiences, how one feels, chooses to act or not to act. Since a subject is always multiply positioned in relation to a whole range of discourses, many of which do not concern gender, women do not always live in the prison house of gender.

Indeed, the currency of non-gendered or gender-neutral identifications should emphatically be kept in mind in our search for understanding the variability and diversity of media consumption practices, both among and within women and men. How, otherwise, to understand women who like watching the weekend sports programme, the news, or hard-boiled detectives, men reading women's magazines or watching *Cagney and Lacey*, couples watching pornography or reading travel guides together, and so on? Indeed, it is questionable whether we should always foreground the articulation of masculinity and femininity in analyzing media consumption practices.[10] For example, in his analysis of the cross-cultural reception of *Dynasty*, Kim Schrøder (1988) concludes that the pleasure of regularly watching *Dynasty*, for his male and female interviewees alike, has to do with the pleasure of solving narrative enigmas, what he calls 'the weekly reconstruction of self-confidence'. Similarly, we might ask whether the pleasure of watching sports is really in all its aspects that different for men and for women; we might consider that discourses of nation and nationalism may play a more significant role in sports viewing than discourses of gender (Poynton and Hartley 1990). Of course, this doesn't mean that gender positionings are totally absent from either *Dynasty* or sports programmes; what we do want to point out however is that non-gendered identifications may sometimes take on a higher priority than gendered ones, allowing for a much more complex and dynamic theorization of the way media consumption is related to gender.

In this sense, we oppose Susan Bordo's (1990) dismissal of the idea of gender neutrality as purely ideological. 'In a culture that is in fact constituted by gender duality (. . .) one cannot simply be "human", she states (Bordo 1990: 152). But if we acknowledge that culture is not a monolithic entity but a shifting set of diverse practices, we must assume that partiality of gender as a structuring principle in culture. Furthermore, the taking up of positions in which gender is not necessarily implicated – for example that of professional, hostage, teacher, or citizen – always transcends the 'simply human'; these are overdetermined social positions in which identities may – temporarily – be articulated in non-gendered ways, dependent upon context.[11] Indeed, given the dominant culture's insistence on the all-importance of sexual difference, we might arguably want to cherish those rare moments that women manage to escape the prison house of gender.

The Instability of Gender in Media Consumption

Our theoretical explorations have led us to recognize the fundamental instability of the role of gender in media consumption practices. We cannot presume *a priori* that in any particular instance of media consumption gender will be a basic determining factor. In other words, media consumption is not always a gendered practice, and even if it is a gendered practice its modality and effectivity can only be understood by close examination of the meanings that 'male' and 'female' and their interrelationships acquire within a particular context.

What we have tried to clarify, then, is the importance of recognizing that there is no prearticulated gender identity. Despite the force of hegemonic gender discourse, the actual content of being a woman or a man and the rigidity of the dichotomy itself are highly variable, not only across cultures and historical times, but also, at a more micro-social and even psychological level, amongst and within women and men themselves. Gender identity, in short, is both multiple and partial, ambiguous and incoherent, permanently in process of being articulated, disarticulated, and rearticulated.

The consequences of this particularist perspective for research into gender and media consumption are not too difficult to spell out. In our view, the ethnographic turn in the study of media audiences is, given its spirit of radical contextualism and methodological situationalism (Ang 1990b), well suited to take on board the challenge of problematizing and investigating in which concrete situations which gender positions are taken up by which men and women, with what identificatory investments and as a result of which specific articulations. But in order to do this, the ethnographic project needs to be radicalized even more, since not only gender, but also media consumption cannot be conceptualized in static terms. To be sure, this claim gives this article a final destabilizing twist.

The current emphasis on the social experiences of audience subjects as starting point for understanding practices of media consumption is ethnography's major contribution to audience studies. However, in their focus on women's reception of women's genres most existing studies of gender and/in media consumption have not pushed the ethnographic thrust far enough. Since the main interest of these studies, as we have seen, has been in text/reader relationship, they tend to decontextualize the reception process from the ongoing flow of everyday life. But in our media-saturated world media audiences can no longer be conceived as neatly demarcated categories of people, collectively set in relation to a single set of isolated texts and messages, each carrying a finite number of subject positions. This insight can only lead to a more radical 'anthropologization' of the study of media consumption, in which the text is radically decentered and the everyday contexts in which reception, consumption and use take place are more emphatically foregrounded (e.g. Radway 1988; Silverstone 1990; Morley and Silverstone 1990; Ang 1990b).

To do justice to such a perspective, then, we need to go beyond the boundaries of reception analysis and develop new forms of 'consumption analysis'. In everyday life, media consumption cannot be equated with distinct and insulated activities such as 'watching television', 'reading a book', 'listening to a record', and so on. Since people living in (post) modern societies are surrounded by an ever-present and ever-evolving media-environment, they are always-already audiences of an abundance of media provisions, by choice or by force. Thus, media consumption should be conceptualized as an ever proliferating set of heterogenous and dispersed, intersecting and contradicting cultural practices, involving an indefinite number of multiply-positioned subjects: 'everyone is constantly exposed to a variety of media and forms, and participates in a range of events and activities' (Grossberg 1988a: 20/21).

Hermann Bausinger (1984) has summed up a list of phenomenological considerations which illuminates the enormous complexity of the field opened up here, although the list is also helpful in beginning to map the terrain. To understand day-to-day media use in contemporary society, Bausinger states, it is necessary to take the whole 'ensemble' of intersecting and overlapping media provisions into consideration. Audiences piece together the contents of radio, television, newspapers, and so on. As a rule, media texts and messages are not used completely or with full concentration. We read parts of sports reviews, skim through magazines, and zap from channel to channel when we don't like what's on TV. Furthermore, media use, being an integral part of the routines and rituals of everyday life, is constantly interrelated with other activities such as talking, eating, or doing housework. In other words, 'mass' communication and 'interpersonal' communication cannot be separated. Finally, according to Bausinger, media use is not a private, individual process, but a collective, social process. Even when reading the newspaper one is often not truly alone, but interacting with family, friends, or colleagues. In short, comprised within the deceptively simple term 'media consumption' is an extremely multifarious and differentiated conglomerate of activities and experiences.

Against this background, we need to perform an even further particularization in our research and interpretive endeavour. Since media consumption takes place in the 'the complex and contradictory terrain, the multidimensional context, within which people live out their everyday lives' (Grossberg 1988a: 25), no two women (or men) will have exactly the same experiences in 'the ever-shifting kaleidoscope of cultural circulation and consumption' (Radway 1988: 361), although of course specific overlapping interests and commonalities in past and present circumstances are not ruled out. In such a context, we must accept contingency as posing the utter limit for our understanding, and historical specificity as the only ground on which continuities and discontinuities in the ongoing but unpredictable articulation of gender in media consumption can be traced. In other words, such continuities and discontinuities only emerge *post facto*. Within this horizon, ethnography's task would be the production of accounts that make these historically specific continuities and discontinuities explicit, thereby lifting them out of their naturalized day-do-day flow.[12]

This brings us back to the hazardous episode of daily life in the Meier family with which we opened this article. In unexpectedly ending up watching the sports programme, Mrs Meier simultaneously places herself outside the gendered discourse of 'televised football is for men', and reproduces the traditional definition of femininity in terms of emotional caretaking by using the viewing of the game as a means of making contact with her son. It is not impossible that such accidental events will lead Mrs Meier to eventually like football on television, thereby creating a gender neutral zone within the family's life with the media. After having finished doing the dishes while watching a favourite soap opera on a small black and white TV set in the kitchen, she might watch the sports programme in the sitting room because she and her husband have become involved in a debate over the technical qualities of United's new goalkeeper (thereby developing a 'masculine' interest in sports). Or else, she might watch the game for human interest reasons (which would be a 'feminine' subject position). At the same time, whether she takes up a masculine, feminine or gender neutral position in relation to TV football, this very development would only reinforce Mr Meier's investment in a discourse which sees masculine preferences as natural.

Postscript: on Feminist Critique

It is clear that our exposition of the instability of gender/media consumption articulations draws a great deal from postmodern theory, energized as it is by a wariness of generalized absolutes and its observance of the irreducible complexity and relentless heterogeneity of social life (see also Corner, in this volume). However, doesn't this stance make theory and politics impossible? Doesn't postmodern particularism inevitably lead to the resignation that all there is left viable are descriptions of particular events at particular points in time? And doesn't radical endorsement of particularity and difference only serve to intensify an escalating individualism? If we declare 'women' to be an indeterminate category, how can a feminist politics still assert itself?

These questions are certainly valid and understandable, although we think they need not have to remain unanswered. For one thing, we believe that the dangers of easy categorization and generalization, so characteristic of mainstream traditions in the social sciences (including mass communication theory and research), are greater than the benefits of a consistent particularism. The earlier feminist tendency to speak for and behalf 'women' as if this were a unified category with a uniform identity has already been eroded by a gradual acknowledgement of differences between different sorts of women, positioned in different relations of class, ethnicity, generation, sexual orientation, and regionality. But postmodern feminism, building up a poststructuralist theory of subjectivity, goes further than this sociological differentiating move by adopting a more profound sense of gender scepticism, thereby eradicating any pregiven guarantee for female unity. In this sense, postmodern feminism is itself a critical reaction to the normative and moralist absolutism in earlier feminisms: 'a critical vision consequent upon a critical positioning in unhomogeneous gendered social space' (Haraway 1988: 589) [13]

As Jane Flax (1990: 56) has noted, '[f]eminist theories, like other forms of postmodernism, should encourage us to tolerate and interpret ambivalence, ambiguity, and multiplicity'. She even adds to this that '[i]f we do our work well, reality will appear even more unstable, complex and disorderly than it does now' (Flax 1990: 56/7). In political terms, this means that we can no longer afford to found a feminist practice upon the postulation of some fixed figure of 'women' without risking to be totalizing and excluding the experiences and realities of some. Arguably, such unifying feminist politics will only be ultimately unproductive: the fact that many women today refuse to call themselves feminists is symptomatic of this. Another example would be the sharp contrast between the critical feminist condemnation of Steven Spielberg's film *The Color Purple* as white middle-class cooptation of Alice Walker's novel, and the impressive positive responses to the film from black women viewers (Bobo 1988; Stuart 1988). This example also clarifies the political importance of local, contextualized ethnographic studies: the production of 'situated knowledges' whose critical value lies in their enabling of power-sensitive conversation and contestation through comparison rather than in epistemological truth (Haraway 1988).

Indeed, any feminist standpoint will necessarily have to present itself as partial, based upon the knowledge that while some women sometimes share some common interests and face some common enemies, such commonalities are by no means universal. Asserting that there can be no fixed and universal standards for political 'correctness' does not mean relativist political reticence nor submission to a pluralist free of all. On the contrary, it is an acknowledgement of the fact that in order to confront 'sexism in all its endless variety and monotonous similarity' (Fraser and Nicholson 1990: 34), a flexible and pragmatic form of criticism might be more effective than one based upon predefined truths, feminist or otherwise. What is at stake here then is not relativism, but a politics of location:

> [L]ocation is about vulnerability; location resists the politics of closure, finality, or (. . .) 'simplification in the last instance'. (. . .) We seek [knowledges] ruled by partial sight and limited voice – not partiality for its own sake but, rather, for the sake of the connections and unexpected openings situated knowledges make possible. (. . .) The only way to find a larger vision is to be somewhere in particular [and through] the joining of partial views and halting voices into a collective subject position that promises a vision of the means of ongoing finite embodiment, of living within limits and contradictions – of views from somewhere.
>
> (Haraway 1988: 590)

Notes

1   For example, several authors have pointed to the fact that feminine subject positions constructed in mass cultural texts do not simply reproduce patriarchal definitions of femininity, but also offer utopian opportunities for fantasmatic transgression. Allison Light, for example, sees in romantic fiction 'explorations and productions of desires which may be in excess of the socially possible or acceptable' (Light 1984: 7). See also Modleski (1982), McRobbie (1985), Kaplan (1986), Ang (1990a).

2   This is not to say that generalizations as such should at all cost be avoided (indeed, this would make the production of knowledge virtually impossible); it is merely to point to the importance, in understanding social phenomena, of complementing the generalizing tendency with an opposite, *particularizing* one (see Billig 1987).

3   Frow's (1987) criticism of Bourdieu comes despite the latter's explicit rejection of objectivist sociology and its 'substantialist' conception of reality, and his commitment to

apply a relational mode of thinking in his analysis of cultural differentiation. See e.g. Bourdieu (1989)).

4 See Potter and Whetherell (1987) for the importance of paying attention to inconsistency and variation in discourse analysis.

5 It won't come quite as a surprise that what we know about men and media consumption has for a greater part been written by or about homosexual men (Dyer 1980; Easthope 1986, Gross 1989).

6 For an introduction to poststructuralism and feminism, see Weedon (1987).

7 It is exactly these terms that were used by uses and gratifications theorist to describe individuals' media uses and consumption.

8 Personal communication of Joke Hermes with Ann Gray, July 1990.

9 In our view, this would be a viable way of theorizing the mechanisms of 'routines' and 'regularities' in everyday life.

10 Obviously, genres such as the news and travel literature, and certainly pornography, do contain gendered subject positionings in the way they substantially and formally address their spectators. But such positionings cannot be assumed to exhaust the textual effectivity of these genres. Here, work in the field of textual analysis can offer us much more detailed insight. For example, Charlotte Brunsdon (1987) has explored this issue in her analysis of the British crime series *Widows*.

11 That such positions are often in the second instance articulated in gendered terms, for example in the stereotyping of professional women as unfeminine or in the call for treating male and female hostages differently (as, for example, in the Gulf crisis), is precisely the result of the hegemonic work of patriarchal discourse. It is important for feminism to *disarticulate* such discursive genderings.

12 For conceptualizations of ethnography as story-telling, see e.g. Clifford and Marcus (1986); Van Maanen (1988); Geertz (1988).

13 Nicholson (1990) is an excellent collection of articles pro and contra the feminism/postmodernism connection.

References

ALLEN, ROBERT, C., 1985: *Speaking of Soap Operas*. Chapell Hill and London: University of North Carolina Press.

ANG, IEN, 1988: 'Feminist Desire and Female Pleasure', *Camera Obscura*, 16: pp. 179–191.

——1990a: 'Melodramatic Imaginations: Television Fiction and Women's Fantasy', pp. 75–88 in Mary Ellen Brown (ed.), *Television and Women's Culture*. London: Sage.

——1990b: *Desperately Seeking the Audience*. London & New York: Routledge.

BAEHR, HELEN, and GILLIAN DYER (ed.), 1987: *Boxed In: Women and Television*. London: Pandorra Press.

BARTOS, RENA, 1982: *The Moving Target: What Every Marketer Should Know About Women*. New York: Free Press.

BAUSINGER, HERMANN, 1984: 'Media, Technology and Daily Life', *Media, Culture and Society*, 6(4): pp. 343–351.

BILLIG, MICHAEL, 1987: *Arguing and Thinking*. Cambridge: Cambridge University Press.

BOBO, JACQUELINE, 1988: 'The Color Purple: Black Women as Cultural Readers', pp. 90–109 in E. Deidre Primbam (ed.), *Female Spectators: Looking at Film and Television*. London: Verso.

BORDO, SUSAN, 1990: 'Feminism, Postmodernism and Gender-Scepticism', pp. 133–156 in Linda J. Nicholson (ed.), *Feminism/Postmodernism*. New York and London: Routledge.

BOURDIEU, PIERRE, 1984: *Distinction*. Trans. Richard Nice. Cambridge, MA: Harvard University Press.

——1989: 'Social Space and Symbolic Power', *Sociological Theory*, 7(1): pp. 14–25.

BROWN, MARY ELLEN, 1990: 'Motley Moments: Soap Operas, Carnival, Gossip and the Power of the Utterance', pp. 183–198 in Mary Ellen Brown (ed.), *Television and Women's Culture*. London: Sage.

BRUNSDON, CHARLOTTE, 1987: 'Men's Genres for Women', pp. 184–202 in Helen Baehr and Gillian Dyer (ed.), *Boxed In: Women and Television*. New York and London: Pandora.

CANAPE, CHARLENE, 1984: 'Split Image', *Madison Avenue*, (August): pp. 38–44.

CLIFFORD, JAMES and GEORGE MARCUS (ed.), 1986: *Writing Culture: The Politics and Poetics of Ethnography*. Berkeley, CA: University of California Press.

CORNER, JOHN, 1991: in this volume.

COWARD, ROSALIND, 1983: *Patriarchal Precedents: Sexuality and Social Relations*. London: Routledge and Kegan Paul.

——1984: *Female Desire: Women's Sexuality Today*. London: Paladin.

CURRAN, JAMES, 1990: 'The New Revisionism in Mass Communication Research: A Reappraisal', *European Journal of Communication*, 5(2–3): pp. 135–164.

DE LAURETIS, TERESA, 1984: *Alice Doesn't: Feminism, Semiotics, Cinema*. Bloomington: Indiana University Press.

——1987: *Technologies of Gender*. Bloomington and Indianapolis: Indiana University Press.

DOANE, MARY ANNE, 1987: *The Desire to Desire*. London: MacMillan.

DYER, RICHARD (ed.), 1980: *Gays and Film*. London: FBI.

EASTHOPE, ANTHONY, 1986: *What a Man's Gotta Do: The Masculine Myth in Popular Culture*. London: Paladin.

FISKE, JOHN, 1987: *Television Culture*. London: Methuen.

——1991: 'In this volume'.

FLAX, JANE, 1990: 'Postmodernism and Gender Relations in feminist Theory', pp. 39–62 in Linda J. Nicholson (ed.), *Feminism/Postmodernism*. New York and London: Routledge.

FRASER, NANCY and LINDA J. NICHOLSON, 1990: 'Social Criticism Without Philosophy: An Encounter between Feminism and Postmodernism', pp. 19–38 in Linda J. Nicholson (ed.), *Feminism/Postmodernism*. New York and London: Routledge.

FROW, JOHN, 1987: 'Accounting for Tastes: Some Problems in Bourdieu's Sociology of Culture', *Cultural Studies*, 1(1): pp. 59–73.

GAMMAN, LORRAINE and MARGARET MARSHMENT (ed.), 1988: *The Female Gaze: Women as Viewers of Popular Culture*. London: The Women's Press.

GEERTZ, CLIFFORD, 1988: *Works and Lives: The Anthropologist as Author*. Cambridge: Polity Press.

GITLIN, TODD, 1991: 'In this volume'

GLEDHILL, CHRISTINE, 1988: 'Pleasurable Negotiations', pp. 64–89 in E. Deidre Pribam (ed.), *Female Spectators: Looking at Film and Television*. London: Verso.

GRAY, ANN, 1987: 'Behind Closed Doors: Video Recorders in the Home', pp. 38–54 in Helen Baehr and Gillian Dyer (ed.), *Boxed In: Women and Television*. New York and London: Pandora Press.

——(forthcoming) *Video Playtime: The Gendering of a Communications Technology*. London: Comedia/Routledge.

GREER, GERMAINE, 1971: *The Female Eunuch*. London: Paladin.

GROSS, LARRY, 1989: 'Out of the Mainstream: Sexual Minorities and the Mass Media', pp. 130–149 in Ellen Seiter, Hans Borchers, Gabriele Kreutzner and Eva-Maria

Warth (ed.), *Remote Control: Television, Audiences, and Cultural Power*. London and New York: Routledge.

GROSSBERG, LAWRENCE, 1988a: *It's A Sin*. Sydney: Power Publications.

——1988b: 'Wandering Audiences, Nomadic Critics', *Cultural Studies*, 2(3): pp. 377–392.

HALL, STUART, 1982: 'Encoding/Decoding', pp. 128–138 in Stuart Hall, Dorothy Hobson, Andrew Lowe and Paul Willis (ed.), *Culture, Media, Language*. London: Hutchinson.

——1986: 'On Postmodernism and Articulation', *Journal of Communication Inquiry*, 10(2): 45–60.

HARAWAY, DONNA, 1985: 'A Manifesto for Cyborgs: Science, Technology, and Socialist Feminism in the 1980s', *Socialist Review*, 15(80): pp. 65–107.

——1988: 'Situated Knowledges: The Science Question in Feminism and the Privilege of Partial Perspective', *Feminist Studies*, 14(3): pp. 575–599.

HENRIQUES, JULIAN, WENDY HOLLWAY, CATHY URWIN, COUZE VENN and VALERIE WALKERDINE, 1984: *Changing the Subject*. London and New York: Methuen.

HOLLWAY,WENDY, 1989: *Subjectivity and Method in Psychology*. London: Sage.

KAPLAN, CORA, 1986: '*The Thornbirds*: Fiction, Fantasy, Femininity', pp. 142–166 in Victor Burgin, James Donald and Cora Kaplan (ed.), *Formations of Fantasy*. London and New York: Methuen.

KAUFMAN, MICHAEL (ed.), 1987: *Beyond Patriarchy: Essays by Men on Pleasure, Power and Change*. Toronto and New York: Oxford University Press.

KUHN, ANNETTE, 1982: *Women's Pictures: Feminism and Cinema*. London: Routledge and Kegan Paul.

——1984: 'Women's Genres', *Screen*, 25(1): pp. 18–29.

LACLAU, ERNESTO and CHANTAL MOUFFE, 1985: *Hegemony and Socialist Strategy*. London: Verso.

LIGHT, ALLISON, 1984: 'Returning to Manderley: Romantic Fiction, Female Sexuality and Class', *Feminist Review*, 16(3):

LIVINGSTONE, SONIA, 1991: 'In this volume'.

LULL, JAMES (ed.), 1988: *World Families Watch Television*. Newbury Park, CA: Sage.

MCROBBIE, ANGELA, 1982: 'The Politics of Feminist Research: Between Talk, Text and Action', *Feminist Review*, 12(4): pp. 46–57.

——1985: 'Dance and Social Fantasy', pp. in Angela McRobbie and Mica Nava (ed.), *Gender and Generation*. London: McMillan.

MODLESKI, TANIA, 1982: *Loving with a Vengeance: Mass Produced Fantasies for Women*. London: Methuen.

MOI, TORIL, 1985: *Sexual/Textual Politics*. London: Methuen.

MORLEY, DAVID, 1986: *Family Television: Cultural Power and Domestic Leisure*. London: Comedia/Routledge.

MORLEY, DAVID and ROGER SILVERSTONE, 1990: 'Domestic Communications: Technologies and Meanings', *Media, Culture and Society*, 12(1): pp. 31–55.

MORRIS, MEAGHAN, 1988: 'Banality in Cultural Studies', *Block*, 14: pp. 15–25.

MULVEY, LAURA, 1975: "Visual Pleasure and Narrative Cinema', *Screen*, 16(3): pp. 6–18.

——1990: 'Afterthoughts on 'Visual Pleasure and Narrative Cinema" inspired by Duel in the Sun', pp. 139–188 in Tony Bennett (ed.), *Popular Fiction: Technology, Ideology, Production, Reading*. London and New York: Routledge.

NICHOLSON, LINDA J. (ed.), 1990: *Feminism/Postmodernism*. New York and London: Routledge.

NIGHTINGALE, VIRGINIA, 1990: 'Women as Audiences', pp. 25–26 in Mary Ellen Brown (ed.), *Television and Women's Culture*. London: Sage.

POTTER, JONATHAN and MARGARET WHETHERELL, 1987: *Discourse and Social Psychology*. London: Sage.

POYNTON, BEVERLEY and JOHN HARTLEY, 1990: 'Male-Gazing: Australian Rules Football, Gender and Television', pp. 144–157 in Mary Ellen Brown (ed.), *Television and Women's Culture*. London: Sage.

PRESS, ANDREA L., 1990: 'Class, Gender and the Female viewer: Women's Responses to Dynasty', pp. 158–182 in Mary Ellen Brown (ed.), *Television and Women's Culture*. London: Sage.

PRIBRAM, E. DEIDRE (ed.), 1988: *Female Spectators: Looking at Film and Television*. London and New York: Verso.

RADWAY, JANICE, 1984: *Reading the Romance: Women, Patriarchy and Popular Literature*. Chapell Hill, NC: University of North Carolina Press.

——1988: 'Reception Study: Ethnography and the Problems of dispersed Audiences and Nomadic subjects', *Cultural Studies*, 2(3): pp. 359–376.

RAKOW, LANA, 1988: 'Women and the Telephone: The Gendering of a Communications Technology', pp. 207–228 in Cheris Kramarae (ed.), *Technology and Women's Voices*. London: Routledge.

RILEY, DENISE, 1988: *'Am I That Name?' Feminism and the Category of 'Women' in History*. Houndsmills, Basingstoke and London: MacMillan.

ROSS, ANDREW, 1989: *No Respect: Intellectuals and Popular Culture*. New York and London: Routledge.

SCHRØDER, KIM, 1988: 'The Pleasure of Dynasty: The Weekly Reconstruction of Self-Confidence', pp. 61–82 in Philip Drummond and Richard Paterson (ed.), *Television and Its Audience*. London: BFI.

SCOTT, JOAN W, 1988: 'Deconstructing Equality-Versus-Difference: Or, the Uses of Poststructuralist Theory for Feminism', *Feminist Studies*, 14(1): pp. 33–50.

SEIDLER, VICTOR J., 1989: *Rediscovering Masculinity: Reason, Language and Sexuality*. London: Routledge.

SEITER, ELLEN, BORCHERS, HANS, KREUTZNER, GABRIELLE and WARTH, EVA-MARIA, 1989: '"Don't treat us like we're so stupid and naïve": Towards an Ethnography of Soap Opera Viewers', pp. 223–247 in Ellen Seiter, Hans Borchers, Gabriele Greutzner and Eva-Maria Warth (ed.), *Remote Control: Television, Audiences, and Cultural Power*. London and New York: Routledge.

SHARPE, SUE, 1976: *'Just Like a Girl': How Girls Learn to be Women*. Harmondsworth: Penguin.

SILVERSTONE, ROGER, 1990: 'Television and everyday Life: Towards an Anthropology of the Television Audience', pp. 173–189 in Marjorie Ferguson (ed.) *Public Communication: The New Imperatives*. London: Sage.

STUART, ANDREA, 1988: 'The Color Purple: In Defence of Happy Endings', pp. 60–75 in Lorraine Gamman and Margaret Marshment (ed.), *The Female Gaze: Women as Viewers of Popular Culture*. London: The Women's Press.

TUCHMAN, GAYE, 1978: 'Introduction: The Symbolic Annihilation of Women by the Mass Media', pp. 3–38 in Gaye Tuchman, Kaplan Daniels and James Benét (ed.), *Hearth and Home: Images of Women in the Mass Media*. New York: Oxford University Press.

TUCHMAN, GAYE, ARLENE KAPLAN DANIELS and JAMES BENÉT (ed.), 1978: *Hearth and Home: Images of Women in the Mass Media*. New York: Oxford University Press.

TURKLE, SHERRY, 1988: 'Computational Reticence', pp. 41–62 in Cheris Kramarae (ed.), *Technology and Women's Voices*. London: Routledge.

VAN MAANEN, JOHN, 1988: *Tales of the Field*. Chicago: Chicago University Press.

VAN ZOONEN, LIESBET, 1991: in this volume.

WEEDON, CHRIS, 1987: *Feminist Practice and Poststructuralist Theory*. Oxford: Basil Blackwell.

16

The Politics of Communication and the Communication of Politics

Todd Gitlin

1 The Uses of Bad Writing

Historically, the social sciences have been coupled to social criticism.[1] Social theory began, in fact, as an attempt to find footing for criticism – to identify groups who, because of their situation in society, would be able to convert criticism into practice. This was Marxism's achievement, as it was Saint-Simon's and, in a different way, Weber's. These were much different theories and ways of theorizing, but they had in common a faith in the practical meaning and motives of theory. Even as social science has tied itself to more modest policy goals in recent decades, it has retained its commitment to criticism, albeit now criticism of a moderate and manageable sort.

But in recent years, surely one thing that has rent theory and criticism asunder is the self-insulation of professional social science. And no factor has contributed to that self-insulation more than the quality, if that is the right word, of academic writing. Which raises the question of why academics write routinely, hermetically, in clotted prose, ridden with jargon and the passive voice, even enthusiastically crossing the line from complexity to obscurity. The alarm has been sounded by Russell Jacoby, whose ill-tempered clavier in *The Last Intellectuals* (1987) perhaps prematurely presumes that the public intellectual is an endangered species. It is easy enough to make sport of bad writing as Jacoby does. I wish, rather, to climb Jacoby's ladder and to inquire into the causes and social uses of bad writing. This is not to say that inaccessible writing automatically incapacitates social science for social criticism: Marx himself is the counter-example, although when he set his head to pamphleteering he was the most lucid of polemicists. But most recent academic writing, unlike Marx's, fails to spawn social criticism on the part of the less brilliant but more writerly. Considering the thousands of intelligent people absorbed in media studies around the world, their collective output does not do a great deal of criticism at all. Failing to speak to a larger public, we are, by and large, ill-equipped to mobilize ourselves into criticism. Accessibility is not sufficient but it is necessary for social criticism and for the larger project which criticism ought to serve – enlarging the prospects of a democratic society.

Why bad prose? There is, in the first instance, an institutional explanation: Bad prose flourishes because academic institutions and professional gatekeepers tolerate, even encourage it. Graduate students are rarely encouraged, let alone required, to write more accessibly, let alone more clearly, eloquently, subtly or excitingly. Teaching those arts is difficult in the best circumstances; as it is, there is no premium for trying. Nor, in general, are students necessarily rewarded for it. Bad writing is plainly no impediment to publication in the profession's journals. Rather, there is a case to be made for the contrary. There are even penalties for writing well – one can be tarred with the brush of 'journalism', which can even result, in the cause of Paul Starr of the Harvard sociology department, in dismissal. (What a misunderstanding this anathema is of journalism, by the way, most of which is badly written in other ways than the academic – simplistic, obvious, cliche-ridden, short-sighted, historically thin, repetitious, condescending – and which polices its own boundaries by branding superior work as, what else, sociology or that even more hilarious laughing stock, communications.) Social science is sanctified by profaning what lies on the other side of the social science border – a move familiar to sociologists of deviance. You tangle yourself up in the opaque prose in order to establish credentials. The academia/journalism either/or impoverishes both.

The self-reproducing, closed-in, professional tendencies of academic life are part of the story, then. But inward-turning, hard-to-decipher prose has a larger functional reason. It is a mystery that enshrines the authority of the clerisy – albeit an underemployed publicly chastised clerisy frowned upon in recent years. (But the mystery compensates the profession for its sense of futility.) The cipher can be broken, but that takes a specialist in cryptography. The existence of the cipher certifies that the speciality has a point. The aura of mystery may go so far as to insulate the work from the larger conversation with society – the very conversation which is our business as social intellectuals. But the arcana, if suitably located at prestigious institutions, attract cohorts of students who proceed to widen the circle of influence, at least until countercircles organize and free themselves of the grip and regroup. Whatever else quasi- and pseudoscientific, poststructuralist, and other specialist languages are about, they are united in self-regard.

Not all styles of self-regard have the same sweep and function, of course. The master form, resurrected totalist project of the last twenty years, is what has been called, immodestly, 'theory' – the imitation of Parisian varieties of poststructuralist, especially deconstructionist, literary, cultural and social theory. While breaking academic literary study away from the literature which is ostensibly its object, and downgrading literature to one among many types of 'text', 'theory' proclaims the centrality, indeed supremacy, of the theorist as not only interpreter but master of ceremonies and even director of the entire critical enterprise – even as the theorist loudly proclaims that no master discourse exists. Theory's clotted but occasionally elegant and certainly ambitious form of discourse has one distinct virtue: it breaks down parochial boundaries. Like psychoanalysis and Marxism before it, the poststructuralist avant-garde makes its mark across the boundaries of the humanities and social sciences–history, philosophy, political science, sociology, anthropology, women's studies, law, film and television, as well as literary works. It attracts accomplished and ambitious students to a common academic culture and an aura of currency which literature itself can no longer provide. It radiates subversion, interdisciplinary span and international reach at once. It flatters itself for deep insurgency and promises international conferences. Insisting that interpretation is intrinsically political, its writing style incapacitates its practitioners for political and intellectual action that extends beyond the protected grazing fields of academe. Wonder of wonders, this subversion requires not the slightest engagement in the polity. Breaking the spell of literature, identifying the authority of texts with their methods of crystallizing power, 'theory' gathers authority through its own texts and their miracle, mystery, and deauthorizing authority.

2   Two Styles of Bad Writing

The kind of bad writing that concerns me is not just the fruit of carelessness. Nor am I concerned with *difficult* writing which conveys intricate thought. The academy now routinely spawns bad writing which is bad not because the argument traced is intrinsically difficult but because the expression is ungainly, tangled, and hermetic – full of knowing genuflections, high on cloistered display, low on conveyance of meaning. Dependent clauses pile up not because the quality of mind is baroque, as in Henry James, but because the writer cannot be troubled to clarify matters for readers who are not adepts–though they may become so by dint of their immersion in the arcana. The voice is passive because the writer has bowed before a society apparently so formidable and adamant it seems beyond human power to change; or because the writer abdicates responsibility for observing, and wishes to engrave his or her perceptions in stone, or perhaps I should say, hard disc. In this sort of bad writing, the jargon does not convey elusive concepts but rather the writer's pleasure in neologism or club membership. This sort of bad writing is, indeed, a 'discourse'. It has its audiences, subtexts, assurances. It has its reasons. By now, it also has its traditions. Not incidentally, this sort of bad writing has become a credential which proves to crusty academia that the Marxist or poststructuralist scholar is a safe acquisition – safely enclosed within the charmed circle of those who are comprehensible only to each other, and incapable of rousing any rabble at all.

In communication studies I am concerned with two principal types of obscurantist writing. I want to suggest that the two, whose motivations are very different and even appear to be diametrically opposed, share complementary flaws and, indeed, a common model of the relation of ideas to action.

The first obscurantism is the style of research and writing which Paul Lazarsfeld (1941) called 'administrative research' and C. Wright Mills (1959) later dubbed 'abstracted empiricism'. Thirty years after he savaged it, abstracted empiricism has become normal procedure in most of our communications and social science departments. Computers and statistical advances have multiplied the means of obfuscation. If you read Mills' essay with care, you see he is not objecting to empirical research, any more than Adorno and Horkheimer did. Mills has such a healthy respect for 'fact' that he could even be accused of making a fetish of the concept. The nature of Mills' objection is that empiricism has become abstracted from general ideas about social structure. It has tended to restrict study to that which can be measured. It has lost what ought to be its motives in larger, historically based studies of the drift and thrust of social life. It is a collection of means that have become end. To which, more than a quarter century after the publication of Thomas S. Kuhn's *The Structure of Scientific Revolution* (1962), one should add that abstracted empiricism takes for granted an impoverished and in many ways misleading model of progress in the natural sciences.

Why the rise of abstracted empiricism? As Norman Birnbaum points out in his provocative book *The Radical Renewal* (1988), during the postwar period (1946–1964 by his dates) when abstracted empiricism swept through the American social sciences, its dominance stemmed not so much from its pseudoscientific language but rather from its utility to centers of power in an era of presumably manageable problems: 'The American social sciences constituted a social technology, and (I would say elements of – T.G.) a legitimizing ideology, for the larger society – more precisely, for many of its elites. Connected to the corporate structure, to the foundations, and to government by intermediaries recruited from the university not despite but because of their utter absence of critical distance from the distribution of power, the social sciences in the end delivered much of what was required of them'. (Birnbaum: 13) A similar process has operated in much of the rest of the world.

But the rise of abstracted empiricism is behind us, and the situation today is different. Rampant quantification is normalized – and not only in the United States. Government spending on the social sciences has declined considerably, yet the hegemony of abstracted empiricism continues throughout the West – challenged here and there, yet scarcely undermined. As 'social technology', abstracted empiricism has a life of its own, even as its market value has declined. There are even critical rationales. The justification for quantitative content analysis, an apprentice practitioner once told me, is that it 'holds up in court'. It can be harnessed to direct practical use – so many violent acts, so many male Caucasian faces, and so on. Fair enough – quantitative analysis has its uses. But what this practical reason overlooks is that research driven by countability too easily becomes hostage to the political project deemed thinkable, fundable and feasible at the moment – which often turns out to be precisely the safe or trendy project. The modem wags the computer.

This much is to be expected. But more surprising, perhaps, is the default of radical social science. Veterans of the student movements of the 1960s who subsequently flocked into the social sciences expected to reorient scholarship in several respects – not least, to produce critical-minded, ambitious, overarching theory, to counter the abstractedness of a scattershot empiricism unified only by its commitment to the administration. But theory has, in many ways, betrayed the hopes which critics (especially of my generation) reposed in it. In place of the old-line functionalist Grand Theory, our theorists have gone in for certain varieties of self-enclosure. Promethean effort has built theoretical ghettoes – elaborate Marxisms, poststructuralisms, Franco-feminisms, recondite deconstructionisms. Granting fruitful ventures among them, I detect method in the obscurantism. For one thing, there is sheer pleasure in belonging to the club whose collective insight enables it to pierce all veils. The private and parochial tone becomes, in effect, elevating. More troubling still, smug and parochial tones and vocabularies carry a politics which goes largely unexamined. The unspoken and unthought premise is that once the happy few arrive at the correct class map (or a determination of the composition of surplus value, or a theory of imperialism or of housework or the male gaze), they will call it to the attention of the plebes, who will, if they know what is good for them, snap to attention. Plebes are implicitly the recipients, not the makers, of history. History, if it belongs to anyone, belongs to specialists in theory. The unstated (even unfelt) premise is that the theorists will be vindicated once their party comes to power. The impenetrability of the writing is acceptable, then, because the proprietors of the discourse are insiders in training to be managers: in effect, a party of the right-minded. The point of the self-insulating discourse is vicarious mastery of an otherwise intractable world. Or, for those who have rightly ceased to find in a total Marxism the master system which makes sense of all subsidiary phenomena, if history belongs to no one, or if 'history' itself 'defrocked and re-dressed' is nothing more than a defunct metanarrative, as postmodern theorists would have it, then one has at least the satisfaction of enjoying the special protections university culture accords to subversive gestures; one gets to be a critic committed to the defrocking of the critical enterprise – having one's subversion and eating it too.

The curious thing is that, for all their differences, abstracted empiricism and Promethean theory share a commitment to a management model of knowledge. To exaggerate: abstracted empiricism wants to be on tap – wants to roll up its sleeves and go to work for management; Promethean theory wants to be on top – wants to represent the uninitiated within management. But at a deep level, all of these tend toward the same structural model of the relation between knowledge and power. The ideal is that knowledge moves the world by serving a center of power. In the case of abstracted empiricism, the center is an institution that actually exists: government, corporation, or foundation. In the case of abstracted, Promethean theory, the center is hypothetical: a revolutionary class, an active audience. In either case, obscurantist language masks a commitment to a model in which knowledge serves active power.

In recent years, researchers and theorists, many working the precincts of 'cultural studies', have sought refuge from such a model in a romance of audience resistance. Indeed, in this model, popular culture is already political action of an important sort. The rediscovery of the audience comes from several directions, but converges on a consensus. There is recovery from, and correction of, the excesses of manipulation models of Frankfurt inspiration – models which in turn derived much of their force from their rejections of Lazarfeld-style behaviorist pluralism. There is an attempt to find sources of vitality in apparently conservative societies, especially the US under the Republicans and the UK under the Conservatives. There is a populist revulsion against crude Marxist imputations of class consciousness. All good reasons for taking cover from a bad political climate. There are especially good reasons why post-sixties theorists would want to break out of a Marxist Puritanism in which the play of images – the functional equivalent of sex, drugs, and rock 'n' roll for our time – is condemned as frivolous or worse because the signs belie 'the real', which is taken to reside in the sphere of production. But I think it is worth noting what happens when a style of theorizing develops which is driven by an odd combination of, on the one hand, the encapsulation of university life and, on the other, a self-marginalizing style of radical politics. I refer to the cultural theory of stylistic rebellion – a flirtation for some, a torrid affair for others, possibly cohabitation. A riot of this kind of writing has come out of British, then American popular culture and film studies in the last decade, exalting, in particular, the punk style. Dick Hebdige's influential *Subculture: The Meaning of Style* is the canonical text.

Eventually I hope someone tries to place this work more carefully in a history of time – the crisscrossing problems of the British Left, the rise of feminism, the decay of the Labour Party, a particular university situation, and so on. The intellectual and political roots of what became known as cultural studies are inseparable. From Raymond Williams came the program of understanding culture as a field of political action and yet also as a force in itself. From Richard Hoggart came the recognition or argument that traditional forms of working class solidarity were breaking down and being remade by immersion in mass media, so that mass media became a central focus of attention. From Gramsci came a continentally certified theoretical underpinning for a de-Stalinized Marxism, and the idea of the centrality of culture and conceptions of 'common sense' in forming and reforming 'historical blocs', which prevailed in society by establishing and policing the boundaries of legitimate thought in a process called 'hegemony'. The political setting was that of the Labour Party torn between two possibilities: (1) becoming a part of the industrial working class minority, and thereby doomed to remain out of power, political action therefore coming to be seen – out there on the horizon – as a swindle; or (2) on the other hand, becoming a middle-class party and thereby foregoing its place in the socialist lineage. At the same time, social movements of the marginalized were organizing and becoming prominent – nuclear disarmament campaigns in the late Fifties, and eventually working class youth, Afro-Caribbeans, feminists, gays. The project of cultural studies was, in part, to defend the marginalized and to find a theoretical warrant for their significance – eventually, to give them a self-understanding which would make them legitimate heirs to the Marxian version of the ascendent proletariat.

British cultural studies was transplanted to the United States under similar circumstances, in the 1970s. For the generation of the 1960s, which was on its way to becoming the academic generation of the 1980s, the Democratic Party was discredited and any third party was a mirage. By this time, the radical impulses of the New Left were played out, and insurgencies of women and minorities were fragmented and embattled. Moreover, the radical politics of the 1960s had been rooted in popular culture, especially rock music – making it easy to overvalue the political significance of popular art forms. Cultural studies emerged to continue radical politics by other means. *Critics and students of the field began to look to popular culture for signs of oppositional energy they could not find in political activity more strictly considered.* This approach counterposed itself to the one-dimensional critique of one-dimensionality, in the Frankfurt writings of Adorno, Horkheimer and Marcuse. Intellectually, it seemed to preserve the possibility of radical action, while priding itself on the subversion of cultural hierarchy. It stood with the marginal and rambunctious against the stuffy and hegemonic. Indeed, in this way, the 'resistance' turn in cultural studies tried to circumvent certain weaknesses in the use of the concept of hegemony – the tendency to see ideological uniformity either as a sort of fog that flows from nowhere in particular or as a lockstep imposed by irresistible structures. Cultural studies thus took seriously the idea that hegemony is a process which includes collaboration (Gitlin 1987: pp. 205–6) – and inquired into the conditions in which collaboration can be challenged. My sense is that after the 1960s in the United States as in Britain, two things happened simultaneously: youth revolt became an institution – each cohort revolting against previous styles – and various more conventional forms of radical politics were stymied. Whereupon radical theories went searching for substitute proletariats, and found them in popular culture.

Under these pressures and influences, cultural studies in the Eighties developed an either/or language of 'resistance' vs. 'the cultural dominant', borrowing its affirmative term from the prestige and glory of antifascism. There are two versions. First, there is the search for the radical potentials in marginal or 'alternative' or 'oppositional' culture, especially that which expresses the pride of marginalized groups – rap music, so called 'women's music', and so on. One upshot is the prayer, or conviction, that a sufficiently angry youth culture would constitute, by itself, radical politics – keeping alive a flame that the industrial working class had long let flicker out. This fantasy is based on a serious misreading of the relation between radical politics and youth culture in the 1960s. Then, the two movements converged, thanks to the Vietnam war. The trinity of drugs, sex, and rock 'n' roll seemed to promise that avant-garde culture would fuse with a revolutionary assault on capitalism – or even become that assault all by itself. The surrealist manifesto came back to earth, this time destined for a constituency extending beyond the intellectual coteries of the avant-garde – legions of baby-boomers to carry the old hope that you could shock the bourgeoisie and overthrow them at the same time. Culture *was* politics, in their eyes – and in the 1960s a case could be made.

Twenty years on, avant-garde shock has become routine, and avant-gardists have to go farther and farther out to prove they haven't been taken in. Therefore, some of yesterday's outriders of youth culture, along with others, have become theorists scavenging the clubs, the back alleys and video channels for a 'resistance' they are convinced, a priori, must exist. Failing to find radical potential in the politics of parties or mass movements, they exalt 'resistance' in subcultures, or, one step on, in popular styles, or even – to take it one step further – in the observation that viewers watch TV with any attitude other than devoted rapture. This is the second version of resistance theory: the search for signs of political insurgency in mainstream culture, as in David Marc's *Demographic Vistas* or John Fiske's *Television Culture*, and Janice Radway's *Reading the Romance* (though at her best she is more subtle). In the influential work of Frederic Jameson (1979) the claim is that popular culture contains 'moments' of both 'reification' and 'utopia' – as if the two-termed class struggle had been transposed to the artifacts of popular culture. True, criticisms of the structure of wealth and power are often detectable, or interpretable, in popular culture – but in the new criticism there is an eagerness to find them, and a neglect of less exalted possibilities within the text, which bends traces of ideological complexity in a film like *Rambo* into intimations of 'opposition' – as if all opposition were democratic, egalitarian, or in other ways socially fruitful. At times, then, the unstated operating assumption is that popular culture is *already politics* and, moreover, some sort of insurgency.

Resistance, meaning all sorts of grumbling, multiple interpretation, semio-logical inversion, pleasure, rage, friction, numbness, what have you – 'resistance' is accorded dignity, even glory, by stamping these not-so-great refusals with a vocabulary derived from life-threatening political work against fascism – as if the same concept should serve for the Chinese student uprising and cable TV grazing. Some have found the new theoretical grail in sitcoms, some in slash and cult movies, some in the pace of MTV, some in the long tracking shot – some in pun, pornography, and the list grows with the ingenuity. Hegelian to the core, this line of thought agrees that somewhere in the culture 'the resistance' must exist.

Note: the resistance. I am troubled by language predicated on the existence of a bipolar world – opposition vs. elites, which tremendously oversimplifies American culture and, I would say, the whole human enterprise. This splitting represents a refusal to abandon an apocalyptic model of political change. It represents the continuation of revolutionary fantasy by other means.

The language of opposition or resistance and domination I find especially misleading insofar as it substitutes for political activity, radical or otherwise. Whenever I hear some style in youth culture defended as 'resistance' or 'opposition', I reach for my common sense. What kind of opposition is this? What does it stand for, what is its consequence? Does it engage in politics in the strict sense – the politics of state and global policy, political-economic struc-ture, allocations of public goods, and so on – or does it simply make the most of consumption? What does it have in mind for people whose aesthetic is different? Culture, of course, is streaked with politics. So, indeed is pleasure. But it is pure sloppiness to conclude that culture *is* politics. Culture is mistaken for politics only by default – only in a society stripped of opportunities for serious politics. In this sense, the preoccupation with popular culture is a measure of the bankruptcy of democratic politics, the decline of the public, and an unfavorable political situation. It is a curious form of reconciliation. It is also a way of accommodating radical longings to the structure of academic life. For those who expected dramatic political and cultural change toward the values of the 1960s, it is music to lick wounds by – but only that.

Better than romanticizing 'resistance' would be to face the depoliticization of society and to take refuge in the consolations of cultural celebration. Beneath the romance of style, I suspect that the revolutionary Other has been smuggled back into the schema as the unwitting carrier of historical rationality. Scholastic radicalism, in other words, serves the theorist as a shield against practical resignation. The prototype is T. W. Adorno's style of burrowing away beneath the social quicksand. Adorno would chortle over the way his mood has been borrowed by radical celebrators of Public Enemy or Madonna.

One of the appeals of the fetishism of audience 'resistance' is, in fact, political – laudably so. Theories that spot resistance throughout popular culture imply that management doesn't matter, whoever's on top, the beat goes on, and long live the Sex Pistols; in this model knowledge accepts political marginality and making the most of it. But the fetishism of style can slide over to a childish celebration of the marginal – cheering the partisans of insurgent style simply because they are, at least by imputation, 'anti-capitalist'. To oppose power simply because it is power accommodates power; it is bondage of a sort – power still writes the script.

Critical social thought cannot be left to dance attendance upon power. Neither can it be left to celebrate the cultural powers of the subordinated as they dance the night away. Voyeurs have only spotted signs of resistance in popular culture; the point is to change the world. Critical social thought requires a public which does not depend upon the largesse of power either actual or anticipated. It requires, that is – or aims to bring about – a democratic domain where ideas contend. The domain is its audience, its raison d'être. Criticism checks power and outdistances it; it instigates and goads and also creates; it acts impertinent to itself as well as to power. Whoever is in power, criticism would be impious. The decline of social criticism and the self-encapsulation of theory is therefore part of a larger crisis. It is inseparable from the decline of the public at large.

3 The Missing Public

One striking thing about the academic communications discourse – critical *or* administrative – is how little it is committed to engaging, animating, provoking a general public. The self-enclosure of university culture obstructs public intellectual life – as the erosion of public intellectual life renders self-enclosure comfortable.

Self-enclosure is by no means the exclusive doing of communications departments. The channels of discourse which have been termed, sometimes confusingly, 'the public sphere', have been eroding throughout the West as they have been reinvented, thankfully, throughout the East. American public television has been largely arid, though with oases dotted here and there, while the commercialization of television proceeds apace in Europe, leaving the public service tradition embattled. Consider, meanwhile, the decline of serious magazines in the United States. For more than two centuries, magazines have been pipelines for the public circulation of social criticism. (Thus this comment from 1775: 'It has always been the opinion of the learned and curious, that a magazine, when properly conducted, is the nursery of genius; and by constantly accumulating new matter, becomes a kind of market for wit and utility. The opportunities which it affords to men of abilities to communicate their studies, kindle up a spirit of invention and emulation. An unexercised genius soon contracts a kind of mossiness, which not only checks its growth, but abates its normal vigour. Like an untenanted house it falls into decay, and frequently ruins the possessor'. Thus said Thomas Paine in the founding issue of *Philadelphia Magazine*.) As culture goes specialized and professional, general-circulation magazines and intellectual journals decline. General thought is so distinctive a taste, now, as to qualify as a special interest alongside personal computing, running, etc. at the serious news-stand.

Where have the journals and magazines gone? To specialty. Journals of film, feminism, Marxism, theory, etc., etc. abound, but my sense is that the number and circulation of *general* journals of analysis and opinion have shrunk in relation to the college-educated public. The length of articles and pieces of fiction have also shrunk – Saul Bellow (1989) was recently driven to publish a novella as an original paperback for lack of a magazine to publish it; essays over seven or eight thousand words regularly go begging. In the commercial magazines, formats are confining; shortness and slickness is the norm. When the left adapts – as with the celebrity covers of *Mother Jones* and *Ms.* – some of the muckraking strengths remain but the weaknesses on institutional analysis, theoretical conundrums, and practical alternatives stand out all the more starkly. Part of the left's problem, of course, is money. Postal increases, the rising cost of paper, etc. have hurt. Left-wing philanthropy, in the wake of the 1960s and the promise of mobilization at the grass roots, has concentrated on practical political and social payoffs – community projects and the like. Only *Dissent*, of the long-running American journals, has been able to sustain, even increase its circulation – without benefit of an angel-in-charge; it struggles to distribute more than ten thousand copies. But the problem is more than financial. The more accessible weeklies on the left – *The Nation*, *In These Times*, *The Village Voice* – are erratic, awkwardly stapling the agendas of activists to the agendas of academics. *The New York Review of Books* is apparently allergic to media studies and the social sciences generally, and most of all to writers under fifty. The success of the Jewish political-cultural bimonthly *Tikkun* (roughly one-third of whose subscribers are apparently not Jewish) must be partly a result of a widespread hunger for intellectually serious criticism of politics and social problems.

But the problem, I fear, is one of demand as well as supply. There is a shortage of common culture. How often does one hear undergraduates discussing a novel they have read outside class? Or a newspaper article? Reading for pleasure seems a quirky taste, the equivalent of building model railroads. College students seem ignorant of literary, philosophical, and artistic traditions; they don't read newspapers; maleducated students become maleducated teachers. The shortage of both accessible writers and interested readers is worsened by the thousands of childhood hours spent saturated with TV.

But imagine, despite the hurdles, a well-read young academic, setting out to make a career as a public intellectual with an academic niche, possessed of a writing talent and possessed by a finite amount of energy (indeed, for feminist men, considerably less than in early decades, when domestic responsibilities were left to the wife). She or he makes choices. Why look to an unprofessional or cross-disciplinary journal when the reward is meager and there is even a certain risk? Young academics mapping careers are preoccupied by the advantages of publishing in refereed professional journals. Academic journals hospitable to post-New Left and interdisciplinary tendencies have been at pains to maintain their professional standing – at least in part for tenure-getting purposes – and have, to that end, maintained strictly, even baroquely scholastic styles. The readable feminist journal *Signs*, which cuts across academic boundaries, probably because of the trans-departmental esprit still remaining in feminist circles, gets short shrift from promotion committees despite being refereed – the assumption is that a feminist journal must be the property of a coterie. Meanwhile, for scholarly writers who cultivate accessible styles, there is something dispiriting about publishing an article in a public journal only to have it thunderously neglected. (Don Marquis said about an analogous literary exercise: 'Publishing a book of verse is like dropping a petal down the Grand Canyon and waiting for the echo.')

I speak deliberately of the *cultivation* of accessible, let alone felicitous style. Writers are encouraged to write in the styles they see published in the journals that serve as gatekeepers for their professions. Forced into disuse for long enough, accessible style withers.

4 Criticism In Search of Its Own Footing

Many are the pressures and motives, in short, which drive communication studies – and for that matter the humanities and social sciences alike – toward closed loops. The decline of a vigorous public confirms the academic turn towards a preoccupation with 'methodology' (why not 'method'?) – either in celebration (mistaking the discipline's scientific or theoretical 'progress' for society's) or resignation (the dashing of revolutionary hopes for society having led toward hopes that, if nothing else, *theory* might be perfected – a hope often followed by a ritual genuflection toward the idea that 'correct' theory will produce 'correct' practice).

Social criticism, meanwhile, comes unmoored from a larger theory of society and a vision of social change – dilemmas that parallel those of the self-shrivelling academy. In the sixties, the most effective social critics operated outside the academy, and for the most part reached ready made constituencies: Michael Harrington, Betty Friedan, James Baldwin, Paul Goodman, Ralph Nader. In the seventies and eighties, by contrast, freelance critics with flair and scope have been scarce. Among academics, the drive to reach beyond the academy is unusual. In practice, the dilemmas of public-minded criticism (leaving aside its considerable strengths) match those of cloistered communication studies. When sweeping criticism of society (for example, Christopher Lasch's [1979]) does find a considerable readership, it fails to generate serious debate; it also fails to make itself practical – its accusations are too global, its eye for reform too jaundiced. Overarching critical frameworks like social ecology and cultural feminism remain ghettoized – they fail to collide with their contraries in a public domain.

At the same time, the narrower, ad hoc criticism of particular policies and practices – call it abstracted criticism – is either squandered on the op-ed pages and talk shows or remains confined among specialists: circles of policy elites, lobbyists, and trainees. Ad hoc criticism fails to accumulate into a more general critique or a vision of society and transformation. This is particularly troubling when it comes to the burning need for media reform. In a time of deregulation, conglomeration, and proliferation in telecommunications, the left in the United States is not heard nearly or coherently enough in debates, such as they are, about policy. This is partly the responsibility of the established media, of course, whose choices of talking heads are predictably skewed toward respectable opinion; but it is also the responsibility of the left, much of which is trapped in I-told-you-so self-marginalization.

From the late seventies through the eighties and into the early nineties, it was the right that proved artful and confident in framing political debate – in no small part because both the Reagan administration and media elites were receptive. Think of the vulgarized New Class theories of Daniel Patrick Moynihan, Irving Kristol and others, as they made their way to a larger public via the *Wall Street Journal* and the widely quoted commentators of the Committee on the Present Danger, the American Enterprise Institute and the Heritage Foundation. Think of Jeane Kirkpatrick's famous *Commentary* article (1979), which rationalized right-wing dictatorships in a manner tailor-made for the incoming president. While scholars of the left buried themselves beneath piles of statistics or scatter-gun disapprovals of authority – whether of texts or teachers – it was left to Allan Bloom (1987) and Secretary of Education William Bennett to address public anxieties with sweeping, if quarter-baked, ideas about Father, Pentagon, and Canon, touting the virtues of a grand Western tradition as if this were, or had ever been, fixed in perpetual arrest. For its part, too much of the left has trapped itself in the various pieties of Marxism and balkanization, abdicating its responsibility to look for ways of seeing the whole. When in doubt about the adequacy of their sacred texts, Marxists, like Ptolemaic purists, multiply epicycles to rescue the notion that history is, in essence, class struggle, while balkanizers repeat the class/race/gender litany, leaving it to the right to claim a view of the whole (Gitlin 1990). I would like to think that we have seen the higher water mark of this intellectual tide.

We have fragmented theory aplenty – fragments which have not accumulated into overarching vision. But possibly overarching vision is not in the cards – who knows? – and possibly that would not be such a bad thing. A modest politics – what I have called elsewhere a politics of limits (Gitlin, 1989) – might spare us some of the fevers and catastrophes that have accompanied the politics of fixed ideas in the twentieth century. The parallel point can be made about social criticism – there is actually plenty of it, modestly focused, and plenty more is possible, if for no other reason than that many of us are rampantly dissatisfied with precisely the conditions that Russell Jacoby has bashed away at. But healthy criticism requires more than improved prose. Criticism proceeds *from* interests which carry the viewpoints of constituencies; but to replenish the democratic ideal it must proceed *to* a general public. Neither more specialist journals nor more talk shows will accomplish that. The restriction, fragmentation, and distraction of the general public, along with the shrinkage of the electorate, set a decisive limit on the larger resonance of *any* critical discourse now. If we are serious about being critics we have to stare at the damage, have to take it seriously.

I have been told that the area designated for free speech at the University of Texas, Austin, is so inaccessible it is only infrequently used. I am asking: What shall it profit critics if their soapboxes occupy the periphery and they speak in tongues?

Notes

1 This is the revised text of a paper delivered to the International Communication Association, San Francisco, May 26, 1989. An earlier version was published in *Critical Studies in Mass Communication* (June 1990).

References

BELL, DANIEL, 1962: The End of Ideology. New York: Free Press.

BELLOW, SAUL, 1989: A Theft. New York: Viking Penguin.

BIRNBAUM, NORMAN, 1988: The Radical Renewal. New York: Pantheon.

BLOOM, ALLAN, 1987: The Closing of the American Mind. New York: Simon and Schuster.

ENGELS, FRIEDRICH, [1880] 1975: Socialism, Utopian and Scientific. New York: International Publishers.

FISKE, JOHN, 1987: Television Culture. London and New York: Methuen.

GITLIN, TODD, 1982: Television's Screens: Hegemony in Transition. In Michael W. Apple, ed., Cultural and Economic Reproduction in Education. London: Routledge and Kegan Paul. pp. 202–46.

——1987: The Sixties: Years of Hope, Days of Rage. New York: Bantam.

——1989: Postmodernism: Roots and Politics. Dissent (Winter): pp. 100–108.

——1990: All Quiet on the Western Front? Tikkun 5 (July/August 1990): pp. 47–48.

HEBDIGE, DICK, 1979: Subculture: The Meaning of Style. London: Methuen.

JACOBY, RUSSELL, 1987: The Last Intellectuals. New York: Basic.

JAMESON, FREDERICK, 1979: 'Reification and Utopia in Popular Culture'. Social Text: 1 (Winter) 130–148.

KIRKPATRICK, JEANE, 1979: 'Dictatorships and Double Standards'. Commentary 68: pp. 34–45.

KUHN, THOMAS S., 1962: The Structure of Scientific Revolutions. Chicago: University of Chicago Press.

LASCH, CHRISTOPHER, 1979: The Culture of Narcissism. New York: Norton.

LAZARSFELD, PAUL F., 1941: 'Remarks on Administrative and Critical Communications Research'. Studies in Philosophy and Social Science IX: pp. 2–16.

MARC, DAVID, 1984: Demographic Vistas: Television in American Culture. Philadelphia: University of Pennsylvania Press.

MILLS, C. WRIGHT, 1959: The Sociological Imagination. New York: Oxford University Press.

RADWAY, JANICE, 1984: Reading the Romance: Feminism and the Representation of Women in Popular Culture. Chapel Hill: University of North Carolina Press.

Index